W9-CRM-084

A Bibliography of Drug Abuse, Including Alcohol and Tobacco

A Bibliography of Drug Abuse, Including Alcohol and Tobacco

Theodora Andrews
Professor of Library Science
Pharmacy Librarian
Purdue University

1977

Libraries Unlimited, Inc.
Littleton, Colorado

LIBRARIES UNLIMITED, INC.
P.O. Box 263
Littleton, Colorado 80160

Library of Congress Cataloging in Publication Data

Andrews, Theodora.
A bibliography of drug abuse, including alcohol and tobacco.

Includes index.
1. Drug abuse–Bibliography. 2. Alcoholism–Bibliography. 3. Tobacco habit–Bibliography. I. Title.
Z7164.N17A52 [HV5801] 016.3622'9 77-22606
ISBN 0-87287-149-5

TABLE OF CONTENTS

INTRODUCTION

The abuse of drugs by large segments of society all over the world has received an enormous amount of attention during the past decade or two. In view of the large number of publications on the subject, it seemed appropriate to compile this annotated bibliography to help interested individuals, particularly librarians, select the materials they need from the large number of titles offered. It is hoped that those who wish to build collections in the drug abuse field will find the publication helpful not only in selection but in providing guidance for reference service.

The drug abuse problem is far from being solved, and a number of groups are concerned with it. These include parents, community workers, law enforcement officers, employers, and teachers who are being challenged to find the right approach to the difficult task of drug education. In addition, students, researchers, and clinicians also need to find materials to aid them in their pursuits. The titles listed are those which are suitable for most libraries: university, college, public, school, and many special collections.

Representative titles have been selected for inclusion on all levels and on virtually all aspects of the subject. In addition, an attempt has been made to include books that exhibit various points of view. The compilation is fairly comprehensive, though some selectivity was exercised in order to keep the book to a reasonable size.

Drug abuse concerns cut across many subject areas, including psychology, sociology, medicine, physiology, pharmacology, education, law, public health, production and manufacture of drugs, religion and anthropology, and public health. Most of the materials included in this bibliography were published during the past ten or fifteen years, although a few older titles, classical works particularly, have been listed. The bibliography is limited to English language literature (although a few translations have been included), most of it American. Although titles on alcohol and tobacco have been listed, the emphasis is on other drugs of abuse, which reflects the trend currently shown in the media.

Reference works and treatises make up the bulk of the materials reviewed; a section on periodicals has been included, however, and a few pamphlets and annuals are listed. Indexing and abstracting tools, bibliographies, other reference sources, and periodicals have been grouped in Part I; the treatises are in Part II. No audiovisual materials have been included, since these are more usefully listed in separate publications, a few of which are reviewed in Part I, Section 1.

Brief general comments about the nature and characteristics of the drug abuse literature may be of value. A great many of the publications available were written because of the sensational publicity surrounding drug abuse and the newsworthiness of the topic; such publications are themselves written in sensational style. Others provide insights and are intended to help individuals who are involved in one way or another with the drug problem. Many reports of research are beginning to appear also.

It is important to realize that all drugs probably have deleterious effects. Some groups tend to minimize those that are caused by drugs of pleasure (such as alcohol and marihuana) and to maximize or overemphasize those caused by medicinal drugs. Since the latter are ordinarily used only under professional guidance, this would appear to be an incongruous attitude. Nevertheless, this view pervades some of the literature.

It seemed likely that, during the course of reviewing the 725 titles listed in this work, one might glean significant insights into the causes and cures for the drug abuse problem. Such was not the case, however, and the literature showed few encouraging signs regarding the problem. Why it developed and how to solve it still remain largely a mystery. Various points of view were revealed in the items examined for this bibliography. One somewhat novel view is that because there are no physical frontiers anymore, but only those frontiers that exist in the mind, drugs may be an outlet for the pioneering spirit. In addition, there is an attempt to fix the blame for drug abuse. Various factors and groups have been accused: society, poverty, laws, lack of education, peer pressure, the breakdown of the family, even drug manufacturers and advertisers. Most agree, however, that strong family ties are needed for prevention and cure. It has been pointed out that the addict is not necessarily a product of our society. He has always existed. His behavior, however, is likely an expression of deep malaise. The quotation at the end of Alfonsi's book (see entry 155) may provide the best clue to the basis of the drug problem: "I was twenty. Let no one say it was the best time of my life."

A large number of the books reviewed—indeed, almost all that deal with how to approach young people—warn against using "scare tactics" because such efforts "will not work." The authors of these books deny the value of all the "other books" that denounce drugs and their users on the basis of moral, psychological, and biological grounds and threaten doom to all who experiment with them. These authors invariably say that they themselves have written a book with a "common sense" and "realistic" approach and are giving "real evidence." They are presenting "facts" and allowing the youthful reader to decide for himself about drug use. Curiously, virtually no books were found that used the "scare tactics." No books of the last two or three decades, at least, attempt to frighten young people from using drugs. This approach, which seems to be an obvious one, is perhaps the only one that hasn't been tried. In view of the limited success achieved to date in the prevention and cure of drug abuse, or even in curbing increased spread of abuse, a different tactic might be worth investigating. Instead, the assumption is made that "scare tactics" don't work. Drug abuse does have frightening consequences, and much of the literature fails to make this point clear.

Each section of this bibliography is preceded by specific remarks that attempt to characterize the literature of that section. It is hoped that these comments and the reviews of the titles listed will throw some light on the important problem of drug abuse, which has been so muddied by sensationalism, propaganda, and false hopes.

January 1977 — Theodora Andrews

PART I

GENERAL REFERENCE SOURCES

1. Bibliographies, Indexes, and Abstracts

This section lists a number of well-known publications that cover subject areas broader than drug abuse alone but that include references to such material. Among these are such familiar works as *Abstracts for Social Workers, Bibliographic Index*, *Biological Abstracts*, *Business Periodicals Index*, *Chemical Abstracts*, *Current Contents: Life Sciences*, *Index Medicus*, and many more. Indexes that cover just drug abuse (such as *Excerpta Medica Section 40: Drug Dependence and Speed*) are also included. Many bibliographies listed here, such as *Annotated Bibliography of Marihuana, Drug Themes in Fiction*, *Audio-Visual Materials on Alcohol and Alcoholism*, and *Polydrug Use*, among others, cover special aspects of drug abuse.

1. **Abstracts for Social Workers.** Washington, National Association of Social Workers, 1965– . Four times per year.

This publication covers nearly 200 journals in the field of social work and related areas. There is a section on alcoholism and drug addiction. An author and subject index is furnished for each issue as well as annually.

2. Advena, Jean Cameron, comp. **Drug Abuse Bibliography for 1970.** Troy, N.Y., Whitston Publishing Co., 1971. 198p. index. $10.00. LC 79-116588. ISBN 0-87875-016-9.

This bibliography is the first annual volume supplementing an earlier list compiled by Joseph Menditto, *Drugs of Addiction and Non-Addiction, Their Use and Abuse: A Comprehensive Bibliography, 1960-1969*, by the same publisher (see entry 29).

The annual supplementary volumes cover 1973 at this writing.

The arrangement of the material listed has varied somewhat from volume to volume, and the 1971, 1972, and 1973 volumes have been noticeably larger than that for 1970. The recent volumes have included lists of periodical abbreviations and subject heading lists. Most of the references are to periodical literature, but some books also have been included. The listing seems to be rather complete; a large number of bibliographies and periodical indexes were searched in compiling the work. The series will serve the needs of researchers in medical and social sciences and also those of undergraduate students and laymen.

3. Ajami, Alfred M., ed. **Drugs: An Annotated Bibliography and Guide to the Literature.** In collaboration with the Sanctuary, Cambridge, Mass. Boston, G. K. Hall and Co., 1973. 205p. index. $15.00.

This bibliography focuses on drugs of absue and the so-called "drug culture," with references on neurological, pharmacological, historical, social, and political implications. The 529 references are divided into several categories: 1) Drugs in physiological psychology, 2) Pharmacology, 3) Drugs in society, and 4) Cultural and philosophical overviews. The appendices offer a summary of scientific information about a limited number of common drugs, and a guide to bibliographic and search services available. The work should prove quite useful, particularly on the university level, since large numbers of the references come from the more scholarly scientific journals. There is, however, a sprinkling of the popular.

4. **Bibliographic Index.** New York, H. W. Wilson Co., 1938– . Published in April and August with a bound cumulation each December.

This is a subject list of bibliographies that have been published separately or that have appeared as parts of books, pamphlets, and periodicals. It includes a number of bibliographies on drug abuse.

5. **Biological Abstracts.** Philadelphia, BioSciences Information Service of Biological Abstracts, 1926– . Semi-monthly.

This comprehensive work covering all areas of the biological sciences includes references and abstracts to scientific drug abuse articles. The keyword index included in each issue provides easy access, and there are semi-annual cumulated indexes. Older volumes had annual cumulated indexes.

The publishers of *Biological Abstracts* provide many services as extensions of their publication. These include such things as collective indexes on microfiche, an on-line data base for computer searches (available through commercial suppliers), and the *BioResearch Index.*

6. Burg, Nan C. **Forces against Drug Abuse: Education, Legislation, Rehabilitation; A Selected Bibliography.** Monticello, Ill., Council of Planning Librarians, 1971. 11p. (Council of Planning Librarians. Exchange Bibliography 231). $1.50pa.

This bibliography, whose purpose is to point out what counterforces are coming to the fore to cope with the problem of drug abuse and how strong these are or may become, lists both articles and books. The compiler has divided these counterforces into three groups (Education, Legislation, and Rehabilitation), and entries are arranged under these topics. The articles listed appear to be well selected from a wide variety of sources.

7. **Business Periodicals Index.** New York, H. W. Wilson Co., 1958– . Monthly except August with cumulations.

This is a subject index to about 125 English language periodicals in all areas of business. Since drug abuse is of concern in business at the present time, articles on drug abuse are frequently included.

8. **Chemical Abstracts: Key to the World's Chemical Literature.** Easton, Pa., American Chemical Society, 1907– . Weekly.

This publication attempts to include abstracts of all scientific and technical papers containing new information of chemical and chemical engineering interest and to report new chemical information revealed in the patent literature. Since the publication is very comprehensive, it contains much material regarding the chemistry of drugs of abuse.

The indexing of the material is excellent. There are author, patent, and keyword indexes in each issue. The semi-annual and five-year collective indexes available are of several types. In addition to the author and subject indexes, there are formula, ring system, chemical substance, numerical patent, and patent concordance indexes. Some access to the material is available through a computerized data base.

9. **Current Contents: Life Sciences.** Philadelphia, Institute for Scientific Information, 1958– . Weekly.

This current awareness publication reproduces title pages from more than 1,000 journals that report the results of worldwide research in the life sciences, allowing users to keep up with new developments in their fields. An author index and an address directory are supplied as well as a keyword subject index for each issue.

Current Contents publications in other subject areas also include references to drug abuse materials; these are *Current Contents: Clinical Practice*, *Current Contents: Physical and Chemical Science*, and *Current Contents: Social and Behavioral Sciences.*

10. **Dissertation Abstracts International. Section A, Humanities; Section B, Sciences.** Ann Arbor, Mich., Xerox University Microfilms, 1938– . Monthly.

This publication is a compilation of abstracts of doctoral dissertations submitted to the publisher by more than 300 cooperating institutions in the United States and Canada. A list of the institutions is given in each issue. However, not all institutions send all their doctoral dissertations, and they began submitting them at different times. Copies of the dissertations listed are available for purchase from the publisher as microfilm or Xerox prints. Each issue contains a keyword title and author index, and there are some cumulated indexes. Both Sections A and B include abstracts of dissertations in the area of drug abuse; the emphasis of the dissertation in question determines the section in which it will be listed.

11. **Drug Abuse Current Awareness System (DACAS).** Rockville, Md. National Clearinghouse for Drug Abuse Information, 1972– . Biweekly.

This is a comprehensive listing of citations of the recent drug abuse literature, taken from the major publications in the field, including scientific and technical journals, popular periodicals, underground newspapers, books, legal journals, and government project reports. The citations are categorized under major subject areas, then listed alphabetically by author within each category.

In 1974 a cumulated issue was published entitled *A Bibliography of Drug Abuse Literature, 1972.* The citations are also entered into the

Drug Abuse Resources and Materials File, which is part of the Clearinghouse computerized information storage and retrieval service.

12. Eckert, William G., ed. **The Medical, Legal and Law Enforcement Aspects of Drugs and Drug Abuse: A Bibliography of Classic and Current References.** Wichita, Kansas, Laboratory of St. Francis Hospital, 1972. 97p. index. $12.00.

The bibliography is preceded by brief text material on narcotic drugs, hallucinogens, and depressants and stimulants. The material was reprinted from recent issues of newsletters of INFORM (The International Reference Organization in Forensic Medicine and Sciences). The compiler is the editor of INFORM. The bibliography includes 2,500 items, with references taken from many sources (such as the National Library of Medicine publications, and selected abstracts and articles published by INTERPOL and the *Legal Index*). A subject and author index has been provided. The list should prove of value to physicians in general practice, psychiatrists, clinical toxicologists, lawyers, law enforcement officers, forensic scientists, and laymen.

13. **Education Index.** New York, H. W. Wilson Co., 1929– . Monthly except July and August.

This is a cumulative author and subject index to material in English. Though it indexes primarily periodical articles, some proceedings, yearbooks, bulletins, monographs, and government publications are also included. It is an important source for locating articles on drug abuse education.

14. **Excerpta Medica Section 17. Public Health, Social Medicine, and Hygiene.** Princeton, N.J., Excerpta Medica Foundation, 1955– . Ten times per year.

This abstracting journal, which is part of the Excerpta Medica International Medical Abstracting service, indexes and abstracts material in the areas indicated. Drug abuse material that has public health emphasis can be found.

15. **Excerpta Medica Section 30. Pharmacology and Toxicology.** Princeton, N.J., Excerpta Medica Foundation, 1949– . 10 times per year. (title varies).

This section of the Excerpta Medica abstracting service includes highly scientific research material in all areas of pharmacology and toxicology. It abstracts articles that pertain to drugs of abuse and their effects.

16. **Excerpta Medica Section 36. Health Economics and Hospital Management.** Princeton, N.J., Excerpta Medica Foundation, 1970– . 10 times per year.

This journal, which is part of the comprehensive Excerpta Medica set of international medical abstracting services, includes drug abuse materials, particularly those relating to such matters as hospital care and health economics.

17. **Excerpta Medica Section 40. Drug Dependence.** Princeton, N.J., Excerpta Medica Foundation, 1973– . Monthly.

This publication indexes and abstracts international literature pertaining to the non-medical use of drugs and related subjects. More than 5,000 journals are indexed, covering the following subject areas: general materials, drugs with material arranged by type of drug, individual response, diagnosis, medical treatment, rehabilitation, epidemiology, social aspects, and prevention.

18. Gamage, J. R., and E. L. Zerkin. **A Comprehensive Guide to the English-Language Literature on Cannabis (Marihuana).** Beloit, Wisc., STASH Press, 1969. 265p. index. $5.95.

This comprehensive bibliography deals with all areas of the subject including the medical, psychiatric, psychological, pharmacological, chemical, biochemical, botanical, sociological, anthropological, religious, and legal. The main section is arranged alphabetically by author, and an abstract accompanying each entry gives significant findings, the general position of the author, and the methodology used in reports of research. The subject section gives full citations also but not the abstracts. The author index seems to be of limited value, since the main list is arranged by author. However, it does assist in locating articles by co-authors. The journals covered, which are listed, are mostly on the scholarly research level.

19. **Health Education: Drugs and Alcohol; An Annotated Bibliography.** Prepared in cooperation with the ERIC Clearinghouse on Teacher Education. John Aquino, Senior Information Analyst; Lorraine Poliakoff, Editor. Produced in cooperation with Department of School Nurses, NEA. Washington, National Education Association, 1975. 32p. LC 75-5753.

This booklet contains a section of suggestions for educators who need to help students facing the drug/alcohol problem. The remainder of the publication presents annotated bibliographies on drug abuse, drug education, alcoholism, alcohol education, and venereal disease. It lists periodical articles, pamphlets, and reports that come from the ERIC data base. Some of the annotations are brief; others are about one-third of a column long.

20. **Hospital Literature Index.** Chicago, American Hospital Association, 1945– . Quarterly. (title varies).

This is an author and subject index to hospital literature covering all areas of the field. There are annual and five-year cumulations. The cumulated issues list the periodicals indexed—an impressive number; they are all English language publications. The hospitals' concern with drug abuse comes under such headings as "narcotic care," "narcotic control," and "alcoholic care."

21. **Index Medicus.** Washington, U.S. National Library of Medicine, 1960– . Monthly.

This is a comprehensive bibliographic listing of articles appearing in current biomedical journals. All medical subjects are covered, and approximately 2,200 periodicals from all over the world are indexed. There is a subject and author section and a separate *Bibliography of Medical Reviews* in each issue. A complete key to title abbreviations and a list of subject headings used are issued annually in January each year, and a cumulated edition is published annually. The indexing is also available on-line through the computer data base MEDLINE. Medical aspects of drug abuse are very well covered.

22. **Index to Legal Periodicals.** New York, H. W. Wilson Co., 1909– . Monthly except September.

This publication indexes periodicals published in the United States, Canada, Great Britain, Ireland, Australia, and New Zealand. The references are mostly to periodical articles, but some yearbooks, annual institutes, and annual reviews are indexed also. There are both subject and author approaches. Annual and three-year cumulated volumes are provided. Much on alcohol is included, with somewhat less on drug abuse.

23. **International Pharmaceutical Abstracts.** Washington, American Society of Hospital Pharmacists, 1964– . Semi-monthly.

This publication, devoted to all phases of the development and use of drugs and to the professional practice of pharmacy, presents abstracts of articles from a large number of periodicals. Besides the subject index in each issue, there is a semi-annual cumulated subject index and an annual author index. A rather large number of articles on various aspects of drug abuse are abstracted.

24. **Iowa Drug Information Service (IDIS).** Iowa City, College of Pharmacy, University of Iowa, 1966– . Monthly.

This microfiche service provides drug and disease indices to the drug literature of about 140 medical and pharmacy English language journals. The service covers all drugs, including drugs of abuse, with an emphasis on adverse reactions. The articles indexed are reproduced on microfiche, and on-demand computer searches of the data base are available. For the first years the index to the microfiche file was produced on cards, but recently it has been available only on microfiche.

25. Kalant, Oriana Josseau, and Harold Kalant. **Amphetamines and Related Drugs: Clinical Toxicity and Dependence; A Comprehensive Bibliography of the International Literature.** With the assistance of Lydia Vegers. Toronto, Addiction Research Foundation, 1974. 210p. index. $5.50pa.

This bibliography collects references to papers in all languages dealing with clinical toxicity and dependence of the amphetamines and related drugs. Material on both therapeutic and non-medical uses has been included, as has that on psychiatric as well as physical complications. Systematic search of the literature was carried to the end of 1972, though a few papers published in 1973 are included. Of the 802 references, 342 are accompanied by abstracts. A brief analysis of the literature has been included, and there is a list of the journals cited.

26. Kalant, Oriana Josseau. **An Interim Guide to the Cannabis (Marihuana) Literature.** Toronto, Canada, Addiction Research Foundation, 1968. 39p. index. (Addiction Research Foundation Bibliographic Series. No. 2). free.

This guide presents two short monographs, one on the effects of marihuana and the other on the history of the literature on Cannabis. However, the main part of the guide is a review of eleven books and seven review articles. Summaries and critical appraisals are presented. Material is arranged chronologically, from 1900 to 1966. The reviews are of high quality and important since objective appraisals of publications in this field are rare, and many of the publications reviewed are difficult to obtain now as they are old.

27. Keller, Mark, ed. **International Bibliography of Studies on Alcohol. Vol. 1, References, 1901-1950**, prepared by Sarah Spock Jordy. **Vol. 2, Indexes, 1901-1950**, prepared by Vera Efron and Sarah Spock Jordy. **Vol. 3, The Literature of 1951-1960, References and Indexes.** New Brunswick, N.J., Publications Division, Rutgers Center of Alcohol Studies, 1966– . 3v. (Vol. 3 in prep.) $100.00/set. LC 60-14437. ISBN 0-911290-34-6; 0-911290-35-4; 0-911290-40-0.

The general purpose of this monumental work is to provide a broad multidisciplinary and interprofessional bibliography. The listing is very comprehensive, including materials on all aspects of the subject, covering 31 languages and taken from many kinds of publications. Volume 1 contains over 25,000 entries. The bibliography is part of a total documentation system. Other parts of the system are the "Current Literature" section of the *Quarterly Journal on Studies of Alcohol* and the Classified Abstract Archive of the Alcohol Literature, whose headquarters are located in the Rutgers Center of Alcohol Studies. Sets of the Archive are also maintained in a number of other locations about the world. The bibliography under review indicates the location of an abstract within the system. Entries are arranged alphabetically by year.

At this writing Volume 3 of the bibliography, which is to be the first decennial supplement, has not yet appeared. Additional decennial supplementary volumes are planned, and it is also hoped that a historical bibliography for the period before 1901 can be produced.

The bibliography is a much-needed, high-quality work from a center internationally known for its work in the alcohol field.

28. **Medical Socioeconomic Research Sources.** Chicago, American Medical Association. Division of Library and Archival Services, 1971– . Four times per year.

A forerunner of this index, which began in 1962, was called *Index to The Literature of Medical Socioeconomics.* From the beginning the publication was valuable as it filled a gap in indexing. Many of the journals included are not indexed in *Index Medicus.* Each issue lists, in subject arrangement, references to articles from a wide variety of sources covering the economics and sociology of health care. Each issue has an author index. An annual cumulation contains a list of journals and serials indexed during the year, subject headings used, and a subject section and author index with the format of the regular issues. It is easy to scan the subject section for articles of interest. There are sections on alcoholism, drug abuse, drug addiction, drugs–hallucinogenic, and the like.

29. Menditto, Joseph. **Drugs of Addiction and Non-Addiction, Their Use and Abuse: A Comprehensive Bibliography, 1960-1969.** Troy, N.Y., Whitston Publishing Co., 1970. 315p. index. $10.00. LC 79-116588.

This bibliography of about 6,000 entries is a comprehensive guide to research materials in the field of addiction. It includes citations to books and essays, doctoral dissertations, and periodical literature, the latter being divided into "general" and "scientific" categories. References are arranged under the following headings: amphetamines and stimulants, barbiturates and tranquilizing drugs, lysergic acid diethylamide, marihuana, narcotic addiction, narcotic rehabilitation, narcotic trade, narcotics, narcotic control, narcotic laws and legislation, narcotics and crime, and narcotics bibliography.

This basic volume has been supplemented annually by a *Drug Abuse Bibliography*, compiled by Jean Cameron Advena (see entry 2).

30. Mercer, G. W. **Non-Alcoholic Drugs and Personality: A Selected Annotated Bibliography.** Toronto, Canada, Addiction Research Foundation, 1972. 77p. index. (Addiction Research Foundation Bibliographic Series No. 4). $2.00.

This selected bibliography of 181 items is a listing of publications that meet the following criteria: 1) they deal with cannabis, psychedelic, amphetamine, tranquilizing, and narcotic drugs; 2) they deal with human beings rather than animals; 3) they deal with hard data in the form of tests, interviews, comparative sampling and the like; and 4) they are not just philosophical treatises on drugs and drug use. For the most part the publications included have been published in the last 20 years. Most of the references are to journal articles, although some books are included. The annotations are well written, and the bibliography should prove quite useful.

31. **Monthly Catalog of United States Government Publications.** Washington, U.S. Superintendent of Documents, 1895– . Monthly.

This is a current bibliography of publications issued by all branches of the government, including congressional as well as department and bureau publications. Arrangement is by issuing agency. Each issue contains general information and instructions for ordering documents. For each publication listed is given its full title, date, paging, price, Library of Congress card number, etc. There is an annual index by subject and agency, and since 1945 there has been a monthly index in each issue. In addition, since 1974 the subject index has been improved (previously it was by broad category rather than by specific subject), and a title index has been added. A great deal of drug abuse material is included, since much in this area is published by various government agencies.

32. National Coordinating Council on Drug Education. **Drug Abuse Films.** 3rd ed. Washington, National Coordinating Council on Drug Education, 1972. 117p. index.

This publication, which lists and evaluates drug abuse audiovisuals, is intended as a guide only and will not eliminate the need to preview films. Most of the titles reviewed are films, but other audiovisuals, such as filmstrips, are also included. The preface states that *all* the materials reviewed have been found wanting in some degree. Thirty-one percent have been classified "unacceptable" because of inaccuracies, distortion, obsolescence, or conceptual unsoundness. Audiovisuals for minorities are listed in a separate section of the work; they are small in number and poor in quality, according to the preface. In addition to introductory material the following sections are included: 1) NCCDE review process, 2) how to select a drug abuse film, 3) recommended films and audiovisuals, 4) restricted films and audiovisuals, 5) unacceptable films and audiovisuals. 6) films and audiovisuals aimed at minority groups, 7) evaluation panel members, 8) background on National Coordinating Council on Drug Education, and 9) member organizations. The following information is given for each title in the review section: year, intended audience, producer, source, rental price, purchase price, details (such as running time, color or black and white, sound or silent, etc.). There follows a synopsis and an evaluation.

It is interesting that some members of the evaluation panel are well-known individuals in the drug abuse and education field, a few are scientists, and a surprisingly large number are students, well-known entertainers, and producers of avant-garde movies.

It has been felt recently that much of the educational material designed to discourage drug use has had no effect or an opposite effect. There is a growing feeling that the approach formerly used is all wrong. It is not evident what the right approach is, however, so those who use materials such as those listed here are advised to do so with caution.

33. National Institute for Drug Programs. Center for Human Services. **Bibliography on Drug Abuse: Prevention, Treatment, Research.** Washington, Human Service Press, 1973. 222p. index. $7.95. LC 73-77472.

This volume is the first of a series of publications intended to provide information in the field of drug abuse, prevention, rehabilitation, and research. The work is made up of 366 references to publications, each with an abstract of the cited material. The references are divided into two large groups, drug treatment approaches and society and drugs. Under each there are numerous subheadings. The references are to books and periodical articles.

The compilers feel that the bibliography points up at least two important facts. The first is that there is a trend toward developing a variety of approaches to treatment of drug abuse; the second is that there is a notable lack of crucial research and analyses in the field, so that there are few publications of value.

34. **New York Times Index: A Book of Record.** New York, New York Times Company, 1851– . Twice per month.

This well-known index gives good coverage of articles that have appeared in the *Times* newspaper. The indexing is by subject, persons, and organizations. Much has appeared on the subject of drug abuse. Annual cumulations of the publication are available. A microfilmed edition is published, and the indexing is available in a computerized data base.

35. Polacsek, E., and others. **Interaction of Alcohol and Other Drugs.** 2nd ed. rev. Toronto, Addiction Research Foundation, 1972. 560p. index. (Addiction Research Foundation Bibliographic Series. No. 3). $17.50.

This publication is "an annotated bibliography of the scientific literature on the interaction of ethanol and other chemical compounds normally absent in vivo, the influence of congeners in alcoholic beverages, conjunctive addiction to ethanol plus other drugs, and cross-tolerance between ethanol and other compounds." It focuses on the problems of drug use by people, especially combinations of drugs, in ways that threaten individuals and society. The coverage is quite comprehensive, and material in about 20 languages is included. About 45 percent of the papers annotated are in languages other than English. The bibliography is to be supplemented from time to time to keep it current. The titles are arranged alphabetically by the senior author's name. Keyword, author, and drug name indexes are furnished.

Designed for scientists, the work is important, since drug interactions, particularly with alcohol, are a serious, growing problem.

36. Popham, Robert E., and Carole D. Yawney, compilers. **Culture and Alcohol Use: A Bibliography of Anthropological Studies.** 2nd ed. Toronto, Addiction Research Foundation, 1967. 52p. (Addiction Research Foundation Bibliographic Series No. 1). index. free.

The purpose of this bibliography is to bring together the principal anthropological literature on drinking behavior in different cultures, whether it is customary or pathological. The principal sources of references were the periodicals: *Alkoholpolitik*, *American Anthropologist*, *British Journal of Addiction*, *Human Organization*, and *Quarterly Journal of Studies on Alcohol.* Also used were the *Classified Abstract Archive of the Alcohol Literature*, Rutgers Center of Alcohol Studies, and references from relevant books and articles. The bibliography is arranged by broad topics as follows: 1) non-literate peoples, 2) literate peoples, 3) ancient peoples, and 4) theoretical studies.

37. **Psychological Abstracts.** Washington, American Psychological Association, Inc., 1927– . Monthly.

This publication provides non-evaluative summaries of the world's literature in psychology and related disciplines. Over 850 journals, technical reports, monographs, and other scientific documents provide the materials for coverage. Drug and alcohol usage, drug stimulation and psychopharmacology, and drug and alcohol rehabilitation are sections included.

38. **Psychopharmacology Abstracts.** U.S. National Clearinghouse for Mental Health Information. 1961– . Irregular.

This publication is a specialized service designed to help the National Institute of Mental Health meet its obligation of fostering and supporting laboratory and clinical research into the nature and causes of mental illness and methods of treatment and prevention. The materials abstracted assist investigators in the field of psychopharmacology by providing information on new developments and research results. Since drugs of abuse are of the psychoactive type, the material indexed is of considerable interest to those involved in drug abuse research.

Subject and author indexes appear in each issue, and cumulated ones are provided at the end of volumes.

39. **Public Affairs Information Service Bulletin.** New York, Public Affairs Information Service, Inc., 1915– . Weekly except for the last two weeks of each quarter.

This publication is cumulated five times a year, the fifth cumulation being a bound volume for permanent reference. Books, pamphlets, government publications, reports of public and private agencies, and periodical articles are indexed. English language publications only are included. The fields covered are economic and social conditions, public administration, and international relations. There are often references to drug abuse material.

40. **Readers' Guide to Periodical Literature.** New York, H. W. Wilson Co., 1905– . Semi-monthly Sept.-June; monthly in July and August; with cumulations.

This index is a cumulated author and subject listing of periodical articles of general interest from American periodicals of broad, general, and popular character. Also included are some non-technical magazines representing the important scientific subject fields. Since a great deal of information on drug abuse has appeared in popular periodicals, this is a rather good source of material on the subject.

41. Richardson, Winnifred, and Byran E. M. Cooke. **A Bibliography on Drugs; By Subject and Title.** Minneapolis, Burgess Publishing Co., 1972. 60p. index.

This brief bibliography lists references on drug abuse, by title, under about 15 broad subject categories. Book, periodical, and pamphlet references are included. There is a special section of bibliographies, a list of pertinent periodicals, and a list of sources where free and inexpensive materials may be obtained. Most of the references are to articles about drug use among young people and about educating them regarding the hazards of drug use.

42. Rickles, William H., Benjamin Chatoff, and Charlotte Whitaker. **Marijuana: A Selective Bibliography, 1924-1970.** Los Angeles, UCLA Brain Information Service, 1970. 34p. $3.00.

This annotated bibliography is selective rather than comprehensive, but it attempts to cover several facets of the problem in a representative way. Scientific literature has been selected for the most part.

The bibliography lists alphabetically by author 192 references, mostly to periodical articles, with brief annotations. Also included is a detailed table of contents that can serve as an index; referring to articles by number, it is divided by type of article. The following categories have been identified: Cannabis and its origin, pharmacological effects, clinical studies and case reports, therapeutic assessment, sociological and legal issues, and reviews and overviews.

43. **Science Citation Index.** Philadelphia, Institute for Scientific Information, 1961– . Quarterly with annual cumulation. (A five-year cumulation covering 1965 to 1969 is also available.)

This comprehensive publication covers nearly 2,600 international journals and virtually all scientific disciplines. The set includes a source index, a citation index, and a permuterm subject index. The permutation subject index, which began in 1967, is a list of journal articles that uses a permuterm-word indexing system, allowing a conventional subject approach to the material in addition to the citation approach which originated with *Science Citation Index*.

The advantage of the citation index approach to material is that it makes it easier to identify cross-disciplinary relationships missed by conventional subject indexes. This is important in the drug abuse field. Citation indexing also has the unique ability to search forward in time from previously published articles.

A *Social Sciences Citation Index* has recently been made available by the same publisher.

44. Sells, Helen F., comp. **A Bibliography on Drug Dependence.** Fort Worth, Texas Christian University Press, 1967. 137p. index. $2.25pa.

Most of the material listed in this bibliography deals with the treatment of narcotic addiction. However, a few references are to works on alcoholism and on drugs other than opiates. The coverage is international although titles to non-English references have been translated. The period covered is from the 1800s through 1966. The arrangement of the bibliography is alphabetical by subject category. There is an author index only, although the detailed table of contents serves somewhat as a subject index. Other bibliographies have been included in the listing.

45. **Social Sciences Index.** New York, H. W. Wilson Co., 1974– . 4 times per year with cumulations.

This publication is an author and subject index to some 260 periodicals in the fields of psychology, physical anthropology, area studies, classical studies, economics, geography, history, nursing, political science, environmental sciences, sociology, and related subjects. The coverage is international, with an emphasis on American periodicals. This index and *Humanities Index* have developed from and replaced *Social Sciences and Humanities Index* (1916-1974). Much material on drug abuse has been included in the *Social Sciences Index*, but there is only a little in the *Humanities Index*.

46. **Sociological Abstracts.** San Diego, Calif., Sociological Abstracts, Inc. 1952– . Five times per year.

This is a major index publication in the field of sociology. It is co-sponsored by the American Sociological Association, Eastern Sociological Society, the International Sociological Association, and the Midwest Sociological Society. Over 400 periodicals are covered. Drug abuse articles are frequently included.

47. **Speed: The Current Index to the Drug Abuse Literature.** Madison, Wisc., Student Association for the Study of Hallucinogens, Inc. (STASH), 1973– . Semi-monthly.

This publication comes as part of the *Grassroots* subscription (see entry 184), but it can also be subscribed to separately. It supplies prompt bibliographic data on drug abuse articles from about 4,000 professional journals, books, and monographs. The arrangement is by subject and/or form. No indexes have been supplied to date. The publication is most useful as a selection aid for monographs or as a current awareness tool for periodical articles.

48. Sprecher, Daniel. **Guide to Films (16mm) about the Use of Dangerous Drugs, Narcotics, Alcohol and Tobacco.** (With a separate section on Filmstrips). Alexandria, Va., Serina Press, 1971. 61p. index. LC 77-148162.

Most of the reviews presented in this booklet are quite short, but a few are perhaps half a page long. Little effort is made to evaluate the material; reviews are descriptive. Sources for the films are indicated; most can be secured on a rental or sales basis, while others are available on a free loan basis.

49. Tompkins, Dorothy Campbell, comp. **Drug Addiction: A Bibliography.** Berkeley, University of California Bureau of Public Administration, 1960. 130 p. index. $3.00pa.

This bibliography contains a selection of materials relating to the legal, medical, psychological, and regulatory aspects of drug addiction. The period covered is approximately 1930 to 1960. The references are grouped by subject category. There is an author index only; the table of contents must be used to locate specific subject materials.

50. **Toxicity Bibliography: A Bibliography Covering Reports on Toxicity Studies, Adverse Drug Reactions, and Poisoning in Man and Animals.** Washington, U.S. National Library of Medicine, 1968– . Quarterly.

This bibliography provides health professionals working in toxicology and related areas with access to the world's journal literature in the field. The citations come from the MEDLARS system, through which *Index Medicus* is also produced by computer. The material included in the bibliography is one of the files contained in the TOXLINE bibliographic retrieval service. Although indexing drug abuse material is not a prime responsibility, the bibliography does include many citations to articles on abused drugs.

51. U.S. National Clearinghouse for Drug Abuse Information. **A Bibliography of Drug Abuse Literature, 1972.** Washington, GPO, 1974. 236p. index. (DHEW Publication No. (ADM) 74-85) $2.55. S/N 1724-00369.

This publication is a cumulated issue of the *Drug Abuse Current Awareness System (DACAS)* which includes all the citations published in 1972. The citations are categorized into subject areas and then arranged alphabetically by author within each category. The author index which is included contains only the names of the first-mentioned author for each article. Over 4,300 citations are listed, derived from such sources as scientific and technical journals, popular magazines, underground publications, books, legal journals, and government project reports.

52. U.S. National Clearinghouse for Drug Abuse Information. **The CNS Depressant Withdrawal Syndrome and Its Management: An Annotated Bibliography, 1950-1973.** Washington, GPO, 1975. 55p. index. (DHEW Publication No. (ADM) 75-206; Special Bibliographies, No. 2).

It is the intent of this annotated bibliography to provide an introduction to the literature concerning the central nervous system depressant withdrawal syndrome including its etiology, symptomatology, intervention, and management. The substances considered include the barbiturates and the non-barbiturate sedative-hypnotics (including the minor tranquilizers). Most of the 182 publications cited and reviewed are from scientific and medical periodicals.

53. U.S. National Clearinghouse for Drug Abuse Information. **Drug Dependence and Abuse: A Selected Bibliography.** Washington, GPO, 1971. 51p. $0.60pa.

This selected list of references provides an overview of the type of literature published in the drug abuse field, including scientific as well as substantial popular literature. The items selected meet the following criteria: 1) 1969 or 1970 books by recognizable and authoritative authors, 2) current research articles which reflect responsible factual conclusions and add to existing knowledge, 3) items which were cited in two or more significant bibliographies, 4) classic books, articles or studies, and 5) factual literature in popular periodicals which are meaningful additions to the literature. In addition, professionals in the field suggested some materials. The entries are listed under 21 major subject areas. No annotations have been included.

54. U.S. National Clearinghouse for Drug Abuse Information. **LSD Research, an Annotated Bibliography: 1972-1975.** Washington, GPO, 1975. 102p. index. (DHEW Publication No. (ADM) 76-293; Special Bibliographies No. 5).

There is still interest in LSD, although its use has declined as a result of reports of its causing genetic damage. Limited research is being carried out to determine possible therapeutic value of the drug. This bibliography is a collection of abstracts of scientific literature on the drug published from about 1972 to 1975. The 315 abstracts included average about one-half column in length. The literature is primarily for the professional audience. There are three sections: 1) clinical studies, 2) animal studies, and 3) LSD chemistry. A number of data bases were utilized in assembling the citations. The material included in the abstracts can serve as a summary of current LSD research.

55. U.S. National Clearinghouse for Drug Abuse Information. **Methadone and Pregnancy.** Washington, GPO, 1974. 31p. (DHEW Publication No. (ADM) 75-152; Special Bibliographies. No. 1).

Some concern has been shown regarding methadone treatment for addicted young women because of possible ill effects to infants born to them. It has been firmly established that these infants display withdrawal signs at birth, and other complications may arise more frequently than is normal. The references collected for this annotated bibliography span the period from the introduction of methadone in the late 1940s to mid-1973. Most of the articles cited are from medical journals and most are in English. The number of references included is rather limited, but the annotations are of good length, about one-half page each.

56. U.S. National Clearinghouse for Drug Abuse Information. **Polydrug Use: An Annotated Bibliography**. Washington, GPO, 1975. 35p. index. (DHEW Publication No. (ADM) 75-225; Special Bibliographies, No. 3).

This selected bibliography is of note because multiple drug use is a growing trend and problem. The bibliography is not comprehensive, but an attempt was made to include recent literature. A number of computerized data bases were used in assembling the citations. Articles were selected for inclusion only if they treat polydrug use exclusively or as a major point of focus.

57. U.S. National Clearinghouse for Drug Abuse Information. **Women and Drugs: An Annotated Bibliography**. Washington, GPO, 1975. 62p. index. (DHEW Publication No. (ADM) 76-289; Special Bibliographies, No. 4).

The references included in this bibliography span the period from 1937 through June 1975. The coverage is not comprehensive, but an attempt is made to include as much of the recent literature as possible. The annotations average about one-third to one-half page in lenth. The introductory material explains, among other things, that little attention was paid to women drug abusers until the advent of the women's movement.

The bibliography is divided into sections as follows: 1) general articles, 2) women and narcotics, 3) women and psychotherapeutic drug use, and 4) women and alcohol. The sections are subdivided under such headings as sociocultural aspects, treatment service delivery, psychotherapeutic drug advertising, personality studies, and psychological aspects.

58. U.S. National Clearinghouse for Mental Health Information. **Bibliography on Drug Dependence and Abuse, 1928-1966.** Washington, D.C., National Institute of Mental Health, 1967. 258p.

This bibliography of more than 3,000 entries was compiled primarily for specialists and research workers in the field. It includes citations to books, monographs, journal articles, legal documents, and reports of congressional hearings and investigations relating to drug dependence and abuse. The materials are organized under categories as follows: general material, incidence and prevalence, sociological factors, treatment and rehabilitation, attitudes and education, pharmacology and chemistry, psychological factors, and production control and legal factors. The bibliography is not entirely complete for the period covered, but it is quite comprehensive.

59. U.S. National Institute of Mental Health. **Bibliography on Psychotomimetics, 1943-1966.** Washington, GPO, 1968. 524p.

This work reprints bibliographies originally issued by Sandoz Pharmaceuticals, who produced the material in separate publications. The following bibliographies have been combined into this one volume: 1) Annotated Bibliography on Delysid (LSD 25) (d-lysergic acid diethylamide); 2) Five addenda to the aforementioned; 3) Catalogue of the Literature on Delysid (LSD 25) (d-lysergic acid diethylamide); 4) Delysid (LSD-25) Bibliography; 5) BOL-148 Bibliography; and 6) Bibliography on Psilochybin.

For the most part, the references listed are to articles in scientific journals, many in languages other than English. Almost all the entries are annotated.

60. U.S. National Institute on Alcohol Abuse and Alcoholism. **Alcoholism Treatment and Rehabilitation: Selected Abstracts.** Washington, GPO, 1972. 202p. index. (DHEW Publication No. (HSM) 72-9136). $2.75pa. S/N 1724-0239.

This bibliography covers literature on a wide range of treatment modalities, techniques, and rehabilitation and treatment programs. It includes abstracts of world literature since 1960. The presentation is in two parts, books and journal articles. The book section is rather short, reviewing only 37 books. The journal article section, which makes up the bulk of the publication, has been divided into four sections as follows: 1) reviews of the literature, 2) variables in management and treatment, 3) treatment modalities, and 4) treatment programs, rehabilitation, and special techniques. Abstracts are about one-third of a page long. Research investigators, clinicians, therapists, and students will find the bibliography of use.

61. U.S. National Institute on Alcohol Abuse and Alcoholism. **Audio-Visual Materials on Alcohol and Alcoholism.** Washington, GPO, 1974. 34p. illus. index. (DHEW Publication No. (ADM) 74-32).

The National Institute on Alcohol Abuse and Alcoholism and the National Clearinghouse for Alcohol Information (an information service of the Institute) prepared this guide to provide information on films dealing with alcoholism. The materials listed have been produced since 1960. With each entry the following information is usually included: title, medium, date, running time, color or black and white, audience, sale and/or rental price, and an annotation. Indication is also given as to whether or not the medium is cleared for use on commercial-sponsored television. There is a general subject index and some supplementary material such as a listing of additional films (unannotated), television announcements, radio announcements, radio programs, and additional resources.

62. U.S. National Institute on Drug Abuse. **A Cocaine Bibliography–Nonannotated.** Prepared by Joel L. Phillips and Ronald D. Wynne. Washington, GPO, 1974. 131p. (DHEW Publication No. (ADM) 75-203; Research Issues Series No. 8). $2.00pa.

This extensive bibliography includes over 1,800 references from scientific and popular literature covering early times to the present. Many aspects of the subject are covered: the socio-psychological, biomedical, political, and economic. To a lesser extent coca is covered also. The bibliography is subdivided as follows: 1) news-media articles, 2) books, 3) documents, and 4) journal articles from scientific and technical publications, with a special subsection listing anonymous articles from the *Journal of the American Medical Association*. A list of journals included in the bibliographic references has been given. Also included is an analysis of the cocaine bibliography.

63. U.S. National Institute on Drug Abuse. **Drug Themes in Fiction.** By Digby Diehl. Washington, GPO, 1974. 40p. bibliog. index. (DHEW Publication No. (ADM) 75-191; Research Issues Series No. 10). $1.05pa.

This pamphlet includes an essay on drug themes in fiction, a list of references, and an annotated bibliography of fictional works with drug-related thematic content. The bibliography is divided into periods as follows: Post-Victorian; Post-World war II–Late 1950's; Rock 'n' Roll Flower Children of the late 1960's; and the Disillusionment of the 1970's. The roots of the drug themes are explained briefly. Also an indication of the viewpoint toward drug use is given as either positive, negative, or neutral.

64. U.S. National Institute on Drug Abuse. **Drug Themes in Science Fiction.** By Robert Silverberg. Washington, GPO, 1974. 55p. bibliog. index. (DHEW Publication No. (ADM) 75-190; Research Issues Series No. 9). $1.20pa.

This publication, written by a successful author of science fiction, contains a bibliographic essay or overview of drug themes in science fiction and an annotated bibliography of science fiction stories that have a drug theme. The bibliography is divided into periods: Primitive Period, c. 1900-1935; Predictive Period, c. 1935-1965; and Contemporary Period, c. 1965-1973. The author's view is that science fiction is more often a reflection of existing societal trends than a prediction of trends to come. He feels that the current upsurge in drug use is precisely mirrored by the upsurge in the use of such themes in science fiction.

65. U.S. National Institute on Drug Abuse. **Drugs and Attitude Change; Nonmedical Drug Use: Attitudes and Attitude Change.** Edited by Patricia Ferguson, Thomas Lennox, and Dan J. Lettieri. Washington, GPO, 1974. 152p. bibliog. index. (DHEW Publication No. (ADM) 75-185; Research Issues Series No. 3). $2.25pa.

This publication is an annotated bibliography of the major research findings in the field of the past 15 years, formulated in such fashion as to provide a summary, methodology, findings, and conclusions for each of the studies. The material is classified and arranged under three headings as follows: 1) information about drugs, 2) attitudes toward drugs, and 3) communication processes. The publication will be useful for those who seek a quick overview of the subject.

66. U.S. National Institute on Drug Abuse. **Findings of Drug Abuse Research.** An annotated bibliography of NIMH and NIDA-supported extramural grant research 1967-74. Rockville, Md., National Institute on Drug Abuse, 1975. 2v. index. (National Institute on Drug Abuse Research Monograph Series 1: DHEW Publication No. (ADM) 75-255).

These volumes list the drug abuse research literature supported by the National Institute of Mental Health and the National Institute on Drug Abuse. Abstracts or summaries of the articles are provided in most instances. There are 3,500 titles provided by 650 researchers. The intent of the compilation is to give some sense of the diversity and scope of the federal impact on drug abuse research. More specifically it will 1) help NIDA program personnel review the findings of previous drug abuse grants in order to plan future research, and 2) serve as a retrospective indication of the findings from supported research that have been disseminated to the scientific community and the general public.

Volume 1 contains sections on 1) methodology of drug research, 2) drug chemistry and metabolism, and 3) mechanisms of action of different drugs, while Volume 2 covers 4) behavioral studies, 5) adverse effects, toxicity and genetic effects, 6) drug use/abuse prevention, 7) treatment-related research, 8) psychosocial studies, 9) education, 10) epidemiological studies and surveys, 11) peripherally related.

67. Waller, Coy W., and Jacqueline J. Denny. **Annotated Bibliography of Marihuana (Cannabis sativa L.) 1964-1970.** University, Miss., Research Institute of Pharmaceutical Sciences, School of Pharmacy, University of Mississippi, 1971. 301p. index. $7.00.

Most of the 1,112 publications listed in this bibliography are from scientific periodicals. Materials from the lay press have been omitted in most instances. Many foreign language materials have been included. The articles are arranged alphabetically by author. The plan is to supplement the basic list from time to time, and a 1971 supplement has been issued. Using this work, its supplement, and an earlier work, *The Question of Cannabis, Cannabis Bibliography*, by N. B. Eddy (United Nations Commission on Narcotic Drugs, E/CN7/479, 1965), one can trace the literature up to 1972.

68. Weber, David O. **99+ Films on Drugs.** New York, Educational Film Library Association, 1970. 68p. index. $3.00pa.

This booklet presents reviews of recent 16mm films on drug abuse. In addition to the description and summary, an evaluation, a rating, and the level of each film is given. A directory of distributors and their addresses is included. There is some introductory text material, and a few films are listed but not reviewed. The reviews presented include comments made by young people as well as adults. Good films on drug abuse are said to be scarce. It is evident, too, that opinions vary regarding the quality of the drug abuse films that are produced.

69. Weise, C. E., comp. **Teratogenic and Chromosomal Damaging Effects of Illicit Drugs: An Annotated Bibliography with Selected Related Citations Involving the Effects of Licit Drugs.** With assistance from S. Busse and edited by R. J. Hall. Toronto, Addiction Research Foundation, 1973. 175p. index. $5.50pa.

This bibliography is important because a number of substances, particularly illicit drugs, have been linked to chromosomal damage and birth defects in offspring.

The literature cited includes research studies, clinical reports, review articles, letters to the editor, and other commentaries. The material is arranged alphabetically by senior author. The work is in two parts. The first contains 241 citations and annotations of publications about illicit drugs; the second is an unannotated listing of references to materials about the effects of licit drugs. Almost all the articles are available on microfiche from the publisher. Keyword, author, and drug name indexes have been furnished.

70. Wells, Dorothy, comp. **Drug Education: A Bibliography of Available Inexpensive Materials.** Metuchen, N.J., Scarecrow Press, Inc., 1972. 111p. bibliog. index. $5.00. LC 72-317 ISBN 0-8108-0507-3.

This partially annotated bibliography was compiled by a librarian in an attempt to meet the demand of college students for pamphlet materials. All the items listed are free or inexpensive (up to $2.50). The compiler has starred titles that she feels will make a significant contribution to library files. The material is arranged under the following headings: 1) general publications, 2) government publications, 3) reprints, and 4) late additions. Entries in the government publications section are arranged by title, those in the other sections by publisher or issuing agency. There are good author, title, and subject indexes. This is a useful well-selected list.

2. Dictionaries, Glossaries, and Directories

This section lists a number of publications designed to familiarize the reader with the street language of the drug abuser. Communication with drug abusers can be difficult without such knowledge—for example, many abusers know only the street names of the drugs they use, and emergency medical assistants need to recognize these drug names immediately. Most of the directories included list organizations, agencies, and services that offer help to the troubled addict. The *Grassroots Directory of Drug Information and Treatment Organizations* (see entry 71) is perhaps the most outstanding of these. There is also a *Directory of Halfway Houses for the Mentally Ill and Alcoholics* (see entry 82).

71. **Grassroots Directory of Drug Information and Treatment Organizations.** Madison, Wisc., Student Association for the Study of Hallucinogens, Inc. (STASH), 1971– . looseleaf.

This publication comes with a subscription to the *Grassroots* publication, which is reviewed separately (see entry 184). The directory consists of looseleaf volumes; new listings are added and corrections are made from time to time. Arrangement is alphabetical by state. Included are such organizations as counseling and referral services, detoxification programs, drug analysis programs, education and information services, free clinics, government agencies, hot-lines, in-patient services, law enforcement agencies, methadone maintenance and out-patient services, and religions using drugs. The information about each agency includes name, address, phone, description of programs and services, publications, clientele, financial data, and names of staff and officers.

72. Hardy, Richard E., and John G. Cull. **Drug Language and Lore.** Springfield, Ill., Charles C. Thomas, 1975. 171p. $7.95. LC 74-16450. ISBN 0-398-03245-9.

This is a dictionary of the language used by drug abusers. Though no claim is made that it is complete, the list is fairly long and includes frequently used words and phrases.

Besides providing information for those who work with abusers, works like this one also reveal much about the addict's personality and lifestyle as seen through his language.

73. Keller, Mark, and Mairi McCormick. **A Dictionary of Words about Alcohol.** New Brunswick, N.J., Publications Division, Rutgers Center of Alcohol studies, 1968. 236p. bibliog. $7.50. LC 68-64841.

The authors of this authoritative work who are editors of the *Quarterly Journal of Studies on Alcohol,* define a great variety of words pertaining to all aspects of alcohol and alcohol problems. Also included are etymologies (when they throw some light on the basic meaning of the word) and citations showing the word or term in context. In some instances historical accounts are also included to show changes of meaning. A list of works cited has been appended. The work is unique, interesting, and of high quality.

74. Keville, Kathleen, ed. **Where to Get Help for a Drug Problem.** New York, Award Books; London, Tandem Books, 1971. 237p. $1.25pa.

This guide lists, by state and then by city, facilities where one may go for help with a drug problem. It includes hundreds of agencies, community organizations, hospitals, clinics, and similar facilities in the United States that are involved with the treatment of drug addiction and drug problems. The information given about each agency usually includes name, address, phone number, eligibility, kind of facility and services available, cost, and names of directors. Lacking consistent financial support, many drug agencies lead transitory existences, so the information given in directories like this one is often inaccurate. The *Grassroots Directory of Drug Information and Treatment Organizations* (see entry 71) and *Narcotics and Drug Abuse A to Z* (see entry 77) are better publications (although more expensive) because they are updated with looseleaf supplements.

75. Landy, Eugene E. **The Underground Dictionary.** New York, Simon and Schuster, 1971. 206p. $2.70pa. LC73-139637. ISBN 0-671-20803-9pa.; 0-671-21012-2 casebound.

This dictionary was compiled by a clinical psychologist who has had many professional dealings with drug abusers and others of the counterculture and subcultures. Definitions of terms include indications of the subcultures they come from, such as: blacks; drug users; homosexuals; motorcycle groups; medical, scientific or chemical personnel; musicians; prisoners and police; and prostitutes. Many Spanish terms are included. The book, which contains more terms than most glossaries of drug abuse terms, is somewhat like a dictionary of slang.

76. Lingeman, Richard R. **Drugs from A to Z: A Dictionary**. Rev. and updated 2nd ed. New York, McGraw-Hill Book Co., 1974. 310p. bibliog. $6.95. LC 74-13363. ISBN 0-07-037913-0; 0-07-037912-2pa.

Most of the terms included here are from the world of drug abuse, though some scientific and pharmacologic information about drugs, normal medical doses, history and lore surrounding drugs of abuse, and quotations from the literature of the drug world are also included. The origins of the many slang terms listed are traced when possible. Eric Partridge's works on slang were consulted along with other works. The dictionary contains the following appendices: nonsynthetic derivates of opium, morphine, and cocaine; generic names of synthetic opiates; Schedule I drugs under the Controlled Substances Act of 1970; Schedule II drugs under the controlled Substances Act of 1970, as revised in 1973; and Schedules III, IV, and V drugs under the Controlled Substances Act of 1970, as revised in 1973.

77. **Narcotics and Drug Abuse A to Z.** Vols. 1-3. Queens Village, N.Y., Social Service Publications Division of Croner Publications, Inc., 1971. Looseleaf. Kept up to date with quarterly supplements. $18.00 per year per volume. LC 78-173860.

This is a looseleaf directory, dictionary, and guide to information sources concerned with drug abuse. Each volume consists of six sections: 1) dictionary—a compilation of terms germane to the field of drugs, narcotics, and drug addiction; 2) drugs and narcotics—the most frequently abused dangerous drugs are profiled; 3) who's who, which attempts to list medical and program directors of the facilities given in the book as well as executives of "umbrella" agencies, and those involved in various drug addiction programs; 4) bibliography, listing better known works; 5) miscellaneous, which gives the more important facts and dates regarding drugs and addiction in telegram style, as well as a list of organizations; 6) directory of facilities and organizations.

All sections are identical in each of the volumes except Section 6, the directory of facilities and organizations, which varies according to the section of the country covered. Volume 1 covers facilities in Connecticut, New Jersey, and New York; Volume 2, facilities in Alaska, Arizona, California, Colorado, Hawaii, Idaho, Montana, New Mexico, Nevada, Oregon, Utah, Washington, and Wyoming; and Volume 3, the remaining states and Puerto Rico.

The publication should be of particular value to judges, law enforcement agencies, guidance counselors, teachers, clergymen, and parents.

78. National Coordinating Council on Drug Abuse Education and Information, Inc. **Directory.** Washington, National Coordinating Council on Drug Abuse Education and Information, Inc., 1970. 90p. $3.00.

This is an alphabetical list of Council members (organizations, not individuals), with separate listings for federal agency members and state affiliates. Position statements of some of the organizations are provided. Information given about the Council itself includes history, purposes, support, officers, and trustees. There is no index, but the table of contents is alphabetical and will serve as such. The listing of the member organizations includes information on purposes, officers' names, and lists of publications.

79. Student Association for the Study of Hallucinogens. **Directory of Drug Information Groups.** Directory staff, Risa Grossman and others. Beloit, Wisc., STASH Press, 1970. 183p. index. $4.50 LC 75-136212.

This directory serves as a resource guide to organizations concerned with drugs and drug information, including data on drug education and counseling and treatment programs. The information included with the entries was prepared from questionnaires sent to the organizations. Arrangement is alphabetical by name under the states. Some entries include a good deal of information, some very little. Besides address, most give the name of a person to contact. The longer entries include such information as purpose of the organization, publications, programs, services, research, financial data, and officers. It was planned that the list would be updated frequently.

80. U.S. Food and Drug Administration. **Listing of FDA Approved Methadone Treatment Programs for Narcotic Addiction, Current as of July 1975.** Washington, GPO, 1975. 1v. (unpaged).

The agencies listed in this publication are arranged by state. Each entry includes an identifying number, phone number, name of program, name of sponsor, mailing address, and site address. There is no additional information and no text material.

81. U.S. National Clearinghouse for Drug Abuse Information. **National Directory of Drug Abuse Treatment Programs.** By Deena D. Watson. Washington, GPO, 1972. 381p. $2.75.

The directory is an expansion of an earlier listing called *Directory of Narcotic Treatment Agencies in the United States 1968-1969.* Descriptive outlines of 1,300 treatment programs are given, arranged by state. The object of the compendium is to present a referral source for people who need services as the result of abuses of opiates, amphetamines, barbiturates, hallucinogens, solvents, and other substances (excluding alcohol). The listing is restricted to treatment and rehabilitation facilities; services related to drug abuse education and prevention were not included. Information given about each program includes: name, address, phone number, name of officer in charge, type of program, services, admission requirements, clientele, and number and type of staff.

82. U.S. National Institute of Mental Health. **Directory of Halfway Houses for the Mentally Ill and Alcoholics.** Washington, GPO, 1973. 133p. (DHEW Publication No. (HSM) 73-9008.). SuDocs No. HE 20.2402:H13. $2.50.

Providing information on the availability of halfway houses throughout the United States, this directory was designed for use by referring professions, families of potential residents, or the individuals for whom this kind of facility would be appropriate. The facilities provide residential service to the emotionally disturbed, alcoholics, or combinations of these. The directory is arranged by state, and within each state by the primary resident group served. Data given for each facility are as follows: name, address, phone number, year established, geographic area served, auspices, capacity, ages served, sex served, persons served, maximum stay permitted, number of readmissions permitted, and admission requirements.

83. U.S. National Institute of Mental Health. **International Directory of Investigators in Psychopharmacology.** Edited by Alice A. Leeds. World Health Organization/National Institute of Mental Health. Washington, GPO, 1972. 439p. (DHEW Publication No. (HSM) 72-9091).

The names of the persons listed in this compilation were collected by means of questionnaires sent to those on various mailing lists. Approximately 2,200 names have been included. The purpose of the work is to alert researchers to on-going work in other parts of the world and in their own country and to stimulate an exchange of ideas among the investigators. In addition to the alphabetically arranged biography section, which makes up the bulk of the work, there is a geographical index, an index of research activities, and a major fields index.

84. U.S. National Institute on Drug Abuse. **National Institute on Drug Abuse Training Grants Directory.** By Stuart L. Nightingale and Lonnie E. Mitchell. Washington, GPO, 1976. 31p. (DHEW Publication No. (ADM) 76-285).

This publication provides a convenient resource and catalog of the training grants supported by the Institute. There are three sections: 1) Developmental, 2) Career Teacher, and 3) Research Fellowship Training Grants. Each section is arranged alphabetically by state, then by institution. Universities and colleges will be interested in this publication.

85. Winek, Charles. **1971 Drug Abuse Reference.** Bridgeville, Pa., Bek Technical Publications, Inc., 1971. 100p. $2.00. LC 73-155732.

This small book is intended for parents, teachers, and students. It attempts to define words used by drug abusers, scientists, and others concerned with drug use. There are five sections: 1) general terms, 2) drug abuse terms, 3) user slang, 4) a list of drugs and chemicals commonly abused, and 5) an educational source guide, which includes short lists of books, pamphlets, and films on drug abuse. The latter is perhaps the least useful section as it is short and provides little information about the material. The dictionary sections are quite useful. The compiler is a toxicologist and professor of pharmacology.

3. Handbooks, Manuals, and Guides

This section contains a variety of materials aimed at several different groups—parents, law enforcement officers, physicians, lawyers, social workers, students, first-aid squads dealing with overdose victims, commanders in the military services, and drug abusers themselves. Those for the latter, such as the *Hippy's Handbook* (see entry 96), are intended primarily to assist the addict in living with his habit and the drug counterculture. Most publications in this section contain a good deal of practical information about drug effects and how to deal with the abuser and his problem.

86. Alexander, C. J., and Sandy Alexander. **How to Kick the Habit! The Drug Withdrawal Handbook**. New York, Frederick Fell, Inc., 1972. 176p. $5.95. LC 72-175424. ISBN 0-8119-0208-0.

This somewhat flamboyant book is for the general reader, particularly the teen-ager or older youth. However, the senior author is a physician who has had a good deal of experience with youthful drug offenders, and he takes a no-nonsense realistic approach. The chapter headings are as follows: 1) The killer drugs: what you should know about their use; 2) the symptoms: how you can recognize a drug user and his drug; 3) Crossing the bridge: the way to communication and help; 4) Back to reality: is methadone the way? 5) The right diet: what it can do for the addict; 6) To keep your children off drugs: permissiveness, over-protection, or discipline?; 7) Some popular misconceptions: former addicts speak up; 8) Double jeopardy: the drug war in Vietnam.

The second part of the book, "Tell me Doctor," is made up of questions and answers that young people often ask. In addition, the following useful appendices are included: glossary of slang terms associated with today's youth and the drugs they abuse; a list of halfway houses for drug information; "The Westport Drug Story"—an ABC television production.

The authors believe that there is no panacea for treatment of the drug problem. However, they believe that at the present time there is no better therapy than methadone use for treating withdrawal symptoms of heroin addicts. The stress of the book is on preventing the use of dangerous drugs in unsupervised settings.

87. American Hospital Association. **Desk Reference on Drug Abuse**. 2nd ed. Chicago, American Hospital Association, 1971. 76p. bibliog. $1.65.

This book, prepared mainly for hospitals and their personnel involved in providing treatment to drug abusers, is in four sections. The first is on diagnosis and treatment and has its own separate index. The second section is on the hospital and the law. The third section is an extensive bibliography arranged by type of drug. The last section is a good glossary of "drug culture" language.

88. American Hospital Association. **Who Cares about an Alcoholism Program in the General Hospital?** Chicago, American Hospital Association, 1972. 49p. bibliog. $1.50. ISBN 0-87258-088-1.

The first section of this pamphlet-sized manual asks a number of questions about the care of alcoholics and presents some related facts. The second section presents a number of responses to problems and outlines attendant steps. There are several appendices including a statement of admission to the general hospital of patients with alcohol and other drug problems, a typical history of a chronic alcoholic, physical conditions associated with alcoholism, and others.

89. American Medical Association. **Drug Dependence: A Guide for Physicians.** Chicago, American Medical Association, 1969. 186p. bibliog. $1.00pa.

This small publication consists of papers and statements made by the Council on Mental Health and the Committee on Alcoholism and Drug Abuse of the American Medical Association. The statements and papers, originally published in journals of the American Medical Association, have been somewhat abridged to eliminate duplication. Pharmacological, psychological, and sociological bases for drug abuse are taken up. Following are sections on medical treatment and management, the role of law and of education in deterring abuse, and lastly the need for ongoing research in a number of areas. Although the book is intended for physicians, it can easily be understood by laymen. In spite of the fact that the booklet was published a few years ago, the material is still valid, authentic, and worth reading.

90. American Medical Association. **Manual on Alcoholism.** Chicago, American Medical Association, 1973. 72p. bibliog. $2.50pa.

This manual, intended to help physicians treat individuals afflicted with alcoholism, presents a good general view of the subject. The material is divided into sections as follows: 1) the problem, 2) the causes, 3) alcohol: its metabolism and pharmacology, 4) diagnosis and treatment, and 5) an appendix, consisting of a joint statement of principles concerning alcoholism by the American Bar Association and the American Medical Association, and a bibliography.

The text is easy to read and may be of interest to anyone concerned with the problem.

91. Andrews, Matthew. **The Parents' Guide to Drugs.** Garden City, N.Y. Doubleday, 1972. 186p. illus. bibliog. index. $6.95. LC 78-144245.

This guide, prepared by a former drug addict who is a novelist and journalist, is for parents, teachers, and concerned adults. It is surprisingly well done. The first part is a short discussion of the drugs of abuse. The scientific information in this section is a bit weak, but some insight is given into the "drug culture," and there is also information on how the illicit drugs are packaged, prepared, priced, and used. The second part is a discussion of the environment—that is, the home, the school, the street, and the law. The third part discusses therapy, with short sections on the public hospital, private clinics, psychiatric or individual therapy, and encounter or group therapy. Part four, on the parent, gives a glossary of terms used by addicts, a list of organizations and associations interested in drug education, a state-by-state directory of agencies giving emergency aid, suggested readings, recommended films, and not recommended films.

92. Birdwood, George. **The Willing Victim: A Parent's Guide to Drug Abuse.** 2nd ed. London, Secker and Warburg, 1971. 208p. bibliog. $7.75. ISBN 0-436-04300-9.

This book was written primarily for parents of teenagers. Since drug use has been given so much sensational publicity in the press, the author attempts to bring the matter down to earth and strip drug abuse of its mystical aura, which in his view makes abuse appear attractive to the young. The first five chapters of the book describe origins and actions of the drugs, showing why some individuals become their willing victims. Chapter headings are as follows: 1) Who gets addicted?; 2) The soft drugs; 3) The hard drugs; 4) LSD and other hallucinogens; 5) Community addictions; 6) The teenage addict–why?; 7) What has been and could be done. There are several appendices: first-aid in cases of overdosage; drugs and the police–what to do if a teenager is involved; addicts' slang; and trade names and brief descriptions of commonly used drugs that could be abused. The last chapter "What has been and could be done" gives a good brief account of how the United States and Great Britain have handled the drug problem in the past and currently. No plan has been really satisfactory, although the author feels that some could be if minor changes were made.

93. Blakeslee, Alton. **What You Should Know about Drugs and Narcotics.** n.p., The Associated Press, 1969. 48p.

This pamphlet presents an accurate and factual account of today's drug scene and the dangers associated with drug abuse. The approach is largely psychological, and there are good suggestions on how to deal with young people and drug abusers. The work should appeal to both parents and young people. Chapter headings are as follows: 1) The drug scene in America, 2) The scope and signs of drug use, 3) The major mind-affecting drugs, 4) Fuses of the mind-drug explosion, 5) The appeal of drugs, 6) "Mind" drugs–their human price, 7) What parents can do, 8) Law and the "mind" drugs, and 9) The outlook for "mind" drugs. Several films on drugs and narcotics are reviewed briefly.

94. Bludworth, Edward. **300 Most Abused Drugs: A Pictorial Handbook of Interest to Law Enforcement Officers and Others.** Rev. ed. Tampa, Fla., Trend Publications, 1974. 30p. illus. (col). index. $2.00. ISBN 0-88251-018-5.

This small booklet contains excellent color photographs of the most commonly abused drugs, most of them prescription tablets and capsules. Trade names, chemical names, ingredients, and amounts of each are indicated, with supplementary descriptions and a glossary of terms in separate sections. Handbooks such as this one are quite useful in helping laymen as well as law-enforcement officers to identify abused drugs. Many publications on drug abuse contain sections with similar photographs, but this compact booklet should prove as valuable as any.

95. Bogomolny, Robert L., Michael R. Sonnenreich, and Anthony J. Roccograndi. **A Handbook on the 1970 Federal Drug Act: Shifting the Perspective.** Springfield, Ill., Charles C. Thomas, 1975. 182p. index. $13.50. LC 74-8452. ISBN 0-398-03190-8.

This publication analyzes the major revisions of 1970 of the federal drug laws in the United States. The book deals particularly with the control of stimulant, depressant, hallucinogenic, and narcotic drugs.

The work is presented in two sections. The first, which is called an introduction, presents a legislative history of the act, and the meanings of its provisions are pointed out. Chapter headings are: 1) Development of the act, 2) Getting the bill through Congress, 3) Unresolved issues, and 4) Effective dates. The second part presents a section-by-section analysis of the act. Chapters in this part are: 5) Title I–Rehabilitation programs relating to drug abuse, 6) Title II–Control and enforcement, and 7) Title III–Importation and exportation: amendments and repeals of revenue laws.

This book promises to be very useful to a number of groups, particularly lawmakers and persons who must comply with federal laws, such as physicians, drug researchers, pharmacists, and manufacturers of drugs. It will also be of considerable value to librarians, since questions about drug laws are frequent and few sources present the material in reasonably simple layman's language, as this book does.

96. Bronsteen, Ruth. **The Hippy's Handbook.** New York, Canyon Book Co., 1967. 63p. $1.00pa.

This booklet is said to be "the first and only complete guide to the underground today–with up-to-the minute regional data from the East Village to Haight-Ashbury." Although the hippy society has changed a great deal since this booklet was written, it provides a good view of what it was like in the 1960s.

The publication contains the following: a glossary of drug abuse terms; a list of underground newspapers and newsletters (with addresses); an underground movie guide; who's who of the underground (all unknown to the reviewer except for a few such as Joan Baez and Allen Ginsberg); a cookbook of supposed psychedelic substances; a list of drug antidotes; a list of clinics and/or rescue centers; a chapter on how to live on a minimum budget; how to dress like a hippie; how to survive on the streets; how to cope with the police; a directory of shops carrying hippy-oriented merchandise; and a section on hippy churches.

Obviously this is a unique publication.

97. **Controlled Substances Handbook.** Arlington, Va., Controlled Substances Information, Inc., 1972. 1v. (various paging). looseleaf. $20.00. LC 72-75168.

The purpose of this handbook is to provide information to Bureau of Narcotics and Dangerous Drugs registrants. The publication contains the text of the Controlled Substances Act, P.L. 91-513 of 1970, an updated version of the regulations, and an explanation of the regulations written in everyday language that can be applied to real situations. Virtually every person who handles drugs must register with the Bureau. This includes manufacturers, distributors, wholesalers, practitioners such as physicians, dentists, veterinarians, scientists, pharmacies (not pharmacists), and hospitals. Sections are included on labeling and packaging requirements, records and reports, order forms, schedules of controlled substances, and other like matters.

The handbook is supplemented by a periodical publication called *Controlled Substances Quarterly,* published as a service to assist in keeping abreast of the latest regulatory actions. Each issue includes text material and update pages for the handbook.

98. Dawtry, Frank, ed. **Social Problems of Drug Abuse: A Guide for Social Workers.** Edited on behalf of the National Association of Probation Officers. New York, Appleton-Century-Crofts; London, Butterworths, 1968. 115p. illus. (col). bibliog. index. $2.65pa.

This book was written as an aid to practicing social workers. Although it is British, most of what is said applies to situations in the United States as well. The first part covers the social problem of drugs and the second provides background information on drugs. There is useful information on the role of the probation officer, clinics, treatment, and law; and a social workers' dictionary lists medical, trade, and popular terms in drug lore and literature. In addition, there is a list of treatment and rehabilitation facilities located in Great Britain included.

99. Dorris, Robert T., and D. F. Lindley. **Counseling on Alcoholism and Related Disorders.** With the editorial assistance of Tobias S. Annenberg. Beverly Hills, Calif., Glencoe Press, Division of The Macmillan Co., 1968. 123p. bibliog. $5.95pa.

This handbook is intended primarily for counselors in business and industry. The authors, who are recovered alcoholics, hope they can contribute to a better understanding and cooperation between the experienced, recovered alcoholic and the professionally trained person, both of whom are involved with treatment of the disturbed person. The chapter headings are as follows: 1) Basic information about alcoholism, 2) A new approach: lay group therapy, 3) Beverage alcohol: what it is and what it does to the human body, 4) The progressive symptoms of alcoholism, 5) Disorders resulting from alcoholism, 6) Counseling the alcoholic employee, 7) Community resources: lay groups, 8) Community resources: the professionals, and 9) Current trends in treating alcoholism: the national picture. There are also appended materials as follows: affiliates of the National Council on Alcoholism; summer schoools of alcohol studies; and definitions and explanations.

The book is quite well written, interesting, and practical in approach. There are particularly good sections on Alcoholics Anonymous, Al-Anon, and Alateen.

The authors conclude on a hopeful note. They point out that very often people do better for having "had a problem," since overcoming their difficulties often leaves them better than ever to assume leadership. Several famous examples are named such as Abraham Lincoln, William James, and Helen Keller. It is suggested that comfort and relief in periods of stress must be sought in faith rather than in mind-changing chemicals—the idea which is basic in Alcoholics Anonymous.

100. Gannon, Frank. **Drugs: What They Are, How They Look, What They Do.** New York, Third Press, 1971. 182p. illus. bibliog. $6.95. LC 148361 ISBN 0-89388-002-7.

This book gives basic information about drugs, making use of the question and answer technique. It is a book for those who have little prior knowledge of drugs. Although the author seems to have had little scientific education, a good deal of scientific material is presented and quoted, and it is reasonably accurate and pertinent. The appendix is a list of places where one may find drug help and information (by state). Also there are a few pages of colored pictures of drugs commonly abused.

101. Goldhill, Paul M. **A Parent's Guide to the Prevention and Control of Drug Abuse.** New York, Popular Library, 1971. 191p. bibliog. $0.95pa. LC 76-143853.

This book, written by a psychiatrist, is based on the premise that drug abuse is psychological in origin. The author does not believe that making known the alarming facts of drug abuse will necessarily prevent their use. The book attempts to show that drug use stems from emotional problems caused by poor family relationships. The first five chapters presented are headed as follows: 1) Why drug abuse: Questions and answers; 2) Prevention of drug abuse; 3) When you think your child is taking drugs; 4) Professional care and special drug situations; and 5) Drugs and the community. Chapter 6, "A Primer on Drugs," presents basic material about each type of abused drug. There is also a chart, "Selected Drugs and Their Effects," and a short glossary of slang terms. The guide presents sound psychology, authentic information about drugs, and good advice to parents.

102. Hofmann, Frederick G., and Adele D. Hofmann. **A Handbook on Drug and Alcohol Abuse: The Biomedical Aspects.** New York, Oxford University Press, 1975. 329p. bibliog. index. $10.95; $6.95pa. LC 74-83987

This excellent book was written by a pharmacology professor and a professor of clinical medicine. It provides a comprehensive source of information about drugs that are commonly abused, and the discussions are very well written. An attempt is made to separate facts from fiction. Such issues are raised as: why people start using drugs in the first place; why some abstain from use or abandon drugs after preliminary experimentation; whether LSD or marihuana causes chromosomal damage and teratogenic effects; and whether we need stricter laws or some kind of legalization of drug use. Major emphasis is on the clinical effects of drug use on human beings. Animal studies have not been stressed.

The handbook covers the following topics: 1) introduction; 2) general aspects of drug abuse; 3) narcotic drugs; 4) generalized depressants of the central nervous system: alcohol, barbiturates and other drugs exerting similar effects; 5) general depressants of the central nervous system: volatile solvent and aerosol inhalation ("glue sniffing"); 6) hallucinogens: LSD and other agents having similar effects; 7) hallucinogens: marihuana, hashish, and atropinic drugs; 8) central nervous system stimulants; 9) the medical diagnosis of drug abuse; 10) management of selected clinical problems: pharmacological aspects; and 11) drug abuse and the law.

Chapters 9 and 10 present some very practical information on the medical diagnosis of drug abuse and the management of certain problems. The last chapter, which considers the legal aspects of the drug problem, is also notable, pointing out very good and not often mentioned reasons for not legalizing marihuana, at least at the present time. Not enough is known about the consequences of various patterns of cannabinoid usage; the potency of marihuana varies; it is difficult to analyze the material or even describe it in regard to its composition; it is possible to determine the active principles of marihuana (or metabolites of them) in blood only with the resources of a modern research laboratory. The book is highly recommended for students and practitioners of the health professions particularly, but it is also suitable for educators and others who may be interested.

103. International Research Group on Drug Legislation and Programs. **Controlling Drugs: International Handbook for Psychoactive Drug Classification.** By Richard H. Blum, Daniel Bovet, James Moore, and associates. San Francisco, Jossey-Bass Publishers, 1974. 378p. bibliog. index. $25.00. LC 73-9070. ISBN 0-87589-203-5.

This handbook was prepared under the auspices of the United Nations Social Defense Research Institute. Drug classification schemes are used as a basis for national and international legislation. These schemes influence penal actions, manufacturing controls, commercial regulation, and prescription requirements because they are based on assumptions about the benefits and dangers of drug effects. This book provides information that may be helpful in determining how drugs are or can be classified and also what kinds of data, logic, and analysis are useful in the classification. Special attention is given to international aspects of drug control.

Several major themes recur in the book. One is that a state of uncertainty characterizes estimates of drug effects. Another is that policy-makers in the field of drug legislation and control should consider as many alternatives as possible. A third theme is evaluation, which implies knowledge of the various standards that can be used to judge drugs, people, programs, and laws. A fourth theme, related to the third, is the expectation that policy be based on knowledge. There are five sections of the book: 1) overview, 2) basic science and medical considerations, 3) research design and clinical considerations, 4) epidemiological and behavioral science considerations, and 5) economic, legal, and administrative considerations.

The information included in this rather weighty volume may prove useful to lawmakers, officials, professionals, and individuals whose duties or interests have to do with control of psychoactive drugs. The implications of the book are that present drug classification schemes are not accurate and consistent and that major changes should be considered.

104. Jenkins, David P., and Robert Brody. **Facts about Commonly Used Drugs: A Non-Abuser's Guide to Pharmacological and Non-Medical Use of Drugs.** 2nd ed. Phoenix, Do It Now Foundation, 1973. 68p. bibliog. $1.25pa.

The authors of this small booklet feel that they present the material on commonly abused drugs "realistically." The reviewer doesn't know about the realism, whatever that may be, but the material seems to be reasonably accurate—although it seems likely that the authors obtained a good deal of it from the street in spite of the attempt at documentation. There are some freak elements about the publication, particularly the cover picture. There are better places to get information about drugs.

105. Johnson, Robert B., Maurice S. Tarshis, and Thomas M. Colasuonno. **What to Know about Drugs: A General Classification of Drugs and Volatile Chemicals of Potential Abuse.** Corvallis, Ore., Continuing Education Books, 1970. 26p. bibliog. $2.50pa. ISBN 0-87678-407-4.

This manual on drugs and volatile chemicals of potential abuse presents brief, concise, basic information about each drug family. The introduction provides a short historical outline of drug problems and limited information about the drugs themselves. The main part of the presentation is a set of nine tables that give details about each class of drugs and the use and abuse of each drug. Rather extensive bibliographies have been included. The publishers have made the nine drug classification charts (which are suitable for bulletin board displays) available in a separate packet, printed on one side only of 11" x 17" paper.

106. Kline, Nathan S., Stewart F. Alexander, and Amparo Chamberlain. **Psychotropic Drugs: A Manual for Emergency Management Overdosage.** Oradell, N.J., Medical Economics Co.; distr. New York, Van Nostrand Reinhold Co., 1974. 136p. illus. (col.) $12.95.

This pocket-sized manual was designed to help physicians, nurses, and first-aid emergency squads deal with a patient who has received an overdose of a psychotropic drug. This kind of drug is often purchased illicitly on the street. The book spells out what lifesaving actions should be taken for each symptom of overdosage, describes the clinical signs and symptoms for major drug classifications, and recommends appropriate treatment.

The actions that non-medical trained personnel may take and the treatment that they may safely administer are indicated separately from those suitable only for physicians or trained individuals to use.

The main sections of the manual are: 1) a discussion of the treatment of severe complications; 2) clinical signs and treatments arranged by the various classes of drugs; 3) a table of drugs giving type, uses, manufacture, street names, and packaging data; 4) a table of approximate child and youth doses; 5) identifying color photographs of psychotropic drugs; and 6) a list of Poison Control Centers arranged alphabetically by state.

This concise, effective manual should help save many lives. The problem dealt with is a serious one, since over 50,000 deaths a year occur from drug overdosage. The material presented is authentic; the senior author is a noted psychiatrist and educator.

107. Kramer, J. F., and D. C. Cameron, eds. **A Manual on Drug Dependence.** Compiled on the basis of reports of WHO expert groups and other WHO publications. Geneva, World Health Organization, 1975. 107p. bibliog. S. Fr. 24.–pa. ISBN 92-4-154048-1.

This manual was prepared for use by health workers and others professionally involved in efforts to reduce the health and social problems associated with drug abuse. Chapters on the following topics have been included: 1) basic concepts and the use of terms, 2) patterns of use, 3) types of drug dependence: clinical syndromes, 4) circumstances of use, 5) special features associated with age, 6) social attitudes and responses, 7) management, and 8) research.

The manual provides a good overview of the topic. The need for more research is stressed, with certain areas listed as most urgently in need of study: 1) the nature and extent of the problems associated with drug-taking behavior, 2) the evaluation of the effectiveness of different policies, approaches, and methods used in the management of these problems, and 3) the development of improved means for their management.

108. Pace, Denny F., and Jimmie C. Styles. **Handbook of Narcotic Control.** Englewood Cliffs, N.J., Prentice-Hall, Inc., 1972. 95p. illus. bibliog. (Prentice-Hall Essentials of Law Enforcement Series). $3.50pa.; $7.50. LC 75-37962. ISBN 0-13-380469-0(pa.); 0-13-380477-1(cl.).

This publication is an overview of problems concerned with drug abuse. The basic information given will be of particular help to law enforcement officers. While some attention is given to the educational efforts of social agencies and the referral of drug abusers to hospitals and agencies that attempt to rehabilitate drug users, there is an emphasis on making arrests when other efforts have failed to cope with the problem user. The book contains sections on identifying the common drugs, a brief history of them, how to conduct a drug investigation, handling crimes associated with drug usage, and the role of police in drug education. Also included is a brief glossary of scientific terms, a discussion of the Comprehensive Drug Abuse Prevention and Control Act of 1970, sections from federal laws governing drugs, and a list of references, films, and other audiovisual media.

109. Patterson, James A. **Study Guide for Emergency Medical and Drug Abuse Technicians.** Comp. for use by and for Terros, Inc. Phoenix, Do It Now Foundation, National Media Center, 1973. 1v. (various paging). looseleaf. $3.00 (without binder); $4.00 (with binder).

This publication was written and compiled for use in the training program of an emergency drug treatment facility. The material has been produced in looseleaf format so that other drug treatment organizations can incorporate it in their own training programs. The 28 brief sections presented cover a wide variety of topics. In addition to some general sections, there are also sections on such topics as first aid, basic physiology and pharmacology, drug combinations, street drugs and trends, management of overdoses, drug-related medical problems, basic communication skills, suicide intervention, referral resources, and police procedures. Much of the information presented is sketchy and not well organized. However, material of this kind is unique and practical and is undoubtedly much needed.

110. Pawlak, Vic. **Conscientious Guide to Drug Abuse.** 4th rev. ed. Phoenix, Do It Now Foundation, 1973. 48p. $1.00pa.

This is "a manual written and researched expressly for drug users, abusers, and many others." A short monograph on each drug includes information such as classification, overdose potential, physical addiction properties, and common methods of consumption. It covers somewhat unusual drugs of abuse, such as belladonna, morning glory seeds, aerosol sprays, glue, and several petroleum products.

The material presented is probably as accurate as could be learned from contact with street drugs and addicts, but the book could scarcely be called an authentic guide. The author, who assumes that the reader will be taking many chances with drugs, gives advice on how to be as careful as possible. It is a curious book, a cross between the far-out freaky and a serious discussion.

111. Smith Kline and French Laboratories. **Drug Abuse: A Manual for Law Enforcement Officers.** New rev. 5th ed. Prepared under the direction of Donald K. Fletcher. Philadelphia, Smith, Kline and French Laboratories, 1968. 68p. illus. bibliog.

This manual provides information on both the legal and illegal use of abusable drugs and other chemical agents (such as solvents). The following topics are discussed: what drug abuse is, drug groups subject to abuse, drugs and driving, the drug abuser, illegal traffic in dangerous drugs, drug law, investigative techniques, and contact with newsmen. In addition, the following appended materials have been included: 1) a drug identification chart, 2) SK&F's free services for law enforcement officers, 3) a glossary of terms, 4) handling the Addict Report Forms, 5) regional offices of enforcement agency, 6) selected references, and 7) selected films.

112. Sonoma County Drug Abuse Council. **Drug Abuse: Information and Resource.** Santa Rosa, California, Sonoma County Drug Abuse Council, 1971. 142p. bibliog. $4.50pa.

The miscellaneous information about drugs of abuse presented here is useful for reference. Main sections cover: 1) classification of drugs, 2) glossary of slang terms, 3) cocaine, 4) hallucinogenic drugs, 5) marihuana, 6) narcotics, 7) sedatives, 8) stimulants, 9) volatile liquids, 10) history of federal drug laws, 11) California drug laws, 12) usage and arrest figures, 13) effects of arrest and conviction (adults and juveniles), 14) motivation, 15) treatment of drug dependence, 16) referrals, and 17) bibliography (books, periodicals, and pamphlets).

113. U.S. Armed Forces Information Service. **Drug Abuse: Game without Winners; A Basic Handbook for Commanders.** 2nd ed. Washington, GPO, 1972. 71p. illus. $0.55pa.

This official publication, written primarily for commanders in the military services, presents brief material under the following chapter headings: 1) Command relationship to drug abuse; 2) Drugs: 2700 B.C. to now; 3) What is a drug and what does it do? 4) Marijuana and health; 5) Identifying the drug abuser and recommended action; 6) Illicit channels of distribution; 7) The comprehensive drug abuse prevention and control act; 8) Definitions of drug terminology; 9) Identification, detoxification, rehabilitation. A reference chart on drug abuse products has been provided.

The booklet contains good basic information about drugs and indicates the actions that commanders should take in dealing with the problem of drug abuse among military personnel.

114. U.S. Bureau of Narcotics and Dangerous Drugs. **Public Speaking on Drug Abuse Prevention: A Handbook for the Law Enforcement Officer.** Washington, GPO, 1970. 40p. $0.30pa.

This book gives valuable tips to assist the law enforcement officer in making effective addresses to audiences in his local community (a role he is encouraged to assume). The following chapters are included: 1) The purpose and uses of the handbook, 2) Knowing your audience, 3) Helpful hints for the public speaker, and 4) Suggested talks: "Drug Abuse: A Community Problem," "Understanding Addiction," "A Discussion of Marihuana." The "Suggested Talks" included are to be supplemented with local references. The booklet makes good suggestions and should prove useful.

115. U.S. National Clearinghouse for Drug Abuse Information. **A Treatment Manual for Acute Drug Abuse Emergencies.** Peter G. Bourne, ed. Washington, GPO, 1974. 178p. bibliog. index. (NCDAI Publication No. 16). $2.15pa. S/N 1724-00303.

This treatment manual was developed to assist those who are dealing with the drug abuser, particularly for the practicing physician. A growing number of emergency problems have been associated with the abuse of drugs, so a manual like this one can be very valuable. It covers the most commonly encountered drug abuse emergencies. Each chapter was written by an outstanding physician who describes his own preferred method for treating the condition in question. Chapters are arranged under the following headings: 1) Differential diagnosis, 2) Emergency treatment of opiate overdose, 3) Treatment of acute CNS depressant emergencies, 4) Emergency treatment of adverse reactions to CNS stimulants, 5) Emergency treatment of adverse reactions to hallucinogenic drugs, 6) Emergency treatment of acute reactions to cannabis derivatives, 7) Emergency treatment of inhalation psychosis and related states, 8) Emergency treatment of acute alcohol intoxication, and 9) Special problems. The subject is covered competently and comprehensively.

116. U.S. National Institute of Law Enforcement and Criminal Justice. **Methadone Treatment Manual.** Washington, GPO, 1973. 104p. bibliog. $1.20pa. S/N 2700-00227.

This manual is primarily for those who are initiating methadone treatment programs for heroin addicts or who are currently involved in such programs. It is also suitable for community leaders and as supplementary reading in drug education. Although the treatment has limitations and drawbacks, the compilers believe that both the patient and society are far better off than they would be if no treatment were provided. The manual consists of nine sections: 1) The nature of methadone treatment, 2) The patients and their treatment, 3) Medical considerations, 4) The staff, 5) Physical facilities, 6) Security considerations, 7) Termination of methadone treatment or after methadone, what? 8) Community relations, 9) A concluding comment. Also included are several appendices, such as sections on federal regulations.

117. U.S. National Institute of Mental Health. **Psychotropic Drugs and Related Compounds.** 2nd ed. By Earl Esdin and Daniel H. Efron. Washington, GPO, 1972. 791p. bibliog. index. (DHEW Publication No. (HSM) 72-9074). $7.50. S/N 1724-0194.

This publication provides research workers, clinicians, and students with a comprehensive listing of compounds that have psychotropic properties. Included is information about their chemical structure, pharmacologic activity, and therapeutic classification. The compounds are arranged by chemical structure; chemical formulas and all names (generic, chemical, trade, and synonyms) have been included. Names of manufacturers and distributors are given when possible. In addition, the entries include lethal dose (LD_{50} values), human dose, and literature references. A section on drug combinations, a bibliography of 1,764 references, and indexes by compound name and by Wiswesser Line Notation have been provided. The compilation is very useful for reference.

118. U.S. Special Action Office for Drug Abuse Prevention. **Residential Drug-Free Manual.** Executive Office of the President. Washington, GPO, 1974. 77p. (Special Action Office Monograph, Series C, No. 5.) $1.45pa. S/N 4110-00017.

Prepared to assist in the setting up of residential drug-free programs similar to the well-known Synanon, Daytop Village, or Phoenix House, this manual describes a model therapeutic community, outlining goals, treatment plans, and methods of operation. All aspects of the program are treated, such as facilities, budget, security, staffing, and treatment regimen. In this kind of therapeutic community, drug addiction is treated as a personality disorder. The guidelines that are presented are consistent with the Federal Funding Criteria. This monograph is important because the treatment described seems to offer the best chances for successful cures for addicts.

119. Williams, John B., ed. **Narcotics and Hallucinogenics—A Handbook.** Rev. ed. Beverly Hills, Calif., Glencoe Press, 1967. 277p. bibliog. $5.95.

The information in this handbook was obtained from people who have had actual experience in various phases of drug abuse problems, particularly law enforcement officers. Many topics are covered, but emphasis is on the addict; the drugs; controls; the local, state, federal, and international efforts to control drugs; the illegal sale and use of drugs; and drug addiction. The three main parts are: 1) general problems; 2) causes of addiction, descriptions of addicts, and criminal behavior; and 3) treatment of addicts. The handbook will be of particular value to physicians, educators, psychologists, sociologists, investigators, and police officers.

120. Winek, Charles L. **Everything You Wanted to Know about Drug Abuse . . . But Were Afraid to Ask.** New York, Marcel Dekker, Inc., 1974. 213p. bibliog. index. $12.75. LC 73-92518. ISBN 0-8247-6145-6.

The author of this book, who is Chief Toxicologist, Allegheny County Coroner's Office, and Professor of Toxicology at Duquesne University, is well qualified to write about drug abuse. He has been much involved in investigating drug related deaths, in providing a community drug analysis service, and in teaching about drug abuse on several levels. The material is presented in question-and-answer format, and questions frequently answered elsewhere have been omitted. Many of the questions reveal that there is much misinformation about drugs. The author dispels myths and tackles questions that many young people would be embarrassed to ask. His answers are based on generally accepted scientific information, and the book is interesting, informative, and authentic. Chapter headings are as follows: 1) The size and scope of the drug problem; 2) Reasons for the drug problem; 3) Sources of drugs; 4) Route of administration of drugs; 5) Drugs, sex, and promiscuity; 6) Heroin and other narcotics; 7) Barbiturates and other depressants; 8) Amphetamines and other stimulants; 9) Hallucinogens; 10) Marihuana and hashish; 11) Over-the-counter drugs and chemicals; 12) Alcohol is a drug, is a drug, is a drug; 13) Miscellaneous "stuff"; and 14) Solutions . . . Are there any? A glossary of drug abuse terms has been provided.

4. Periodicals

Not many periodicals deal exclusively with drug and alcohol abuse, and most of those that do began publication in the 1960s and '70s. Alcoholism, however, has been studied a good deal longer than other types of drug abuse. The majority of periodicals in the field are newsletters; they are often ephemeral in nature, and are not generally retained in libraries. As many as could be located have been listed. Several substantial journals are included, and a few good scientific ones exist such as the *Journal of Studies on Alcohol* (entry 143) and *Psychopharmacology* (entry 150). There is also a growing number of government-sponsored titles. Probably the reason for the paucity of periodicals on drug abuse is that relatively little research has been done in the field until recently. It is of note that the general acceptance of alcoholism and drug abuse as medical problems is proceeding slowly. It is also well to remember that much of the material on the subject appears in more general periodicals in the fields of medicine, biology, psychology, sociology, law, education, pharmacology, and other related areas.

121. **ADIT: Approaches to Drug Abuse and Youth.** New York, APS Publications, Inc., 1972– . 11 issues per year.

This newsletter publication is of special interest to counselors, teachers, psychologists, lawyers, social workers, and law enforcement officials. Included are ideas and reports of resources, experiments, successes, and failures.

122. **Addiction and Drug Abuse Report: A Confidential Newsletter Covering All Aspects of Drug Abuse, Its Prevention, and Treatment of Its Victims.** In two parts. New York, Grafton Publications, Inc., 1970– . Monthly.

The aim of this newsletter is to keep readers up to date on the constantly changing addiction scene, the progress of treatment methods, and community action in the field. A good deal of attention is given to alcoholism as well as to other drug abuse. The publication is particularly useful for those working closely with addicts.

123. **Addictive Behaviors.** Elmsford, N.Y., Pergamon Press, 1976– . Quarterly.

This interdisciplinary journal publishes articles reporting original research, theoretical papers, and critical reviews in the field of drug and other substance abuse. The emphasis is on alcoholism, drug abuse, tobacco use, and obesity of the type in which psychological or physical dependence plays a large part. Research in the fields of biochemistry, psychology, sociology, psychiatry, neurology, and pharmacology is covered.

124. **Alcohol Health and Research World.** Rockville, Md., U.S. National Institute on Alcohol Abuse and Alcoholism, 1974–. Quarterly.

This periodical was originally an experimental publication, but beginning with the fall 1976 issue it has been an approved federal periodical. It features survey articles and in-depth reports on all aspects of research, prevention, treatment and rehabilitation of alcohol abuse and alcoholism. Articles from allied fields are included when they are significant. Book reviews and bibliographies are included. The articles are of high quality, suitable for those engaged in research, treatment, or prevention work in the field.

125. **Alcoholism Digest.** Rockville, Md., Information Planning Associates, Inc., 1972– . Monthly.

This rather expensive periodical ($75.00 per year at this writing) summarizes current articles, books, and reports on various aspects of alcoholism. These reviews or summaries have also been collected into annual volumes called the *Alcoholism Digest Annual* (see entry 647). Special areas covered are: alcohol abuse education and research by schools, universities, and scientific institutions; treatment and rehabilitation of alcoholics in corporations, institutions, and rehabilitation centers; counseling of alcoholics and families by churches, courts, and clinics; driver education and drunk-driving presentations by law enforcement agencies and safety organizations; and federal, state, and local government programs for treatment and rehabilitation. The publication is of special value to educators, administrators, clergymen, physicians, and researchers.

126. **American Journal of Drug and Alcohol Abuse.** New York, Marcel Dekker, Inc., 1974– . 4 times per year.

This journal takes a medically oriented, comprehensive view of the field. Articles dealing with preclinical and clinical facets of the problem are included in the scope of the publication. Such subjects as drug abuse trends, pharmacology of abused drugs and drugs used in treatment, cultural attitudes, treatment methods, funding sources, criminal laws, community approaches, and self-help techniques are all covered. The journal is intended to appeal to all workers in the field.

127. Association of Food and Drug Officials of the United States. **Quarterly Bulletin.** Topeka, Kans., Editorials Committee of the Association of Food and Drug Officials of the United States, 1937– . Quarterly.

This bulletin publishes papers presented at meetings of the Association, such as the Annual Conference, and sectional and local conferences of Food and Drug Officials. Complete proceedings of the meetings of the National Association, abstracts of meetings of sectional and local organizations, and news items relative to food and drug control appear from time to time. Most of the material published concerns food rather than drugs.

128. **Attack on Narcotic Addiction and Drug Abuse.** Albany, New York State Narcotic Addiction Control Commission, 1967– . Quarterly.

This tabloid-sized news publication contains information on developments in drug-related problems in New York State. There are articles about legal matters, treatment of addicts, education, rehabilitation, and similar matters. Directories of agencies that provide help to drug users are included from time to time.

129. **Bulletin on Narcotics.** United Nations, Division of Narcotic Drugs, 1949– . Quarterly.

This international journal is published in English and French. Selected articles are subsequently published in Spanish and Russian, and a summary of each volume is issued in Chinese every year. The publication covers all aspects of drug control, the work of international groups responsible in this field, and developments in treatment, rehabilitation, and social reintegration of addicts. Some scientific articles that describe original research are published.

130. **Contemporary Drug Problems: A Law Quarterly.** New York, Federal Legal Publications, Inc., 1971– . Quarterly.

While most of the articles in this periodical are concerned with the legal aspects of drug abuse, some material is included on education, policy, social problems, treatment, employment, and other aspects of the drug problem. Book reviews are included also.

131. **Drug and Alcohol Dependence: An International Journal of Biomedical and Psychosocial Approaches.** Lausanne, Switzerland, Elsevier Sequoia S.A., 1975– . Bimonthly.

This journal is published under the auspices of the International Council on Alcohol and Addiction. The intention is that the publication will be multidisciplinary and promote relational approaches in research and intervention activities. Original research papers in English are preferred, but those in French and German are considered. The journal should interest those in the area of biomedical research as well as those engaged in clinical, epidemiological, psychosocial, sociocultural, educational, and medico-legal research.

132. **Drug Enforcement.** Washington, Drug Enforcement Administration, U.S. Department of Justice, 1973– . Quarterly.

This publication continues the *BNDD Bulletin*. Articles on miscellaneous matters of drug enforcement are presented with many photographs, some in color. There is usually a section on notable cases and also photographs and descriptions of persons wanted by the Drug Enforcement Administration. There have been special issues, such as one on international drug traffic.

133. **Drug Forum: The Journal of Human Issues.** Farmingdale, N.Y., Baywood Publishing Co., 1971– . Quarterly.

This journal investigates the psychological, medical, sociological, and cultural factors of drug abuse and their solution. The journal presents practical solutions and alternatives for changing drug-oriented ways of living, and it is especially valuable for those involved in treatment and rehabilitation programs and in supervision. Program failures as well as successes are presented. The publication is indexed in *Psychological Abstracts*, *Excerpta Medica*, *Biological Abstracts*, and *Abstracts on Criminology and Penology.*

134. **Drug Survival News.** Phoenix, Do It Now Foundation, 1970– . Bimonthly.

This tabloid-type publication first appeared in 1970 as *Vibrations–Drug Survival News*, and in 1974 it became a quarterly newsletter called *Street Drug Survival.* Offering news of interest to paraprofessionals, directors, workers, instructors, and those interested in the field of drug abuse, it covers traditional drugs of abuse (both legal and illegal), alcohol, and other chemicals which have physiologic effects. The general tone of the material published is sympathetic to drug use, although an attempt is made to give unbiased reports of current research. Publications such as this are of value in keeping one up to date on the current "drug scene."

135. **From the State Capitals, Drug Abuse Control.** Asbury Park, N.J., Bethune Jones, 1973– . Monthly.

This reporting service, issued in concise mimeographed form, provides factual data on current and prospective legislative, administrative, and judicial action at the state and local levels. Stressing the significance of action, it offers a continuing picture of trends.

136. **High Times: The Magazine of High Society**. New York, High Times Corporation, 1975– . Monthly. (Send mail to Box 386, Cooper Station, New York, N.Y. 10003; offices at 116 East 27th St., New York, N.Y. 10016 $14.00 for 12 issues).

Although this periodical presents underground material, it is attractive and conventional in format. Each issue includes a number of feature articles on matters of interest to drug users (such as information on marihuana smuggling), along with special features such as letters to the editor, record and book reviews, and a column on health. There is even a page of market quotations on illicit drug products from all over the world. The articles are for the most part accurate in their presentation of material but are favorably biased toward the use of drugs.

Perhaps the most outstanding aspect of the magazine is the advertising, which includes a wide range of drug paraphernalia products, drugs themselves, books, jewelry, clothing, and art objects for the drug enthusiast. Many of the ads are in full color.

This is undoubtedly the most amazing and unusual publication of its kind we have seen. A great deal of money and effort obviously go into its production.

137. **International Journal of the Addictions.** New York, Marcel Dekker, 1966– . Six times per year.

This journal is sponsored by the Institute for the Study of Drug Misuse, Inc., New York. It publishes scholarly articles on all aspects of addiction, including narcotics, alcohol, and tobacco. In addition, each issue usually contains a section of research notes, with brief descriptions of research being carried out.

138. **The Journal.** Toronto, Addiction Research Foundation, 1972– . Monthly.

This tabloid-sized publication is designed to familiarize professionals and other interested persons with recent developments in the alcohol and drug dependence field. It reports and interprets news in the areas of research, treatment, education, enforcement, and social policy.

139. **Journal of Altered States of Consciousness.** Farmingdale, N.Y., Baywood Publishing Co., 1973– . Semi-annual.

This journal deals with alterations in the pattern of mental functioning, such that the experiencer feels when his consciousness is radically different from the way it ordinarily functions. Characteristics of such conscious experiences are investigated. In addition to the field of psychopharmacology, others such as yoga, dream research, parapsychology, and such states as trance, hypnosis, general anesthesia, and mystic rapture are given attention.

140. **Journal of Drug Education.** Farmingdale, N.Y., Baywood Publishing Co., 1971– . Quarterly.

Covering the physiological, psychological, pharmacological, legal, and social aspects of drug use, this journal provides information and data of importance in organized educational drug programs. Subjects dealt with include the role of the educator in drug education; innovations in drug education; school and community drug education programs; drug research information; and drug education as applied to business and industry, law enforcement, the clergy, military, and other areas sensitive to the misuse of drugs. The journal is of special interest to such groups as administrators in educational institutions, teachers, guidance counselors, law enforcement officials, personnel supervisors, social workers, and military personnel. The periodical is indexed in several major tools, including *Psychological Abstracts*, *Excerpta Medica*, *Biological Abstracts*, and *Abstracts on Criminology and Penology*.

141. **Journal of Drug Issues.** Tallahassee, Fla., Journal of Drug Issues, Inc., 1971– . Quarterly.

This journal provides a forum for the presentation of drug issues. Papers selected cover a wide range of topics and appeal to a wide audience. Book reviews are included. The articles are of rather high quality, and many report research findings.

142. **Journal of Psychedelic Drugs: A Multidisciplinary Forum for the Study of the Drug Culture.** Beloit, Wisc., STASH Press, 1967– . Quarterly.

This journal is a cooperative venture between the Haight-Ashbury Free Medical Clinic and the Student Association for the Study of Hallucinogens (STASH). The goal of the journal when established was said to be to provide a method for dissemination of honest, objective drug information and to alert workers in the field to the rapidly changing drug abuse pattern which developed in the Haight-Ashbury district of San Francisco and spread to other parts of the country. In more recent issues emphasis has been on special themes and what is called the "politics of drug abuse." Still more recently the increasing amount of research on the subject encouraged the expansion of the journal from a semi-annual publication to a quarterly, and each year there has been one theme issue and three non-theme issues. The journal accepts a wide variety of articles–including critical and historical reviews, theoretical analyses, speculative papers with a systematic focus, and limited numbers of reports of research. Film reviews and bibliographies are included from time to time.

143. **Journal of Studies on Alcohol.** New Brunswick, N.J., Journal of Studies on Alcohol, Inc., at the Center of Alcohol Studies, Rutgers University, 1940– . Monthly.

Before 1975 this publication was called the *Quarterly Journal of Studies on Alcohol, Pts. A and B.* It publishes reports of new research on all aspects of alcohol and alcohol problems, including alcoholism. The type of material published alternates monthly. Original articles appear in the odd-numbered months; and abstracts, book reviews, bibliographies, and indexes appear in the even-numbered months.

The original articles report findings of researchers in such fields as medicine, physiology, biochemistry, psychiatry, psychology, pathology, sociology, economics, statistics, education, and law. The issues that review current literature cover books as well as periodical articles. Abstracts and reviews of over 1,300 items are published in each volume. Supplements on special subjects are occasionally published with the journal. This is one of the leading publications of the field.

144. **Narcotics and Drug Abuse–A to Z: A News Digest.** Queens Village, N.Y., Croner Publications, 1971– . Quarterly.

Subscribers to *Narcotics and Drug Abuse–A to Z* (see entry 77) receive this newsletter free of charge with the quarterly amendment services to the publication. The purpose of the newsletter is to keep readers informed of articles dealing with narcotics and drug abuse which have appeared in the press and national magazines. Pertinent articles are reproduced and studies cited.

145. **National Council on Drug Abuse: Newsletter.** Chicago, National Council on Drug Abuse, 1972– . Monthly.

This newsletter attempts to tell what is current in drug abuse prevention, education, treatment, rehabilitation, and research all over the world. It includes ideas on funding sources, and the names of people who might be needed resources. Supporting members of the Council receive the *Newsletter* as part of their membership. Those interested in the news disseminated include counselors, libraries, crisis centers, treatment centers, physicians, educators, social workers, hospitals, and law enforcement officers.

146. **National Drug Reporter.** Washington, National Coordinating Council on Drug Education, 1971– . Semi-monthly.

The publisher of this newsletter is the country's largest private non-profit drug consortium of 130 national professional, law enforcement, government, youth and service organizations, and corporations. The aim of the Council is to make a coordinated effort to find workable approaches to drug abuse prevention. The newsletter contains information on pertinent national projects, laws and proposed legislation, meetings, publication, and other related matters. At one time issues of this publication were included in the *Grassroots* subscription, but this practice was discontinued at the end of 1975.

147. **Pacific Information Service on Street Drugs.** Stockton, Calif., School of Pharmacy, University of the Pacific, 1971– . Irregular.

Each issue of this small publication usually contains one monographic article on some subject related to drug abuse. These review-type articles are usually written by a faculty member of a pharmacy school. They are brief but of high quality.

148. **PharmChem Newsletter.** Palo Alto, Calif., Pharm Chem Research Foundation, 1972– . Monthly.

Issues of this unique publication usually contain a few short articles about drugs that are frequently abused, with the intention of supplying factual information. The emphasis, however, is on determining and publishing the actual content of "street" drugs. Long lists are published in each issue giving the following information: alleged content, actual content, description, origin (city), date, and street price. The primary objective of the Foundation is to provide at a nominal cost and on an anonymous basis an analysis service on illicit drugs. The information supplied seems to be authentic as well as unique.

149. **Psychedelic Review.** New Hyde Park, N.Y., v.1, no. 1 issued by the International Federation for Internal Freedom, 1963–1971. Quarterly.

This publication was inaugurated as a forum for the exchange of information and ideas regarding psychedelic drug use, particularly social aspects. Since attitudes changed regarding such drug use and the dangers became more apparent, the journal began to publish a somewhat different kind of material and broadened its scope to include research reports, scholarly essays, pharmacologic and therapeutic reviews, artistic and poetic works, and accounts of non-chemical methods of consciousness expansion such as hypnotism, yoga, zen, and the like. A few well-known literary and scientific writers have contributed to the journal, as have the proponents of psychedelic drugs, although mostly in articles reprinted from other sources.

150. **Psychopharmacology**. New York, Springer-Verlag, 1960– . Monthly.

This is a publishing medium for scientific articles that analyze and synthesize information on the effects of drugs on behavior. Some contributions are of a clinical nature; some deal with specialized investigations in the fields of experimental psychology, neurophysiology, neurochemistry, general pharmacology, and related areas. The material included is of high quality.

151. **Registrant Facts.** Washington, U.S. Drug Enforcement Administration, 1974– . Quarterly.

This newsletter is published as part of the Drug Enforcement Administration's registrant information and self-regulation program. The registrants involved are agencies (such as pharmacies) that are registered to handle controlled substances. The newsletter reports regulations, information, and news of interest.

152. **STASH Capsules.** Madison, Wisc., Student Association for the Study of Hallucinogens, Inc. (STASH), 1969– . Monthly.

Issues of this newsletter usually present a well-documented review article on some aspect of drug use. Occasionally there are special issues, such as the Jan.-Feb., 1975, issue (vol. 7, no. 1), which was entirely made up of a Cannabis bibliography. The articles printed are, in general, sympathetic to drug use. The publication is distributed as part of the *Grassroots* subscription but is also available separately.

PART II

SOURCE MATERIAL BY SUBJECT AREA

5. General Discussions, Reviews, Histories, and Personal Narratives

Much material of this kind exists; in particular, there are numerous publications of the personal narrative type, which are usually drug abusers' first-hand reports of their experiences with drugs and of the "drug culture." Many are sensational, many sordid, and some merely factual (at least as the authors see the facts). The section also contains a number of titles that present general information on drugs and the drug abuse problem and that review the present state of affairs. The most all-inclusive publication available is *Grassroots* (see entry 184), a reference work which covers virtually all aspects of the drug abuse field except perhaps the scientific. Several of the historical titles included are classics—for example, Huxley's *Doors of Perception* (entry 193), Lewin's *Phantastica* (entry 200), Moreau's *Hashish and Mental Illness* (entry 208).

153. Adair, James R., ed. **Unhooked.** Grand Rapids, Mich., Baker Book House, 1971. 159p. $3.95; $1.25pa. LC 71-152901. ISBN 0-8010-0017-3pa.; 0-8010-0018-1cl.

This publication, intended primarily for parents and young people, presents a number of personal accounts of teenage drug users who found the way out of their trouble through religious experience. The reader may be skeptical about the "cures," since the tales make it seem too simple and easy to shake the drug habit. However, the book extends hope, and religion has proved as successful in reaching the addict as any other means. Included is a list of centers and agencies that offer a helping hand to drug abusers.

154. Adelstein, Michael E., and Jean G. Pival, eds. **Drugs.** New York, St. Martin's Press, 1972. 122p. bibliog. $2.25pa. LC 72-80021.

This is a collection of articles on various aspects of drug abuse, chosen so that there are at least two views on each topic. The three sections cover the problem, the controversy, and the solution. The following essays are included: 1) Selections from *Drugs on the College Campus*, by Helen H. Nowlis; 2) Selections from *The Drug Epidemic*, by Wesley C. Westman; 3) The heroin plague: What can be done? from *Newsweek*; 4) Heads and seekers: Drugs on campus, countercultures and American society, by Kenneth Keniston; 5) Flying high or low, by Joseph Brenner, Robert Coles, and Dermot Meagher; 6) What this country needs is a safe five-cent intoxicant, by Marvin M. Katz; 7) What we know about marijuana—so far, by Edmund K. Faltermayer; 8) The question of legalization, by Lester Grinspoon; 9) Drugs without crime, by Edgar May; 10) Drug pushers:

a collective portrait, by Richard Blum; 11) Selections from *Understanding Drug Use*, by Peter Marin and Allan Y. Cohen.

The first section includes discussions of the major categories of drugs, their effects, statistics, and case studies, stressing the seriousness of the problem. The "controvery" section includes articles on what motivates drug users and the question of legalization of marijuana. The "solution" section offers three possible approaches: first, the British solution, which allows maintenance doses of heroin; second, doubts are expressed that strong persecution of pushers will help the problem; and finally, a plea is made for parental understanding and guidance for the young. After each essay there is a list of good questions for discussion. The book contains well-selected material.

155. Alfonsi, Philippe, and Patrick Pesnot. **Satan's Needle: A True Story of Drug Addiction and Cure.** Translated by June P. Wilson and Walter B. Michaels. New York, William Morrow and Co., Inc., 1972. 284p. $6.95. LC 76-151924.

This is an account of the day-to-day lives of two young French women who were drug addicts. It was written by two male journalists who became interested in the women while working on a radio report on another addict. The reporters describe the lives and adventures of the addicts as accurately as they can, making use of tape recordings and diaries and letters of the women. Also they kept rather close personal contact with the addicts for several months. The account tells of the girls' continuous search for drugs: marijuana, hashish, opium, LSD, alcohol, anything that was available. They roam from one country to another; from France to Turkey, to Iran, Greece, and back to France. They spend time in prison and hospitals, occasionally attempting to be cured of the habit.

It is a sordid, disturbing, and discouraging tale. Neither girl permanently stops using drugs, although one is stronger than the other. At the end of the story the authors make some interesting observations. They speculate that drug addicts may be by definition incurable. They got rid of some preconceived notions about addicts. First of all, they point out that addicts are not students as has been supposed. The two roles are basically incompatible. The authors met no student addicts during their association with the drug culture, although some addicts had previously been students. The experience also convinced the authors that psychiatrists had no idea how to treat addicts. They did no better than the police in coping with the problem. The American experiment at Daytop, a community of addicts curing each other, something like Alcoholics Anonymous, was felt to be quite successful. It appears that this success is due to the resocialization rather than detoxification of the addict. The addict in such an environment must undergo rigorous community discipline and give up faking. In conclusion, the authors say they do not suggest that the addict is necessarily a product of our society; the history of drug use, especially in poorer countries, indicates otherwise. However, his behavior is an expression of a deep malaise. The old Hindu quotation, given at the end of the book, may be worth repeating as it explains to some extent drug use, "I was twenty. Let no one say that it was the best time of my life."

156. Andrews, George, and David Solomon, eds. **The Coca Leaf and Cocaine Papers.** New York, Harcourt Brace Jovanovich, 1975. 372p. index. $13.95. LC 75-12988. ISBN 0-15-118237-X.

This work is primarily a collection of historical papers on the subject of coca and cocaine. In addition, a few recent papers have been included on how coca is grown and cured and on the chemistry and effects of the plant's constituents. A number of outstanding older classical and historical papers are reprinted in the book. The newer papers are of perhaps less value, as the information in them is readily available.

The viewpoint of the editors seems to be that the public needs to be better educated on the value of cocaine and that its ill effects have been overemphasized.

157. Arndt, Jack R., and William L. Blockstein. **Problems in Drug Abuse.** Madison, Wisc., University Extension, University of Wisconsin, Health Sciences Unit, 1970. 176p. $3.00. LC 75-628904.

This publication is a compilation of the lectures initially presented over the Wisconsin Educational Telephone Network dealing with the problem of abuse of chemicals and drugs. The lecturers are experts in various aspects of the field. Their papers will be of interest to a wide audience, particularly pharmacists, nurses, lawyers, physicians, educators, law enforcement officers, clergy, counselors, social workers, and parents. The following papers are included: 1) Historical background and basic issues of drug abuse, 2) The U.S. Bureau of Narcotics and Dangerous Drugs, 3) Psychological functions of drug use, 4) Basic problems in the social psychology of drug use, 5) Narcotics, 6) Hallucinogens and marihuana, 7) Drug dependence: alcohol-sedative type, 8) Stimulants, 9) Solvents, 10) Youth on a trip (confessions of an LSD tourist), 11) Treatment and rehabilitation of abusers of hallucinogens and amphetamines, 12) Narcotics and the law, 13) Current status of programs in drug abuse education. The material presented here is very good; it is objective, authentic, and realistic.

158. Ashley, Richard. **Heroin: The Myths and the Facts.** New York, St. Martin's Press, 1972. 276p. bibliog. index. $7.95. LC 72-89417.

This book was written by a user or former user of heroin, who writes in the authoritative tone of an expert, although he appears to have had little formal education in such matters. His viewpoint is that nearly all the "well-known facts" about heroin are false, and he sets out to right matters. Although many literature references and notes have been included, a large proportion of the "true facts" seem to be the author's own opinions. Typically the "establishment," the government, society, the military, etc., are blamed for the problems. At the present time it does not appear that the much-publicized drug use among the returning Vietnam War veterans has resulted in the problems the book predicts.

159. Austrian, Geoffrey. **The Truth about Drugs.** Garden City, N.Y., Doubleday and Co., Inc., 1971. 131p. illus. $3.50. LC 70-103729.

This book is unusually interesting and is particularly suitable for young people in their teens. It is an accurate, straightforward account of the use of drugs, their effects, history, reasons for their use, and what is being done about the problem. The author, who is a newspaper reporter, pleads no cases for or against the use of drugs; he simply tells the facts, which are pretty depressing.

160. Bergel, Franz, and D. R. A. Davies. **All about Drugs.** With the collaboration of Peter Ford. London, Thomas Nelson and Sons, Ltd., 1970. 203p. illus. bibliog. index. 42s.

The aim of this book is said to be to present as objectively as possible all the major facts concerning drugs of abuse and their different origins and effects and to look at the justification for legislation as it stands in Europe, Great Britain, and the United States. Chapter titles are as follows: 1) Introductory; 2) Alcohol: the products of fermentation; 3) Cannabis: the hemp resins from the East; 4) Opium, the opiates, and the mild analgesics; 5) Cocaine and the coca leaf; 6) The mental stimulants: amphetamines and anti-depressants; 7) The sedatives: tranquilizers and barbiturates; 8) The hallucinogen: LSD and the products of the sacred cactus; 9) Further enjoyments and hazards. The five appendices cover: notes on chemistry and analysis; principles of gas chromatography; alcohol limits in selected countries; table of main drugs; and table of main hallucinogens.

The book makes the point that the longer a bad habit's history, the closer it has moved to being a good habit. Tradition seems to be able to brainwash whole societies, making their members ignorant of the dangers of psychic dependence.

161. Blachly, Paul H., ed. **Drug Abuse: Data and Debate.** Springfield, Ill., Charles C. Thomas, 1970. bibliog. index. $12.50. LC 78-119970.

The papers that make up this publication were presented at the Second Annual Western Institute of Drug Problems Summer School held at Portland State University, August 11-14, 1969. The participants were a very diverse group: educators, physicians and other health professionals, policemen, students, clergymen, pharmacologists, social workers, youth counselors, drug addicts, and others. Consequently, the book will appeal to a wide audience. Many aspects of the problem were discussed, including the subculture of the criminal narcotic addict, the development of treatment programs, the role of laboratory work in the analysis and control of drug dependence, the psychology of drug abusers, laws, drug use and students, society and drugs, and speculation on where we should go from here.

162. Blachly, P. H., ed. **Drug Abuse—Now.** Proceedings of the Western Institute of Drug Problems Summer School, August 9-13, 1971, Portland, Oregon. Corvallis, Ore., Oregon State University, 1972. 230p. $5.00pa. ISBN 0-87678-414-7.

The papers printed in this publication were presented at the Fourth Annual Western Institute of Drug Problems Summer School. Numerous aspects of the subject were discussed, including moral dilemmas of physicians operating treatment programs; problems of the mass media; education; drugs in the military, the ghetto, and the work place; and drug use among parents. Even drugs and fashion were discussed. The speakers for the most part are recognized authorities.

163. Blachly, Paul H., ed. **Progress in Drug Abuse.** Proceedings of the Third Annual Western Institute of Drug Problems Summer School. Springfield, Ill., Charles C. Thomas, 1972. 321p. bibliog. index. $15.50. LC 74-180803. ISBN 0-398-02233-X.

The individuals who contributed the papers presented here are all professionals in their fields. Each paper presents current developments and thinking on the topics in question, and the way is pointed to additional research studies, new legislation, or educational techniques that should help improve the present unsatisfactory methods for dealing with drug abuse. The following papers are presented: 1) the community–conditioning the scene of drug education; 2) Why people use drugs and what should be done about it; 3) Today's drug problem–what's happening in 1970; 4) The American and British drug problem–some comparisons; 5) Synanon: How it works, why it works; 6) Drug use among high school students and their parents in Lincoln and Welland counties; 7) Patterns of drug abuse in young adults: an empirical study of clients of a free clinic; 8) The sociology of a multimodality strategy in the treatment of narcotic addicts; 9) Sociological and economic aspects of drug dependence in India and the United States; 10) Today's drug abuse laws at work; 11) Utopia at High Dudgeon, 12) The viewpoint of the Bureau of Narcotics and Dangerous Drugs on legislation; 13) Alternative viewpoints regarding drug legislation; 14) Discussion; 15) Drug abuse and crime; 16) New approaches to the use of drugs in the treatment of drug addiction; 17) A current view of the amphetamines; 18) Marijuana and adverse psychotic reactions; and 19) Implications and direction. Appended are articles on medical progress with marijuana and management of "bad trips" in an evolving drug scene.

164. Bourne, Peter G., ed. **Addiction.** New York, Academic Press, 1974. 239p. index. $17.50. LC 74-1642. ISBN 0-12-119535-X.

Leading authorities in the field of drug abuse express their feeling on key issues of addiction in this book. There are continual changes in the manner in which addiction is perceived, and this book brings out some of the recent thinking. Chapter headings are as follows: 1) Issues in addiction, 2) On the nature of opiate reinforcement, 3) Hypotheses concerning the etiology of heroin addiction, 4) Evaluating the success of addiction programs, 5) Rational planning for drug abuse services, 6) Beginning to dissect a heroin addiction epidemic, 7) Involuntary treatment of drug addiction, 8) Three critical issues in the management of methadone programs, 9) The search for rational approaches to heroin use, 10) Early history of heroin in the United States, and 11) Drug abuse: changing perspectives in long-term social and political strategies.

The book is intended for all who wish to gain an understanding of addiction, particularly psychiatrists, psychologists, social workers, and law enforcement and correctional officers. The book successfully poses many questions about the drug problem but offers few answers.

165. Brecher, Edward M., and the Editors of Consumer Reports. **Licit and Illicit Drugs: The Consumers Union Report on Narcotics, Stimulants, Depressants, Inhalants, Hallucinogens, and Marijuana–Including Caffeine, Nicotine, and Alcohol.** Boston, Little, Brown and Co., 1972. 623p. index. bibliog. $12.50. LC 75-186972. ISBN 0-316-15340-0.

This report was undertaken because the editors felt that the illicit drug scene in the U.S. was becoming intolerable. All aspects of drug abuse are taken up—the pharmacology, the effects of drug laws, drug policies, and drug attitudes. Each drug is presented in historical perspective. It is interesting to note that the "licit" drugs referred to are caffeine, nicotine, and alcohol; many readers may feel that caffeine and nicotine are not quite in the same class as alcohol. The work is well documented and thorough. It ends with recommendations that the authors hope will point the way to both short-term and long-term improvements in the critical situation. There is no claim that they constitute a panacea. Many readers may feel that implementing the recommendations will not improve matters at all but may indeed make them worse. The primary recommendation is that marijuana use be made legal although subject to regulation.

166. Brill, Leon, and Ernest Harms, eds. **Yearbook of Drug Abuse.** New York, Behavioral Publications, 1973. 386p. bibliog. $19.95. LC 70-174271. ISBN 0-87705-060-0.

The first of a projected series, this yearbook is designed to keep individuals working in the drug abuse area apprised of major developments in the United States and foreign countries. The editors hope to offer a forum for the wide-ranging problems involved in drug abuse, and to present some of the solutions found. This volume covers the current situation in the United States and a few foreign countries regarding treatment programs and research. The papers included, written by well-known authorities, are as follows: 1) Federal. Drug abuse—the need for a rational pharmacologic approach; 2) Federal. Civil commitment in the federal medical program for opiate addicts; 3) Federal. Narcotic antagonists as analgesics of low dependence liability—theoretical and practical implications of recent studies; 4) The treatment of drug abuse: experiences and issues; 5) New York City. Addiction Services Agency of the City of New York; 6) New York City. Phoenix House: a therapeutic community program for the treatment of drug abusers and drug addicts; 7) Chicago. The Illinois Drug Abuse Program; 8) Philadelphia. Drug abuse in Philadelphia: current treatment, legislative and research activity; 9) California. California drug scene; 10) California. The drug abuse problem in California; 11) Puerto Rico. The drug scene in Puerto Rico; 12) England. Drug abuse in present-day England; 13) General perspectives on drug abuse; 14) A perspective on heroin: the genesis of the American system of narcotics control; 15) Multiple drug use among heroin users; 16) Perspective on marijuana; 17) A perspective on LSD and the psychedelics.

167. Chapin, William. **Wasted: The Story of My Son's Drug Addiction.** New York, McGraw-Hill Book Co., 1972. 216p. $6.95. LC 71-38812. ISBN 0-07-010535-9.

This is an account, written by the father, of a family's experience with a drug-using son. Although the boy was bright enough and seemed to have a good family background, he began at the age of 14 to use drugs. The family desperately sought cures, but by the age of 21 the boy had to be confined to a mental hospital, evidently a hopeless case. The father was extremely anguished and made great efforts to understand and deal with the son's condition.

The book is touching and quite well written. Some readers may gain insights from the story. Possibly the parents, in spite of good intentions, did not set good examples for their children and were somewhat unstable themselves. The father, for example, seemed to be an alcoholic or near alcoholic. However, his own diagnosis of the root of the problem was that he had failed to express his love for his son enough.

168. Clark, Evert, and Nicholas Horrock. **Contrabandista!** New York, Praeger, 1973. 231p. $6.95. LC 72-87296.

This book, which reads somewhat like a novel, is the story of a scheme for smuggling heroin wholesale into the United States by light plane from South America. Eventually the contrabandistas were outmaneuvered and caught by a small but determined group of U.S. narcotic agents and international intelligence operatives. The kingpin of the heroin ring, Auguste Joseph Ricard, was extradited to the United States from Paraguay and was tried and convicted in New York federal court. The authors, a *Newsweek* magazine team, have related the story in a fascinating manner.

169. Cook, A. Bramwell. **Drugs? What You Should Know.** East Melbourne, Australia, Citadel Press, 1971. 56p.

The author of this short publication is a physician who has been a medical missionary and Salvation Army leader. The booklet discusses the following topics: 1) The situation today, 2) What makes addicts, 3) Drug dependence, 4) The use of sedatives, 5) The use of marijuana 6) Marijuana, 7) LSD, 8) Narcotics, 9) Tobacco—a warning, and 10) Alcohol. Basic, authentic material is presented with religious overtones.

170. Cortina, Frank Michael. **Face to Face.** New York, Columbia University Press, 1972. 301p. $10.00. LC 76-184745. ISBN 0-231-03635-3.

This book contains several personal narratives of drug abusers' lives told by means of interviews with the author. The narratives were taped and played back as part of the therapy for the abuser. The stories are interesting, depressing, and perhaps enlightening.

The suggestion is made that drug abusers are such perverse individuals that they renunciate life, that which separates them from the lower orders. The suggestion is also made that what is necessary for cures is intervention in the life of the addict. However it is pointed out that there is no one available who has the time to intervene perpetually in another person's life.

171. Cortina, Frank Michael. **Stroke a Slain Warrior.** New York, Columbia University Press, 1970. 231p. $7.50. LC 70-133197. ISBN 0-231-03481-4.

The author of this work wrote under a pseudonym because of his confidential relationship with a large number of drug users. He wrote the book at the suggestion of a former addict friend who felt that addicts had received so much adverse publicity that it would be well to show what kind of people drug abusers really are. The work is made up of 17 vignettes, each of which covers a different type of person involved in drug abuse. Following are the individuals described: 1) The pusher, 2) The epileptic, 3) The call girl, 4) The musician, 5) The rich girl, 6) A badly made doll (a prisoner), 7) Rosa-Rosey (a prostitute), 8) The too-present father, 9) The artist, 10) The pickpocket, 11) The old-timer, 12) The mother, 13) The gamester, 14) The old tale, 15) The fourteen-year-old, 16) The younger-brother syndrome, 17) The prophet.

The stories are interesting but sad and depressing. Few could kick the habit; most died young.

172. Crowley, Aleister. **The Diary of a Drug Fiend.** New York, Samuel Weisner, Inc., 1973. 368p. $3.00pa. LC 79-142495. ISBN 0-87728-035-5.

This novel tells the story of a devoted couple and their adventures and experiences with drug abuse. The book, which originally came out about 1923, was shocking to the reader of that time. Along with the love story (which is quite touching), it gives a picture of the post-World War I era and the freaked-out world of the drug addict in Europe. The story is well written, if disturbing. It is interesting that the life-style of the drug addict has changed so little from the 1920s and 1930s until today. The attitudes and actions of the couple seem very familiar.

173. De Ropp, Robert S. **Drugs and the Mind.** Foreword by Nathan S. Kline. New York, Gnome Press, 1957. 310p. bibliog. index. $0.95pa.

This widely known book is very readable and interesting. At the time it was written there were few books available on the subject, particularly for the general reader. Much historical material is included, and there are numerous case reports and quotations from self-observations by such writers as Baudelaire, Gautier, Havelock Ellis, and Aldous Huxley, who used drugs. Though drugs of abuse are discussed (such as mescaline, marihuana, LSD, alcohol, and heroin), there is also much discussion of mind-altering drugs that are used legitimately, such as tranquilizers and psychic energizers. Both De Ropp and Kline seem to have high hopes that the use of drugs that affect the mind will have some good results. New research into mental processes will be possible, they say, and perhaps man can reach spiritual maturity. However, proper medical supervision of the use of such drugs is stressed. From today's vantage point, it does not appear that these hopes are being realized. There has been too much abuse of the materials, and efforts are being directed toward solving that problem.

174. Drug Abuse Survey Project. **Dealing with Drug Abuse: A Report to the Ford Foundation.** Foreword by McGeorge Bundy. New York, Praeger Publishers, 1972. 396p. $8.95. LC 77-189472.

This book summarizes the findings and conclusions of a survey conducted under the auspices of the Ford Foundation in the latter part of 1970 (with updating). The study group was composed of experts in medicine, psychiatry, law, and economics. The volume contains, in addition to the findings, conclusions, and recommendations, and staff papers as follows: 1) The drugs and their effects, 2) Drug education, 3) Treatment and rehabilitation, 4) The economics of heroin, 5) Federal expenditures on drug abuse control, 6) Altered states of consciousness, and 7) Narcotics addiction and control in Great Britain.

No startling new discoveries were made. The group feels that alleviation of the drug abuse problem will come "through a slow and painful process of social change and accommodation." The major recommendations called for the establishment of an independent Drug Abuse Council to sponsor research, fund treatment and education programs, evaluate treatment approaches, and disseminate information. Such a council was formed under the aegis of the Carnegie Corporation, the Commonwealth Fund, and the Henry J. Kaiser Family Foundation, in addition to the Ford Foundation.

175. **Drugs: For and Against.** Introduction by Harold H. Hart. New York, Hart Publishing Co., Inc., 1970. 239p. illus. index. $2.45pa. LC 71-131980. ISBN 0-8055-1078-8.

This book presents a broad spectrum of thought in regard to the use/abuse of drugs. Each chapter is by a different author, many of whom are well known, and each presents that author's views. Extreme views, pro and con, have been included as well as those that are moderate. The viewpoints expressed differ on the seriousness of the problem and on how drugs should be controlled. There is some agreement among the contributors that more intensive research into the problem is needed in order to allow one to form sounder opinions. The contributors are: Sidney Cohen, Max Rafferty, Alan Watts, Roswell Johnson, Michael Aldrich, Bernard Barber, Judianne Densen-Gerber, Fritz Redl, Joel Fort, Edward Bloomquist, Michael Rossman, and Robert de Ropp.

176. Ebin, David, ed. **The Drug Experience: First-Person Accounts of Addicts, Writers, Scientists, and Others.** New York, Grove Press, Inc., 1961. 385p. bibliog. $1.75pa.

This is a collection of excerpts about the personal drug experience of various writers—most of them well known. The editor has added an introduction and notes. A few of the accounts included have not been published before, and there is a translation of a work that has not previously appeared in English. The collection is limited to works on hallucinogenic drugs, with the possible exception of two sections—"Opium" and "Opiates, Addicts, and Cures." The other sections are: "Hemp," "Peyote," "Mushrooms," and "LSD." Each section is preceded by a one-page introduction on the character of the drug, and each account in a section is preceded by editorial comments that place it in perspective.

Some of the classic selections included are works by Théophile Gautier, Charles Baudelaire, Thomas De Quincey, Jean Cocteau, Havelock Ellis, and Aldous Huxley. Writings of more modern drug users (such as Billie Holiday, Alexander King, and Allen Ginsberg) are also included. A number of the writers relate their involvement with drugs in scientific fashion, some are highly literary accounts, and others resemble the ravings of lunatics. It is an interesting collection of materials not easy to find elsewhere.

177. Efron, Daniel H., Bo Holmstedt, and Nathan S. Kline, eds. **Ethnopharmacologic Search for Psychoactive Drugs.** Proceedings of a symposium held in San Francisco, January 28-30, 1967. Sponsored by the Pharmacology Section, Psychopharmacology Research Branch, National Institute of Mental Health. Washington, GPO, 1967. 468p. illus. bibliog. index. $4.00. (Workshop Series of Pharmacology Section, N.I.M.H., No. 2; Public Health Service Publication No. 1645).

This symposium was organized to review and explore what is known about plant sources of psychoactive drugs and their effects. It was felt that these substances have not been utilized to the fullest extent for medicinal purposes. However, their use for religious ceremonial purposes is in many cases very old. The participants, well-known scientists in a number of areas, included pharmacologists, pharmacists, chemists, biochemists, psychiatrists, and anthropologists. They exchanged information, presented various points of view, and pointed to new research objectives for the future.

There were six sessions on the following topics: 1) An overview of ethnopharmacology; 2) Piper Methysticum (Kava); 3) Myristica Fragrans (Nutmeg); 4) South American snuffs; 5) Ayahuasca, Caapi, Yagé; and 6) Amanita Muscaria (Fly Agaric). Much historical and anthropological background has been included in each section, in addition to recent scientific material. The illustrations and documentation are excellent. The publication brings together interesting information in a field of growing importance.

178. Elgin, Kathleen, and John F. Osterriter. **The Ups and Downs of Drugs.** New York, Alfred A. Knpof, 1972. 63p. illus. index. $3.95. LC 75-168994. ISBN 0-394-92378-2, library edition; 0-394-82378-8, trade edition.

This book for children was written by an author of many juvenile books and a physician. The senior author did the illustrations also. Straightforward facts, in simple language, cover many aspects of drug use. Chapter headings are as follows: 1) What is a drug? 2) Barbiturates: the downers; 3) Amphetamines, the uppers; 4) Hallucinogens; 5) Narcotics; 6) Stimulants and other problem drugs; 7) Quotes of 6-10 year olds; 8) Quotes of 10-19 year olds; 9) It's up to you. There is also a simple glossary of terms and a drug chart. The material is well presented and authentic.

179. Emboden, William A., Jr. **Narcotic Plants.** New York, Macmillan, 1972. 168p. illus. (part col.) bibliog. index. $12.95. LC 77-173691.

This book was written by the Senior Curator of Botany at the Los Angeles County Museum of Natural History who also is Professor of Biology at San Fernando Valley State College. It is a historical, botanical, and chemical account of psychoactive plants and their derivatives. Separating myth and legend from the known attributes of the plants, the author discusses a wide variety of plants—minor ones as well as major—in the following sections: 1) Hallucinogens, 2) Stimulants, 3) Inebriants, 4) Tobacco and snuffs, 5) Hypnotics: tranquilizers and sedatives. The two appendices cover the chemistry of hallucinogens and botanical descriptions.

Plants are described within each section, along with an account of the drug's history and use, and recent information on its chemistry and pharmacology. The illustrations (95 in beautiful color and 39 line cuts) are outstanding.

180. Fixx, James F., general ed. **Drugs: The Great Contemporary Issues.** New York, New York Times Arno Press, 1971. 757p. illus. bibliog. index. $25.00. LC 78-169196.

This large volume contains reprinted *New York Times* articles that deal with the drug problem. Much history is included. The material is not arranged chronologically, however, but is organized so as to point up trends and interrelationships that the editors believe are illuminating. The material is arranged under the following topics: 1) The problem, 2) Where drugs come from, 3) The rising tide, 4) Marijuana, 5) Science and drugs, 6) The war on drugs, 7) The drug culture. Also included is a glossary of drug terms, a brief chronology of the drug problem, and suggested readings. The book's primary value is that it presents some raw material for examination.

181. Gibbins, Robert J., and others, eds. **Research Advances in Alcohol and Drug Problems.** Vol. 1. New York, Wiley, 1974. 428p. bibliog. index. $22.00. LC 73-18088. ISBN 0-471-29737-2.

This is the first volume of a new annual series whose purpose is to review the many aspects contributing to an understanding of drug abuse and its problems. The critically evaluative papers stress interdisciplinary inquiry. Material is drawn from the areas of biochemistry, pharmacology, physiology, medicine, sociology, anthropology, psychology, and jurisprudence. This volume contains the following chapters: 1) The use of animal models for the study of drug abuse, 2) Chemical and biochemical methods of drug detection and measurement, 3) Organic pathology related to volume and pattern of alcohol use, 4) Preclinical pharmacology of marihuana, 5) Clinical pharmacology of marihuana, 6) Treatment and rehabilitation of narcotic addiction, 7) The epidemiology of psychoactive and hallucinogenic drug use, and 8) Validity of survey data on alcohol use.

182. Girdano, Dorothy Dusek, and Daniel A. Girdano. **Drugs: A Factual Account.** Reading, Mass., Addison-Wesley Publishing Co., 1973. 216p. illus. bibliog. index. $3.95pa. LC 75-171431. ISBN 0-201-02373-3.

This book depicts the historical, social, and legal impact of drugs on society and also attempts to give a basic understanding of the physiology of the nervous system, the pharmacology of drugs, and how these things relate to behavior changes. Some explanation is made of sleepiness, alertness, appetite loss, physical dependence, and drug tolerance, although the mechanism of the action of many drugs is not well understood, and the authors are teachers of health education rather than scientists.

Written for a wide audience, the book covers most areas of the subject reasonably well. Some of the views expressed, however, are a bit too simple (for instance, it is suggested that drug abuse is a manifestation of our technological bureaucracy; yet it is evident from the historical accounts that drug abuse has always been with us and has existed in all societies).

183. Gorodetzky, Charles W., and Samuel T. Christian. **What You Should Know about Drugs.** New York, Harcourt Brace Jovanovich, Inc., 1970. 121p. illus. (col.) index. $4.95. LC 74-128366. ISBN 0-15-295510-0.

The authors of this book are both researchers in the field of drug abuse. Their aim in writing the book was to fill the need for a book on drugs for children in the upper elementary grades. Parents and teachers will also find it useful and accurate. Information is given, in plain language, on a number of different drugs of abuse including glue, solvents, marihuana, LSD, sedatives, stimulants, heroin, narcotics, and alcohol. Also included are personal accounts of young people and quotations about their drug experiences. There is a good glossary of drug abuse terms, and the illustrations, which are color photographs, are outstanding.

184. **Grassroots.** Madison, Wisc., published by the Student Association for the Study of Hallucinogens, Inc. (STASH), 1971– . About 9 volumes, looseleaf. $100.00 per year.

This publication, although curious and unconventional in format, is invaluable for those wanting information on drug abuse. Materials covering all aspects of the subject are sent out monthly to subscribers to be inserted in the looseleaf binders. The material is reprinted from many sources. In addition, some pamphlet and newsletter publications are included with the subscription. Materials are divided into well-chosen subject areas, such as history, sociocultural aspects, psychology, epidemiology, drug education, speakers' clearinghouse, on-going research, prevention, community action, underground digest, treatment and rehabilitation, law and public policy, street drugs, grants and contracts, up-coming meetings, alcohol, narcotics, stimulants, hallucinogens, cannabis, and other drugs. Books, films, and other audiovisuals are evaluated.

Two of the *Grassroots* volumes are special publications that are reviewed separately in this bibliography. See *Grassroots Directory of Drug Information and Treatment Organizations*, a state-by-state listing of drug group services (entry 71), and *Speed: The Current Index to the Drug Abuse Literature*. (entry 47).

The *Grassroots* materials are of particular use to students preparing papers on various aspects of drug abuse, to community groups, and to speakers.

185. Greenberg, Harvey R. **What You Must Know about Drugs.** New York, Scholastic Book Services, 1971. 160p. illus. index. $1.25pa.

This book successfully guides the reader through the entire drug scene. The numerous case histories included make the work interesting to the general reader. The author, a psychiatrist, presents varying viewpoints on drug use when they exist, and indicates where he stands and why.

The author's conclusion is that there is nothing wrong with young people living simple "accepting" lives like their parents live. However, if they do want to explore inner horizons, this is all right also, but using drugs is not the way to do it. He tells the reader that one can "pick up the tools without having to undergo the torment, and horror, and the essential emptiness so many found with drugs instead of what they were really searching for." Unaided by drugs, man has reached into his own inner self to create masterpieces and make great discoveries. This book is sensible and persuasive.

186. Hafen, Brent Q., comp. **Readings in Drug Use and Abuse.** Provo, Utah, Brigham Young University Press, 1970. 525p. bibliog. $6.95.

This book of readings was compiled from a variety of sources especially for teachers and other individuals who work with young people. The readings fit into one of the following general categories: the medicinal value of drugs; the nature and characteristics of drug abuse; the motivation behind the misuse of drugs; drugs and related social problems, including laws and enforcement; major drugs of abuse, including alcohol and tobacco; and prevention and rehabilitation. There are two appendices: a general classification of some of the major narcotics, other dangerous drugs and chemical compounds, and a glossary of slang terms.

This is a good collection of material, but there is no index of authors, titles, or subjects to assist one in finding a certain paper. The table of contents does not list authors' names or source of material.

187. Hall, Pamela. **Heads: You Lose.** New York, Hawthorn Books, Inc., 1971. 148p. $4.95. LC 78-148035.

This book was written by a young woman who started using drugs when in her early teens. She relates what are said to be true experiences with other young drug users in the hope that the reader will see what mistakes her parents, other families, and the young people made and that they will be able to avoid some of them themselves.

The author says she became involved with drugs as a way to escape loneliness and overcome shyness. The drug scene became a security blanket, a circle one belonged to. The experiences related and the author's reasoning seem to be all too typical of immature teenagers.

188. Healy, Patrick F., and James P. Manak, eds. **Drug Dependence and Abuse Resource Book.** Chicago, National District Attorneys Association, 1971. 581p. bibliog. $10.00pa. LC 78-149765.

The editors read and evaluated many hundreds of articles, then selected and reprinted in this volume the ones they thought represented the best on a topic, regardless of the age of the article. The papers are grouped under four classifications: 1) The problem of drug dependence and abuse and the role of law in a free society, 2) The problem of drug dependence and abuse and the role of education and preventive programs, 3) The problem of drug dependence and abuse: the social perspective, 4) The problem of drug dependence and abuse: the medical perspective. In addition, there are some useful appendices; especially valuable are an annotated bibliography of books, pamphlets, paper presentations and articles and an annotated listing of films, filmstrips, video tapes and film distributors. A glossary of slang terms is included.

The position of the National District Attorneys Association is that the only solution to the drug problem is education, and it hopes that this presentation will assist in that task.

189. Hoch, Paul H., and Joseph Zubin, eds. **Problems of Addiction and Habituation.** New York, Grune and Stratton, 1958. 250p. illus. bibliog. index. $6.50. LC 58-11835.

This book contains the proceedings of the Forty-Seventh Annual Meeting of the American Psychopathological Association, held in New York, February 1957. The purpose of the meeting was to allow representatives of the different approaches to the addiction problem to meet face to face so there could be an interchange of ideas. Addiction was broadly defined, and there are papers on unusual topics, such as coffee use and the disease called pica (abnormal appetite for substances not fit for food). Although the book is rather old, the papers are of high quality, and most are still of interest.

190. Horman, Richard E., and Allan M. Fox, eds. **Drug Awareness.** New York, Avon Books, 1970. 478p. bibliog. $1.45pa.

This book contains 31 articles and papers selected from over 2,000 articles, books, and pamphlets collected by staff members of the Drug Education Activities project at Temple University. The compilers' intention was to assemble a comprehensive volume of material that would answer questions currently asked about the "drug scene." There are seven sections, each containing several papers: 1) Background information; 2) Drugs, the student, and his environment; 3) Position statement; 4) Drug dependence; 5) LSD and the hallucinogens; 6) Marijuana; 7) Educational strategy. Each section begins with general material and then becomes more technical as one reads further into the chapter. This increases the value of the work, since it can be used by both lay and professional people. There are two glossaries, one of slang terms and one of scientific terms associated with drug abuse.

The book provides the reader with expert opinions concerning the effects of marijuana and LSD, looks at the drug scene in perspective, attempts to provide an understanding of what the problem may be a symptom of, and indicates how it can best be dealt with.

191. Houser, Norman W. **Drugs: Facts on Their Use and Abuse.** In consultation with Julius B. Richmond. New York, Lothrop, Lee and Shepard Co., 1969. 48p. illus. (col.) bibliog. $4.25. LC 74-82103.

The purpose of this book, like that of so many others, is to provide concise but accurate answers to questions on drugs of abuse, particularly for young people. Written by an educator with the assistance of a physician, it is rather nicely done. The primary aim of the book is to discourage drug experimenting, and possibly it will do so. The publication is attractive with unusual illustrations and art work, but drug use is not made attractive.

192. Hozinsky, Murray. **Is This Trip Necessary? Drug Information for Students.** Denver, Love Publishing Co., 1971. 61p. bibliog. LC 77-177989.

This booklet was prepared for young people with the hope that it would clarify the picture of drug usage. Reasonably accurate but simplified information is given about the main drugs of abuse and the problems associated with their use.

193. Huxley, Aldous. **The Doors of Perception** and **Heaven and Hell.** New York, Harper and Row, 1963 (c1954-56). 185p. $5.95. LC 54-5833 and 55-10694.

In the *Doors of Perception* the noted novelist, Aldous Huxley, vividly describes the effects of mescalin on the mind. Although it had long been known that the Indians of Mexico and the American Southwest use peyote (from which mescalin comes) in religious ceremonies and venerate it as though it were a deity, Huxley brought it to worldwide notice when this book was written in the 1950s. Huxley criticized drug use in his *Brave New World* (1932), satirizing a future world in which science has solved all human problems; but in *Doors of Perception* he sees drug use as a gateway to perception and as a means to mystical insight. The work is frequently quoted by those who advocate drug use.

Heaven and Hell (which makes up the last part of this volume) is an extension of the first work. Huxley believed that there is a posthumous heaven of blissful visionary experience and that there is also a hell of the same kind of appalling visionary experience as is suffered by some of those who take mescalin. He also thought there is "an experience, beyond time, of union with the divine Ground."

194. Jones, Kenneth L., Louis W. Shainberg, and Curtis O. Byer. **Drugs, Alcohol, and Tobacco.** San Francisco, Canfield Press, 1970, 113p. illus. bibliog. index. $4.00. LC 70-119010.

This book provides basic information for inquiry into problems relating to drugs, alcohol, and tobacco. It is presumed that the reader will want to pursue the subject further from other sources. The following chapters are presented: 1) Drug use and abuse; 2) Drugs, laws, and treatment; 3) Alcohol and alcohol abuse; 4) Alcoholism; and 5) Smoking and the effects of tobacco. At the end of each chapter are a summary in outline form and a list of questions the reader can consider. In addition, there is a short glossary of technical terms. Although the material presented is brief and concise, all the important basic information is given objectively and factually. This is an excellent presentation.

195. Jones, Kenneth L., Louis W. Shainberg, and Curtis O. Byer. **Drugs and Alcohol.** 2nd ed. New York, Harper and Row, 1973. 162p. illus. bibliog. index. $5.00. LC 72-12003. ISBN 0-06-043429-5.

This book, according to the authors, presents the basic information vital to young people when making important decisions concerning their potential use of drugs, including alcohol. This basic information, a good deal of it scientific, is accurate and well presented. The illustrations and diagrams are unusually helpful. In addition, laws and restrictions governing drug distribution are discussed; medical use of drugs is investigated; and drug groups are placed within a continuum of actions and effects on the central nervous system. The role of emotional and psychological problems in drug and alcohol abuse is taken up. A good glossary is included.

196. Kiev, Ari. **The Drug Epidemic.** New York, Free Press, division of Macmillan Publishing Co., Inc., 1975. 227p. $8.95. LC 74-15367. ISBN 0-02-917240-3.

This book describes the experiences of drug abusers and addicts, presenting personal information from the victims themselves. The evolution of the drug problem is portrayed from experimentation in social groups to entry into the drug subculture. The author's viewpoint is that studying the stages in the development of addiction may lead to new insights that can help in prevention and treatment. Chapter headings are as follows: 1) Introduction: The epidemiology of drug abuse; 2) Antecedents of drug abuse; 3) Drugs: Definitions, symptoms, syndromes; 4) Finally, heroin; 5) Crime; 6) Overdoses, breakdowns, deterioration—and stopping; 7) Therapeutic programs; 8) Treatment and prevention; 9) Prevention; 10) The role of voluntary community organizations; and 11) Final thoughts.

The author suggests in conclusion that a crisis-intervention type system of treatment should be established on a decentralized level. On a more personal level, he feels that people need a "strategy for living" (he wrote a book by that title in 1973). He further suggests that the addict must develop self-reliance, personal responsibility, and goal direction if he is to be cured.

197. Labin, Suzanne. **Hippies, Drugs, and Promiscuity**. Translated by Stephanie Winston. New Rochelle, N.Y., Arlington House, 1972. index. $7.95. LC 70-189375. ISBN 0-87000-156-6.

The author, who is a native Parisian, traveled thousands of miles to observe the hippie members of the counterculture in the United States, Canada, France, England, Italy, Germany, Sweden, the Netherlands, India, Nepal, and Afghanistan. She talked with the young people, policemen, parents, and diplomats, and read the hippie press. The book is well written in a novelistic style with case histories. The reader is given a tour of the hippie world and a view of their drugs, clothes, hygienic habits (or lack of them), and their philosophy of life. There are many descriptions of drug use. At the end the author makes a plea for the young people to change their ways before it is too late. She says the newspapers have not exaggerated the seriousness of the problem. The number of runaways is very large, and never in history has drug abuse been so widespread.

198. Lehrman, Robert L. **Drugs: Use and Abuse.** New York, Cambridge Book Co., 1972. 49p. illus. bibliog. index. LC 77-183783. ISBN 0-842-830-707.

This pamphlet is addressed to the young reader. It is unique among drug education materials, since nearly half the text is background and history about the legitimate and beneficial aspects of drug development and use. The remainder of the publication discusses drug abuse. There are questions posed throughout for thought and discussion. The text is well written and authentic. Young people, in particular, will benefit from reading it.

199. Levin, Peter A., ed. **Contemporary Problems of Drug Abuse.** Acton, Mass., Publishing Sciences Group, Inc., 1974. 196p. $14.95. LC 73-84168. ISBN 0-88416-002-5.

This book is an edited transcript of the proceedings of a symposium held at Villanova University School of Law in 1973. At the meeting, attended by law and medical students, papers were presented by distinguished members of several professions who had been involved with the problems created by drug abuse. Medical, pharmacological, psychiatric, social, political, and legal points of view were represented. Chapter headings are as follows: 1) Introduction, 2) Responses, 3) History, 4) Studies, 5) Advertising, 6) Civil liberties, 7) Marihuana, 8) Education, and 9) Problems. Each chapter contains one or more formal presentations on the particular topic and the discussion that followed. The material presented is readable and informative.

200. Lewin, Louis. **Phantastica, Narcotic and Stimulating Drugs: Their Use and Abuse.** Foreword by Bo Holmstedt. New York, E. P. Dutton and Co., 1964. (Reprint of 1931 ed., translated from the second German ed.). 335p. index.

This classic work, the first of its kind, was reprinted because drug abuse and psychopharmacology are of such vital importance at the present time. The author of the book was an outstanding German pharmacologist who first published his book in German in 1924. It was subsequently published in several other languages and has long been a collector's item.

Dr. Lewin used the term "phantastica" for drugs that give rise to sense illusion; the term now used most often is "hallucinogens." The book describes these drugs as well as stimulants, narcotics, sedatives, soporifics, and lesser known substances of abuse. The descriptions are complete, yet non-technical, and historical material is included. The foreword contains a good deal of biographical material about the author. Dr. Lewin's view was that drugs have created a great problem, an evil from which mankind needs to be freed.

201. Lieberman, Mark. **The Dope Book: All about Drugs.** New York, Praeger Publishers, 1971. 141p. bibliog. index. $5.95. LC 74-122090.

This book, written for young people by a journalist, presents the view that if youths are told the facts about drugs they can draw their own rational conclusions about using them. While this is obviously not a foolproof approach, it is probably as good as any. The book is well written and scientifically correct, although the appeal is psychological. The glamour is taken away from all drug use—nicotine and alcohol as well as illicit drugs.

202. Lindesmith, Alfred R. **Addiction and Opiates.** Chicago, Aldine Publishing Co., 1968. 295p. bibliog. index. $7.50. LC 68-19870.

This work is a revision of a 1947 book, *Opiate Addiction*, by the same author. The bibliography and the glossary have been expanded and updated and much of the text has been rewritten and updated. The author, who is a professor of sociology at Indiana University, maintains that addiction is fixed not by the positive pleasure produced by a drug, but by the relief of withdrawal distress which injection brings about after physical dependence is established. (He is speaking only of addiction to the opiate-type drugs and their synthetic equivalents.) This classic theory of opiate addiction was presented by the author in his earlier work.

The first part of the book presents material on the nature of the opiate habit with a portrayal of the addict and the hows and whys of addiction. The second part of the volume is a study of the social problems of addiction in the United States, with an historical background of the problem, a legislative history, a discussion of the impact of World War II, and opinions on needed reforms.

The book, like many on the subject, is critical of the way addiction problems have been handled in the recent past. Like many others, however, it offers no specific convincing plan that might remedy the situation.

203. Louria, Donald. **Nightmare Drugs.** New York, Pocket Books, Inc., 1966. 96p. $1.00pa.

The physician author wrote this small book in the hope that an understanding of the addicting drugs will aid in prevention, detection, and a realistic approach to the treatment of the addict. The dangers of LSD are stressed. A good deal of basic information about drugs and addiction is given. After separate discussions of the addicting drugs, the author states his views on how to attack the drug problem. He feels that the causes must be sought and corrected and that proper dissemination of facts is necessary. Controls must be realistic and workable, and there must be a crackdown on illicit sales. Above all, prevention is a great responsibility, and the author believes this begins with the parents.

204. Matheson, Douglas W., and Meredith A. Davison. **The Behavioral Effects of Drugs.** New York, Holt, Rinehart and Winston, Inc., 1972. 277p. bibliog. index. $3.95pa. LC 70-186960. ISBN 0-03-085307-9.

This book, designed to familiarize the reader with the behavioral effects of drugs and the behavior of drug users, contains material for the layman and for the professional, particularly in the form of data. There are five chapters: 1) Introduction, 2) Popular social drugs, 3) Uppers and downers: the psychotropic drugs, 4) Hallucinogens, and 5) Narcotic analgesics. The chapters are made up of a collection of articles (mostly reprinted), preceded by brief introductions.

Intended primarily for students, the book can be used in courses in psychology, sociology, medicine, nursing, law, and related areas. Many of the articles are suitable for high school students and parents as well.

205. Maurer, David W., and Victor H. Vogel. **Narcotic and Narcotic Addiction.** 4th ed. Springfield, Ill., Charles C. Thomas, 1973. 473p. illus. bibliog. index. $15.75. LC 73-7879. ISBN 0-398-02906-7.

This book is a recent revision of a work originally published in 1954. Offering no solutions to the problems of drug abuse, it describes the state of affairs in detail and investigates the efforts being made to curb the spread of illicit drug use. The drugs of abuse are described, effects indicated, and methods of administration outlined, with some attention given to methods of treatment. Social implications of drug abuse, especially in the United States, are studied, and the drug subculture is described, with considerable emphasis on linguistic habits of the addicts. The glossary, of terms "commonly used by underworld addicts," is extensive. Intended primarily for government and law enforcement officers, physicians, judges and lawyers, probation officers, social workers, criminologists, teachers, and writers, the book can easily be read by almost any interested person.

The chapter headings are as follows: 1) The nature of drug addiction, 2) Opiates and their synthetic equivalents, 3) Addicting nonopiate sedatives, 4) Stimulant drugs, 5) Identification of drugs and proof of addiction, 6) Treatment of narcotic addiction, 7) Legal controls for drugs of addiction, 8) Drug abuse and crime, 9) Drug addiction and youth, and 10) The argot of narcotic addicts.

Much historical material presented, and drug abuse during earlier periods (1930s through 1950s) is frequently referred to. The senior author is a Professor of English and Humanities who formerly was a Lecturer on Narcotic Addiction and Criminal Argots, Southern Police Institute, Louisville, Kentucky. The co-author is a physician who was formerly Chairman, California Narcotic Addict Evaluation Authority, and formerly Medical Officer in Charge, U.S. Public Health Service Hospital, Louisville, Kentucky.

206. Milbauer, Barbara. **Drug Abuse and Addiction . . . a Fact Book for Parents, Teen-Agers, and Young Adults.** New York, New American Library, 1970. 203p. bibliog. Index. $0.95pa. LC 79-127504.

Presenting both the parents' view and young people's view of drug abuse, this book contains much of interest to both groups. The chapter headings are: 1) Problems of drug abuse and addiction, 2) Drugs that can be physically addictive, 3) Drugs often misused, 4) Types of drug dependence, 5) The life of the middle-class addict, 6) The drug user–visible and invisible, 7) How drugs get to the user, 8) Medical aspects of drug abuse and treatment, 9) Methods of treating drug abuse, 10) "Curing" the addict, 11) Drug taking–arguments pro and con, 12) Drugs and the law, 13) The research dilemma, 14) Suggestions for change, 15) A final word: To parents; to teenagers.

The material is presented very well and covers a broad spectrum: the social, medical, and legal aspects of drug abuse. Case studies are included, facts presented, and questions posed. Little attempt is made to provide a solution to the drug problem, but this is probably a realistic approach, since there appears to be no solution. This is an interesting, well written and informative book.

207. Milbauer, Barbara, and Gerald Leinwand. **Drugs.** New York, Washington Square Press, 1970. 190p. illus. bibliog. index. $0.95pa. ISBN 0-671-47847-8.

This book, one of a series on "Problems of American Society," attempts to show "both sides" of the drug question (although the authors feel that there are not two sides, that drug use is harmful and must be regulated in the common interest). The presentation is in two parts; the first is "The Problem and the Challenge," and the second is a collection of selected readings by addicts, ex-addicts, and authorities on the subject. The book contains a number of case studies that are vivid and insightful. However, not very much factual information has been included.

208. Moreau, Jacques-Joseph. **Hashish and Mental Illness.** Editors: Hélène Peters and Gabriel G. Nahas. Translated by Gordon J. Barnett. New York, Raven Press, 1973. 245p. illus. bibliog. $9.75. LC 76-107227. ISBN 0-911216-14-6. (Translation of *Du Hashisch et de l'aliénation mentale; Etudes psychologiques.*)

This book, written in 1845, documents the results of psychiatrist Moreau's observations on the use of hashish. He described and categorized all the varied effects, both psychic and physical, and used a range of doses on subjects far higher than any modern scientist would dare use today in humans. He enumerated eight main symptom groups of hashish intoxication: 1) general feelings of pleasure; 2) increased excitement combined with a heightening of all senses; 3) distortion of the dimension of space and time, generally a magnification of both; 4) a keener sense of hearing combined with a greater susceptibility to music and the phenomenon that ordinary noise can be enjoyed as though it sounded sweet; 5) persistent ideas verging on persecution mania; 6) disturbances of emotion, most often in the form of an increase in pre-existing feelings; 7) irresistible impulses; and 8) illusions and hallucinations, of which evidently only the former are related to objects in the external world.

Moreau further observed that the psychic effects of the drug take on the characteristics of insanity if the dose is large enough. He warned against chronic use and pointed out what has been suspected recently, that personality changes develop subtly over a few years. For instance, there is diminished drive, lessened ambition and motivation, apathy, shortened attention span, impaired communication skills, introversion, magical thinking, and diminished capacity to carry out plans or prepare for the future. He saw that the drug produced psychoses which would be useful in psychiatric experiments; insights might be offered into physical origins of the psychoses. He also thought the drug might have therapeutic value.

There is much of interest in the book. The experiments described are of importance still, particularly since legal restrictions would make it impossible to undertake many of them today.

209. Multidisciplinary Symposium on Drug Dependence, Strasbourg, 1972. **Report and Conclusions.** n.p., 1972. 208p. $5.50.

This symposium was held by the Council of Europe in conjunction with the World Health Organization. The causes, prevention, treatment, and control of drug abuse were discussed. The main purpose was to arrive at conclusions which would pave the way for the proposal of practical measures within the Council to reduce drug dependence in member states and to increase the effectiveness of prevention and treatment by means of international cooperation. Four consultants presented the plenary sessions, and these reports served as working papers. The participants included pharmacologists, pharmacists, psychiatrists, specialists in other medical fields, public health administrators, jurists, representatives of police, prison or customs authorities, youth leaders, social workers, psychologists or sociologists, teachers, and mass communication experts. Material was presented of interest to all of these groups. A number of recommendations grew out of the symposium, and these are stated along with conclusions.

210. O'Callaghan, Sean. **Drug Addiction in Britain.** London, Robert Hale, 1970. 223p. illus. index. ISBN 0-7091-1463-X.

The author wrote this book because he felt there was a need for a work on drug addiction by a layman with knowledge of the subject. He felt qualified to undertake it because he had investigated the underworld of drug trafficking in the Far East, Middle East, and in North and South America and had published findings about it. Having seen the misery drug use brings and how rapidly addictions spread in places outside Britain, he expresses the hope that parents can be made aware of the growing menace.

The following chapters are presented: 1) Drug addiction–its cause and effect, 2) The growth of drug trafficking in Britain, 3) The drug menace in Britain today, 4) My son's story, 5) Drugs in the schools, 6) Drugs and young people, 7) The "soft" drug smugglers, 8) The pushers, 9) The drug subculture, 10) The acid heads, 11) The treatment of drug addiction, 12) "Addicts die young", 13) Is addiction a crime or a disease? (the case for and against legalizing cannabis), 14) The drug menace in Ireland, and 15) Alcohol–the socially accepted drug.

The book does not preach or moralize, but it makes it difficult to take a permissive attitude toward drug use. The author believes in more education about drugs and their effects. He answers the claim that teaching young people about drugs may lead to more experimentation. He says the young must be made to realize that "something which may start as a 'giggle', to use their own term, could end up in utter degradation and an untimely death."

211. Phillipson, Richard V., ed. **Modern Trends in Drug Dependence and Alcoholism.** New York, Appleton-Century-Crofts; London, Butterworths, 1970. 311p. bibliog. index. $14.50. ISBN 0-407-29040-0.

In this book experts who have worked closely with narcotics addicts and alcoholics write about the problems prevalent in the United States and Great Britain. Practices in both countries are recorded. The following topics are treated: 1) Drug addiction and dependence in New York State: a programme for prevention and control, 2) Treatment of narcotic and non-narcotic drug dependence: the need for research, 3) Antagonists in the treatment of opiate dependence, 4) Drug control in the United Kingdom, 5) The implementation of the Second Report of the Interdepartmental Committee on Drug Addiction, 6) The Narcotic Addict Rehabilitation Act of 1966 and its implications, 7) The role of voluntary organizations in combating alcoholism, 8) The status of alcoholism as a disease, 9) Integrated hospital and community care for alcohol dependents and their families, 10) The forensic aspects of addiction, 11) Nine decades of experience in the treatment of alcoholism and drug dependence, 12) The development and action of drugs of dependence. Several of the papers are written on a scientific level and require some knowledge of chemistry for understanding; others are not technical.

The hope is expressed that this book brings into perspective what is known and what can be done and also how much needs to be done on basic, clinical, and therapeutic research and on treatment programs.

212. Pope, Harrison, Jr. **Voices from the Drug Culture.** Boston, Beacon Press, 1971. 147p. bibliog. $2.45pa. LC 70-184635. ISBN 0-8070-2770-7; 0-8070-2771-5pa.

The author began this book at Harvard College; it seems to have been an undergraduate project, presenting as it does personal accounts by drug users instead of objective research results. The author says that it seemed wiser for a researcher in such a study to reveal his personal feelings and to allow the reader to judge for himself the degree of bias. This reader thinks there is a good deal of bias toward and sympathy with drug use, although the picture drawn of the drug scene is not pleasant. The main theme that runs through the abusers' accounts is that there was something lacking in their home life: the days were dull and boring before they used drugs, and their parents didn't understand them or anything about life. Most accounts by drug users are similar to the ones presented here. Perhaps some insights can be gained into the drug culture by reading them; however, it is well to keep in mind that such accounts simply relate what young people say without indicating whether this is truth or rationalization. There may also be some prompting by the interviewer. All in all, these accounts sound very much like immature youth speaking, although the book is well written.

213. Read, Donald A. **Drugs and People.** Boston, Allyn and Bacon, Inc., 1972. 39p. illus. index. $1.45pa. LC 76-182381.

This booklet presents a simple, total view of drug use with the young reader in mind. At the end of each chapter are questions for review. There is also a question-and-answer section and a brief glossary of terms. The quality of the material presented is good, but it is very brief and elementary.

214. Rice, Julius. **Ups and Downs: Drugging and Duping.** New York, Macmillan, 1972. 214p. index. $5.95. LC 77-183862.

This book, written by a physician, is a story of drugs that are commonly abused, stimulants and sedatives. Marijuana is treated separately. Two classes of abusers are considered: those who receive their drugs from legal sources and those who use illegal sources. The chapter titles are as follows: 1) Psychoactive drugs: ups and downs; 2) The brain and drug mechanisms; 3) The voluntary nervous system; 4) The involuntary nervous system and drug mechanisms; 5) The embryo and fetus; 6) Up, down, and mezzanine; 7) Stimulants; 8) Going up; 9) Sedatives: going down; 10) Marijuana (Mezz); 11) Recognizing the drug users; and 12) What can we do and where should we start? The last chapter discusses ways of alleviating the drug problem, such as responsible prescribing and manufacturing policies by physicians and drug companies. The author criticizes advertising, including that in medical journals. He gives suggestions for educators and parents and encourages the setting up of drug rehabilitation centers.

215. Rosenthal, Franz. **The Herb: Hashish versus Medieval Muslim Society.** Leiden, E. J. Brill, 1971. 212p. bibliog. index.

This work studies the way medieval Muslim authorities tried to curb the use of drugs and examines the resistance to these attempts. The study, which is well documented and scholarly, is based in large part on manuscript materials from famous libraries.

There are five chapters: 1) Introduction, 2) Monographs on hashish and some of the more important sources, 3) The use of hashish, 4) The legal discussion, and 5) Hashish and its users in society. The appendix contains translations of some hashish poems and the Arabic text of a monograph on hashish.

The author concludes that effective countermeasures against drug use were not readily available in medieval Muslim society and that "the conflict between what was felt to be right and morally and socially good and what human nature craved in its search for play and diversion went on." Much of what is written in the book about drug use in medieval Islam society is analogous to the drug scene of today.

216. Rublowsky, John. **The Stoned Age: A History of Drugs in America.** New York, G. P. Putnam's Sons, 1974. 218p. bibliog. index. $6.95. LC 73-93744. ISBN 0-399-11306-1.

The author of this work takes the view that attitudes toward drug use in this country have not been consistent throughout our history. We have given little attention to the use of alcohol and tobacco, but have considered use of other mind-altering drugs a great evil. The book emphasizes the way people have reacted to drug use. In the last chapter, he recommends that politicians not make laws regarding drug use. He feels that the public must protect itself from the politicians' paternalistic efforts, suggesting that the public has not been told the truth about drugs, that the matter might even best be ignored. The author also points out that addiction is a permanent condition once established and that no treatment really cures the addict. He suggests that treatment centers such as the Halfway Houses and Phoenix programs be abolished, and that all drugs should be legally available. He further points out that his reforms would save much money and that they would probably not result in an increase in the number of addicts.

217. Scott, J. M. **The White Poppy: A History of Opium.** New York, Funk and Wagnalls, 1969. 205p. illus. bibliog. index. $5.95. LC 75-76127.

Tracing the history of the opium plant from early times to the present, the author examines its influence on art, medicine, crime, and literature. Arabic, Greek, and Roman uses are explored, as well as the use of opium by writers such as De Quincey and Coleridge and by physicians of the past. There is a section on the Opium War in China. The problem of opium use is brought up to date, and the current situation is described–how one body of opinion believes that drugs such as the opiates should be banned except for strictly medicinal purposes, and another believes they can open up one's consciousness. The author's view is that opium derivatives (there are about 50) should be strictly controlled lest they destroy us.

218. Smith, David E., and Donald R. Wesson, eds. **Uppers and Downers.** Englewood Cliffs, N.J., Prentice-Hall, Inc., 1973. 151p. bibliog. $2.45pa. LC 73-15558. ISBN 0-13-038597-5.

The two editors, who are physicians, and the contributors have all had much experience with drug abusers. Most of the articles have been reprinted from other sources. The titles of the papers are as follows: 1) The politics of uppers and downers, 2) Amphetamine use and misuse: a medicolegal view, 3) An analysis of amphetamine toxicity and patterns of use, 4) The transition to amphetamine abuse, 5) Cocaine: champagne of uppers, 6) Barbiturate toxicity and the treatment of barbiturate dependence, 7) The politics of barbiturate and amphetamine abuse, 8) Legitimate and illegitimate distribution of amphetamines and barbiturates, 9) Methaqualone: just another downer, 10) The corporate pushers, and 11) The ethics of addiction. A glossary of drug terms has been included.

The book stresses the problems of barbiturate and amphetamine abuse because they have not received as much attention as some other drugs of abuse. The editors suggest that the supply of these drugs should be more strictly controlled, since vast quantities of legitimately manufactured drugs evidently reach the street-level black market. Physicians and pharmaceutical manufacturers are criticized for the part they play in allowing these drugs to be abused.

219. Smithsonian Institution. **Drugs in Perspective: A Fact Book on Drug Use and Misuse.** Washington, Smithsonian Institution Press, 1972. 48p. illus. $1.95pa. LC 72-7213. ISBN 0-87474-128-9.

This popular presentation is based on an exhibition held at the Smithsonian. The purpose of the exhibition was to deal with ideas and social issues rather than with objects, and to collect information on all facets of a controversial subject and put them in scientific, historic, and social perspective. Arrangement is in six sections: 1) What do we mean by "drugs"? 2) How do drugs affect us?; 3) What is the drug problem?; 4) How do we deal with the drug problem today?; 5) The drug scene down the ages; and 6) The new decade.

The drug problem is summed up as follows: People will always use drugs, and some will misuse them. The challenge is to find ways to use drugs not to harm life but to improve it. The disease of drug misuse must be dealt with within the individual.

220. Spruce, Richard. **Notes of a Botanist on the Amazon and Andes.** With a new Foreword by Richard Evans Schultes. London, Macmillan and Co., 1908; New York and London, Johnson Reprint Corp., 1970. 2v. illus. index. $56.00. LC 78-117251.

The material in these volumes was collected and first published in 1908, after Spruce's death, from his manuscripts, correspondence, and field data. Until the work was reprinted it was almost a collector's item. It contains references, descriptions, discussions, and theories concerning plants and vegetation in the regions Spruce studied, as well as information on geological, anthropological, linguistic, historical, sociological, and zoological aspects of the regions. All kinds of plants are covered, and perhaps only one chapter is of particular concern to those exclusively interested in drug plants (Chapter XXV, "Indigenous Narcotics and Stimulants Used by the Indians of the Amazon"). Special attention is given to narcotics and stimulants such as ayahuasca, caapi, coca, guaraná, guayusa, and niopo. The beliefs and customs of the Indians who use these drugs and the proceedings of their medicine-men are discussed as well as the plants and the drugs made from them.

221. Stimmel, Barry. **Heroin Dependency: Medical, Economic, and Social Aspects.** New York, Stratton Intercontinental Medical Book Corp., 1975. 304p. illus. bibliog. $27.00; $17.50pa. LC 74-770. ISBN 0-913258-20-2.

This work is divided into three sections. The first begins with an historical narrative, followed by a discussion called "socioeconomics of heroin use." Effects of legislation and law enforcement are also discussed. One chapter is devoted to the need for more precise and standardized reporting procedures—a definite need, since incomplete data are frequently used as the basis of important conclusions. The second section of the book, which discusses the medical aspect of heroin, is of particular interest to physicians. The pharmacology and the medical complications of the drug are discussed. The third section, concerned with treatment and rehabilitation, expresses the prevalent concepts and complex problems in considerable depth.

The book is competently prepared and should have general as well as professional appeal.

222. Strauss, Nathan, III. **Addicts and Drug Abusers: Current Approaches to the Problem.** A publication of the Center for New York City Affairs, New School for Social Research. New York, Twayne Publishers, Inc., 1971. 188p. bibliog. index. $4.80. LC 73-125266.

Nathan Strauss, III, is a New York businessman who has been active in various organizations concerned with the drug abuse problem. He is author of only the first chapter of this publication, the remainder having been contributed by lawyers, doctors, and other well-known professionals who are involved with the drug problem.

Strauss's view is that while we want to prevent addiction and find a cure for it as soon as possible, the urgent requirement at the present time is to reduce the economic and social cost of drug abuse. The book describes current significant approaches and programs, evaluates them, and makes suggestions for changes and improvements. Chapter headings are as follows: 1) An overview, 2) The view of a practicing physician, 3) Criminal justice, 4) The New York City Program, 5) The New York State Narcotic Addiction Control Commission: its program and activities, 6) Group psychotherapy, 7) The community mental health approach, 8) Methadone maintenance treatment, 9) The British experience.

The book presents the problems of drug abuse and its treatment and prevention very realistically. It is a better book than most of the popular presentations, which either emphasize the sensational or express too much idealism.

223. Taylor, Norman. **Flight from Reality.** New York, Duell, Sloan and Pearce, 1949. 237p. bibliog. index.

The author of this book is well known for his classic works in the areas of botany, gardening, and drug plants. This book takes the view that people will never cease to look for things that will offer them some respite from the stark demands of reality. The author discusses the plant materials that have been used for this purpose from all corners of the world. This includes materials commonly used in highly industrialized societies (such as tobacco, alcohol, tea, coffee, and chocolate) as well as those used in exotic places. The latter include marijuana and other cannabis derivatives (which were exotic substances at the time this book was written), opium and its derivatives, peyotl and ololiuqui, cocaine, betel nut, datura, kava, pituri, curare, scopolamine, fly agaric, and caapi.

Not many older books on this subject exist; this title is outstanding among those few.

224. Terry, Charles E., and Mildred Pellens. **The Opium Problem.** With a new Foreword by John C. Ball and a new Preface by Charles Winick. Bureau of Social Hygiene, Inc., 1928; repr. Montclair, N.J., Patterson Smith, 1970. 1042p. bibliog. index. $25.00. LC 76-108232. ISBN 0-87585-115-0.

This classic work, which has generally been regarded as the single most comprehensive work in the field, is also a source book that includes many passages from famous writers of the past. An appraisal of these reports is provided. The work is limited to discussion of what are known today as "hard narcotics"—heroin, morphine, paragoric, codeine, and other narcotic analgesics. Five areas of the drug abuse problem are explored: 1) The history of use in the United States, including the extent of chronic use; 2) The life course of addiction from onset to death, with emphasis on different types of addicts; 3) The medical aspects of addiction, including tolerance, dependence, and withdrawal; 4) American and European treatment programs; and 5) Legal control of opium abuse under local, state, federal, and international auspices. This landmark book serves as a foundation for further current research on the problem.

225. U.S. Drug Enforcement Administration. **Fact Sheets.** Washington, GPO, 1973. 67p. illus. (part col.) $0.60.

This pamphlet, intended for general use, contains some spectacular illustrations and much general information about drugs. Topics include the Drug Enforcement Administration, illegal traffic in narcotics and dangerous drugs, an overview of the drug problem and the drug abuser, prevention education, information about the various types of abused drugs, a special section on audio-visual aids, a list of the agency's publications, and a section on the Special Action Office for Drug Abuse Prevention. A notable feature is a section of colored pictures of abused drugs (crude and in tablet form) and drug paraphernalia.

226. Walton, Alan Hull. **Aphrodisiacs: From Legend to Prescription; A Study of Aphrodisiacs Throughout the Ages, with Sections on Suitable Food, Glandular Extracts, Hormone Stimulation and Rejuvenation.** Westport, Conn., Associated Booksellers, 1958. 267p. illus. bibliog. index. $7.95. LC 58-13948.

This account of the use and misuse of aphrodisiacs throughout history contains a great deal of material taken from obscure medical and literary sources. The author is a learned literary scholar, and the book is laden with footnote references to the literature of all people in all times and places. The volume is in three sections: The first, "Aphrodisiacs through the Ages", starts with the herbs and salves used by ancient Jews, Greeks, and Romans and moves down to modern times. The second section, "The Cookery of Love", describes the effects upon sexual vigor of many foods, beverages, tonics, glandular extracts, and ointments. It includes actual recipes that have been presumed to be of value. The last section, "Medicine and Sexuality", attempts to show how pharmaceutical preparations affect virility, covering such topics as nutrition, vitamin use, and hormones. The major drugs of abuse are mentioned only briefly.

The book is quite interesting as a literary curiosity, but it is not recommended for scientific information.

227. Whipple, Dorothy B. **Is the Grass Greener? Answers to Questions about Drugs.** Washington, New York, Robert B. Luce, Inc., 1971. 224p. bibliog. index. $5.95. LC 73-129135.

The author, a physician who has practiced pediatrics for many years, discusses all drugs in common use (including alcohol) in a question-and-answer style. The language is suitable for young readers. Like many books on drugs written for young people, this one does not argue against drug use in obvious fashion but presents factual information. The implication is that the reader himself will decide whether or not to use drugs from the material presented. Actually, the facts as presented are probably argument enough against drug use.

Chapter headings are as follows: 1) What drugs are and what they do; 2) Marihuana and hashish; 3) LSD and other psychedelics; 4) Opium, morphine and heroin; 5) Amphetamines; 6) Down drugs–the barbiturates; 7) Cocaine; 8) Glue, nutmeg and others; 9) Alcohol; 10) The people who use drugs today; 11) Prevention, treatment and rehabilitation; 12) Drug laws and how they came to be passed; 13) What the drug laws have accomplished; and 14) Other ways of tackling the drug problem.

228. White House Conference on Narcotic and Drug Abuse. **Proceedings.** September 27-28, 1962. Washington, GPO, 1962. 330p. illus. $1.00pa.

This conference was called at the request of President Kennedy because of his concern over the drug abuse problem. Chaired by Attorney General Robert F. Kennedy, it was attended by more than 400 representatives of public and private agencies concerned with the control and treatment of drug abuse. The mission of the conference was not to arrive at solutions to the problem but rather to point out the aspects of it that required intensive analysis and inquiry. Representatives of all relevant disciplines were involved. The proceedings are made up of five panel discussions: 1) Law enforcement and controls, 2) Current and experimental methods of treatment, 3) Research, 4) Civil commitment and parole, and 5) Legislation.

The report contains some useful information and data, with suggestions for research investigations. The numerous conclusions at the end of the report fall into major categories of history, pharmacology, incidence and prevalence of drug abuse, characteristics of the drug abuser, treatment, and rehabilitation.

229. White, William, Jr., and Ronald F. Albano, eds. **North American Symposium on Drugs and Drug Abuse.** Philadelphia, North American Publishing Co., 1974. 376p. illus. bibliog. index. (North American Reference Encyclopedia Series, v.3). $27.50. LC 72-84735. ISBN 0-912920-04-1.

The aim of this publication is to gather together in one reference source the best available facts and opinions on the drug abuse issue. New articles are included as well as some reprinted from other sources. The views expressed are those of rather widely known physicians, psychiatrists, pharmacists, chemists, social scientists, and religious and legal scholars.

The 22 articles, most of which are of high quality, are presented in three groups. The first covers scientific facts and opinions about drugs, the second presents psychological facts and opinions, and the third surveys the drug abuse problem in three representative societies (the United States, Great Britain, and Israel). Excellent lists of materials have been included, and there is an annotated guide to films and a 60-page bibliography of books and articles.

Some of the chapters of the book present valuable special materials, such as tables that aid in identifying unknown drugs in capsule and tablet form. This is important information because unknown drugs are frequently found in the possession of overdose victims who need immediate treatment. One article includes a good glossary of drug abuse terms. This work contains much of value to a wide audience.

230. Williams, John B. **Narcotics and Drug Dependence.** Beverly Hills, Calif., Glencoe Press, 1974. 422p. $7.95pa. LC 72-85762. ISBN 0-02-47950-8.

The two main parts of this work are "The problems of drug abuse—dimensions and responses" and "The drugs and chemicals of abuse." Discussing the most commonly abused drugs, including their authorized medical uses, the book indicates signs and symptoms of drug abuse and discusses rehabilitation. There is a glossary of technical and slang terms.

Designed to inform the reader, to help him recognize when another person is using drugs, and to equip him to render personal help or to alert others who can assist more expertly, the book can also show the drug abuser himself a way out of his difficulty. It is recommended reading for all those interested in the drug problem. Much authentic medical material has been included as well as legal information.

6. Incidence and Prevalence

This section, containing books on the incidence and prevalence of drug abuse, includes titles covering the United States, Great Britain, India, Canada, a small town in England, several different states of the United States, medium-sized American cities, the military, and students. Publications in this section frequently refer to drug abuse as an "epidemic" that has reached a "crisis state."

231. Ball, John C., and Earl D. Chambers, eds. **The Epidemiology of Opiate Addiction in the United States.** With a preface by Griffith Edwards. Springfield, Ill., Charles C. Thomas, 1970. 337p. bibliog. index. $15.50. LC 70-126466.

Following a precedent set in other areas of trouble, the term "epidemiology" is extended in this book beyond the realm of infectious diseases to include addiction. Tracing the history of drug addiction in the United States to the present time, the work considers questions of etiology and prevention. Research findings are presented, and there are many statistical tables. Research workers, planners of health services, and legislators should be interested in the book. The material is divided into the following parts: 1) History and present epidemiology, 2) Patterns of drug use in the United States, 3) Opiate use in selected populations, and 4) Medical aspects of opiate addiction.

232. Blum, Richard H., and associates. **Drugs II: Students and Drugs, College and High School Observations.** San Francisco, Jossey-Bass, Inc., 1969. bibliog. index. $12.50. LC 73-75936. ISBN 0-87589-034-2.

This publication is a companion volume to *Drugs I: Society and Drugs, Social and Cultural Observations* by the same authors. The emphasis in *Drugs II* is on student drug abuse. Chapter headings are as follows: 1) Prologue: Students and drugs; 2) Drugs on five campuses; 3) Those who do, those who do not; 4) Student characteristics and major drugs; 5) Student characteristics, minor drugs, and motivation; 6) Correlations and factor analysis; 7) Users of approved drugs; 8) Users of illicit drugs; 9) Bad outcomes on campus; 10) Students' drug diaries; 11) A follow-up study; 12) Student ideologies compared; 13) Life style interviews; 14) Psychological tests; 15) Horatio Alger's children: case studies; 16) Predicting who will turn on; 17) Psychiatric problems; 18) Drugs and Catholic students; 19) Drugs and high school students; 20) Overview for administrators; and 21) Epilogue: Students and drugs.

An attempt is made, though not very successfully, to characterize the kind of student who uses or experiments with drugs. It is evident, however, that drug use was very prevalent in schools at the time the book was written, at least in the West Coast area.

233. Btesh, Simon, ed. **Drug Abuse: Nonmedical Use of Dependence-Producing Drugs.** New York, Plenum Press, 1972. 289p. bibliog. (Advances in Experimental Medicine and Biology. Vol. 20). $16.50. LC 76-190227. ISBN 0-306-39020-5.

This publication presents the Proceedings of the Sixth Round Table Conference organized by the Council for International Organizations of Medical Sciences with the participation of the United Nations Educational, Scientific, and Cultural Organization and the World Health Organization, Geneva, Switzerland, October 20-21, 1971. It includes the papers presented as well as the discussions that followed them. A humanistic approach was taken to the drug problem, although the conference was interdisciplinary and a number of professions were represented (such as psychiatry, epidemiology, public health, sociology, law, and pharmacology). The material was presented under the following subject headings: 1) Factors associated with the use of dependence-producing drugs, 2) Current patterns of abuse of dependence-producing drugs, 3) Preventive approaches to drug dependence.

Three major conclusions were reached at the conference. The first was that research on drug abuse should be carried out by interdisciplinary groups. The second was that a wide variety of lay and professional groups should be educated in order to provide understanding of the spectrum of non-medical drug usage and the necessity of bringing the patients into the society of the majority. And the third was that the general medical community must be involved in the management of drug abuse patients.

234. Chambers, Carl D., James A. Inciardi, and Harvey A. Siegal. **Chemical Coping: A Report on Legal Drug Use in the United States.** New York, Halsted Press (a Division of John Wiley and Sons), 1975. 157p. illus. $10.95. LC 74-30196. ISBN 0-470-14326-6.

The authors of this work are members of the Department of Epidemiology and Publis Health, University of Miami School of Medicine. Their aim is to present a picture of the legal use of drugs in the United States. However, "legal" uses are sometimes abuses. Psychoactive drugs such as hypnotics, tranquilizers, stimulants, and alcohol are discussed. The book analyzes several of the dimensions of chemical coping in American society, providing a base from which to formulate the implications and costs of such behavior. Some of the results of the study are interesting. About 7 percent of everyone in the United States over the age of 13 regularly uses at least one prescription psychoactive drug to stimulate, sedate, or tranquilize themselves. About 65 percent are regular users of alcohol, and about 10 percent can be classified as heavy drinkers. To make matters worse, alcohol can potentiate the effects of many psychoactive drugs. The authors fear that chemical coping will prevent the adaption of non-chemical coping mechanisms and may lead to the extinguishing of non-chemical coping skills. Mention is also made of the wide use of non-prescription drugs and the dangers that attend overuse of them. The book makes a valuable contribution to a comprehensive picture of the drug phenomenon in the United States. The medical professions and the lay public should be interested in it.

235. Chopra, R. N., and I. C. Chopra. **Drug Addiction: With Special Reference to India.** New Delhi, Council of Scientific and Industrial Research, 1965. 264p. bibliog. index.

The authors point out that although drug abuse has not reached the epidemic proportions in India that it has in the United States, there is danger that this might come about. Therefore, a book such as this one is important. The authors discuss the problem of drug addiction and alcoholism from the point of view of both the medical profession and the layman.

Part I, which deals with the general aspects of drug abuse as a world problem, contains chapters on addiction-producing drugs, psychiatric and clinical aspects of addiction, treatment, minor drug habits, tobacco, alcohol, and barbiturates. Part II deals with the problem of drug addiction with reference to India, especially the use of cannabis drugs, opium, and cocaine, as well as control of the drug problem. There are three appended sections: international control of narcotic drugs, drugs under international narcotics control (a list), and drug dependence (a report of a WHO scientific group).

Informative and interesting for both laymen and professionals in the health field, the book contains a great deal of historical material.

236. Deedes, William. **The Drugs Epidemic.** New York, Barnes and Noble, Inc., 1970. 160p. bibliog. $4.00 ISBN 0-389-04107-6.

This book, written by a member of Parliament in Great Britain, is aimed at young people who can perhaps be kept from misusing drugs. Chapter headings are: 1) Approaching the problem, 2) The size of the threat, 3) Drugs and the law, 4) The American conflagration, 5) Who takes drugs and why? 6) Cannabis, 7) LSD, 8) Punishment or treatment? 9) Laws which will work, 10) Combating the drug traffic, 11) What action? An appendix reproduces the Schedule in the Misuse of Drugs Bill and lists controlled drugs in three new classes. A second appendix sets out the offenses and their penalties proposed in this British bill.

The book is rather interesting and well written. Its message is essentially a plea for individuals to have faith in God and build a better spiritual world. The author sees society now as basically decent but devoid of faith.

237. Geller, Allen, and Maxwell Boas. **The Drug Beat.** New York, Cowles Book Company, Inc., 1969. 278p. bibliog. index. $6.50. LC 70-78408. ISBN 0-402-12201-1.

This book, written by two journalists, presents a sympathetic and somewhat sensational picture of the drug scene. It also attempts to answer questions regarding the effects of drugs of abuse. The material is grouped into three sections: 1) Marijuana, 2) LSD, and 3) Amphetamines.

The book concludes that repressive laws are largely responsible for the seamy side of drug abuse, leaving the impression that there is a good (or at least better) side. The dangers inherent in drug use are pointed out from time to time in the text, but the book does not seem likely to discourage drug experimenting among youth.

Much of what is pictured is out of date now, particularly with respect to attitudes. The drug scene has changed since the late 1960s, at least as presented in the literature, and the glamour and excitement have been replaced by a feeling of hopelessness regarding treatment and cures.

238. Gormely, Sheila. **Drugs and the Canadian Scene.** Toronto, Pagurian Press Ltd., 1970. 186p. $6.50. ISBN 0-919364-01-2.

This is a Canadian newspaper reporter's story of the drug scene as she saw it in her work. The writing is somewhat sensational, but the picture presented is not glamorous. The writer is sympathetic both to the young people and to their parents, and it is difficult to tell just what her point of view is. Perhaps her intention is just to show a bad situation vividly. She thinks that "truth and love" will provide a solution but doesn't know how to translate this to young people. The reviewer found few insights from the book except to recall that adolescent fads have been with us for at least several generations, but most of them have not been as damaging and as permanent as drug addiction.

239. Illinois Legislative Investigating Commission. **The Drug Crisis: Report on Drug Abuse in Illinois; To the Illinois General Assembly.** Chicago, 1971. 363p. illus. bibliog.

In the hope of expanding the knowledge of drugs among citizens, this report covers many aspects of drug abuse, using these chapter headings; 1) Legislation, 2) The drug problem, 3) The youthful drug culture, 4) Marihuana, 5) Narcotics, 6) Dangerous drugs (includes history and types), 7) Law enforcement, 8) Drug education, 9) Treatment and rehabilitation, 10) Briefing from federal authorities, 11) Interviews of Los Angeles authorities, 12) Interviews of San Francisco authorities, 13) Interviews of New York City authorities, 14) Chicago hearings: an overview, 15) Chicago hearings: law enforcement, 16) Chicago hearings: the drug revolution, Part 1, 17) Chicago hearings: the drug revolution, Part II, 18) Chicago hearings: legislation, Part I, 19) Chicago hearings: legislation, Part II, 20) Springfield hearings: legislation, Part III, 21) Conclusions, 22) Recommendations. A pictorial section (in color), "Drugs of Abuse," is a reprinting of a pamphlet originally published by the U.S. Bureau of Narcotics and Dangerous Drugs; it provides identifying photographs and explanations of controlled substances and marihuana. A good glossary of terms used by drug users has been included, and there are numerous appendices, primarily of laws. A unique section, Appendix 17, gives the words of popular songs that refer to drug use. A large number of authorities were consulted in compiling the work, and these persons are listed in Appendix 18. The bibliography is impressive. The report is thorough, authentic, and realistically presented.

240. Louria, Donald B. **The Drug Scene.** New York, McGraw-Hill Book Company, 1968. 215p. bibliog. $5.95. LC 68-27509.

The author states in his introduction that he hesitated to add another book to an already overburdened literature, but he thought it was a good time to analyze the drug scene. When this book was written, statistical data had become available on the prevalence and trends in drug abuse. Also the initial thrust of the psychedelic cult had lost a great deal of its vigor. The author felt that the proliferation of magazine and newspaper articles, television shows, and books had not done much to inform the public on the subject. This book presents factual data to dispel myths and in addition states the author's interpretations and opinions. His feeling, in brief, is that proper education in the home and school is needed to heal a troubled society.

241. Nurco, David. **Drug Abuse Study 1969.** Sponsoring agencies: Maryland Commission to Study Problems of Drug Addiction and the Maryland State Department of Mental Hygiene; scientific, financial and administrative agencies: National Institute of Mental Health and Friends of Psychiatric Research. Baltimore, 1969. 360p.

The main purposes of this study were: 1) to assess the feasibility of collecting data from a wide spectrum of agencies in Maryland, and 2) to interpret these data and evaluate their usefulness in helping community agencies assess the extent of the drug problem. Special studies were made to evaluate five classes of community agencies: training schools and health, educational, social, and correctional agencies. Several supplementary areas were studied, such as the state's Psychiatric Care Register, the emergency rooms in three hospitals, drug deaths reported to the medical examiner, the feasibility of locating addicts, and a study of Montgomery County physicians.

The study was quite comprehensive, presenting much useful material concerning the extent and nature of drug abuse in the state of Maryland. Attitudes and practices needed to cope with the problem are discussed. The study identifies individuals who seem to have the highest risk of becoming addicts, and it explores the reasons why people use drugs.

242. Plant, Martin A. **Drugtakers in an English Town.** London, Tavistock Publications, 1975. 319p. bibliog. index. £6.50; £2.95pa. ISBN 0-422-74650-9; 0-422-74660-6pa.

This book looks at drug users in their everyday settings in the town of Cheltenham, England, where the author spent two years studying in depth the lives of 200 admitted drug users. The users are differentiated into three categories: students, middle-class bohemians, and low-status unemployed and manual workers. The latter group is closest to the conventionally held view of drug abusers.

There is some indication that the prescribing practices of physicians have influenced drug use: the availability of amphetamines has been reduced, but sedatives and tranquilizers are prescribed frequently for respectable middle-aged parents. Young people see cannabis use in the same light as their parents' use of these prescribed drugs; at least they say they do. The author concludes that drug use itself does not constitute a problem, at least not in the town of Cheltenham at the time of the study.

243. U.S. Domestic Council Drug Abuse Task Force. **White Paper on Drug Abuse, a Report to the President.** September 1975. Washington, GPO, 1975. 116p. $1.55pa. S/N 041-010-00027-4.

This paper documents the principal findings of the Task Force, assesses the current status of drug abuse in America, and presents a number of recommendations for improving the federal government's program to reduce drug abuse. The Task Force believes that the optimism expressed so confidently a few years ago regarding the drug problem was premature and that a national commitment to the effort will be required if we are ultimately to succeed. The major recommendations of the White Paper are as follows: 1) priority should be directed toward abuse of the most destructive drugs, 2) the drug supply and distribution systems should be attacked, and 3) education and prevention efforts should be emphasized. In addition, the report delineates the responsibilities and programs of various government agencies concerned with drug abuse.

244. U.S. National Institute on Drug Abuse. **Young Men and Drugs—A Nationwide Survey**. By John A O'Donnell and others. Springfield, Va., National Technical Information Service, 1976. 144p. (NIDA Research Monograph 5; DHEW Publication No. (ADM) 76-311) bibliog. index. $6.75pa. $2.25 microfiche. LC 75-4388.

Presenting significant statistical data that provide many possibilities for further study, this survey is made up of both tabular and text material on drug use among young men 20 to 30 years old in 1974. Use of the following drugs is considered: tobacco, alcohol, marihuana, psychedelics, stimulants, sedatives, heroin, opiates, and cocaine. Chapter titles are: 1) Introduction; 2) Lifetime prevalence; 3) Current prevalence; 4) Estimates of drug use in the population of young men; 5) The drug epidemic; 6) Attitudes, motivations, and contexts; 7) Problems and benefits attributed to drug abuse; 8) Drugs, crime and criminal justice; 9) Multiple drug use; 10) A total drug use index; 11) Drug use and military service; 12) Treatment for drug use; and 13) Regional variation in use.

The findings of the study are summarized: there has been some decline in the use of cigarettes; there has been no decline in prevalence in the use of other drugs except possibly psychedelics; veterans show no higher use rates than non-veterans; reported involvement in criminal behavior varies directly with drug use; drug use was found to be higher among those who lived in large cities, were unemployed, unconventional in behavior, and had achieved lower educational levels only; Among those drug users who entered college, most majored in social sciences, fine arts, and the humanities.

245. U.S. Special Action Office for Drug Abuse Prevention. **An Assessment of the Diffusion of Heroin Abuse to Medium-Sized American Cities**. By Mark H. Greene and others. Washington, GPO, 1974. 106p. bibliog. (Special Action Office Monograph, Series A, No. 5.) $1.80pa. S/N 041-010-00020.

This is a report of a survey conducted in June 1974 to determine the extent that heroin abuse had spread from large metropolitan areas to medium-sized cities, the so-called "Ripple Theory." The following ten cities were studied: 1) Austin, Texas; 2) Boulder, Colorado; 3) Des Moines, Iowa; 4) Eugene, Oregon; 5) Greensboro, North Carolina; 6) Jackson, Mississippi; 7) Macon, Georgia; 8) Omaha, Nebraska; 9) Pensacola, Florida; and 10) Racine, Wisconsin. Previous data had shown that the heroin epidemic peaked in most coastal cities by 1968-69, then moved to less populous areas and inland regions, where addiction rates climaxed as late as 1972-73. The study gives a good deal of attention to the methodology used to collect the data, since it is difficult to determine heroin use. For the most part, the Ripple Theory was validated. It took about one year for drug epidemics to spread from large cities to smaller ones.

246. Westin, Av, and Stephanie Shaffer. **Heroes and Heroin: the Shocking Story of Drug Addiction in the Military**. Based on an ABC-TV News Documentary. New York, Pocket Books, 1972. 284p. illus. ISBN 0-671-78245-2.

An expansion of a TV news documentary, this work includes eyewitness accounts, statistics, documentation, and personal interviews made by journalists of military and medical experts, servicemen, and people back home involved with the men of the Vietnam War. As the journalists covered the war front they found much evidence of a growing drug epidemic. The data collected are accompanied by many pictures. It is difficult to assess the book, since so many conflicting opinions and beliefs have been evident regarding the Vietnam War, and, for that matter, the whole drug scene. In retrospect, it does not appear that the drug abuse problem among Vietnam veterans has been any greater than among young men who did not serve.

247. Zacune, Jim, and Celia Hensman, compilers. **Drugs, Alcohol and Tobacco in Britain**. London, William Heinemann Medical Books, Ltd., 1971. 239p. bibliog. index. £4.00. ISBN 0-433-39880-9.

This book is an outgrowth of a WHO questionnaire that collected data on the problems of alcohol and drug dependence in various countries and on each nation's efforts to contain the situation. Many experts contributed the data that form the basic framework for the book, which focuses on England, Wales, Scotland, and Northern Ireland. The book is in six sections: availability and control of alcohol and drugs; normal use of alcohol and medical use of drugs; misuse of alcohol and non-medical use of drugs; treatment and rehabilitation; education, advertising, prevention and research; tobacco and the nation's health.

Besides providing a one-stop source for data that otherwise would have to be searched for, this book portrays a country's total response to the fact of its inevitable and continuing co-existence with substances that act on the mind. It is an attempt "to lay a range of facts side by side, and see then what sort of portrait emerges of a complex co-existence, of accidents and intentions, of implementations and inactions, of governmental and voluntary and commercial and criminal activities, which together go to make up a National Response."

The material is well presented, and the book should be very useful for research workers, physicians, college and university libraries, social workers, and all those involved with formulating policies on drug, alcohol, and tobacco use.

7. Prevention, Rehabilitation, and Community Action Programs

Many books deal with the treatment and prevention of drug abuse and with community programs that have been developed to cope with the problem. So far no plan of treatment has been notably successful; the outlook is not encouraging. The trend is to use a variety of approaches in treating the condition, since one plan might be successful with some patients and not with others. The "therapeutic community" has proved itself in many instances. This approach can be compared to some degree with Alcoholics Anonymous, which is generally considered the most successful method of treating alcoholics. The drug methadone is used with limited success for heroin addiction, but it is rather dangerous and is itself addicting. However, when the drug is substituted for heroin the dose can be lowered and controlled.

Mention is made in some books of "intervention" in the addict's life as being important in the treatment processes. This is presumed to be a successful approach, although few have the time to intervene perpetually in another's life. Therapeutic communities and Alcoholics Anonymous take the time to intervene, which is perhaps why they are the best of the treatment plans. The concept of "alternatives" has been stressed in the prevention and treatment of addiction. Instead of escaping with drugs, the potential victim is encouraged to seek other means of finding satisfaction in his life.

248. **ABC of Drug Addiction: A collection of articles most of which appeared in 'Community Health' September-October, 1969, and November-December, 1969.** Bristol, England, John Wright and Sons Ltd., 1970; distr., Baltimore, Md., Williams and Wilkins Co., 93p. bibliog. $5.25. ISBN 0-7236-0290-5.

The first section of this booklet is a glossary of slang drug terms. Although the publication is British, many of the same terms seem to be used in the United States. The remainder of the publication contains these articles: 1) The nature and properties of drugs which give rise to dependence, 2) Politics of drug dependence, 3) Social work and drug dependence, 4) The drug scene and the Christian community, 5) Drug offenders and the courts, 6) Drug taking, myth or reality? 7) The working of a drug dependence treatment clinic, 8) Thoughts on drug dependence, 9) The police aspect of drug abuse in Hampshire, 10) Talking about drugs, 11) A community drug project, 12) The spread of heroin abuse in a community, 13) Drug dependency–a community responsibility, 14) Polydrug abuse. The emphasis in most of the articles is on the state of mind of those who become or are drug abusers.

249. Addiction and Drug Abuse Report. **What You Need to Know about Anti-Drug Abuse Work: Special Report**. New York, Grafton Publications, Inc., 1972. 22p. $5.00pa.

This is a summary of information that will help individuals who are working with drug abusers and addicts. It will be particularly useful for those who have had experience with this kind of activity, presenting information on such matters as the psychology of the abuser, the drug treatment scene, do's and dont's of creating confidence, what to say to young people, where to go for assistance in establishing treatment centers, and how to raise money for programs. The report is realistic and practical.

250. Barnette, Henlee H. **The Drug Crisis and the Church**. Philadelphia, Westminster Press, 1971. 176p. bilbiog. $2.95. LC 73-148563. ISBN 0-664-24921-3.

This book presents an objective and accurate overview of the drug problem in terms of the nature, etiology, and effect of drugs, along with some suggestions for rehabilitating the drug dependent person. The author is a theologian who has had experience in working with addicts, although he himself has been a user only of caffeine, nicotine, aspirin, and an assortment of painkillers after two surgical operations.

The book begins by describing our drug-oriented society. The next chapter identifies some drugs of abuse, while Chapter 3 discusses causes of drug abuse. Chapter 4 deals with legal aspects of the problem, Chapter 5 is for parents who are concerned about their children, and Chapter 6 deals with treatment and rehabilitation of addicts. Chapters 7 through 10 take up religious aspects of the drug problem.

The author's conclusion is that the churches of today should educate themselves about the drug problem and cooperate with other agencies in community efforts to handle the problem. The material, the documentation, and the author's viewpoint are unusually well presented. This is the kind of book that is frequently found in church libraries; it is highly recommended for them.

251. Bejerot, Nils. **Addiction: An Artificially Induced Drive**. Springfield, Ill., Charles C. Thomas, 1972. 78p. bibliog. index. $7.50. LC 72-75906. ISBN 0-398-02527-4.

The author's theory is that the early stage of drug abuse may be a symptom of social or psychological maladjustment, but that the person then loses control of the situation, since a deep-seated pathological state develops, with dynamics of its own. Because an individual's reason for beginning to take drugs thus has nothing to do with why he continues, treatment of the initiating condition will not be effective after the dependence on drugs is well developed. The author, a Swedish psychiatrist, has classified addiction into three kinds of cases: 1) single cases, where the addiction is developed through medical treatment or self-medication; 2) epidemic cases, where the individual is introduced to drugs by another abuser; 3) endemic cases, in which the addiction is to socially accepted drugs like alcohol. Treatment is discussed on the basis of these theories.

The conclusion is that public opinion is the most important factor in stamping out drug addiction. This excellent short book provides many insights and makes sensible suggestions.

252. Bejerot, Nils. **Addiction and Society**. Springfield, Ill., Charles C. Thomas, 1970. 299p. bibliog. index. $9.75. LC 75-122199.

Though authored by a Swedish scientist who has had much experience with addicted persons in Sweden, this book takes an international view. Amphetamine drug abuse is considered almost exclusively, but comparisons are made with other kinds of commonly abused drugs.

The author's view is that the short-term treatment usually administered to drug-dependent individuals is almost always futile, and he presents a treatment program that he thinks would be more effective. The basic points of this program are as follows: 1) There should be an attack on the agent of abuse itself. Many of the drugs of abuse should not be manufactured. There must be strict narcotic legislation and heavy punishment for offenders. 2) We must attempt to get control of the paths by which dangerous agents are spread; in particular illegal production, import, and sale must be blocked. 3) Preventive measures should be taken to localize groups and individuals who are susceptible to drug epidemics. 4) Isolation and long-term care of the highly contagious addictive cases should be enforced as with other epidemic cases. In conclusion, the author states that it will probably take a long time before society is ready to tackle this extremely complicated problem on a broad front.

253. Bell, R. Gordon. **Escape from Addiction.** New York, McGraw-Hill Book Co., 1970. 201p. index. $5.95. LC 70-118794.

The author, a physician and a recognized authority on addiction, is president of the Donwood Institute in Toronto, which operates a hospital for research and treatment of addiction. The chapter headings are as follows: 1) The drinking crisis, 2) The chemical trap, 3) Patterns of dependence, 4) Booze and taboos, 5) Attempts at social management, 6) The psychological labyrinth, 7) Medical treadmills, 8) No Man's land, 9) Toward total care, 10) The Donwood Treatment Plan (phase one), 11) The Donwood Treatment Plan (phase two), 12) The Donwood Treatment Plan (phase three), 13) The territorial concept, 14) The Donwood Health Program, 15) Community action, and 16) Escape into what?

The book is primarily concerned with alcoholism. The author is optimistic that something can be done about chemical addiction. He defines the problem, describes methods he has used successfully in dealing with it, and suggests some approaches that should help prevent such dependence. He feels that his suggestions are practical. The reviewer is somewhat skeptical, but it is likely that the treatment plan outlined is as good as any.

254. Berry, James. **Heroin Was My Best Friend.** New York, Crowell-Collier Press, 1971. 128p. bibliog. $4.95. LC 70-153761.

This book presents the case histories, based on interviews, of several drug addicts who lived in a therapeutic community in New York. The stories are well told and are probably typical. Some insight into the behavior patterns of drug abusers can perhaps be gained by reading the accounts. Probably of more importance, however, is the view of the therapeutic community and its successes and failures. There is a strong appeal throughout the book for drug abusers to seek help.

255. Blachly, P. H., ed. **Methadon.** Proceedings of the Methadon Workshop, March 27-28, 1971, Portland, Oregon. Sponsored by the Western Institute of Drug Problems, the Division of Continuing Education, State of Oregon, University of Oregon Medical School, and the Alcohol and Drug Section, Mental Health Division, State of Oregon. Corvallis, Ore., Continuing Education Publications, 1971. 115p. bibliog. $5.00. ISBN 0-87678-413-9.

For this workshop, the usual spelling, "methadone," was replaced with the original spelling of the term, "methadon," to symbolize that simplification was the focus of the workshop. Organized to improve the efficiency and reduce the redundancy of drug treatment efforts, the workshop brought together those involved in methadone drug abuse treatment programs so that they could share experiences. Most of the papers were presented by physicians who had had reasonably good results using the drug to treat heroin addicts. Many aspects of the subject were covered.

256. Brill, Leon, and Louis Lieberman, with the assistance of Stephen A. Green. **Authority and Addiction.** Boston, Little, Brown and Co., 1969. 318p. bibliog. index. $13.50. LC 73-82920.

It has been nearly impossible to treat and rehabilitate drug addicts on a permanent basis; they usually slip back into drug usage after treatment. This book deals with a new approach to true rehabilitation. It reports on a program conducted for five years by the Washington Heights Rehabilitation Center in New York City and sponsored by the National Institute of Mental Health, the New York City Department of Health, and the New York City Community Mental Health Board. In this program rational authority was the most important factor in the treatment. The Center stressed joint management by probation officers, who used coercive techniques, and caseworkers, who used somewhat permissive techniques.

Most of the book analyzes and evaluates the findings of the study. Included in appendices are questionnaires and forms, and "Selected Characteristics of Addict Population." This information may be useful for insights, for setting up other studies, and as a base for future comparison.

The authors of this book do not claim to have found an easy answer to the problem of addict rehabilitation. As a matter of fact, the patients in the control group did almost as well as those in the experimental group. However, some insights can probably be gained from the report, which will be useful to those working with addicts.

257. Brill, Leon. **The De-Addiction Process: Studies in the De-Addiction of Confirmed Heroin Addicts.** With a Foreword by Carl D. Chambers. Springfield, Ill., Charles C. Thomas, 1972. 166p. bibliog. index. $9.50. LC 72-75910. ISBN 0-398-02532-0.

This study of the processes by which a number of heroin addicts succeeded in quitting drugs presents case studies of a number of long-term addicts of varied backgrounds. In most cases help was achieved through a treatment modality such as methadone maintenance.

A "Findings" section summarizes the psychosocial factors, conditioning, and other factors that determine whether a person becomes an addict. Next, the book traces the de-addiction process through the case studies, pointing out strains that finally impel the addict to seek a cure and find his way back to conventional living. Also studied is a recently emerged younger group of multiple-drug users, who pose new problems for treatment. The following treatment methods are described: 1) methadone maintenance; 2) the narcotic antagonist, cyclazocine; 3) therapeutic communities such as Synanon and Phoenix House; and 4) religious approaches. Some success was reported in de-addiction when no formal treatment program was instituted.

258. Brill, Leon, and Louis Lieberman, eds. **Major Modalities in the Treatment of Drug Abuse.** New York, Behavioral Publications, 1972. 313p. $12.95. LC 77-174270.

The objective of this book is to describe the major modalities currently used in treating drug abusers. It is confined to a discussion of what is being done in the way of treatment and what additional efforts are required to solve the problem of drug abuse and addiction. The authors of the various articles that make up the book present the treatments they prefer, though it is felt that no one treatment is suitable for every case, since addicts have different social and psychological characteristics as well as physical ones.

Among the institutions and agencies discussed are the U.S. Public Health Service and Institutional Treatment Program for Narcotic Addicts and the National Institute of Mental Health Clinical Research Center at Lexington, Kentucky, and the Addiction Services Agency of the City of New York. Methadone maintenance is covered, as is the role of religion in the treatment of opiate addiction. The reports on the agencies usually include the following information: brief history, staffing, treatment goals, treatment methods, typical case study, findings, pros and cons, and implications for other problems. This book should have implications in the treatment of other social problems, such as alcoholism, vagrancy, prostitution, criminality and delinquency, and mental illness.

259. Burkhalter, Pamela K. **Nursing Care of the Alcoholic and Drug Abuser.** New York, McGraw-Hill Book Co., 1975. 297p. bibliog. index. $7.95pa. LC 74-10697. ISBN 0-07009051-3.

Designed to provide a foundation that will help the practicing and student nurse care for alcoholics and drug abusers, this work discusses new and innovative programs that meet the needs of these people. Nursing care as it applies to hospitals, psychiatric areas of practice, and community facilities is emphasized, but the book may be useful to other health professionals as well as to nurses.

The presentation is in three parts: 1) Alcoholism: nature, treatment, and nursing care; 2) Drug abuse: background, treatment, and nursing care; 3) Rehabilitation and the changing role of the nurse. The chapter headings are as follows: 1) Alcohol, culture, and society; 2) Alcoholism: definition, theories of causation; 3) Treatment: what and where is it? 4) Nurses' attitudes and the alcoholic patient; 5) Caring for the alcoholic in the general hospital; 6) The detoxification unit; 7) Psychiatric nursing and the alcoholic; 8) Nursing care of the alcoholic in the community; 9) Defining drug abuse; 10) Sociocultural aspects of drug abuse; 11) Drugs associated with drug abuse; 12) Theories of causation and characteristics of drug abuse; 13) Drug abuse: how is it treated? 14) Nursing care of the drug abuser in the general hospital; 15) Psychiatric nursing and the drug abuser; 16) Nursing care of the drug abuser in the community; 17) Rehabilitation and the changing role of the nurse; 18) Rehabilitation of the drug abuser; and 19) Future trends. The book incorporates much practical information as well as theories and philosophies.

260. Burns, John, and others. **The Answer to Addiction.** New York, Harper and Row, 1975. 232p. bibliog. $7.95. LC 74-4630. ISBN 0-06-061255-X.

This book was written by four editors of *24 Magazine*, all recovered alcohol and/or drug addicts. The theme of the work is as follows: the world has abandoned God, but God is real after all, and men cannot live without Him without going out of their minds. Those who are going out of their minds need relief and therefore turn to drugs and drink, bringing about addiction. The only possible solution to the problem is to return to God. All other resources have failed and will continue to fail (such as medicine, professional assistance, and the government), because their attempts are materialistic and take no account of spiritual reality. God historically has proved to be the answer to addiction. The idea is expressed that God is real, that materialistic things are not.

Chapters are arranged in the following sections: I) The reality of the answer and the hindrances that surround it, II) The strange miscasting and consequent confusion of the professionals, and III) The stunning success and ensuing difficulties of the amateurs.

The authors say in conclusion that Alcoholics Anonymous has done a fine job in the recovery of alcoholics, but that the overall alcohol problem is more insoluble than ever because such a large percentage of individuals drink. The situation since Alcoholics Anonymous is better for alcoholics, but worse for the general public. Again, turning to God is said to be the answer.

261. Canada. Commission of Inquiry into the Non-Medical Use of Drugs. **Report. Treatment.** Ottawa, Information Canada, 1972. 125p. illus. bibliog. index. $1.75. Catalogue No. H21-5370/3.

This is a final report on findings, conclusions, and recommendations with respect to treating the effects of non-medical drug use. A final report of all findings and recommendations is to be made later. This report discusses the various methods of treating the adverse physical and psychological conditions resulting from drug use. After a discussion of the concepts of the sickness and treatment, there is a brief description of those conditions which call for medical intervention. The various goals and kinds of therapeutic intervention are then outlined. Other chapters cover treatment of opiate dependence, treatment of high dose amphetamine (speed) dependence, treatment of alcoholism, hallucinogens, short-term medical management, therapeutic communities, organization and coordination of community treatment services, other therapeutic approaches, and cost estimate of a treatment complex.

262. Casriel, David, and Grover Amen. **Daytop: Three Addicts and Their Cure.** New York, Hill and Wang, 1971. 150p. $5.95. LC 73-163566. ISBN 0-8090-3777-7.

This book is about Daytop, a Staten Island home for drug addicts who are seeking a cure. Daytop is similar to Synanon, the progressive therapy center in California. The book presents personal accounts of the lives of three residents, vividly showing the addict's world, his problems, and the details of his eventual cure. The treatment used in centers such as this has probably been more successful than any other. The addicts provide for each other the motivation and other support needed to bring about change within the individual so that he can face his problem realistically.

The Daytop philosophy, which is read every day at morning meeting, says in part: "We are here because there is no refuge, finally, from ourselves. Until a person confronts himself in the eyes and hearts of others, he is running. Until he suffers them to share his secrets, he has no safety from them. Afraid to be known, he can know neither himself nor any other—he will be alone. . . . Here, together a person can at last appear clearly to himself. . . ."

In Epilogue the senior author, a psychiatrist, explains why therapy like that used at Daytop is effective.

263. Cassens, James. **The Christian Encounters Drugs and Drug Abuse.** St. Louis, Concordia Publishing House, 1970. 136p. bibliog. $1.50pa. LC 70-123890.

The author of this work says he is not categorically condemning drugs but has chosen to "tell it straight" from various vantage points. It may be that he is telling it that way, but he has little to say that hasn't been said many times before. His point of view is one that is typical of many writers; he takes a lenient attitude toward the abuser and blames society for the drug problem. In spite of the title, there is little about religion in the book except at the end, where it is suggested that Christianity can be an alternative to drug experience.

264. Chambers, Carl D., and Leon Brill, eds. **Methadone: Experience and Issues.** New York, Behavioral Publications, 1973. 411p. bibliog. $19.95. LC 72-6122. ISBN 0-87705-072-4.

The experimental drug methadone can now be used (under federal regulations set forth in 1971) to treat heroin addiction under closely supervised conditions. Methadone itself is an addicting narcotic, and questions have been raised regarding its safety and efficacy and the advisability of substituting one narcotic for another as the lesser of two evils. The essays in this book, which discuss past and current experiences, were written by contributors knowledgeable in the field of drug abuse treatment. The book is divided into the following parts: 1) Early experiences and issues, 2) Maintenance therapy: recent experiences and issues, 3) Detoxification therapy: recent experiences and issues, 4) Methadone versus other chemical substitution therapies, 5) Innovative programs, 6) Opposition of methadone maintenance therapy: a study of recent sources of criticism, 7) International maintenance programs, and 8) Summary and conclusions. Also included is an appendix, Proposed Special Requirements for Use of Methadone.

The authors of this work contend that the approach to methadone programs has become too rigid and that any hope for success within the program must be based on adapting the therapy to each individual's needs, which calls for rehabilitative follow-up not provided at the present. The authors also feel that research and utilization of other treatments is called for.

265. Cross, Jay N. **Guide to Community Control of Alcoholism.** New York, American Public Health Association, 1968. 128p. bibliog. index. LC 68-25573.

This book is written for professional health workers at the local level who wish to develop community programs to deal with alcoholism. Principles of program development are presented rather than descriptions of specific services and activities, since the author feels that each community must tailor its programs to meet its own needs. The guide should also function as a teaching reference in schools of public health and in continuing education activities, among other places. The work is divided into three parts: 1) Beverage alcohol use in American society, 2) Alcoholism, and 3) Alcoholism program development. The first deals with social, physical, and psychological aspects of drinking; the second is a general discussion of the problem; and the third presents principles for planning community programs.

266. Cull, John G., and Richard E. Hardy. **Organization and Administration of Drug Abuse Treatment Programs: National and International.** Springfield, Ill., Charles C. Thomas, 1974. 342p. index. $15.75. LC 73-22452. ISBN 0-398-3114-4.

Rehabilitation programs for drug abusers have received much attention recently, but there is no consensus regarding what approach is the most effective. Though there are differences in the philosophies of treatment and care, the goals are universal. The primary purpose of this book is to communicate the universality of drug problems to professionals, paraprofessionals, and lay people. In addition, it will provide help in the practical aspects of setting up drug abuse programs.

The book is divided into three sections: 1) Programs administered by state or municipal bodies; 2) Private, non-profit, drug rehabilitation programs; and 3) International programs of drug abuse rehabilitation. Since many programs are described, the book can also serve as a directory of rehabilitation centers.

267. Danaceau, Paul. **Methadone Maintenance: The Experience of Four Programs.** Washington, Drug Abuse Council, Inc., 1973. 109p. $1.25. LC 73-81224.

This publication is the first report of the Council's monograph series. Since the methadone treatment has become more important during the last decade in treating heroin addiction, this report is of special interest. Four programs are summarized: 1) The Adolescent Development Program in New

York City, which is a clinic caring exclusively for adolescents from one large urban high school. Supportive services are emphasized. 2) The Drug Rehabilitation Clinic in New Orleans, a "fee for service" clinic providing mathadone without supportive services. 3) The East Boston Drug Rehabilitation Clinic, which has a primarily white, working-class patient population and emphasizes psychological services. 4) La Llave (The Key) Drug Rehabilitation Program in Albuquerque, which developed from the concern of the Chicano community and which operates primarily within that culture. The issue of community control has influenced this program's development. The author of the report is a journalist and a former staff director of a U.S. Senate subcommittee. The reports of the programs do not evaluate them scientifically; they are reports of the experience of the programs.

268. Densen-Gerber, Judianne. **We Mainline Dreams; The Odyssey House Story**. Garden City, N.Y., Doubleday and Co., Inc., 1973. 421p. illus. $9.95. LC 72-89302. ISBN 0-385-00371-4.

This is a description of one of the most successful programs in the country for curing drug addicts, the Odyssey House. Written by the founder and director, the book tells of the rigorous and often unorthodox methods of treatment and of the early difficulties in getting support for the program. Much of the book is taken up with biographical accounts, a personal story about the author herself and about the ex-addicts and professionals who run the program. The author is a distinguished physician and lawyer who showed special concern for child addicts and addicted mothers when the program was getting underway. Odyssey House has now grown to include 33 establishments, which are flourishing in six states. The treatment seems to work; it is claimed that most of the addicts treated can return to the community. The book is unusual and fascinating, with some insight into the handling of addicts. The houses are tough-minded, structured psychiatric therapeutic communities. They are most effective with addicts who don't want treatment but who must stay because the courts have sent them there, refuting the idea that an addict must seek treatment himself in order for it to be successful. The Odyssey Houses believe in accountability. Residents are held responsible for their actions. It is felt that accountability is part of getting addicts well, since the fundamental cause of most addiction is an inability to think in terms of consequences.

269. **Drug Dependence**. Papers given at the 15th series of the Institute for the Study of Treatment of Delinquency Lectures at the Caxton Hall, London, October 1969–March 1970. London, The Institute, 1970. 39p. $0.50pa.

The booklet presents the following papers: The International Background, by Sir Harry Greenfield; What Are Drugs?, by Michael Ginsburg; The London Drug Scene, by Kenneth Leech; The Drug Problem in a Provincial Setting, by H. N. Rathod; and Treatment and Rehabilitation in the Community, by P. A. L. Chapple. All the papers are of high quality. The first concludes that the lesson of the past 40 years has been that no nation can protect itself single-handedly against drug abuse and that preventive measures can be effective only if they are internationally based. In the second paper the author concludes that he prefers, like most people, to experience elation through life rather than with drugs, and he is deeply concerned that some unfortunate persons cannot do likewise. Reverend Leech in the third paper sees the role of his church as a caring ministry operating from the inside. The fourth paper presents a general sketch of narcotic abuse in a small town near London, in the hope that this will help in understanding the total picture. The last paper concludes that everything points to the need for a community for the chronic addict.

270. Einstein, Stanley, ed. **Methadone Maintenance.** Papers presented at the Second National Methadone Maintenance Conference, New York, October 26-27, 1969. New York, Marcel Dekker, Inc., 1971. 249p. bibliog. index. $17.50. LC 79-149717. ISBN 0-8247-1165-3.

The papers presented in this volume were first published in the *International Journal of the Addictions* in September 1970. The conference where they were presented was originally sponsored by the National Association for the Prevention of Addiction to Narcotics and by the National Institutes of Mental Health. The reason for holding such a conference was to impart the experiences, knowledge, and problems that are inherent in the methadone maintenance treatment programs being used for heroin addicts. The contributors have reviewed questions and issues and suggested areas where further research is needed. Tables, copies of interviews, and schedules pertinent to the programs have been provided. The titles of the papers are as follows: 1) Treatment of narcotic addicts in New York City, 2) Research on methadone maintenance treatment, 3) Further experience with methadone in the treatment of narcotics users, 4) Methadone maintenance programs in Minneapolis, 5) Methadone maintenance in St. Louis, 6) The Man Alive Program, 7) Two methods of utilizing methadone in the outpatient treatment of narcotic addicts, 8) Low and high methadone maintenance in the outpatient treatment of the hard core heroin addict, 9) The New Haven methadone maintenance program, 10) Methadone in New Orleans: patients, problems and police, 11) Methadone related deaths in New York City, 12) Methadone in Miami, 13) Blockade with methadone, cyclazocine, and naloxone, and 14) Evaluation of methadone maintenance treatment programs.

The book is particularly valuable for those working in the field of methadone maintenance and other treatment methods for addicts. Community leaders, health professionals, and interested laymen can also profit from reading it.

271. Feagles, Anita MacRae. **The Addicts.** Chicago, Cowles Book Co., 1971. 107p. $4.95. LC 79-144213.

The author of this work has written a number of notable books for young readers. Though this book is not directed particularly to young people, it is suitable for them as well as others. It is a narrative presentation that illustrates one approach to the treatment of addiction—the outpatient encounter therapy method, conducted primarily by former addicts with the guidance of a psychologist. The stories related by the addicts are depressing but human. Some hope for the future comes through in the idea that if the old life-style of the addict is discarded the individual may be able to find a new, rewarding life.

272. Fisher, Seymour, and Alfred M. Freedman, eds. **Opiate Addiction: Origins and Treatment.** Washington, V. H. Winston; distr. New York, Halsted Press (a division of John Wiley and Sons), 1974. 247p. bibliog. index. $11.95. LC 73-19073. ISBN 0-470-26153-6.

This book, based on a 1972 meeting of the American College of Neuropsychopharmacology, includes material from the areas of pharmacology, physiology, neurochemistry, sociology, law, and psychology, among others. The first part of the book takes up the psychosocial and pharmacological aspects of opiate addiction, the second the clinical approaches to the treatment and control of addiction.

The editor feels that, although the possibilities for simple and ready solutions to drug abuse are not immediate, some rewarding and productive avenues appear to be open. The hope is that the book will stimulate and encourage further thought and research in the field.

273. Glatt, M. M. **A Guide to Addiction and Its Treatment: Drugs, Society, and Man.** New York, Halsted Press (a division of John Wiley and Sons, Inc.), 1974. 346p. bibliog. index. $15.95. LC 74-8421. ISBN 0-470-30322-0.

The author, who has had many years of experience treating alcoholism and drug dependence, writes from his experience. The addictive personality, psychological dependence, morbidity and mortality, treatment, prevention, and control of drugs are all discussed. There is also a section on types of addictive drugs. Throughout the book the author emphasizes the similarities between alcohol and drug problems; and the use of tobacco, compulsive overeating, and pathological gambling are presented as related problems.

Dr. Glatt pleads for "a middle-of-the-road, comprehensive, co-ordinated multi- and interdisciplinary approach to the complex problems of drug dependence." He believes that in the long run it is psychic (and possibly social) dependence which is much more important than physical dependence. Finally, he asks adults, parents, and teachers to adopt a morally superior attitude to their children and pupils who have, after all, learned their drug habits from drinking, smoking, pill-taking adults.

274. Hardy, Richard E., and John G. Cull. **Drug Dependence and Rehabilitation Approaches.** Springfield, Ill., Charles C. Thomas, 1973. 236p. bibliog. index. $8.95. LC 72-88480. ISBN 0-398-02690-4.

This collection presents both theoretical and practical information contributed by professional persons who are practicing in the field of rehabilitation of the drug abuser. The editors/authors interviewed 200 teenage and pre-teenage drug abusers as a basis for their work. In general, what they discovered is not new—that there is social acceptance of drug abuse by young people, that the strongest influence on children and young adults is peer group pressure or the pressure of conformity behavior, and that young people are rather contemptuous of professionals who have worked with them regarding their drug problem. Since it was found that young people felt that professional persons did not understand drugs, drug abuse, and the drug culture (a premise open to question), the authors developed this book to give workers in the field a basic understanding of drugs, drug abuse, and guidelines for reintegrating abusers into society.

Chapters cover the following subjects: 1) the effects of mood altering drugs: pleasures and pitfalls, 2) the causes of drug abuse, 3) types of narcotic addict, 4) drug use in the military service, 5) the public vocational rehabilitation program and the drug abuser, 6) clinical and counseling problems in drug dependence, 7) treatment in drug abuse: counseling approaches and special programs, 8) using work therapeutically, 9) a therapeutic approach to the rehabilitation of the youthful drug abuser, 10) case studies, and 11) language of the drug abuser.

275. Hardy, Richard E., and John G. Cull. **Rehabilitation of the Drug Abuser with Delinquent Behavior: Case Studies and Rehabilitation Approaches in Drug Abuse and Delinquency**. Springfield, Ill., Charles C. Thomas, 1974. 196p. index. $9.75. LC 73-216. ISBN 0-398-02823-0.

Most of this book consists of case study accounts of drug abusers who have experienced difficulty in adjusting to society. Emphasis is on rehabilitation, and programs of this sort are discussed, especially those supported through federal and state sources.

There is little in the book except the case studies. They are interesting and well written, and the reader can easily discover the rewards and frustrations of the professional practitioner when he deals with the drug abuser. There is a glossary included, "Language of the Drug Abuser."

276. Hentoff, Nat. **A Doctor among the Addicts**. New York, Rand McNally and Co., 1968. 136p. $4.95. LC 68-11406.

This book, written by a journalist, is the story of Dr. Marie Nyswander, who is known for her work with drug addicts. A physician and psychiatrist, she pioneered in using the methadone maintenance treatment for heroin addicts in New York City. The book contains biographical information on Dr. Nyswander, and it goes into detail about her work and success with "storefront" psychiatry and the treatment of addicts. The author quotes Dr. Nyswander as saying that methadone is not a cure-all for heroin addiction, since other approaches may prove more effective for some patients. However, the drug, which is a long-acting synthetic narcotic, blocks the euphoric action of some opiates and satisfies the craving for narcotics, making readdiction unlikely. Unfortunately, the drug itself is addicting, and many feel that for this reason it is not a good treatment modality. However, it is possibly the lesser of two evils as a small dose satisfies, and it can be used to aid in the withdrawal of narcotics. At the time this book was written, it was looked upon favorably, and it probably still offers the best possibility for successful treatment known, particularly if used with a rehabilitation program.

The material in the book appeared previously in a briefer form in the *New Yorker* magazine.

277. Institute on New Developments in the Rehabilitation of the Narcotic Addict, Ft. Worth, Texas, February 16-18, 1966. **Rehabilitating the Narcotic Addict**. Washington, GPO, 1967. 392p. $2.25.

This work reports on an institute sponsored jointly by the Division of Hospitals of the U.S. Public Health Service, Vocational Rehabilitation Administration and Texas Christian University. The contributors were leaders in treating and rehabilitating narcotics addicts. The hope was that the material presented here would be useful in planning guidelines for future rehabilitation and treatment programs. The subject is thoroughly explored.

There are several sections of the report as follows: I) Treatment of narcotic addiction and new laws for drug addicts; II) Psychological, social and epidemiological facotrs; III) New developments in federal narcotic treatment hospitals; IV) New developments in non-federal hospitals and institutions; V) Social psychology in the treatment of mental illness: a model approach for treatment of addiction; VI) Return to community living: the halfway house; VII) Community programs of rehabilitation of narcotic addicts; VIII) Research and evaluation; and IX) Research and evaluation panel discussion.

278. James, W. Paul, Clifford E. Salter, and H. George Thomas. **Alcohol and Drug Dependence.** London, King Edward's Hospital Fund for London, 1972. 98p. illus. bibliog. index. £1.50pa.

This report correlates therapeutic principles with the planning and design of facilities for treating alcoholism and drug dependence. The authors who have studied facilities in England, Scotland, and the United States, describe some of these and include floor plans. Considerable attention is given to the staff/patient ratio. There are recommendations as to what should be done in the future to cope with the problem, and the need for prevention measures, training of staff, and additional research is pointed out.

279. Josiah Macy, Jr. Foundation. **Medical Education and Drug Abuse: Report of a Macy Conference.** New York, Josiah Macy Jr. Foundation, 1973. 17p. $2.50pa.

This small pamphlet is a summary report of a conference held October 16-18, 1972, in New York City. The Foundation and Rockefeller University invited 30 individuals representing broad interests in medical education to meet in conference to consider the problem of drug abuse and to emphasize prevention and treatment. The participants were well-known individuals from the basic sciences and clinical departments of medical schools, federal and state agencies, professional associations, and the pharmaceutical industry. The report is very short, but it points out the major responsibilities and the role of medical education where drug abuse is concerned.

280. Kaplan, Harold I., and Benjam J. Sadock, eds. **Groups and Drugs.** New York, Jason Aronson, Inc., 1972. 181p. (Modern Group Book III.) $10.00. LC 72-96935. ISBN 0-87668-079-1.

This is one volume of a series that provides a survey of the theories, hypotheses, and therapeutic techniques dominating contemporary group psychotherapy practice. The emergence of group psychotherapy is one of the most significant developments in the field of psychiatry at the present time. There are five chapters: 1) Clinical diagnosis in group psychotherapy, 2) Group therapy with narcotic addicts, 3) Group therapy with alcoholics, 4) Group psychotherapy and psychopharmacology, and 5) Phoenix Houses: therapeutic communities for drug addicts. Also included is an extensive glossary of psychological terms.

The first chapter has been included because the editors believe the diagnostic interview is very important to effective treatment outcome. The second chapter discusses methadone maintenance as well as group therapy with addicts. The third chapter discusses traditional group therapy with alcoholics (such as Alcoholics Anonymous) and includes a large number of case studies. The fourth chapter surveys, discusses, and lists drugs used in the therapy of mental disorders. Dosages, indication, contraindications, and side effects are outlined. Chapter five discusses one of the most successful therapeutic communities for addicts, Phoenix House in New York City.

281. Kolb, Lawrence. **Drug Addiction: A Medical Problem.** Springfield, Ill., Charles C. Thomas, 1962. 183p. bibliog. index. LC 62-12049.

The author of this work was formerly an Assistant Surgeon General of the U.S. Public Health Service. The purpose of the book is to further understanding of the addiction phenomenon and development of programs of control and treatment. The chapter headings are as follows: 1) A perspective on drug addiction, 2) Drug addiction and crime, 3) Types and characteristics of drug addicts, 4) Behavior and characteristics of cases of medically-induced addiction, 5) Juvenile addiction, 6) The struggle for cure and conscious reasons for relapse, 7) Pleasure and deterioration from narcotic addiction, 8) Effects of addiction on health, 9) Treatment of narcotic addiction, 10) Highlights in the history of addiction, 11) Propaganda about addiction, its cause, nature and effect, and 12) Solution of addiction problem. In regard to the solutions to the problem, the author suggests that there should be less propaganda regarding punishment and more attention given to addiction as a medical problem. He believes there should be improvements in treatment facilities and the practical management of maintenance dose programs.

282. Kolton, Marilyn, and others. **Innovative Approaches to Youth Services.** Madison, Wisc., STASH Press, 1973. 131p. $5.00pa. LC 73-90978.

In recent years communities have undertaken action programs to assist young people, particularly those involved with the drug scene. Because programs are independent of one another, each needs to learn about the activities and ideas of others. This book is an attempt to help with the communication problem among these groups. The material presented is based on information gained through a "participatory learning conference," in which small groups discuss a variety of topics. In 1971 and 1972 three of these conferences were held, and material stemming from them has been synthesized into this book. The focus is on ethics, philosophy, tactics, and integrity in program development. Specific matters such as funding, facilities, organizational issues, special programs, evaluation, staffing, community relations, political involvement, and police-program relations are discussed.

The book is not solely about drug programs for youth. It also considers to some extent other problems of young people who are representative of the new youth subculture.

283. Leech, Kenneth. **Pastoral Care and the Drug Scene**. London, S.P.C.K., 1970. 165p. bibliog. index. $2.42.

This book was written for "straights"—that is, for individuals who do not belong to the drug scene but who wish to have a better understanding of it, to have accurate information about it, and to be of help with the problems involved in it. The work is aimed particularly at ministers, priests, and others who are involved with the pastoral care of young people who use drugs. Assuming that accurate knowledge is necessary for true pastoral care, the author has devoted the first part of the book to a summary of data about drugs of abuse. There are chapters on the pill scene, the junk scene, the pot scene, and the acid scene. Part two is on pastoral care in the drug scene. The author has drawn upon his experience in Soho and on the London scene. Social structure of the scene, its spirituality, and the priest and the drug scene are specifically discussed.

284. Louria, Donald B. **Overcoming Drugs: A Program for Action**. New York, McGraw-Hill Book Co., 1971. 233p. bibliog. $6.95. LC 74-151499.

The author of this book, a physician and noted authority on the drug problem, gives advice on how to deal with drug abuse. He addresses a number of specific social groups, as can be seen from the chapter headings: 1) Where it's at—and why, 2) Approaching young people, 3) Questions and answers, 4) A program for parents, 5) An approach to education, 6) Proposals for communities, 7) Rules and regulations, 8) The laws—proposals for legislators, and 9) Final thoughts. The author's point of view is that education, both preventive and remedial, is the best approach to ending drug abuse. He suggests a curriculum for schools and special training for teachers. He also presents a fifteen-point program for communities. The book will be of most value to parents, educators, legislators, and physicians.

285. Love, Harold D. **Youth and the Drug Problem: A Guide for Parents and Teachers**. With a Foreword by William H. Osborne. Springfield, Ill., Charles C. Thomas, 1971. 101p. index. $9.50. LC 79-143748.

This book is primarily for parents and teachers, but it may also interest physicians, ministers, and counselors who work with youth. The first part of the presentation consists of the following chapters: 1) Defining the drug problem, 2) The abusable drugs, 3) How can you tell if your child is taking drugs?, 4) Treatment of drug abusers, and 5) The role of parents and teachers in drug education. The second part of the book, made up of contributions by various individuals who were interviewed because they had had dealings with drug users, contains the following chapters: 6) A teacher looks at drug abuse in the schools, 7) Parents look at drug abuse, 8) Policemen look at drug abuse, 9) Nurses look at drug abuse, 10) A minister looks at drug abuse, 11) School administrators look at drug abuse, and 12) A student looks at drug abuse. The last chapter, which was written anonymously by a student whose physician father was a hopeless addict, is especially poignant because of the way the lives of the whole family were affected.

286. Ludwig, Arnold M., Jerome Levine, and Louis H. Stark. **LSD and Alcoholism: A Clinical Study of Treatment Efficacy**. Springfield, Ill., Charles C. Thomas, 1970. 331p. bibliog. $15.00. LC 77-126481.

The authors of this book received an award from the American Psychiatric Association for their research accomplishment in the area reported on here. The book deals primarily with the evaluation of LSD treatment for alcoholism. There has been some reason to believe that LSD might prove valuable in this respect. The work is divided into six parts: 1) Background for investigation, 2) The treatment study, 3) Special studies, 4) The alcoholic in the community, 5) Overview, and 6) Appendices. The appendices provide more extensive descriptions of the procedures used, the evaluation forms employed, and other documentary material.

Unfortunately, the authors were forced to conclude that on the basis of findings emanating from their investigation, and of other studies, that the various LSD procedures do not offer any more for the treatment of alcoholism than traditional methods used (which are also quite ineffective). Aside from this evaluation, the book is valuable in that it deals with issues relating to the evaluation of all psychiatric therapies, and a section is devoted to the behavior of alcoholics in the community and the problems of follow-up.

287. Mann, Kenneth W. **On Pills and Needles: A Christian Look at Drug Dependence**. New York, Seabury Press, 1969. 36p. bibliog. $0.50.

This small booklet discusses drug dependence simply and briefly from the standpoint of what a church can and should do. The author, a well-trained minister of the Episcopal Church and a specialist in the fields of religion and psychology, discusses the following topics: 1) drugs and their effects, 2) how many people are drug-dependent?, 3) what the government has done, 4) what the Episcopal Church has done, 5) some basic questions, 6) what the individual can do, and 7) what the church must do. The book is basically an appeal to individuals and churches to help solve the drug problem.

288. Meyer, Roger E. **Guide to Drug Rehabilitation: A Public Health Approach**. Foreword by Jerome H. Jaffe. Boston, Beacon Press, 1972. 171p. bibliog. index. $5.95. LC 76-179152. ISBN 0-8070-2772-3.

This book, written by a professor of psychiatry who has had long experience with drug rehabilitation and research, attempts to evaluate and review all the known efforts at drug rehabilitation. The author urges that a multiplicity of approaches be used, depending on needs and resources. The book is divided into three sections; the first is on heroin addiction, the second on treating other forms of drug abuse, and the third, a public health approach to treatment. Treatments discussed are methadone maintenance and narcotic-blocking drugs; civil commitment programs; and voluntary psychological treatments including traditional approaches, confrontation style groups and therapeutic communities, exhortative groups, and aversive treatments. The book is simply written and will be of value to law enforcement officials, clergymen, community leaders, mental health professionals, physicians, and high-level policy makers. The author has hopes that community programs can be effective in dealing with this difficult problem.

289. National Association for the Prevention of Addiction to Narcotics. **Fifth National Conference on Methadone Treatment, March 17-19, 1973. Proceedings.** New York, National Association for the Prevention of Addiction to Narcotics, 1973. 2v. bibliog. index.

The aim of this conference was to promote the exchange of ideas by professionals in the field of narcotics addiction. Topics covered include: 1) Rehabilitation of patients on methadone programs, 2) Dosage comparisons, 3) Discrimination against methadone patients in employment and strategies for change, 4) Education components to methadone maintenance treatment programs, 5) Criminal justice, 6) Treatment selection, 7) Program management, 8) Counselor training, 9) Detoxification, 10) Alcoholism and the methadone patient, 11) Drug associated deaths, 12) Providing treatment for youth, 13) Monitoring of private clinics, 14) Management issues, 15) Clinical experiences with narcotic antagonists, 16) Myth versus fact in long-term methadone maintenance treatment, 17) Physiological complications in addicts, 18) Client characteristics, 19) Larger issues surrounding addiction, 20) Unusual treatment settings, 21) Conceptual issues surrounding maintenance, 22) Medical complications of methadone treatment, 23) Vocational rehabilitation, 24) Data systems, 25) Present and potential relationships between methadone maintenance programs and courts of criminal jurisdiction, 26) The Philadelphia Treatment Alternatives to Street Crime Program, 27) Rational planning, 28) High dose versus low dose, 29) Alternatives to methadone, 30) Poly-drug use, 31) Urinalysis, 32) Problems in evaluation and monitoring of programs, 33) Methadone and pregnancy, 34) Treatment techniques, 35) Cost-benefit analysis of methadone treatment programs, 36) Clinical management, 37) Program description, 38) Psychological issues, 39) Methadone and naloxone in combination for the treatment of heroin addicts, 40) Problems and approaches to treatment program evaluation, and 41) Philosophical issues.

290. **National Drug Abuse Conference, 1974. Proceedings. Developments in the Field of Drug Abuse.** Edited by Edward Senay, Vernon Shorty, and Harold Alksne. Cambridge, Mass., Schenkman Publishing Co., Inc. 1975. In cooperation with the National Association for the Prevention of Addiction to Narcotics (NAPAN). 1129p. bibliog. index. $32.50.

This conference grew out of a series of National Methadone Conferences initiated in 1967 (see entry 289, National Association for the Prevention of Addiction to Narcotics: *Fifth National Conference on Methadone Treatment*). The early focus was on methadone treatment for drug addiction, but the conference now covers minorities, paraprofessionals, women, youth, and the work of therapeutic communities, free clinics, industrial physicians, drug abuse staff concerned with prevention, and those concerned with the interface between enforcement and treatment. This meeting is now the major annual conference in the area of drug abuse.

A large collection of papers by experts are presented in the volume, including (in addition to the Plenary Sessions) the following sections: 2) Evaluation of treatment efforts, 3) Epidemiology of drug abuse, 4) Studies from therapeutic communities, 5) Studies from multi-modality programs, 6) The addicted woman, 7) Treatment of the youthful drug abuser, 8) Community, city and state perspectives on drug abuse, 9) Prevention, education and alternatives, 10) Antagonists, Propanolol, propoxyphene, methadyl acetate and biochemical studies, 11) Drug abuse and the criminal justice system, 12) Critical issues, 13) Drug abuse programs in the private and public sections, 14) Staff issues in drug abuse programs, and 15) Programs combining treatment for alcohol and drug abusers.

291. Nelkin, Dorothy. **Methadone Maintenance: A Technological Fix.** New York, George Braziller, 1973. 164p. bibliog. index. $6.95. LC 72-96071. ISBN 0-8076-0681-2; 0-8076-0680-4pa.

The author's point of view is that methadone maintenance is essentially a chemotherapeutic "fix" for heroin addiction. The methadone treatment consists of giving the drug methadone in place of heroin, and dependence is transferred to methadone. It has become the predominant means of dealing with the heroin problem because there have been no other successful developments for dealing with the poorly understood problems of the addict. The effect of methadone is similar to that of heroin; it is itself addicting. The treatment remains controversial. Many feel that addiction is a moral, psychological, and legal problem as well as medical and that a purely medical treatment, such as methadone maintenance, does not get to the roots of the problem.

A Syracuse, New York, program was selected for the study outlined in this book, although the development of the program is considered in its larger national context. Chapter headings are as follows: 1) The addict and society; 2) Methadone maintenance; 3) Problems, politics, and treatment programs: a community study; 4) The organization of a methadone program; 5) The addict as patient; and 6) The limits of a technological fix.

The book concludes that methadone programs have value and serve to reduce the heroin needs of street addicts. However, more positive rehabilitation measures should be developed to support drug-free programs, including self-help efforts.

292. Nyswander, Marie. **The Drug Addict as a Patient**. New York, Grune and Stratton, 1956. 179p. bibliog. index. $10.50. LC 55-12227. ISBN 0-8089-0351-9.

The author, a physician well known in the field of drug abuse, has been involved in pioneering work with the problem. This book was written before drug addiction reached the high levels of the late 1960s, but it has remained important because of the treatment methods suggested. Approaches to be used by physicians in general private practice are set forth, and the view is taken that forms of therapy used should be removed from the aura of the correctional institution and put under the physician.

The following chapters are presented: 1) Drug addiction in the United States: past and present; 2) Pharmacology; 3) Physiology; 4) Psychology; 5) Social pathology; 6) Clinical diagnosis; 7) Withdrawal treatment; 8) Rehabilitation; 9) The British approach; and 10) Looking forward.

293. Palmquist, Allen, and Frank Reynolds. **The Drug Bug**. Minneapolis, Bethany Fellowship, Inc., 1970. 70p. $0.75pa.

The authors of this small book have had much experience working with drug addicts. The message they preach to young people in an effort to help with the drug problem is a religious one; it is probably as successful as any other.

294. Sells, S. B., ed. **Studies in the Effectiveness of Treatments for Drug Abuse.** Cambridge, Mass., Ballinger Publishing Co., 1974. 2v. $18.50; $16.50. LC 74-1069. ISBN 0-88410-018-9 (v. 1); 0-88410-017-0 (v. 2).

The National Institute of Mental Health contracted with Texas Christian University's Institute of Behavioral Research in 1969 to establish and maintain a patient reporting system for NIMH-supported drug abuse treatment programs as a data base for treatment outcome evaluation research. This program, known as the DARP (Drug Abuse Reporting Program), grew until 1974 when the reporting of new admissions was discontinued. The base is a computerized file of longitudinal records on 43,931 patients from 52 agencies out of over 200 in the total NIMH program. Volume I of the publication under consideration evaluates drug abuse treatments, and Volume II presents research on patients, treatment, and outcomes (studies of the effectiveness of treatments for drug abuse). Drug abuse in these studies is defined as the illegal use of substances (excluding alcohol and tobacco) known or presumed to be psychoactive. Large amounts of data are presented and analyzed in the work; much is presented in tabular and graphic form.

The editor feels that the information in these volumes should be of interest in three respects. First, the information bears directly on the degree of success for various kinds of treatment programs and should interest those with administrative and professional responsibilities in the drug abuse field. Second, data from such a large group of pathological patients should be of interest to psychologists, sociologists, and physicians concerned with deviant behavior. Third, social scientists should benefit from the procedures and results of such "real life" data collection and processing.

The work makes clear the diversity of factors involved in drug abuse treatment and shows that many outcome factors are independent of others. The overall evaluation results were found to be encouraging, particularly with respect to the reduction of alcohol and drug use and criminality during treatment. However, poorer results were obtained with respect to employment and welfare support. Another finding was that the outcomes observed with older patients were superior to those with youth. Critical follow-up studies are planned.

295. Simmons, Luiz R. S., and Martin B. Bold, eds. **Discrimination and the Addict: Notes toward a General Theory of Addict Rehabilitation.** Sponsored by the Institute for the Study of Health and Society, Inc. Beverly Hills, Calif., Sage Publications, 1973. 334p. bibliog. (International Yearbooks of Drug Addiction and Society. Vol. 1). $15.00. LC 72-98048. ISBN 0-8039-0203-4.

This well-documented, scholarly work is an attempt to inspire the public imagination with a recognition of the social and legal obstacles to the rehabilitation process. The book points out how such obstacles influence the attitudes of addicts in and out of treatment. There are three sections: 1) Civil disabilities, 2) The right to treatment, and 3) The limits of treatment. Each section contains several papers, contributed by different authors. Section one is concerned with the need to formulate a strategy of treatment in the light of social and legal impediments. Section two explores the responsibility of a free society in providing treatment of the unfortunate. Section three concludes that all aspects of addiction must be dealt with if a cure is to be realized.

296. Smith, David E., David J. Bentel, and Jerome L. Schwartz, eds. **The Free Clinic: A Community Approach to Health Care and Drug Abuse.** Beloit, Wisc., STASH Press, 1971. 206p. bibliog. $5.00. LC 70-183532.

This three-part publication contains the proceedings of the First National Free Clinic Council Symposium, held January 31 to February 1, 1970, Free Clinic Position Papers, and The National Free Clinic Survey. The "Free Clinics" with which the publication is concerned deal mainly with drug abuse problems, and the term "free" means more than that there is no charge per patient visit. It also means that there is little or no red tape about forms and papers and that there is also freedom from conventional bureaucracy, moral judgments, etc. The publication is of interest because the clinics seem to be surviving in spite of many problems, such as financing, staffing, personnel, and unorthodox approaches. The publication includes a list of 61 such clinics which initiated service during 1967-1969 and were still in operation on January 1, 1971. Many of the institutions of this kind are short-lived, but new ones are being initiated.

297. Smith, David E., and John Luce. **Love Needs Care: A History of San Francisco's Haight-Ashbury Free Medical Clinic and Its Pioneer Role in Treating Drug Abuse Problems.** Boston, Little, Brown and Co., 1971. 405p. illus. bibliog. $8.95. LC 77-121434.

This book tells the story of the Haight-Ashbury Free Medical Clinic, which was the first free community medical center to treat drug abusers. A great deal of material is presented about the Haight district of San Francisco and its decline from a neighborhood of flower children to a crime-ridden ghetto. The book is illustrated with many photographs of the district and its people, many of them shocking and depressing. The multitude of drugs that have to be dealt with and the incredible variety of diseases are described. The only hope offered is that clinics like the one described will reach the alienated groups that have such a desperate need.

The book ends by saying that the free clinics may be clumsy models for the delivery of health services in the future, but that they have demonstrated some important things. They have gained a wide popularity by respecting the needs of the imperfect humanity of their patients; they have minimized red tape in dealing with people; they have pioneered in the use of paramedical volunteers; and in addition they have proven their ability to reach alienated economic, racial, and philosophical minorities. The senior author, a physician, is the medical director and co-organizer of the Clinic. The co-author, a journalist, is the public affairs director of the Clinic.

298. **The Treatment of Drug Abuse: Programs, Problems, Prospects.** Raymond A. Glasscote and others. Washington, Joint Information Service of the American Psychiatric Association and the National Association for Mental Health, 1972. 250p. $7.00. LC 70-187294.

The authors of this work attempt to show realistically what a community can do about a drug abuse problem and how effective a program can be. The book reports on nine programs that exist presently to help drug addicts, concluding that none of the presently available approaches can be expected to be successful with more than a small percentage of drug abusers, and that all approaches combined will have a quite limited effect. Taking no position for or against any particular approach, the authors simply discuss the features of each. They give a great deal of detailed, objective information about the well-known programs discussed. Chapter headings are as follows: 1) Introduction, 2) Drug abusers—then and now, 3) Theories about the cause of drug abuse, 4) The history of treatment, 5) Present approaches, 6) The status of programs in mid-1971, 7) What might be done, and 8) What one gets for the effort. The nine drug treatment programs discussed are: 1) Beth Israel Medical Center, New York City, 2) Daytop Village, New York, 3) California Civil Addict Program, 4) Illinois Drug Abuse Program, 5) Teen Challenge of Northern California and Nevada, San Francisco, 6) Drug Dependency Treatment Program, St. Louis, 7) The Connecticut State Program, 8) Connecticut Mental Health Center, New Haven, 9) Mendocino State Hospital, Talmage, California. The book is highly recommended for individuals involved in community programs that deal with the drug abuse problem.

299. U.S. Department of the Army, the Navy, and the Air Force. **Drug Abuse (Clinical Recognition and Treatment, Including the Diseases Often Associated).** Washington, GPO, 1973. 1v. (various paging). bibliog. (Dept. of the Army Technical Bulletin TD MED 290; Dept. of the Navy Publication NAVMED P-5116; Dept. of the Air Force Pamphlet AFP 160-33). $0.95pa. S/N 0820-00454.

This publication is designed to help medical officers of the armed services who are concerned with the identification, evaluation, and treatment of drug abusers, including interview techniques, recognition and management of intoxication and withdrawal syndromes, and clinical identification and treatment of diseases often associated with drug use. There are four chapters: 1) Clinical recognition and screening for drug abuse, 2) Recognition and management of acute intoxications, 3) The recognition and management of withdrawal symptoms, and 4) Clinical identification and treatment of diseases often associated with drug abuse. Appended materials include ingestion-excretion drug patterns, case examples, suggested format for drug interview, glossary of drug vocabulary, criteria for the diagnosis of alcoholism, and selected bibliography. The material presented is brief, but it furnishes a good outline.

300. U.S. National Institute on Drug Abuse. **Alternative Pursuits for America's 3rd Century: A Resource Book on New Perceptions, Processes, and Programs—with Implications for the Prevention of Drug Abuse.** Washington, GPO, 1974. 233p. bibliog. $2.60pa. (DHEW Publication No. (HSM) 73-9158). S/N 1724-00333.

Presenting alternatives as a road to drug abuse prevention and early detection, this book hopes to get at the roots of alienation and drug abuse.

It is an anthology of articles that offer a cultural perspective on the causes of drug abuse and a glimpse of the ways in which energy and creativity can be directed toward positive alternatives, leaving no place for drugs. Most of the selections presented have been condensed from longer articles. In addition to the articles, there is a Resource Directory with Bibliographic Notes, which lists organizations and publications of interest.

301. U.S. National Institute on Drug Abuse. **Effective Coordination of Drug Abuse Programs: A Guide to Community Action.** Washington, GPO, 1974. 151p. index. (DHEW Publication No. (ADM) 74-119).

This community action manual was drafted for the Center for Studies of Narcotic and Drug Abuse, Division of Narcotic Addiction and Drug Abuse, National Institute of Mental Health, by Ronald D. Wynne and Linton, Mields, and Coston, Inc., under contract. The purpose of the manual is to help communities organize effective and coordinated community-wide drug abuse efforts, based on programs that have been effective. There are three sections: 1) Community action manual, 2) Community action workbook (appendices), and 3) Case studies in drug abuse program coordination.

The book is not a how-to-do-it outline. It presents issues that are likely to arise and options that may be used to help communities develop their own programs. It includes program ideas and some indication of the costs a community might incur for different levels of programming.

302. U.S. Office of Juvenile Delinquency and Youth Development. **A Community Mental Health Approach to Drug Addiction.** By Richard Brotman and Alfred Freedman. Washington, GPO, 1968. 137p. bibliog. $1.00.

This document was issued as part of a training program that provided curriculum materials to help stimulate discussion in training courses. Members of various professions will find it of value in keeping informed about developments in the field of juvenile delinquency prevention and control. There are four sections: 1) The American reaction to narcotic use, 2) Physical, psychological, and social aspects of addiction, 3) The community mental health approach to diagnosis, and 4) Targets, goals, and methods for intervention. More than half of the book consists of appendices: a glossary of dependence producing drugs, a screening instrument, case histories, a research study, and a bibliography.

303. U.S. Special Action Office for Drug Abuse Prevention. **Drug Incidence Analysis.** By Leon Gibson Hunt. Washington, GPO, August 1974. 36p. (Special Action Office Monograph, Series A, No. 3).

This pamphlet brings together information on the best available techniques for helping communities understand their changing drug abuse problems, since that understanding is necessary before they can plan and evaluate programs to solve the problems.

The first section presents "Drug Incidence Data: Its Meaning and Uses in Planning," and the second part is an "Analysis of Incidence Data." The many figures and graphs present statistical data and show comparisons and relationships.

304. U.S. Special Action Office for Drug Abuse Prevention. **Estimating the Prevalence of Heroin Use in a Community**. Mark H. Greene. Washington, GPO, August 1974. 20p. bibliog. (Special Action Office Monograph, Series A, No. 4).

This pamphlet describes the current state of the art for determining the prevalence of heroin use in a community setting. Methods and their applications are discussed, with comments on limitations and shortcomings. The following sections are presented: 1) Introduction, 2) Direct methods, 3) Indirect indices of prevalence, 4) Recommended studies, and 5) Conclusion. Local planners can make use of the material presented to determine how many heroin users are in the area under consideration and how that number changes over a time.

305. U.S. Special Action Office for Drug Abuse Prevention. **The Vietnam Drug User Returns.** Final Report, September 1973. Lee H. Robins, Principal Investigator. Washington, GPO, 1974. 1v. (Various paging). (Special Action Office Monograph, Series A, No. 2). $2.10pa. LC 74-600015.

The White House Special Action Office for Drug Abuse Prevention arranged for and assisted in a follow-up study of army enlisted men who returned from Vietnam to the United States in September 1971. Their assignment was to evaluate concerns about drug abuse among the men and to learn how many would require treatment, the kinds of treatment and social services needed, and identification of the abusers. This detailed report presents the results of the comprehensive study.

The publication is important in that it shows the extent and consequences of the drug crisis in Vietnam. The drug abuse problem is shown in clearer perspective, and something of the natural history of drug abuse is shown.

306. U.S. Strategy Council on Drug Abuse. **Federal Strategy for Drug Abuse and Drug Traffic Prevention 1975**. Washington, GPO, 1975. 102p. illus. index. $1.40pa.

The Strategy Council on Drug Abuse was established in the Drug Abuse Office and Treatment Act of 1972 to develop a strategy for the drug prevention activities of the federal government. The act required a yearly publication, of which this is the third and last. The publication reviews the accomplishments, continuing problems, and future plans of all the federal agencies dealing with drug abuse problems. There is a continued emphasis on balanced treatment, rehabilitation, education, and law enforcement. Some historical material has been included, and there are budget charts showing fund distribution and allocation.

307. Weisman, Thomas. **Drug Abuse and Drug Counseling: A Case Approach.** Cleveland, Press of Case Western Reserve University, 1972. 193p. bibliog. index. $5.95. LC 75-107154. ISBN 0-8295-0223-8.

The intent of this book is to help counselors deal with people who have problems involving drug abuse. It attempts to provide a foundation of pharmacological knowledge that will help the counselor build confidence and skill in his work. Each chapter of the book deals with a different drug or group of drugs.

Chapter headings are as follows: 1) The narcotic analgesics, 2) Alcohol, 3) Hypnotics and tranquilizers, 4) Amphetamines and cocaine, 5) Hallucinogens, 6) Marihuana, and 7) Caffeine and nicotine. There is a short expository section, a true-false question section, and a set of case problems for each chapter. The material presented is easy to understand and practical, and the approaches suggested are probably as effective as any.

308. Westman, Wesley C. **The Drug Epidemic: What It Means and How to Combat It.** New York, Dial Press, 1970. 163p. index. $4.95. LC 70-102832.

The author of this book is a Ph.D. clinical psychologist who has had much experience treating addicts. For the most part, he writes about the new middle class addicts rather than the ghetto variety, since he feels that this new addict exhibits more of the personal, family, and peer-group disturbance that leads to addiction. Some of his observations seem to be valid for addicts in all settings, while others pertain to certain types. He discusses the addiction-prone personality, effective forms of treatment, and harmful effects of the drugs. Also included are a glossary of terms and a list of addiction referral services throughout the United States.

The book offers good psychology in easy-to-understand language.

309. World Health Organization Expert Committee on Drug Dependence. **Twentieth Report.** Geneva, World Health Organization, 1974. 89p. (World Health Organization Technical Report Series No. 55). ISBN 92-120551-2.

This report presents the views of an international group of experts concerning possible future ways to prevent problems associated with the nonmedical use of dependence-producing drugs. It also covers methods of increasing the effectiveness of preventive activities.

Part I outlines the work of several international bodies, Part II (the longest section) discusses prevention of problems associated with drug use, and Part III is a brief report on the international control of an individual drug, difenoxin. The conclusions and recommendations presented at the end of Part II give special attention to the availability of drugs, the individual and small groups, the environment, alcoholic beverages, and research.

310. **Youth Report. Constructive Alternatives to: Apathy, Drugs, Loneliness. Special Report.** New York, Grafton Publications, Inc., 1973. 20p. $5.00pa.

This is "a concise manual of community action to help troubled young people." The word "alternative" suggests that if we can substitute a good activity for a bad one we will have improved the youth situation. This booklet presents "alternatives" to drug abuse and points out ways to make choices possible for young people. A number of youth programs are discussed.

8. Education and Attitudes

Titles listed in this section cover various aspects of drug abuse prevention education, particularly books intended for teachers, parents, counselors, and those concerned with community programs. There has been a strong feeling of late that many programs of drug education have been an "overkill" and that some have even encouraged rather than discouraged drug abuse. Films have been particularly blamed. Many books attempt to show how to get just the right approach. Some works deal with drug education curricula on all school levels, also including teaching methodologies. There is much material to assist the teacher in drug abuse education.

311. Abrams, L. Annette, Emily F. Garfield, and John D. Swisher, eds. **Accountability in Drug Education: A Model for Evaluation**. Washington, The Drug Abuse Council, Inc., 1973. 169p. $2.25. LC 73-92439.

These articles, which cover the evaluation of drug education programs in public schools, provide a good background for planning such programs. All kinds of articles are included–theoretical, those that present research findings, case studies, and so forth. Some emphasis is placed on programs designed to produce in children not abstinence but "rational, well thought out personal positions toward drug use" and to "offer students desirable alternatives to drug use and drug-related lifestyles."

Chapter titles are as follows: 1) Specifying objectives, 2) Evaluation management, 3) Basic experimental design, 4) Research: an evolutionary perspective, 5) Pitfalls in data collection, 6) Stanford University Evaluation Scales, 7) Pennsylvania State University Evaluation Scales, 8) Affect and cognition in drug education, 9) Computers: boons and boondoggles, 10) Consumer feedback: student evaluation results, and 11) Program planning dimensions.

312. American School Health Association and Pharmaceutical Manufacturers Association. **Teaching about Drugs: A Curriculum Guide K-12**. 2nd ed. Kent, Ohio, American School Health Association, 1971. 213p. illus. (part col.) bibliog. index. $4.00pa.

Prepared with the assistance of a large group of scientists and educators, this guide was designed to help teachers plan drug education programs and upgrade the quality of health instruction. The first part of the book suggests curricula for each age group, giving objectives, comments, suggested learning activities, and lists of resources and materials. The second part, "Reference Materials," is an excellent group of review papers, each by a noted educator and/or scientist. The last section, a collection of "Teaching Aids," includes suggestions for discussion groups, a glossary of slang terms related to drug usage, a drug abuse products reference chart, photographs of stimulants, depressants, hallucinogens (in color), and a list of signs and symptoms to help identify drug abusers. Although many feel that there has been an "overkill" on teaching young people about drug abuse, this guide is a good one; it will help teachers plan programs about drugs and drug abuse as part of the regular health education curriculum.

313. Bedworth, Albert, and Joseph A. D'Elia. **Basics of Drug Education.** Farmingdale, N.Y., Baywood Publishing Company, 1973. 271p. bibliog. index. $9.00. LC 72-94344.

The authors of this book take a complete approach to drug education for young people, assuming that the reader has little knowledge about drugs and drug abuse and presenting an entire educational program in this area. They tell what, when, and how to teach, and how to evaluate what is done. The first six chapters are: 1) Toward a philosophy of drug education; 2) Health education: implications for drug abuse prevention; 3) The education community's responsibility in providing drug abuse prevention programs; 4) The risk to health from smoking; 5) Alcohol, people, and society; 6) Essential drug information. Chapter 7, on drug curricula, presents specific behavioral objectives for each developmental level, kindergarten through grade 12, as well as basic concepts and descriptions of student-oriented learning experiences that form the basis of a drug education program. Chapter 8 presents guidelines for evaluating drug education. There are four appendices: a glossary, an example of a state penal code, the New York State Education Law, and a list of additional student and teacher resources, such as publications and organizations involved with drug abuse.

314. Bennett, James C., and George D. Demos, eds. **Drug Abuse and What We Can Do about It**. Springfield, Ill., Charles C. Thomas, 1970. 138p. index. $8.50. LC 71-113785.

The editors of this publication are professional educators who have been involved with drug education programs. The first of the three sections presents the proceedings of a symposium on drug abuse among youth in Riverside County, California. This section covers legal, medical, and community aspects of drug abuse, and a student reaction panel to drug abuse. Section two, which contains papers by a number of different people (most of whom are educators) tells what progress is being made and what implications there are for a new approach to education. Section three presents conclusions, the main one being that the school curriculum should be changed to include a continuous, coordinated, K-12 curriculum entitled "Education for Contemporary Living." It would be involved with drugs, alcohol, tobacco, sex education, family life education, and especially civic responsibility.

The book has much material that will interest and help educators, psychologists, counselors, religious groups, community workers, and young people themselves.

315. Blachly, Paul H. **Seduction: A Conceptual Model in the Drug Dependencies and Other Contagious Ills.** Springfield, Ill., Charles C. Thomas, 1970. 83p. illus. bibliog. $7.00. LC 75-122200.

This work arose from the author's dissatisfaction with the practical value of existing psychiatric, sociological, and psychological conceptions for dealing with behaviors such as drug abuse and others that are wrong, dangerous, destructive, and harmful. He is speaking of situations in which abusers know and agree that certain behavior is ill-advised, but persist in it anyway. He uses the term "seduction" to describe these behaviors.

The author, who is a well-known psychiatrist, makes these phenomena understandable. The book also contains implications for prophylactic education and child-rearing practices. The last chapter, "Treatment of Seductees," presents modifications that should be made in treatment programs if drug dependent individuals are to show any real improvement.

316. Cassel, Russell N. **Drug Abuse Education.** North Quincy, Mass., Christopher Publishing House, 1971. 379p. illus. bibliog. index. $5.95. LC 77-125922. ISBN 0-8158-0245-5.

This programmed text, designed for self-study, presents useful information on dangerous drugs. Intended for use with teenagers and young people in the senior high schools of the country, it can also be used by teachers, nurses, and the police. The following sections are included: 1) Nature and classes of dangerous drugs, 2) States of effect for dangerous drugs, 3) Nature and type of drug addiction, 4) Reasons for illegal use of dangerous drugs, 5) Treatment programs for drug dependence, 6) Drug abuse education based on rules of evidence, 7) Drug control laws in the United States, 8) The drug users' "argot" and vocabulary.

317. Cohen, Sidney. **The Drug Dilemma.** New York, McGraw-Hill Book Co., 1969. 139p. bibliog. $4.95. LC 68-25649.

This small book was written for those who teach or counsel young people, but students and their parents should also find it valuable. The author, a physician whose chief research interest is psychopharmacology, discusses the current drug scene, showing trends and future developments and outlining the effects, side effects, treatment, and prevention of drug abuse. Chapter headings are as follows: 1) "Those who will not learn from history . . . "; 2) Some definitions; 3) The psychedelics. . .LSD & others; 4) The psychedelics. . . marihuana; 5) Witches' brew and the like; 6) The opiates; 7) The sedatives; 8) The stimulants and cocaine; 9) The sniffers; 10) The "head"; and 11) The drug dilemma . . . a partial solution. In addition there is a drug glossary, a table summarizing drug effects, and a list of additional readings.

318. Corder, Brice W., Ronald A. Smith, and John D. Swisher. **Drug Abuse Prevention: Perspectives and Approaches for Educators.** Dubuque, Iowa, Wm. C. Brown Co., 1975. 123p. bibliog. index. ISBN 0-697-07361-0.

Designed to provide perspectives for those interested in developing or revising drug education programs, this book is not a curriculum guide. It consists of three sections: 1) Perspectives, 2) Principles, and 3) Strategies. The first section (three chapters) is designed to provide basic reference materials for those implementing a plan. The remaining chapters present basic principles, strategies, and evaluative techniques for drug abuse prevention programs.

319. Cornacchia, Harold J., David J. Bentel, and David E. Smith. **Drugs in the Classroom: A Conceptual Model for School Programs.** St. Louis, C. V. Mosby Co., 1973. 329p. bibliog. index. $6.95. LC 72-88507. ISBN 0-8016-1053-2.

This book's purpose is to "introduce a conceptual model of a multi-dimensional, differential school drug program designed to meet the needs of a variety of student drug users and abusers as well as the nonusers." It is said to be a new approach that should be useful to school personnel. The emphasis is on the prevention of drug abuse for grades kindergarten through twelve, with special attention given to the behavioral approach. The book synthesizes and organizes the most promising demonstrations, activities, and information available from many sources. Guidelines for school drug programs have been included. The book may also be of value to those involved in community drug abuse prevention programs.

320. Eddy, John. **The Teacher and the Drug Scene.** Bloomington, Ind., Phi Delta Kappa Educational Foundatin, 1973. 42p. bibliog. $0.50pa.

This booklet was prepared to help school personnel (teachers, counselors, administrators, paraprofessionals, and others) deal with the drug abuse problem in their schools and community. The brief chapters cover the following topics: 1) The drug problem in the schoools and society, 2) Facing the known facts about drug use and abuse, 3) Handling personnel in-service training, 4) Managing staff and student confidentiality, 5) Using hotlines and drug centers in student referrals, 6) Dealing with law enforcement officers, 7) Selecting educational resources and developing drug courses, 8) Working with parents, 9) Viewing the changing drug scene, 10) Identifying selected drugs, and 11) Identifying the drug user–by the Committee on Drug Education.

A plea is made to set up programs of drug treatment even if we do not yet know how to cure the drug abuse disease.

321. Frykman, John H. **A New Connection: An Approach to Persons Involved in Compulsive Drug Use.** San Francisco, Scrimshaw Press, 1971. 116p. bibliog. $2.25. LC 74-156775. ISBN 0-912020-12-1.

This guide may be of value to counselors, teachers, social workers, correction officers, and other working with persons who have drug abuse problems. The author sees drug abusers as persons with low self-esteem, high approval needs, and deficient problem-solving techniques. This book, intended for those who want to have a better understanding of these people, suggests ways to create a climate of trust, rapport, and communication in which a troubled person will feel free to examine his feelings. Chapter headings are as follows: 1) Observations on drug abuse and its treatment, 2) Counseling: attitudes and actions, 3) Dependent relationships. bereavement, 4) Group work: comments and suggestions, 5) Basic drug information, 6) Coping with drug crises and withdrawal, 7) Drug treatment programs: organization and operation, 8) Glossary of drug-related slang terms. The author has had much counseling training and experience with drug users.

322. Girdano, Daniel A., and Dorothy Dusek Girdano. **Drug Education: Content and Methods.** Reading, Mass., Addison-Wesley Publishing Co., 1972. 280p. illus. bibliog. index. $5.95pa. LC 75-171431. ISBN 0-201-02369-5.

Written to inform teachers and prospective teachers about drug abuse and how to teach it, this work presents social, psychological, and physiological information. It also contains a collection of "classroom tested" methods, activities, and discussion topics. Chapter headings are as follows: 1) Why drugs?, 2) Physiological basis of drug action on the central nervous system, 3) Alcohol, 4) Marihuana, 5) LSD and other hallucinogens, 6) Amphetamines and other stimulants, 7) Barbiturates and nonbarbiturate sedatives, 8) The opiates, 9) Drugs and the law. A glossary is appended and there are numerous overlay masters–posters on various aspects of drug abuse, which can be converted into plastic overlays to project in classrooms. The book contains useful material.

323. Gross, Jack E., ed. **Respect for Drugs: A Community Service Program.** Sponsored by the College of Pharmaceutical Sciences, Columbia University. Washington, GPO, 1968. 157p. bibliog. $1.25pa.

This instructional manual was prepared by the Columbia University College of Pharmaceutical Sciences faculty and staff to help community pharmacists and communities fill the need for drug education and increased pharmaceutical health service. It is concerned with all aspects of drug education, including drug abuse and misuse.

Included are a number of presentations on miscellaneous subjects: 1) General aspects of pharmacology, 2) Understanding addiction, 3) The patient drug information system, 4) Helpful hints for the public speaker, 5) A children's talk on drugs, 6) What are drugs and how do they work?, 7) Your prescription–what's behind the label, 8) Drug abuse–a community problem, 9) A discussion of marijuana, 10) Intentional abuse and misuse of drugs in general, 11) Biopharmaceutics–therapeutic implications, 12) Addiction control agency reference, and 13) Suggested pamphlets for pharmacy display. Useful material will be found here.

324. Hackett, Peter, Wendell M. Lewis, and Jill B. Pierce, eds. **Educational Perspectives on the Drug Crisis.** Charlottesville, University of Virginia, 1971. 183p. bibliog. index. LC 72-182198.

Prepared as an interdisciplinary textbook on drug education, this work can be used as a basic curriculum guide, and it has been used that way at the University of Virginia. It collects much source material from various areas of the field–education, law, pharmacology, psychiatry, psychology, sociology, and history. Chapters were contributed by various faculty members at the University of Virginia: 1) The cultural context of the drug crisis and the role of the educator, 2) Historical and sociological aspects of drug problems in society, 3) The psychology of drug abuse, 4) Introduction to drugs, 5) General principles of pharmacology, 6) Organization and physiology of the central nervous system, 7) General (nonselective) depressants of the central nervous system, 8) Opiate narcotics, 9) Nervous system stimulants, 10) Hallucinogenic and psychedelic drugs, 11) Marijuana effects, 12) Medical and social implications of marijuana use, 13) Legal implications of drug use and abuse, 14) Implications for educators,

15) Theoretical considerations for curriculum development and policy formation, 16) Epilogue: educational perspectives on the drug crisis. A glossary of pharmacologic terms has been provided, and there are two appendices: "Evaluation of Teaching Materials for Drug Education" and "Classification of Major Psychoactive Drugs with Established Abuse Potential."

325. Hafen, Brent Q., ed. **Drug Abuse: Psychology, Sociology, Pharmacology.** Comments by Eugene J. Faux. Provo, Utah, Brigham Young University Press, 1973. 610p. illus. bibliog. $7.95. LC 73-2263. ISBN 0-8425-0002-2.

These readings have been reprinted from a variety of sources in the medical, health, and educational fields. It is hoped that the collection will be of value to those interested in or responsible for working with young people. The following areas are covered: 1) the medicinal value of drugs; 2) the nature and characteristics of drug dependence; 3) the motivational and psychological aspects of drug abuse; 4) drugs and related social problems, including laws and enforcement; 5) major drugs of abuse, including alcohol and tobacco; and 6) prevention and rehabilitation.

Appended is a programmed instruction course on drugs and their effects, which is a reprint of a National Institute of Mental Health publication, DHEW Publication No. (HSM) 72-9134.

326. Hozinsky, Murray. **Student Drug Abuse: A Rational Approach for Schools.** Denver, Love Publishing Co., 1970. 111p. bibliog. LC 71-138835.

This book is designed for teachers, counselors, administrators, and other school personnel who are planning or hoping to modify drug education programs in their schools. A carefully planned approach is suggested; the reader is warned that some crash programs may have no effect at all or may even promote drug abuse. The following chapters are presented: 1) Introduction, 2) Adolescence and drug use, 3) Teacher preparation, 4) Drug education coordinating committee, 5) Parent involvement, 6) Teaching about drugs, 7) Selected readings. In addition, a "Glossary of Drug and Drug-Related Terms and Slang" and an annotated bibliography have been included.

327. Illinois Interagency Drug Abuse Education Development Committee. **Teaching about Drug Abuse.** Springfield, Ill., 1970. 147p. bibliog.

This guide contains a great deal of information and teaching methodology concerning drugs, so teachers and others interested in education will find it valuable. The following chapters are included: 1) Overview of drug abuse, 2) History of legal and illegal use, 3) Common drugs of abuse, 4) Teaching methodology, and 5) Teaching about drug use and abuse. Appendices cover pertinent laws, methods of therapy, resource agencies, resource materials, a glossary of slang terms, and literature references. Much useful material is found in this work.

328. Jones, J. William. **Drug Crisis: Schools Fight Back with Innovative Programs.** Washington, National School Public Relations Association, 1971. 64p. bibliog. $4.00pa.

This special report deals with several aspects of the drug problem: why schools have had poor success in their educational programs on drug abuse; what is and what is not being accomplished; and why youths turn to drugs. It presents material to aid in planning an effective drug abuse program for a school. The material included is brief but significant.

329. Kurzman, Marc G. **Drug Abuse Education in Pharmacy Schools.** A report prepared for the Drug Enforcement Administration by the American Association of Colleges of Pharmacy. Silver Spring, Md., American Association of Colleges of Pharmacy, 1973. 77p.

This study was sponsored by the Preventive Programs Division, Office of Public Affairs, Drug Enforcement Administration, U.S. Department of Justice, under contract DEA 73-4. It summarizes the results of a comprehensive survey to determine the nature, scope, and extent of drug abuse prevention measures and drug education in schools of pharmacy. Indications are that pharmacy schools have expanded their curricular and extracurricular activities to a great extent in response to the national problem. These activities have taken the form of an increased number of lectures and courses in this area for pharmacy students and other groups, involvement in community projects, drug information and analysis services, and the sponsoring of continuing education courses, research activities, and other projects. A profile is included for each school; arrangement is by state.

330. National Coordinating Council on Drug Abuse Education and Information, Inc. **Common Sense Lives Here: A Community Guide to Drug Abuse Education.** Washington, National Coordinating Council on Drug Abuse Education and Information, Inc., 1970. 104p. $3.00.

Intended for community groups and individuals concerned about the problem of drug abuse, this handbook is not designed for professionals in rehabilitation work, officers of the law, or medical specialists. It includes some basic facts about drugs, discusses the makeup of communities, and shows some links between community life and the forces that lead to drug abuse. The action guidelines and strategies developed can be applied to almost any community. Also included is a list of agencies that can be of assistance and a glossary of slang terms used in the world of drugs. (Note: The issuing body of this publication is now called the National Coordinating Council on Drug Education.)

331. Nowlis, Helen. **Drugs Demystified: Drug Education.** Paris, Unesco Press, 1975. 92p. $2.00. ISBN 92-3-10131-2.

This booklet was prepared at the request of the Unesco Secretariat. The author is a psychologist known for her work in the drug abuse field, and the views and interpretations presented here are based on data collected by Unesco. The work is addressed to an international audience of parents and teachers. The following chapters are included: 1) Introduction and overview, 2) Drugs and drug effects, 3) Drug use and drug users, 4) An expanded psycho-social model, 5) Strategies for prevention, 6) Arenas for growth, 7) Youth's challenge, and 8) Conclusion. In addition there are two appendices: "Questions and Comments on This Pamphlet" and "Sources of Information," which is an international list of agencies concerned with the drug abuse problem.

The author's view is that if the established institutions of society cannot meet the needs of young people, then they will create their own to respond to their needs, or they will resort to deviant and destructive behavior. Communities and nations must continually accept their role in nurturing individuals.

332. Polinsky, Max, and James R. Thompson. **Drug Abuse Education: Teachers and Counselors.** A compilation of the presentations made at the Drug Abuse Institute for Teachers and Counselors, June 7-12, 1970, University of the Pacific School of Pharmacy. Stockton, Calif., School of Pharmacy, University of the Pacific, 1970. 155p.

The purpose of this booklet is to provide teachers and counselors at the junior and senior high school levels with information about comprehensive programs that can give them knowledge and concepts about the misuse of drugs. The papers are arranged under the following subject sections: the drug problem and its dimensions, drug information, legal and moral aspects of drug abuse, and approaches to the drug problem. A good course outline has also been included.

333. Reagen, Michael V., ed. **Readings on Drug Education.** Prepared by the American Foundation for Continuing Education at Syracuse University. Metuchen, N.J., Scarecrow Press, 1972. 271p. bibliog. $7.50 LC 72-7237. ISBN 0-8108-0548-0.

These readings provide a brief, descriptive overview of some of the complexities of the drug abuse problem. Though the material is primarily intended for teachers, other groups, such as parents and clergymen, should also find it valuable. A number of good papers are presented by well-known experts. Included is a good section on how to recognize a drug abuser. In addition, there is an unusually complete "Glossary of the Youth Subculture and Drug Scene for the Establishment and Other Uptight Adults." Included as an appendix is a questionnaire form for a drug use survey in Syracuse schools, along with the results of that survey, which did not reveal that there had been much drug use.

334. Rosenthal, Mitchell S., and Ira Mothner. **Drugs, Parents, and Children: The Three-Way Connection.** Boston, Houghton Mifflin Co., 1972. 182p. index. $5.95. LC 73-162010. ISBN 0-395-12718-1.

This is a parents' guide to understanding the young person who has turned to drugs. The authors feel that too much attention has been given to vast educational campaigns and community treatment programs, and not enough to the role of the family. They think the family remains the best bulwark against drugs (although some help is needed from the community). The first half of the book gives facts and advice for parents. The second half is made up of case studies of drug-troubled families. There are transcripts of sessions with parents, from which one can gain a great deal of insight. The authors take a rather hard line, suggesting that parents must communicate with their children but must stand firm on the question of "no drugs."

335. Smart, Reginald G., and Dianne Fejer. **Drug Education: Current Issues, Future Directions.** Toronto, Addiction Research Foundation of Ontario, 1974. 112p. bibliog. (Program Report Series No. 3). $3.95pa. ISBN 0-88868-006-6.

Pointing out that drug education programs have not been notably successful, the authors take the view that such education should move toward the controlled assessment of experimental programs. They also feel that these programs should stem from studies of communication and persuasion rather than from current educational or cultural fads. The following chapters are presented: 1) Introduction: drug use and drug education, 2) Drug education: an information processing approach, 3) Research into what influences the effectiveness of drug information communications, 4) Unevaluated drug education programs for teachers and students, 5) Audiovisual and printed material evaluations, 6) Results of drug education evaluations, and 7) Summaries of current research needs and aspects of ideal drug education programs. Also included are lists of films and audiovisuals (recommended and not recommended) and a bibliography.

The book provides insight into why some drug education programs fail and shows which approaches are most successful in drug education development.

336. Smith, David E., ed. **Drug Abuse Papers, 1969**. 2nd ed. Berkeley, Continuing Education in Criminology, University Extension, University of California, Berkeley, 1969. 1v. (various paging). bibliog. $5.50pa.

This is a course syllabus compiled for "An American Dilemma: Drug Use and Abuse X 404," given by Continuing Education in Criminology, University Extension, University of California, Berkeley. The course was first offered in 1967. The content has been updated to reflect changing patterns in the drug scene and the latest research findings in drug abuse. The publication contains a collection of papers reviewing the drug field, emphasizing illegal drug patterns; arrangement is under the following headings: 1) Patterns of drug use and abuse, 2) Drug abuse of the sedative-hypnotic type, 3) Drug abuse of the narcotic type, 4) Drug abuse of the stimulant type, 5) Drug abuse of the psychedelic type, 6) Drug abuse: recommendations for treatment and research. Additional sections include an outline of the California Health and Safety Code and an annotated bibliography, "References on the Use and Misuse of Drugs." Much of the material presented is reprinted from other sources.

337. Smith Kline and French Laboratories. **Drug Abuse: Escape to Nowhere; A Guide for Educators.** Washington, National Education Association, 1967. 104p. illus. bibliog. $2.00pa. LC 67-16183.

Designed to provide educators with accurate, reliable information concerning drugs and chemicals of abuse, this guide also hopes to help educators approach young people. It provides information rather than a teaching plan, however. A panel of well-known experts advised on the preparation of the booklet. The material is presented under the following headings: 1) A historical perspective, 2) Drugs of abuse and their effects, 3) The drug abuser and methods of therapy, 4) Educational approaches, 5) Problems of abuser identification. Appendices cover information on drug distribution; legal controls; where to get help; and selected films, books, pamphlets and articles. Technical definitions and glossary of slang terms are included, and there is a drug abuse products reference chart. The booklet should serve its intended purpose very well.

338. Stamford Public Schools, Stamford, Conn. **Stamford Curriculum Guide for Drug Abuse Education.** Chicago, J. G. Ferguson Publishing Co., 1971. 96p. bibliog. $4.25. LC 70-134585.

This guide is intended for use in drug abuse education programs in schools from grades four through senior high school. After presenting objectives and recommendations for the implementation of a program, it provides a curriculum guide for each grade (or grades) worked out in practical detailed fashion. There are also several useful appendices, such as current laws, lists of films, a bibliography, addresses for resource material, and a glossary of drug abuse terms.

339. Tye, Arthur, William M. Dickson, and Robert A. Buerki, eds. **Drug Abuse in Today's Society**. Proceedings of the 15th Annual Ohio Pharmaceutical Seminar held at Columbus, Ohio, March 23-26, 1970. Sponsored by the Ohio State University College of Pharmacy. Columbus, Ohio State University, 1970. 213p. illus. bibliog. $4.50pa. LC 78-632970.

Planned to present a coordinated overall picture of some of the important factors in understanding and dealing with drug abuse, this program used an interdisciplinary approach to relate the social, psychological, political, and pharmacological aspects of the problem. The hope was that this approach would offer a stronger base of knowledge from which to find solutions to the drug situation. The papers were presented by experts in the field of drug abuse, many of them from schools of pharmacy. A short biographical sketch of each participant is included, with a photograph. The papers have a strong educational slant, and the book would be particularly useful to those who teach or plan to teach courses on drug abuse education on the college level. On the whole, the papers and discussions are very good.

340. U.S. Bureau of Narcotics and Dangerous Drugs. **Guidelines for Drug Abuse Prevention Education**. Washington, GPO, 1971. 77p. bibliog. $0.75pa.

The material in this publication was originally prepared by the Bureau's Office of Science and Drug Abuse Prevention, Drug Abuse Prevention Division, for the Workshop for Educators conducted by the Concerned Business Committee of Phoenix in 1970. The work is in three parts. The first is background information. The second presents sample courses of study for kindergarten through high school. The third is an appendix which includes literature and audiovisual resource lists, a chart of drugs, and selected drug curricla.

341. U.S. National Clearinghouse for Drug Abuse Information. **Resource Book for Drug Abuse Education**. 2nd ed. Washington, GPO, 1972. 115p. bibliog. $1.00pa. S/N 1724-0232.

It is hoped that this selection of scientific, philosophical, and educational drug abuse literature can serve as a basis for understanding, trust, and communication between teachers and students regarding drug use. The following sections are presented: I) Drug abuse: insights and perspectives, II) Drug abuse: definition and delineation, III) Drug abuse programs: prevention and intervention, IV) Drug abuse education: principles and practices. There are also two appendices: a list of additional resource materials and a list of state lending libraries. The articles are for the most part reprinted from other sources or abridged from longer reports. A summary of the 1972 Report from the Secretary of Health, Education, and Welfare to the U.S. Congress on "Marihuana and Health" is included in Section II. The authors of the selections are well-known experts in the drug abuse field. Practical information and assistance are provided in Section IV.

There has been a recent emphasis on the concept of "alternatives" to taking drugs, and many in the drug abuse field believe this concept may prove to be the only effective means of dealing with the problem. Two of the articles included here discuss this approach.

342. U.S. National Institute of Mental Health. **The Social Seminar: What Will Happen If . . . A Programmed Instruction Course on Drugs and their Effects.** Washington, GPO, 1972. 51p. $0.55pa. S/N 1724-0233.

The material presented in this self-teaching programmed text is relatively elementary. The following sections are included: 1) Introduction: defining our terms, 2) Narcotics, 3) Stimulants, 4) Depressants, 5) Hallucinogens, 6) Marihuana, and 7) Review. There is a good general review of drug effects.

343. U.S. Senate. 39th Congress. First Session. **Proper and Improper Use of Drugs by Athletes.** Hearings before the Subcommittee to Investigate Juvenile Delinquency of the Committee of the Judiciary. Pursuant to 5 Res. 56, Section 12, Investigation of Juvenile Delinquency in the U.S., Investigative Hearings, June 18 and July 12-13, 1973. Washington, GPO, 1973. 854p. illus. bibliog. $6.60. S/N 052-070-02471-1.

This comprehensive publication presents hearings, chaired by Senator Birch Bayh, which were concerned with getting facts about the extent of the drug problem and effectiveness of drug education for athletes. The hearings explored the drug policies followed by schools and professional teams, attempting to determine what the proper policy should be. This document contains a great deal of very good material, and the subject is thoroughly explored.

344. Vermes, Jean C. **Pot Is Rot (and Other Horrible Facts about Bad Things).** New York, Association Press, 1969. 128p. illus. $1.75pa. LC 69-31328. ISBN 0-8096-1702-1.

Addressed to young people, this book presents the facts they need to know about the dangers of smoking, drinking, drug use, and promiscuous sex relations. Moral, psychological, and physical hazards are discussed. The approach taken is somewhat religious, but it is also in line with professional thinking. The book is a teen-agers' version of a work addressed to parents and other adults called *Helping Youth Avoid Four Great Dangers: Smoking/Drinking/VD/Narcotics Addiction.*

345. Way, Walter L. **The Drug Scene: Help or Hang-Up?** Englewood Cliffs, N.J., Prentice-Hall, Inc., 1970. 119p. bibliog. $1.75pa. ISBN 0-13-220814-8.

One of a series which focuses on important contemporary social and political issues, this title is an in-depth study of the drug abuse problem, presenting material from a number of viewpoints and a variety of sources. The book chapters are as follows: 1) Introduction, 2) How long have drugs been used?, 3) Today's drug scene: what is it?, 4) Why do people use drugs?, 5) Opinions about drug usage, and 6) What should be done? There is also a glossary and a bibliography for further study.

Though no conclusions are drawn from the readings, each one is followed by questions for discussion and reflection. It is presumed that the reader will draw his own conclusions. The book should prove valuable for student use and for discussion groups.

346. Weinswig, Melvin H., and Dale W. Doerr. **Drug Abuse: A Course for Educators; A Report of the Butler University Drug Abuse Institute.** Indianapolis, Butler University College of Pharmacy, 1968. 157p. illus. bibliog. $2.00pa.

These papers were presented at an institute for training educators to deal with the problems of drug abuse and for informing them of the dangers and important medical uses of drugs. Material also was presented to help the educators develop programs of their own, and a teaching outline or course syllabus for classroom use was developed. The speakers were educators, scientists, and government officials.

347. Wittenborn, J. R., and others, comps. and eds. **Communication and Drug Abuse.** Proceedings of the Second Rutgers Symposium on Drug Abuse. Springfield, Ill., Charles C. Thomas, 1970. 542p. illus. bibliog. index. $23.25. LC 75-126494.

This book examines drug abuse from the standpoint of communication phenomena. It includes the papers of the contributors as well as transcripts of the discussion. The participants were representatives of the mass media, behavior and medical scientists, and a few students. Some of the subjects covered were: communications and attitude change, sources of drug information, programs of education and communication, the law as a message, public opinion, and current communication requirements.

The conclusions arrived at during the symposium are not entirely evident, although in general the educational system is blamed for the communication problem with respect to drug abuse.

348. The Yerians. **Rainbows and Jolly Beans: A Look at Drugs.** Illustrated by Harry Garo. Chicago, Childrens Press, 1971. 56p. illus. (col.) index. $4.39. LC 71-173293.

This children's book, which warns them of the dangers of drug use, is colorfully illustrated with psychedelic drawings. Chapter headings are as follows: 1) Drug use, 2) Drug abuse, 3) Narcotics, 4) Sedatives, 5) Stimulants, 6) Hallucinogens, 7) Miscellaneous, 8) Marijuana, 9) Why?, 10) Why not? Because. . . . The glossary-index defines terms in simple fashion.

This is an attractive and informative book, but the thought comes to mind that such books do not always make the intended impression on young people. The accounts of drug use among youth may actually influence children to try drugs.

9. Drugs and Youth

The numerous writings about drugs and youth only attest to the magnitude of the problem. For the most part, the books listed in this section attempt to place the phenomenon of drugs and youth in social perspective. Some authors seem to be writing in desperation, others make suggestions on how the drug problem can be prevented or alleviated, and some present the viewpoint that drugs should be accepted by society. A prevailing viewpoint is that the family is very important in influencing the young. However, peer groups are also of considerable importance, as young people are great conformists. They frequently adopt life styles that are startlingly different from those of their parents. It has been said of the hippies that a curious sort of uniformity was present. Everyone dressed the same, got high on drugs, and lived on handouts. There is some evidence, however, that peer groups have little influence as long as the family is strong.

349. Blum, Richard H., and associates. **Horatio Alger's Children: the Role of the Family in the Origin and Prevention of Drug Risk.** San Francisco, Jossey-Bass, Inc., 1972. 327p. bibliog. index. $10.50. LC 72-186580. ISBN 0-87589-120-9.

This book presents the results of research into the origins of drug use—that is, which individuals are most likely to use drugs, and why. Since the family is the most obvious single influence on the individual, it is the focus of this study. The findings of the study show that drug use among the young can be predicted with accuracy by examining certain characteristics of the family. The key factors were found to be social class, religion, drinking habits, medical practices, and attitudes toward authority.

The authors conclude that the family is *the* institution for forming responsible citizens. The peer group, contrary to popular belief, has little or no influence as long as the family is strong. An excellent family was found to be one of the extended clan where grandparents still play an important role.

This excellent book is readable as well as informative. Attention to the results of the research should throw considerable light on the origin and prevention of the great problem of today.

350. Brenner, Joseph H., Robert Coles, and Dermot Meagher. **Drugs and Youth: Medical, Psychiatric, and Legal Facts.** New York, Liveright, 1970. 258p. bibliog. index. $5.95. LC 72-114383. ISBN 0-87140-501-6; 0-87140-028-6pa.

The authors of this work are two physicians and a lawyer. Each has contributed material in his own area of expertise, and the subject has been viewed from the medical, psychiatric, and legal aspects. The following sections are presented: 1) Definitions; 2) Marijuana; 3) Acid, mescaline, speed, and other drugs; 4) Heroin; 5) Who takes marijuana and why; 6) Growing up; 7) What marijuana does to the mind; 8) Flying high or low; 9) Drugs and the law (this section is about 50 pages long). In addition, there is a section of state-by-state penalties for drug offenses, particularly marijuana; this material rapidly becomes outdated, since states are changing their laws, usually making them more lenient.

The authors do not blame all the evils of society on drug abuse, but neither do they propagandize drug use as the ultimate way to personal salvation. They present documented facts and their own informed opinions. The material is presented in interesting fashion, which includes case studies and accounts from abusers themselves.

351. Cain, Arthur H. **Young People and Drugs.** New York, John Day Company, 1969. 160p. bibliog. $4.75. LC 10816.

The author, a Ph.D. psychologist who has counseled many troubled young people, says his purpose in writing this book is to clarify the many confusions surrounding the whole subject of young people and drugs. He rather effectively strips away the myths, delusions, and wishful thinking that cover the drug scene.

He feels that it is very difficult for a young person to avoid identifying, even if the identification is quite unconscious, with one of the extremist groups of drug users. He further points out that there is also a group of non-extremist young people who seem to feel that, since they are reasonably clean and do not go about in bizarre clothing, their use of marijuana is a perfectly sensible thing. They are sincerely convinced that what they are doing with their intellectual/aesthetic pot parties is an admirable thing, and they feel quite self-righteous about the matter. Both these groups are taken to task for their attitudes and life styles, which set a poor example.

After a survey of the various so-called mind-expanding drugs, there are discussions of the chemical, medical, psychological, social, and religious aspects of their use. The last two chapters are a personal plea to users to take "An Alternate Route," and to take "The Trip Back." The material is well presented and substantiated with authentic medical and psychological facts along with convincing arguments. The author does not pretend that breaking the drug habit is easy; he points out that the percentage of cures is small, but that cures can be accomplished with will power and the right mental attitude. There is a short glossary and a section on antidotes for overdose.

352. Carey, James T. **The College Drug Scene.** Englewood Cliffs, N.J., Prentice-Hall, Inc., 1968. 210p. bibliog. index. $5.95. LC 68-27489.

Written by a university professor, this book presents a sympathetic view of the drug scene of the late 1960s. The work is based on interviews with the young people who were drug abusers in California.

The author does not believe that the "straight" community will either accept drug use or drive it underground, because their own children compose it. The best analysis that can be made is that the movement indicates a vague dissatisfaction with the quality of our lives. The author hopes that we will "heed seriously the call to slow down, to live our life instead of enduring it, to open our eyes to beauty, and finally to humanize the large-scale structures that now victimize us."

353. Child Study Association of America. **You, Your Child and Drugs.** New York, Child Study Press, 1971. 73p. $3.95. LC 77-122013. ISBN 0-87183-238-0.

This small book presents brief guidelines for parents to use in dealing with drug-related problems. It also includes some basic information about the drugs themselves and some quotations from teenagers that may provide insights. The information presented is accurate but oversimplified for many readers.

354. Deschin, Celia Spalter. **The Teenager in a Drugged Society: A Symptom of Crisis.** New York, Richard Rosen Press, Inc., 1972. 181p. bibliog. $3.99. LC 72-190581. ISBN 0-8239-0226-9.

The author of this book sees drug abuse and addiction as symptoms of much that needs improving and changing in American life. She feels emphasis should be on the social roots rather than the symptoms of problems. An attempt is made to place blame for all that is wrong, and many groups are pointed to: pushers, politicians, advertisers, drug manufacturers, the military, society in general, and anyone who does not go along with the reforms usually advocated by those of liberal leanings. The book is well documented, although most of the works referred to are those that take a somewhat favorable view of drug use.

355. Fort, Joel. **The Pleasure Seekers: The Drug Crisis, Youth, and Society.** Indianapolis, Bobbs-Merrill Co., 1969. bibliog. index. $6.50 LC 69-13090.

This book discusses the mind-altering drugs such as marihuana, LSD, barbiturates, tranquilizers, amphetamines, and alcohol. The social policies and laws that have been used to control drugs are criticized. The book is aimed at all those who have contact with drugs abusers: parents, young people, doctors, lawyers, teachers, psychologists, sociologists, journalists, and officers of the law. Although the author of this work is a reasonably well known physician and authority on drugs, the reviewer is not impressed with the book. The viewpoint is not clear and much of the discourse pointless. The chapter headings are as follows: 1) The truth shall make you free; 2) Around the world; 3) Never send to ask who is the drug user; 4) The traveling salesman: drug traffic; 5) But it's against the law; 6) Once upon a time: hard drugs; crime and violence; 7) Demons and demagogues: insanity; sex; birth defects; and dropping out; 8) Better living through chemistry?; 9) Why? Perchance to dream; 10) Youth, American society, and drugs; 11) Beyond drugs: the real problems and how to solve them. An appendix, "Comparison Chart of Major Substances Used for Mind Alteration," has been included.

356. Gamage, James R., ed. **Management of Adolescent Drug Misuse: Clinical, Psychological and Legal Perspectives.** Proceedings of the Second Annual Symposium of the Student Association for the Study of Hallucinogens. Beloit, Wisc., STASH Press, 1973. 139p. $5.00. LC 73-81336.

These seven papers, by noted authorities in several different disciplines concerned with drug abuse, provide perspectives on various means of dealing with young drug abusers. The contents include: 1) "Myths and realities of the college drug scene: adventures in epidemiology," by Samuel Pearlman and others, 2) "Toxic reactions to marihuana," by Andrew Weil, 3) "Management of drug abuse emergencies," by David E. Smith and George R. Gay, 4) "Long-term psychological management of adolescent drug abuse," by Robert E. Gould, 5) "Drugs and the law: a therapeutic dilemma," by Albert Lowenstein, 6) "Relieving acid indigestion: educational strategies related to psychological and social dynamics of hallucinogenic drug use," by Alan Cohen, and 7) "Drugs: information for crisis treatment," by Matthew Lampe.

The authors are more sympathetic to drug use than many; however, their suggestions for dealing with immediate problems of this nature may serve as a useful guide, particularly for those working in drug programs.

357. Garabedian, John. **Drugs and the Young.** New York, Tower Publications, Inc., 1970. 140p. $0.95pa.

Prepared by a newswriter, this is a sensationally written work that includes many quotations and accounts of what drug abusers experience. The chapter headings are as follows: 1) Marijuana, 2) LSD, 3) Amphetamines, 4) Heroin, 5) Life styles, and 6) Why they do it. An appendix provides a glossary of drug abuse terms. The picture drawn of the drug scene is not pleasant, and much silliness and freakiness is played up, but young readers may possibly find it exciting. It isn't entirely clear what the point of the presentation is, although the intention is probably to show the drug scene as it is in the hope that society can find a way to get youth back into the mainstream.

358. Gitchoff, G. Thomas. **Kids, Cops, and Kilos: A Study of Contemporary Suburban Youth.** San Diego, Malter-Westerfield Publishing Company, 1969. 178p. bibliog. $2.95pa. LC 71-91216. ISBN 0-91718-24-9.

This work reports on an investigation (1966-1968) of an upper-middle class suburban area near San Francisco. A major concern of the study was the rapid growth in drug use and abuse among teenagers in a relatively short period of time. The investigation was supported by case study material and direct experience within the sample community. It was found that there was a startling change in attitudes, interests, and activities of the young people during this critical time. They rejected most middle-class suburban values for a drop-out or hang-loose ethic.

The author suggests that it would be wise to listen to the voice of youth (although just what that voice was saying isn't so clear). In any case, looking at the material presented in this book from the vantage point of the present, it is reasonable to say that it does not successfully explain the reasons for the attitudes of the youths of the 1960s or what might have caused youthful attitudes to change in the 1970s.

359. Harms, Ernest, ed. **Drug Addiction in Youth.** London and New York, Pergamon Press, 1965. 210p. bibliog. $11.50.

This is an initial survey of what was known of juvenile drug addiction at the time of writing. Coverage is not systematic, but the book provides a good idea of the situation. Some of the psychological material is particularly noteworthy, such as the chapter "Psychological Characteristics of the Adolescent

Addict," which draws a psychological profile of the addict. One interesting observation is that "both male and female addicts have in common a tendency to overvalue the masculine role. With the male addict this is reflected in excessive masculine posturing to win peer respect." Another comment of note is: "Karl Marx is reputed to have said that 'religion is the opium of the people.' Considering the all-consuming character of narcotic-centered behavior, it is probably at least as true to say that opiates seem to be the 'religion' of some of the people."

The editor of the work indicates that he is dissatisfied because the book does not present as complete a picture as he would like. However, the contributors to the volume are well known and capable and the quality of the work high. The book is still read ten years after it was first published. The editor summarizes the drug abuse problem by saying that treatment and prevention measures have been disappointing. He suggests medical and psychiatric treatment and re-education. Slow-withdrawal appears to offer more hope of success than abstinence withdrawal. On the social side, the greatest hope lies in "narcotics anonymous" measures and group psychotherapy techniques.

360. Harms, Ernest, ed. **Drugs and Youth: The Challenge of Today**. New York, Pergamon Press, 1973. 247p. bibliog. $13.00. LC 72-84115.

This collection of studies and opinions from a number of experts in the field of drug addiction stresses social, cultural, and psychological aspects. The following chapters are included: 1) Drug abuse in pregnancy: its effects on the fetus and newborn infant, 2) The major drugs of use among adolescents and young adults, 3) A survey of the inhaling of solvents among teen-agers, 4) Glue sniffing–a communion, 5) Physical and mental pathology due to drug addiction, 6) Psychopathology in the juvenile drug addict, 7) The social patterns of the teen-age drug abuse, 8) Basic aspects of the drug addict's conflict with law and society, 9) Sex-crazed dope fiends!–myth or reality?, 10) Vocation and social adjustment of the treated juvenile addict, 11) Some approaches to the treatment of adolescent drug addicts and abusers, 12) Withdrawals and methadone treatment, 13) Attitudes toward methadone maintenance, 14) Group therapy in the treatment of the juvenile narcotic addict: a review of the findings, 15) Psychotherapy with the juvenile drug addict, 16) The religious problematic of the juvenile addict, 17) Aftercare problems with the juvenile drug addict.

In 1964 the editor compiled *Drug Addiction in Youth* (see above). The present work follows the pattern of the earlier, though it emphasizes more recent professional speculations. The editor feels that progress has been made in dealing with drug abuse during the last decade but that there is a great deal still to be learned. In particular, he feels that we have learned to listen to the addict and to understand a bit more of his psychology. The papers presented in the book are quite good.

361. Hemsing, Esther D. **Children and Drugs.** Washington, Association for Childhood Education International, 1972. 64p. bibliog. $2.50pa. LC 74-189675.

In the past decade, drug abuse has spread downward to younger children and is now a concern among elementary age children. It is also a concern among babies born to addicted mothers. This booklet presents papers by various authors who attempt to set this problem in social perspective, offering suggestions for ways of working with children and their parents that may help bring about changes in education and society that could eliminate the need for drug taking. A good annotated bibliography is included.

362. Herron, Donald M., and L. F. Anderson. **Can We Survive Drugs**? 2nd ed. Philadelphia, Chilton Book Co., 1972. 81p. bibliog. index. $2.95pa. LC 72-8356. ISBN 0-8019-5752-4.

The authors of this work have had a good deal of experience as law enforcement officers and have lectured frequently to law enforcement agencies, school administrators, and parents about the drug problem. This simply written book, primarily for parents, has a practical approach, telling the parent how best to cope with drug abuse among youths.

Several useful special sections have been appended, including a list of agencies, publications, and films dealing with drug abuse; a narcotics identification chart; and a glossary.

363. International Conference on Student Drug Surveys, First, Newark, N.J., 1971. **Proceedings**. Edited by Stanley Einstein and Stephen Allen. Farmingdale, N.Y., Baywood Publishing Co., 1972. 346p. bibliog. $18.00.

Surveys of student drug abuse have become very prevalent recently, but the results and conclusions do not necessarily tell much. The intent of this conference was to permit interested and concerned lay and professional individuals to discuss the implications and consequences of such surveys on the young people, the school, and the community. The papers are divided into four sections: 1) Drug use in high school, 2) Drug use in college, 3) The drug use survey: how and why, and 4) Interpretation and implications. Some sample questionnaires are also included. In general, the conference showed that it is questionable whether the reinforcing or changing of particular value systems and life styles can be determined from most questionnaries, statistics, and hastily implemented programs.

364. Johnston, Lloyd. **Drugs and American Youth**. A report from the Youth in Transition Project. Ann Arbor, Mich., Institute for Social Research, University of Michigan, 1973. 273p. bibliog. index. $7.00. LC 71-190022. ISBN 0-87944-120-8pa; 0-87944-133-X.

The research presented here was part of a nation-wide study of adolescent boys begun in 1966 under the primary sponsorship of the U.S. Office of Education. The study, called *Youth in Transition*, followed a panel of young men from 1966 to 1970. Though the study's main concern was the causes and consequences of dropping out of high school, several additional areas were studied, one of which is reported in this book. Chapter headings are as follows: 1) An introduction to the study; 2) The use of drugs during and after high school; 3) The attitudes of youth toward drug taking; 4) Background and intelligence related to drug use; 5) Drugs and the high school experience; 6) Paths taken after high school; 7) Drugs, delinquency, and alienation; and 8) Summary and policy implications. The report contains a great deal of valuable statistical data. The most important conclusion reached is that there has been much less use of non-addictive illegal drugs (such as marihuana) among young people of the United States than the media have been suggesting and that its effects have been far less serious than most Americans have assumed.

365. Land, Herman W. **What You Can Do about Drugs and Your Child.** New York, Hart Publishing Co., 1969. 240p. bibliog. index. $7.50. LC 68-29532.

Written for parents who are concerned about their children becoming dangerously involved with drug abuse, this book extends help to them at all stages of the drug problem. Practical matters are discussed: How can you allay your fears: To whom should you go for help: How should the subject be approached with your child? In addition, there is material on how to spot the use of drugs, the treatments available, and preventive measures that can be taken. An appendix lists names and addresses of treatment centers, hospitals, halfway houses, community health centers, state mental health offices, and related agencies. The material presented would be of use to teachers and counselors as well as parents.

366. Leech, Kenneth, and Brenda Jordan. **Drugs for Young People: Their Use and Misuse.** 2nd ed. Oxford, The Religious Education Press, Ltd. (a member of the Pergamon Group), 1967. $2.25pa. ISBN 0-08-017938-X.

This is a factual discussion of the problems that result from the misuse of various types of drugs. The chemical nature of the drugs and how they act on the body are explained. Legal treatment, incidence, and socioeconomic characteristics of the addict population in the United States and England are contrasted. There are chapters on such subjects as the social causes of drug abuse and treatment and cures for addiction. Although the book is primarily for young people, the material is presented on a fairly advanced level, and technical terms are used. The glossary identifies only slang terms, but the technical terms are reasonably well explained in the text. In the hope that the book will be useful for current affairs lessons, the authors have included questions for discussion after each chapter.

The book is well written and contains sensible judgments. It concludes that drug abusers must stop trying to escape but should face and overcome the need to escape. It also concludes that loneliness is at the root of the drug problem, that people feel cut off from God and man.

367. Lieberman, Florence, Phyllis Caroff, and Mary Gottesfeld. **Before Addiction: How to Help Youth.** New York, Behavioral Publications, 1973. 131p. bibliog. index. $7.95. LC 73-7803. ISBN 0-87705-112-7.

Written for parents, this book's purpose is to help prevent drug addiction. The authors are social workers who have had a good deal of experience with drug abusing adolescents. The book is practical and includes a broad perspective of the social environment, a critique of treatments used, and a discussion of the adolescent and his family. The first of the book's three parts deals with the problem, the second with therapy; the third is an exploration of social and philosophical issues and broader concerns.

368. Marin, Peter, and Allan Y. Cohen. **Understanding Drug Use: An Adult's Guide to Drugs and the Young.** New York, Harper and Row, 1971. 163p. bibliog. index. $5.95. LC 69-15318.

On the assumption that most young people will experiment with drugs, the authors of this guide try to help parents understand drug use and find some realistic ways to deal with it. Their suggestions cover what to do if a child is arrested, what to do if a child has a "bad trip" with drugs, what helpful attitudes are, guidelines for drug use, and how to inform yourself on drug use. There is also a section of information on the major drugs–something that almost all books on the subject contain.

The reviewer is not greatly impressed with the book. Although some of the advice is sound, the authors are young themselves and appear to identify with the wayward children rather than the parents. Advice on a matter so serious as drug abuse could be better sought from more mature individuals. The text is full of phrases for which there is no better descriptive term than "kidspeak."

369. Moses, Donald A., and Robert E. Burger. **Are You Driving Your Children to Drink? Coping with Teenage Alcohol and Drug Abuse.** New York, Van Nostrand Reinhold Co., 1975. 235p. bibliog. index. $8.95. LC 75-23097. ISBN 0-442-25583-7.

This is a "new approach" to the understanding and treatment of the drug and alcohol problems of young people, based on the concept that the psychological interaction of parents and children is at the heart of the problem. The authors attempt to get at the causes for drug use, to show how parents may have unwittingly planted the seeds of frustration and rebellion and may have "driven their children to drugs and drink."

The book is in four parts: 1) The roots–drugs and alcohol have come to middle America, but the home is where they got their start; 2) Storm warnings–what children cry out for is seldom what we listen to; 3) Healing–therapy takes many forms, but it must break a vicious circle to succeed; 4) The public problem; let's have an end to public moralizing and find a way to the understanding of individual needs.

The psychology presented in the book is good, though it is perhaps a bit simplified in order to make it suitable for the general reader.

In summary, the major proposition of the book is this: if parents are understanding of their child, yet firm in their setting of limits, if they love their child but are willing to let him grow in his individual way, can that child become a drug abuser? The answer is yes, he can, but he can also be treated far more simply and positively.

370. Nowlis, Helen H. **Drugs on the College Campus.** With an introduction by Kenneth Keniston. Garden City, N.Y., Doubleday, 1969. 144p. bibliog. $1.25pa. LC 69-15579.

Written by a social psychologist who is well known for her work with student affairs, education, mental health, and drug abuse, this book is, in part, a synthesis of material used as background for conferences sponsored by the National Association of Student Personnel Administrators with support from the U.S. Food and Drug Administration. The subject matter was found to be very complex, but the author hopes that the discussion presented will clarify issues and implications raised by college students' use of drugs. The following chapters take up about half the book: 1) Defining the problem, 2) Facts about drugs: problems and issues, 3) The student and his culture, 4) Drugs and the law, 5) The response of the educational institution. The remainder of the book is a discussion of six drugs: barbiturates, ethyl alcohol, amphetamines, marihuana, lysergic acid diethylamide (LSD), and aspirin. There is a comparison chart of major substances used for mind-alteration, a glossary of technical terms, and some information about the Bureau of Narcotics and Dangerous Drugs.

A great deal is said about why student drug use has developed but little about what might be done about it. The general tone of the book is one of acceptance of drug use.

371. Quattrocchi, Frank, and Henrietta Quattrocchi. **Why Johnny Takes Drugs.** Westlake Village, Calif., Aware Press, 1972. 256p. $4.75pa.

The authors, a journalist and an anthropologist, present their material in a journalistic style, and they use short sensational passages to gain attention. This book is an outgrowth of the authors' year-long study of the hippie community in California. The presentation is interesting and readable and the material authentic enough, but there is no clear explanation of "why Johnny takes drugs." He doesn't take them for any clear predictable reason, according to the book. The nearest the reviewer can come to an answer (from the material presented, anyway) is that Johnny is bored with modern life.

372. Roberts, Chester F., Jr. **A Follow-Up Study of the Juvenile Drug Offender.** Sponsored by the Institute for the Study of Crime and Delinquency and the Rosenberg Foundation in cooperation with the California Youth Authority. Sacramento, Calif., Institute for the Study of Crime and Delinquency, 1967. 37p. bibliog.

This publication presents the findings of a study made to test some commonly held views concerning the causes and consequences of drug abuse. Some of the propositions studied were: 1) that there is a relationship between drug involvement and other delinquency, and 2) that there is a relationship between socioeconomic background and drug involvement. Data were collected from the arrest records of 866 youths on such personal characteristics as sex, ethnic background, age at initial arrest, socioeconomic classification of area of residence, and prior arrest record.

Findings and a great deal of information are presented in the pamphlet, particularly in tabular form, and a number of conclusions can be drawn from the findings. A general one is that instead of drug involvement leading to delinquent behavior, it is more likely that delinquent youth frequently become involved with drugs as part of their delinquent behavior. Also, it is doubtful that there is a relationship between lower socioeconomic status and drug abuse.

373. Scott, Edward M. **The Adolescent Gap: Research Findings on Drug Using and Non-Drug Using Teens.** Foreword by Theodore M. Hesburgh with a chapter by Chuck Paulus. Springfield, Ill., Charles C. Thomas, 1972. 143p. bibliog. index. $6.95. LC 73-175084. ISBN 0-398-02403-0.

The suggestion made by the title of this book is that not all young people are alike; there is an adolescent gap. In this book three different groups of the teenage population share their views. These groups are made up of those who have not used drugs, those who have and have stopped, and those who are taking drugs and do not plan to stop. Insights can be found from the accounts; the rationale for the puzzling activity of drug use may become more clear to the reader. A great many facts and figures are presented. The last chapter summarizes the data, reflects on the facts, gives suggestions for prevention and treatment, and offers hints on therapy.

Taking a look at the future, the author predicts that: 1) In general, drug use will decline. The user will learn that drugs are neither a panacea nor a cure for problems, and ill-effects will make more of an impression. 2) Drug use by the normal or average youth particularly will diminish. 3) Use of hard drugs by the seriously maladjusted will continue. 4) Inroads will be made in rehabilitation. 5) Factions will arise advocating new life styles, the counter-culture, etc. 6) Militant groups will survive to some extent, but in fragmented and diminished form.

374. Shedd, Charlie W. **Is Your Family Turned On? Coping with the Drug Culture.** Waco, Texas, Word Books, 1972. 148p. illus. $1.25pa. LC 71-165959.

The author of this title has written several other religious works for young people. The material for this book was secured from entries to a contest sponsored by the author and the publisher; prizes were offered to young people for the best entries on the topic "Why I don't use drugs." The replies to the contest question showed that users and nonusers of drugs have some common traits, but the author also found significant differences. Ten areas of difference were identified, and the nonuser showed the following traits: 1) He has warm feelings toward his home, 2) He anticipates his day with pleasure, 3) He is appreciative, 4) He has a healthy attitude toward himself, 5) He knows the satisfaction of work, 6) He faces hard things with courage, 7) He is preparing himself for responsible citizenship, 8) He respects his sexuality, 9) He has been encouraged to use his own judgment, and 10) He feels responsible to God. A survey of literature that reports what drug users say about their problem showed that in general they have opposite traits.

375. Turkel, Peter. **The Chemical Religion: The Truth about Drugs and Teens.** Glen Rock, N.J., Paulist Press, 1969. 118p. $1.45pa. LC 69-18371.

The aim of the author, a reporter, was to present the unpleasant facts of drug addiction in the hope that potential users would decide against using drugs. The material seems to be authentic and is well presented. The writing is journalistic but not overly sensational.

376. U.S. Bureau of Narcotics and Dangerous Drugs. Office of Scientific Support. **Drug-Taking in Youth: An Overview of Social, Psychological, and Educational Aspects.** By Louise G. Richards and John H. Langer. Washington, GPO, 1971. 48p. bibliog. $0.40pa.

This pamphlet pictures the drug abuse phenomenon as it currently exists. Part I takes up social and psychological aspects; Part II discusses today's youth and drug education. The material is intended for teachers, parents, group workers, and others who deal with or are concerned about young people. The hope is expressed that the pamphlet will lead to a better understanding of the drug epidemic.

The following chapters are included: 1) Extent and patterns of drug use by young people of the United States; 2) The social context of youthful drug use; 3) Delinquency and drug use: trends in arrests; 4) Psychology, mental health, and family conditions; 5) Early educational efforts; 6) Drug education today; and 7) Educational programs and curricula. Each part of the publication includes a good bibliography; in all, it gives a good brief view of the subject.

377. U.S. National Institute on Drug Abuse. **Drugs and Family/Peer Influence: Family and Peer Influences on Adolescent Drug Use.** Edited by Patricia Ferguson, Thomas Lennox, and Dan J. Lettieri. Washington, GPO, 1974. 140p. bibliog. index. (DHEW Publication No. (ADM) 75-186; Research Issues Series No. 4.) $2.10pa.

This booklet summarizes articles reporting major research findings of the last 15 years. All the materials reviewed are in the English language, and American drug issues are stressed. The materials covered have been classified and arranged under various headings: 1) The world of youthful drug use: groups and gangs, 2) Becoming a marijuana user: predictions, 3) The family of the addict: influence and interaction, 4) Horatio Alger's children: parents as models, and 5) Developmental factors: childhood experience. With each citation the following information is usually given: a summary, comments on methodology, findings, and conclusions.

378. U.S. National Institute on Drug Abuse. **Predicting Adolescent Drug Abuse: A Review of Issues, Methods, and Correlates.** Edited by Dan J. Lettieri. Washington, GPO, 1975. 361p. illus. bibliog. (DHEW Publication No. (ADM) 76-299; Research Issues Series No. 11).

This volume of the Research Issues Series comprises some of the recent thinking on the problems and intracies of predicting drug-abusing behaviors. Most of the papers presented focus on predicting adolescent drug abuse, so thre is an emphasis on marihuana use. The publication is divided into the following sections: 1) Conceptual issues, 2) Nosological and clinical approaches, 3) Methodological issues, and 4) Research findings: the search for correlates and predictors. Each section contains several papers. In the last section the following areas are explored: intrapersonal, behavioral/demographic, longitudinal, developmental, and interpersonal.

The illustrations included throughout the work are disturbing but outstanding; they were taken from works by William Blake and Maurits Cornelis Escher that are in the National Gallery of Art.

379. Wiener, R. S. P. **Drugs and Schoolchildren.** New York, Humanities Press, 1970. 238p. bibliog. index. $7.50. ISBN 0-391-0038-1.

This book is of interest because the growing drug use by school children is a serious problem. The book is based on a study of children (aged 14 to 19) in the London area. The study was a sociological investigation to assess the situation and to devise a policy for dealing with it. Questionnaires were given to over 1,000 children, and answers from drug users and non-users were compared. It was found that the behavior, attitudes, and knowledge of the users and non-users differed consistently. The author includes a discussion of what should be done about the drug problem. He also considers the effectiveness of several different educational media, including films. The research methods used are outlined in some detail. The book is in three parts: 1) The problem and the background to the hypotheses, 2) Methodology, and 3) Results, discussion and recommendations.

380. Wilson, Morrow, and Suzanne Wilson, eds. **Drugs in American Life.** New York, H. W. Wilson Co., 1975. 212p. bibliog. (The Reference Shelf. v. 47, no. 1). LC 75-4607. ISBN 0-8242-0569-3.

This is one of a series which reprints articles, excerpts from books, and addresses on current issues and social trends in the United States and other countries. This volume, on the "drug scene," is intended primarily for college and high school students; the emphasis is on youthful involvement with drugs, with some attention given to historical perspective. There are five sections: 1) Overview, 2) Legal aspects of drugs, 3) Social and medical aspects, 4) Personal accounts, and 5) Possible solutions. The authors of the articles are well known, for the most part, and most are professionals in such fields as law, social work, medicine, or psychology. The personal accounts, however, are written by those who have experienced subjective physical, mental, and emotional reactions to various drugs. Among others, there are selections by the author Aldous Huxley; by Mezz Mezzrow, the jazz musician; by William Burroughs, the novelist; and a humorous piece on "How I Stopped Smoking" by caricaturist Al Hirschfeld.

381. Wittenborn, J. P., and others, comps. and eds. **Drugs and Youth.** Proceedings of the Rutgers Symposium on Drug Abuse. Springfield, Ill., Charles C. Thomas, 1969. 485p. bibliog. index. $22.75. LC 74-83841.

This volume is made up of position papers presented by experts in the field of drug abuse at a symposium meeting, comments made by other participants, and reviews by policy makers on current practices. Scientists, legislators, and judges took part in the meeting. The work is in six parts: 1) An overview; 2) Morphine, heroin, and cocaine; 3) Amphetamine type and barbiturate tranquilizer type drugs; 4) Marijuana and LSD; 5) Drug abuse and the law; and 6) Action.

Some of the conclusions of the group were that education in the causes and consequences of drug abuse should be provided for secondary school and college students, the sources of illegal drugs should be suppressed, heroin and marijuana should not be available legally, some laws are too severe (marijuana), and some too lenient (amphetamines).

382. Wolk, Donald J., ed. **Drugs and Youth.** Washington, National Council for the Social Studies, 1971. 96p. illus. bibliog. (Teaching Social Studies in an Age of Crisis, No. 1). $2.25. LC 75-151826.

Prepared for the use of secondary school teachers, particularly social studies teachers, this booklet is of special interest because schools have been adding programs on drug education to their curricula. The book explores aspects of the drug scene, using the following chapter headings: 1) Why drugs?; 2) The drugs of concern; 3) Drugs in the high school: a student research report; 4) Excessive drug use: signs, symptoms, and family-related factors; 5) Social and political aspects of drug use; 6) Socio-legal policies on drugs; 7) Drug education in grades ten, eleven, and twelve; 8) Four rules for teaching about drugs. Appended materials, called "Practical Information for Teachers," consist of a chart listing drugs and giving medical uses, symptoms produced, and their dependence potential; a drug glossary; a selected annotated bibliography; a section on how to use drug films; and examples of drug education curricula.

10. Psycho-Social Aspects

The materials in this section discuss various sociological and psychological aspects of drug abuse. There are more sociological than psychological titles, since more of the former seem to exist. Works that present hard psychological research have been placed in Section 12, "Pharmacology, Chemistry, Research, and Medical Aspects." Many of the titles listed under "Psycho-Social Aspects" deal with the life styles and behavior of addicts; they attempt to acquaint the reader with the "drug culture," and many urge an acceptance of it. The pervading theme of this material is the attempt to explain the sociological basis of drug abuse.

383. Adler, Nathan. **The Underground Stream: New Life Styles and the Antinomian Personality**. New York, Harper and Row, 1972. 135p. $2.25pa. LC 72-83620. ISBN 0-06-13168-3.

The author states that "the study of social and historical context of character structure, personality formation, and sensibility is barely begun," but the papers in this book are, he says, themes and variations for such a work. Although his viewpoint is somewhat difficult to fathom, it seems to be that drug use is not evil but can produce "psychic rebirth, bring new insights and pleasures, intensify feelings, and renew an automated world." Emphasis is on antinomianism, which is defined as a social movement that develops in times of transition and crisis when old moral codes are no longer of value. The titles of the papers are as follows: 1) Psychedelic hoax; 2) Antinomianism in history; 3) Antinomianism: the social context; 4) The tuned organism: body image, sensibility, and self; 5) The phenomenal self and the field; and 6) Ethics, ethos, and actualism: the paradigm of the antinomian therapies.

384. Agar, Michael. **Ripping and Running: A Formal Ethnography of Urban Heroin Addicts.** New York, Seminar Press, 1973. 173p. bibliog. index. $8.50. LC 72-12214. ISBN 0-12-802150-0.

This book attempts to explain what an addict is like and how he adapts to life in the streets, and to show the learning process that enables him to perceive, decide, and act in his drug-oriented environment. The author, an anthropologist, got his material with the help of patients at the Lexington, Kentucky Drug Treatment Center.

The following chapters are presented: 1) Ethnography and the addict, 2) Ethnography and cognition, 3) Methodology, 4) Some informal preliminaries,

5) The events in process, 6) Decision-making in the streets, and 7) Conclusion. Appendices include a sample simulated situation and a glossary of street addict terms. The reader could not get along without the latter, since the text is copiously sprinkled with the language of the addict.

While the study is well presented and gives some insight into an addict's life and thought, the reviewer in general finds the book boring. Addicts do not seem to live interesting day-to-day lives; and their "richly descriptive terminology" is limited and tiresome.

385. Barber, Bernard. **Drugs and Society**. New York, Russell Sage Foundation, 1967. 212p. bibliog. index. $6.50. LC 67-25910.

Allowing a broad definition of the term "drugs," this book is concerned with man's uses and abuses of all substances that have been called drugs. The author gives some historical background, showing that drugs have been used for a variety of purposes: for aesthetic reasons, as implements of war, for relief of pain, for social and psychological escape, and for the control of thought and behavior. The author, who is a sociologist, criticizes the work of such specialists as biologists, medical researchers, pharmacologists, social scientists, pharmacists, health administrators, and just about everyone else involved with the matter. He emphasizes the need for specific new research.

In summary, the author's view is that society has not adjusted to the great changes of the past 25 years or so in respect to drugs, with the result that many problems have developed. Among those discussed in the book are large profits of drug companies, inadequate government controls over testing of drugs, shortage of competent drug researchers, inadequate education of doctors for the newer drug therapeutics, and the persistence of police approaches to the addiction problem when a socio-medical approach is needed.

A great many of the ideas expressed in the book do not impress the reviewer. However, the following quotation, which originally came from another of the author's books, points out a basic dilemma that should be noted: "The problem of the use of drugs is the problem of the use of all human technology. No matter how beneficial some class of technological substance or agents may be, there is always the possibility that they may be . . . used for ill as well as good. The control of the uses of drugs . . . is a problem . . . for which there are no easy solutions."

386. Barber, Theodore Xenophon. **LSD, Marijuana, Yoga, and Hypnosis** Chicago, Aldine Publishing Co., 1970. 337p. bibliog. index. $10.95. LC 73-115935. ISBN 0-202-25004-1.

The author is a psychologist who has conducted a great deal of research and done extensive publishing on yoga, hypnosis, and psychedelic drugs. This book is concerned with the psychological and physiological effects of yoga, hypnosis, and major psychedelic drugs (such as LSD and mescaline), and minor psychedelics (such as marihuana and cannabis derivatives). It is believed that these three things—the drugs, yoga, and hypnosis—give rise to altered states of awareness or consciousness. It is also said that they tap unused potentialities, and they have been viewed as part of abnormal psychology and discontinuous from other known psychological phenomena. The author treats these topics as continuous with other known psychological phenomena and as part of social psychology. The author's view is that psychedelics, yoga, and hypnosis do not necessarily bring out unused mental or physical capacities, heighten awareness, give rise to enhanced creativity, produce altered states of consciousness and the like. These assumptions are analyzed and accepted only if supported by empirical data.

The author says that the main purpose of the book is to illustrate a way of thinking and a method of analysis toward soft areas of psychology. The book should particularly interest experimental, clinical, and social psychologists, sociologists, educators, and those concerned with social problems.

387. Berke, Joseph, and Calvin Hernton. **The Cannabis Experience: An Interpretative Study of the Effects of Marijuana and Hashish.**London, Peter Owen Ltd., 1974. 288p. bibliog. £4.50. LC 74-176430. ISBN 0-7206-0073-1.

The authors of this work are concerned with the experimental domain in which cannabis is perceived to affect its users. Berke is a psychiatrist, and Hernton is a sociologist. Their view is that the effects of cannabis vary from one occasion to the next for the same individual and from one person to another. They believe that three factors must be considered in studying experimental effects of the drug: 1) The drug itself, 2) The individual using it, and 3) The context in which the drug is taken. It is felt that the user's life, memories, dreams, and personal eccentricities determine the effect of the drug, and the setting is also said to be important.

The authors have worked out a methodology for studying the drug's effects: The user's point of view was determined through the use of a questionnaire, then content analysis was used to transfer the information into countable units. Effects were classified. The investigators distinguished more than 150 different groupings which they called effect-categories, and these groupings furnished the building blocks for the discussion of the experimental effects of the drug.

The authors conclude that the typical cannabis user in Great Britain at the present time is male, middle class, highly educated, and either a student or a white collar worker with a fair income. The authors also believe that the paranoid reactions experienced by some users are related to the illegality that surrounds use of the drug. Some of the conclusions reached by the authors are obviously questionable, such as that clarity and profundity of thought are characteristic of the first stages of cannabis intoxication, and that the drug potentiates analytical and critical powers. They have only shown cannabis users as they themselves think they are.

388. Blum, Richard H., and Associates. **Drugs I: Society and Drugs, Social and Cultural Observations**. San Francisco, Jossey-Bass, Inc., 1969. 400p. bibliog. index. $12.50. LC 73-75936. ISBN 0-87589-033-4.

This volume provides a perspective on psychoactive drugs, giving information on marijuana, LSD, heroin, alcohol, and related drugs of abuse. Besides tracing history of drug use, it analyzes patterns of use among groups such as the hippies, more normal citizens, and high school and college students. Comparing drug use among various cultures, the book assesses the results of prolonged use and discusses drug associations with crime, religion, educational status, and other factors. The author, a psychologist, is director of the Psychopharmacology Project at the Institute for the Study of Human Problems at Stanford University. Much of the material presented in the book is based on investigations conducted at the Institute. A companion volume authored by the same group is called *Drugs II: Students and Drugs, College and High School Observations.*

389. Claridge, Gordon. **Drugs and Human Behaviour.** New York, Praeger Publishers, 1970. 266p. bibliog. index. $7.95. LC 78-127139.

The author says that this book is essentially "an attempt to show how, by studying people given drugs, we can learn something about how drugs work as well as about how people work." All drugs that affect behavior (substances that act on the central nervous system) are considered. This includes generally benign substances such as aspirin, coffee, alcohol, and tobacco as well as the dangerous hallucinogens such as LSD and mescaline. The chapter headings are as follows: 1) What is psychopharmacology?; 2) When is a drug not a drug?; 3) Drugs, wakefulness and sleep; 4) Drugs, learning and memory; 5) A sober look at psychedelics; 6) Why drug effects vary; 7) Measuring mental illness with drugs; 8) Drugs, behavior and the brain; 9) Drugs in daily life; and 10) In conclusion. The author is a psychologist who is writing for the intelligent layman.

390. Cockett, R. **Drug Abuse and Personality in Young Offenders.** New York, Appleton-Century-Crofts; London, Butterworths, 1971. 166p. bibliog. index. $9.65pa. ISBN 0-407-15470-1.

This publication is based on a study of over 2,500 young people who have been involved in drug abuse. The author, who is a prison psychologist in Great Britain, studied the personalities of the young offenders in order to find any possible correlation between drug use and crime. He presents a great deal of evidence on such matters as the social setting of drug abuse, its history, its connection with social relationships and adjustment, and the psychological characteristics of young people who use drugs. The material is presented in rather technical language, although the results can be interpreted by the general reader.

The results of the study show several things. For the most part, delinquency began before drug taking, so no obvious causal connection can be seen between the two. The age at which drug-taking began was found to be significant: those who started earliest became the most heavily involved. About 15½ years of age was the average for the heavily involved user. Most users began with cannabis or amphetamine drugs. As to whether or not marihuana use led to the use of other drugs, the research showed that 59 percent of those who began their drug use with marihuana progressed in some measure to multi-drug use. As for the personality of drug abusers, the psychiatric states most frequently noted were underlying depressive factors, anxiety and tension, and psychopathic and hedonistic types of condition. The researchers were able to identify to some extent certain personality elements that constitute vulnerability to drug abuse. These were what is popularity known as inadequacy or weakness of character. This work presents much good data that should interest social workers, physicians, prison workers, and psychologists in particular.

391. Cooperstock, Ruth. **Social Aspects of the Medical Use of Psychotropic Drugs.** Toronto, Addiction Research Foundation, 1974. 179p. (International Symposia on Alcohol and Drug Problems, No. 2.) $10.00. $6.50pa.

This volume is one of a series which presents papers given in 1973 at an International Symposium on Alcohol and Drug Research, co-sponsored by the Department of National Health and Welfare and the Alcoholism and Drug Addiction Research Foundation of Ontario, in association with the International Council on Alcohol and Addictions. The emphasis in this work is on the distribution, use, and regulation of prescription drugs of the psychotropic type (which are often abused). The drugs considered include amphetamines, barbiturates and other sedatives and hypnotics, antidepressants, and tranquillizers; one paper discusses alcohol use as a coping mechanism for psychic distress. Five papers discuss various aspects of physicians, involvement in the distribution and use of drugs; two deal with control of the pharmaceutical industry and the manufacture, distribution, and prescribing of psychotropic drugs; and others consider such things as economic and consumer aspects of prescription drug use, family patterns of use, research, and drug technology. The interaction of all these factors is considered. It is noteworthy that there has been an increased acceptance of the legal use of psychotropic drugs, and there is a growing interest in the problems that have resulted from their use. The population seems to believe that freedom from anxiety characterizes an adjusted life, and avoiding anxiety has become a goal.

392. Council of Europe. European Public Health Committee. **Public Health Implications of Recent Developments in Drug Dependence.** Report prepared by S. Kaymakçalan (Turkey), K. Kryspin-Exner (Austria), and A. Teigen (Norway). presented by P. Kielholz (Switzerland). Strasbourg, 1970. 132p. bibliog. $6.50pa.

The information presented in this report is based on a study made in 1969. The results are given in four sections: 1) A general view of the drug situation, 2) A summary of the situation in all member countries and Finland, 3) Observations made by the study group, and 4) Recommendations.

Six trends were discernible: 1) a growing incidence in young people, 2) new patterns in drug dependence (e.g., central stimulants, administered intravenously), 3) the rapid increase of the well-known drugs in other age groups (hypnotics, anti-pyretic analgesics, and central stimulants), 4) a rising frequency of multiple dependence, 5) an increasing number of women dependents, and 6) a rapidly increasing problem of alcoholism. Among othér observations: the unreported cases of drug dependency were felt to be high; admission to hospitals is limited because of lack of space; and rehabilitation is promoted extensively in the United Kingdom and Sweden. Control measures prevail in all the countries concerned. The publication presents a good general view.

393. Cull, John G., and Richard E. Hardy, eds. **Types of Drug Abusers and Their Abuses.** Springfield, Ill., Charles C. Thomas, 1974. 209p. bibliog. index. $8.95. LC 73-9651. ISBN 0-398-02928-8.

This book is made up of 12 chapters by different contributors; each contributor has had unusual experiences in the drug abuse field and each has knowledge about special populations and their problems. The characteristics of different types of addicts are described in separate chapters: 1) The medical profession addict, 2) The pain prone addict, 3) Opiate addiction, 4) Drug use in the military service, 5) The ex-addict and his alternate subcultures, 6) The hippie drug abuser, 7) The street and the southern addict, 8) The abusers of stimulants and depressants, 9) The marijuana abuser and the abuser of psychedelic-hallucinogens, 10) The alcohol abuser, 11) The abuser of tobacco. In addition, there is a section on the language of the drug abuser.

The editors are experienced rehabilitation psychologists and the contributors are fairly well-known experts. The book is intended primarily for professional practitioners, but is of interest to anyone curious about the characteristics of drug abusers.

394. Dai, Bingham. **Opium Addiction in Chicago**. Reprinted with the following additions: Introductory essay by Lois B. De Fleur, "Chicago Addiction in Contemporary Perspective"; new Preface by the author; index. Montclair, N.J., Patterson Smith, 1970. 212p. index. (Patterson Smith Reprint Series in Criminology, Law Enforcement, and Social Problems). $9.00. LC 72-124503. ISBN 0-87585-126-6.

This classic study, originally published in 1937, was one of the earliest to focus attention on the sociological and social-psychological aspects of drug addiction. It investigated a number of problems, first tracing the origin and spread of opium addiction in the United States (and in Chicago) as a cultural complex. The study then assessed the general characteristics of the addict population as it existed in Chicago. In order to understand how opium addiction spread, the author focused on the social and cultural situations within which this occurred. Lastly, intensive interviews were conducted with selected addicts, seeking insights into the nature of their personality problems and emotional reaction patterns.

The preliminary sections of this edition make a number of comparisons between what was found in the 1930s and the drug abuse situation today. Perhaps the most noteworthy difference is that drug abuse is more and more becoming a problem of the young. Other characteristics that have changed are race and nationality. The majority of Chicago's addicts of the 1930s were members of the white majority (although the number of Negro and Chinese addicts was disproportionately large). Now there is a predominance of minority offenders. In addition, there seem to be proportionately fewer females involved in addiction now than in the '30s. As might be supposed, the link between addiction and crime is now more firmly established. In general, addiction is a problem of larger scope now than formerly. What has not changed is that the addict's troubles stem mainly from his relation with other people and from his failure to meet the requirements made of him as a member of society.

395. Einstein, Stanley. **The Use and Misuse of Drugs: A Social Dilemma.** Belmont, Calif., Wadsworth Publishing Co., Inc., 1970. 86p. bibliog. index. $1.25pa. LC 79-107371.

This small book, part of the series called "Basic Concepts in Health Science," consists of eight chapters: 1) Introduction; 2) Drugs: problems, considerations, and definitions; 3) Drug users: their characteristics, patterns of drug use, and behavior; 4) Drugs: types, uses, and effects; 5) Misuse of drugs and the community's response; 6) Treatment and legal control of drug use; 7) Economics of drug use and misuse; and 8) Further considerations. The author, who is Executive Director and founder of the Institute for the Study of Drug Addiction in New York City, says his guiding philosophy is 1) that alcoholism and drug addiction are but two of a number of behaviors that are tied together generically (drug addiction, gambling, smoking, overeating, alcoholism), and 2) that the most meaningful way to view any of these problems is by use of an epidemiological frame of reference: host, agent, environment, and their interactions. He concludes that the state of scientific knowledge, the skill of caretaker staffs, community attitudes and values, the types and goals of treatment programs, education and training, public policy, and economics must be understood before any large-scale success is experienced in the treatment of drug addiction. Also, the philosophy of progress through chemistry must be kept in mind. And lastly, we must come to terms with the fact that at present our society reinforces rather than inhibits the misuse of drugs.

396. Evans, Wayne O., and Nathan S. Kline, eds. **Psychotropic Drugs in the Year 2000: Use by Normal Humans.** Springfield, Ill., Charles C. Thomas, 1971. 168p. bibliog. index. $7.75. LC 74-151866.

This work was published under the imprimatur of the American College of Neuropsychopharmacology; this group originally conceived its mission to be the consideration of using chemicals to enhance the quality of human life and the review of the effects of these chemicals when prescribed to the nonpsychotic. Therefore, this book is not directed specifically to the problem of drug abuse. Instead, it shows a sample of some of the kinds of drugs that we will be capable of producing by the year 2000. Both the technical capacity and the possible social effects are considered. The last chapter, "Drugs and Society in the Year 2000," is a panel discussion by such noted authorities as anthropoligist Ashley Montagu; John Campbell, editor of *Analog Science Fiction*; Arthur Koestler, lecturer and author; and John Oliver of the federal bench. The types of drugs considered in the book are new intoxicants, chemical aphrodisiacs, psychotropic drugs in gerontological practice, drugs to manipulate life patterns, psychedelic LSD research, and psychedelics used with criminals.

This is an interesting book on a significant topic. The contributions by the panel of experts are especially worth reading. They urge many cautions in the matter of drug use.

397. Fiddle, Seymour. **Portraits from a Shooting Gallery: Life Styles from the Drug Addict World.** New York, Harper and Row, 1967. 360p. index. $7.50. LC 67-13711.

The author is a sociologist with vast experience in ghetto areas. The ideology for this book grew out of a personal confrontation with the drug addict culture at Exodus House in New York City. The book presents first-hand accounts of addicts' lives taken from tape recordings as the author talked with them. Key addict life styles are revealed, anxieties are exposed, and the cycles of need, exploitation, and self-deception are unfolded.

The accounts are fascinating and well presented, and the analyses are clear. The book is of considerable importance for those who care about or who deal with addicts.

The author thinks that there are a number of reasons for the prevalence and growth of the drug problem. He makes a plea that the necessary research be done in the pharmacological, biological, psychological, and social science areas to alleviate the situation.

398. Gable, Fred B. **Psychosocial Pharmacy: The Synthetic Society**. Philadelphia, Lea and Febiger, 1974. 247p. bibliog. $6.00. LC 73-20169. ISBN 0-8121-0478-1.

This book is primarily about pharmacy as a profession at the present time. Pointing out how the role of the pharmacist has increasingly become one of human service, it includes the following chapters: 1) Drugs and society, 2) Addiction and child abuse, 3) Alcoholism, 4) Marijuana, 5) Sexuality, 6) Pharmacist as personal consultant, 7) Contraception and birth control, 8) Terminal patient, and 9) Why drug dependence? A large part of the pharmacist's role is obviously concerned with problems of drug dependence. The material is well presented and suitable for use in courses of study in professional schools as professionals become more socially conscious.

399. Goldberg, L., and F. Hoffmeister. **Psychic Dependence: Definition, Assessment in Animals and Man, Theoretical and Clinical Implications.** New York, Springer-Verlag, 1973. 244p. illus. bibliog. index. (Bayer-Symposium 4). $22.40. LC 73-13497. ISBN 3-540-06478-8.

This work presents papers given at a symposium held at Grosse Ledder near Cologne, Germany, September 27 - October 1, 1972. The papers deal with the factors that underlie the development of psychic dependence. Psychic dependence is defined, or redefined, and the social consequences of the abuse of psychic dependence-producing drugs are discussed, with special emphasis on the dangers to public health in general. The papers give much attention to animal models for the prediction of a drug's capacity to produce psychic dependence in man. Ethical and legal implications of using human clinical trials of dependency producing drugs are considered. Transcripts of the discussions that followed each paper are included.

400. Goode, Erich. **The Drug Phenomenon: Social Aspects of Drug Taking.** Indianapolis, Bobbs-Merrill Co., Inc., 1973. 63p. bibliog. $1.25. LC 73-920. ISBN 0-672-61326-3.

The author points out that there is no broad consensus about drug use. Some view it as a great evil, while those at the other extreme think that it does no harm, that it enhances and stimulates creativity. There are experts on both sides—indeed, on all sides, since every aspect of drug use is controversial. This small book attempts to sort it all out. The following topics are treated: 1) The drug controversy, 2) What is a drug?, 3) Introduction to some drugs and their effects, 4) Turning on, 5) Drug use as deviant behavior, and 6) The social context of drug use.

The author does not entirely "sort it all out." He concludes that the outcome of drug use is highly variable and depends somewhat on the customs of those who use drugs.

401. Goode, Erich. **Drugs in American Society**. New York, Alfred A. Knopf, Inc., 1972. 260p. bibliog. index. $2.95pa. LC 73-179619. ISBN 0-394-31323-2.

The author, a sociologist, treats drug abuse as a sociological problem. The following chapter headings are used: 1) A sociological perspective on drugs and drug use, 2) Marijuana, 3) The marijuana controversy, 4) The psychedelics, or hallucinogens, 5) Stimulants and depressants, 6) Heroin and the narcotics, 7) Drugs and the law, 8) Concluding remarks. There is an appendix entitled "Does marijuana lead to dangerous drugs?"

The inclusion of many accounts by drug addicts makes the work readable. A rather hard sell for the legalization, or at least decriminalization, of marijuana pervades the work.

402. Gould, Leroy C., Andrew L. Walker, Lansing E. Crane, and Charles W. Lidz. **Connections: Notes from the Heroin World.** New Haven, Yale University Press, 1974. 236p. bibliog. $8.95. LC 73-86896. ISBN 0-300-01731-6.

The authors' concern was to present information about the heroin problem in such a way that the reader could form his own impressions and conclusions. The book describes, rather than analyzes, the events that made up the heroin problem in the late 1960s and early 1970s. A number of different styles were used in writing the volume, and each chapter was intended to be an experiment in the presentation of data. In general, the authors used the same vocabulary and grammar that the subjects used. The authors, three sociologists and one lawyer, studied the drug scene for four years. They describe how people are introduced to heroin and street life, the problems of law enforcement, and treatment methods. Three aspects of treatment are taken up; screening and evaluation, methadone maintenance, and a residential therapeutic community.

403. Hammond, Kenneth R., and C. R. B. Joyce, eds. **Psychoactive Drugs and Social Judgment: Theory and Research.** New York, John Wiley & Sons, 1975. 278p. illus. bibliog. $16.95. LC 75-16136. ISBN 0-471-34728-0.

These papers by various experts investigate the effects of psychoactive drugs on sociopsychological behavior, analyzing the findings of investigations. The work is in three parts. The first, "Problem: Theory: Method," reviews the literature of psychoactive drugs and behavior and offers a general overview of the results of research to date. This part considers the therapeutic use of psychoactive drugs and describes the theory and methods intrinsic to social judgment theory. Part two, "Empirical Studies," addresses the question of whether the biochemical changes produced in the nervous system by some well-known psychoactive drugs lead to changes that affect social judgment. Conclusions are drawn about the extent to which a person is a danger to himself and others. In part three, "New Directions," two studies directly address the matter of cognitive control. The first of these reports on new methods for providing cognitively oriented feedback, and the effect of such feedback on cognitive control. The second analyzes the concept of cognitive control, studying methadone's effects on judgment. A third chapter illustrates the role of cognitive control in physicians' judgments of the effect of drugs in clinical trials.

Concluding observations are made concerning possible directions of new research on the subject. It is suggested that we still need to know how drugs influence judgments *of* the drugged, *about* the drugged, and arising from the *interaction* of the drugged with others. The book is highly technical, suitable for graduate students and professionals in psychology, psychiatry, clinical pharmacology, psychiatric nursing, and social work.

404. Hochman, Joel Simon. **Marijuana and Social Evolution . . .** Englewood Cliffs, N.J., Prentice-Hall, Inc., 1972. 184p. bibliog. index. $5.95 LC 72-8952. ISBN 0-13-556217-1; 0-13-556209-0pa.

The author's point of view is that marijuana has replaced alcohol as the "in" drug among young people to regulate human emotions. This book attempts to give more information on the effects of the drug within the context of society. The conclusions are based on surveys, interviews, and literature sources.

405. Imlah, Norman. **Drugs in Modern Society**. Princeton, N.J., Auerbach Publishers, Inc., 1971. 151p. index. $7.95. LC 78-141791. ISBN 0-87769-063-4.

The author of this work, who is a psychiatrist, refers frequently to the two-sided problem of drug use: there are patients who need to take drugs prescribed by physicians and who won't take them, and there are those who take drugs and should not. Paradoxically, these are often the same drugs or similar ones. Learning this confuses many young people. The author feels that physicians have not explained such matters well and have relied on patients' unquestioning willingness to follow their dictates.

The book examines the problems of drugs and their effects upon the mind and behavior, attempting to distinguish between the healthy use of drugs and the unhealthy, and to educate the public. The following chapters are presented: 1) Getting the perspective, 2) The control and movement of drugs, 3) Patterns of drug-taking, 4) Drugs and their properties, 5) Who becomes addicted?, 6) Methods of treatment, 7) Toward an informed public opinion, 8) Current measures, and 9) Future prospects.

Chapter 4 is of particular interest because it creates five categories of drugs of abuse, from the most dangerous to the least. Those of widespread use and those with strongly addictive properties are considered the most dangerous. Each drug is discussed in detail. Classified by the author as most dangerous are opium, heroin, amphetamines, phenmetrazine, barbiturates, LSD, cannabis, and alcohol. The least dangerous are the tranquilizers and antidepressants.

In Dr. Imlah's view, we should recognize that, because of personal deficiencies and social pressures, it is inevitable that the more vulnerable will always resort to drugs. Their reliance on this solution depends on the availability of drugs more than anything else. He seems to believe in a system of airtight international drug control.

406. Jacobson, Richard, and Norman E. Zinberg. **The Social Basis of Drug Abuse Prevention.** Washington, Drug Abuse Council, Inc., 1975. 123p. $1.25.

This is the report of a study of the social and personal factors that initiate the abuse of illicit drugs and that govern the personal control of their use. Interviews were the basis for the study, and the text is heavily illustrated with exceprts from them. Appended materials give details of the methods used, a sample interview, and a summary of interviews.

407. Johnson, Bruce D. **Marihuana Users and Drug Subcultures.** New York, John Wiley and Sons, 1973. 290p. bibliog. index. $12.95. LC 72-8786. ISBN 0-471-44623-8.

This book is based on the author's Columbia University thesis, presented under the title *Social Determinants of the Use of Dangerous Drugs by College Students*. The work is addressed to students, teachers, lawmakers, school administrators, and laymen interested in the causes of drug use and to professional researchers and sociologists interested in the sociology of deviance. Data were collected from students by means of a questionnaire. The author found that, by using such social variables as gender, cigarette use, religious participation, political orientation, and friendships, he could predict accurately who would use marihuana. He also showed that drug selling involved one with the drug subculture more than did the use of marihuana. The author further contends that this is because of present laws which make it impossible to obtain marihuana without becoming involved with the illegal drug trade. Consequently a plea is made for the liberalization of drug laws. Regardless of whether one agrees with Dr. Johnson's solution to drug problems, the book contains much data of significance.

408. Josephson, Eric, and Eleanor E. Carroll, eds. **Drug Use: Epidemiological and Sociological Approaches.** Washington, Hemisphere Publishing Corp.; distr. New York, Halsted Press, a division of John Wiley and Sons, Inc., 1974. 381p. bibliog. index. $13.50. LC 74-19056. ISBN 0-470-45082-7.

These are the papers of an international conference on the epidemiology of drug use held in San Juan, Puerto Rico, February 12-14, 1973. The aim of the conference was to produce state-of-the-art reports on the subject and to find directions for future research. Most of the papers report on original research and present never-before-published data. Titles of the papers are as follows: 1) Drug abuse: a conceptual analysis and overview of the current situation; 2) Addiction, dependency, abuse, or use: which are we studying with epidemiology?; 3) The epidemiology of narcotic addiction in the United Kingdom; 4) Some epidemiological considerations of onset of opiate use in the United States; 5) Is the onset of narcotic addiction among treated patients in the United States really declining?; 6) Epidemiology of heroin addiction in the 1970s: new opportunities and responsibilities; 7) Some aspects of careers of chronic heroin users; 8) Issues in the evaluation of heroin treatment; 9) Methodological considerations for a model reporting system of drug deaths; 10) Trends in adolescent marijuana use; 11) Interpersonal influences on adolescent illegal drug use; 12) Patterns of college student drug use and lifestyles; 13) The epidemiology of hallucinogenic drug use; 14) The epidemiology of stimulant abuse; 15) An overview of psychotherapeutic drug use in the United States. It is noteworthy that the book is much concerned with conceptual and methodological issues. The material presented will be of most value to drug abuse workers from the fields of sociology, epidemiology, public health, psychology, and psychiatry. Also it can be used as a textbook. The papers, written by experts and presented on a scholarly level, are of high quality.

409. Krystal, Henry, and Herbert A. Raskin. **Drug Dependence: Aspects of Ego Function.** Detroit, Wayne University Press, 1970. 127p. bibliog. index. $5.95. LC 76-121920. ISBN 0-8143-1419-8.

The authors of the work are practicing psychoanalysts who have had considerable clinical experience with drug dependent individuals. The book is a study of the personality disturbances that lead to the need for drugs, with some attention given to techniques that may be more effective in the treatment of addicted persons. Although the book is of most interest to mental health personnel such as psychiatrists, psychologists, social workers, sociologists, and counselors, it is not too difficult for the average educated reader. It provides many insights into the personalities of drug dependent persons.

410. Light, Patricia K. **Let the Children Speak: A Psychological Study of Young Teenagers and Drugs.** Lexington, Mass., D. C. Heath and Co., 1975. 95p. bibliog. LC 74-313 ISBN 0-669-92676-0.

The author's work as a consulting psychologist enabled her to study young teenagers, and this book resulted from that opportunity. The study, based on eight children (five drug users and three nonusers), covers the development of drug-taking and the variables associated with use or nonuse. The following chapters are presented: 1) Introduction, 2) Perspective on student drug use, 3) Gathering the data, 4) The children speak, 5) Findings, and 6) Discussion.

What emerges from the study is that, although peer group influence is important, young people use drugs for extraordinarily diverse reasons—some situational, some accidental, some personal. The use of marijuana is no longer limited to one subcategory of youth. The author concludes that for some youngsters using drugs is a shield against the anxiety problems that growing up generates. This use often leads to abusing drugs in a downhill spiral of self-defeating behavior. For many others, however, drug-taking is little different from the "few Saturday night beers" of a generation ago.

411. Malcolm, Andrew I. **The Pursuit of Intoxication.** New York, Washington Square Press Pocket Books, 1971. 276p. bibliog. index. $1.25 LC 70-142249. ISBN 0-671-48104-5.

This book, written by a psychiatrist with the Addiction Research Foundation in Toronto, is a historical and scientific sourcebook on the use of psychoactive drugs. The author examines the use of the substances in many societies throughout history, presenting the material under five broad categories. The first of these is religion, since this seems to have been the basis of the earliest use. Part two takes up medical aspects. Part three deals with endurance, or the use of drugs in war and sports. Part four considers intoxicating substances that can be used to incapacitate or kill; this includes suicide, murder, chemical warfare, and brainwashing. Part five deals with the drugs that have commonly been used in the pursuit of pleasure or recreation.

The material is well presented and for the most part is not controversial. However, the author presents a few theories of his own, the most important being his theory of chemical conversion. This is the hypothesis that certain vulnerable users of mind-altering drugs experience a fixation of their beliefs, usually an alienation, and that this condition tends to be very persistent, if not irreversible. It is a process similar to brainwashing.

412. Malikin, David. **Social Disability: Alcoholism, Drug Addiction, Crime and Social Disadvantage.** New York, New York University Press, 1973. 266p. bibliog. $9.75. LC 72-96468. ISBN 0-8147-5361-2.

This is a scholarly dissertation on each of four social disabilities: alcoholism, drug addiction, crime, and social disadvantage. Included also are four case histories and a review of the literature, which is mainly from the fields of psychology, social work, and rehabilitation. Rehabilitation is stressed throughout, as is the need for immediate attention to the problems of social disability. Writers' and journalists' opinions have been included, and several chapters were written by individuals engaged in various aspects of social work.

The book is easy to read and the case histories interesting. Whether they can be considered typical and whether they reveal any new insights is open to question, but they do show the plight of unfortunate individuals.

413. Martindale, Don, and Edith Martindale. **The Social Dimensions of Mental Illness, Alcoholism, and Drug Dependence.** Westport, Conn., Greenwood Publishing Co., 1971. 330p. bibliog. index. $12.50. (Contributions in Sociology, No. 9). LC 72-133499. ISBN 0-8371-5175-9.

This sociological study examines the physiological, psychological, and social stresses that contribute to mental illness, alcoholism, and drug dependence. The authors' theory is that these illnesses represent a failure of socialization in the development process. They cite evidence that the more successful trends in therapy attack the individual's psychology and at the same time transform the social context in which he is operating into an ego-sustaining therapeutic community. Chapter headings are as follows: 1) Contours of the contemporary problem of mental illness; 2) Mental illness and the law; 3) The trauma of commitment to the primary group; 4) Formal and informal organization of the mental hospital; 5) The career of the mental patient; 6) Mental disorders, treatment methods, and the therapeutic community; 7) Return to the community; 8) Alcoholism; 9) Drug dependence; 10) Toward an integrated theory.

414. Ray, Oakley S. **Drugs, Society, and Human Behavior.** St. Louis, C. V. Mosby Co., 1972. 299p. bibliog. index. $6.50. ISBN 0-8016-4093-8.

Written primarily as a text for college students, this book presents material on the pharmacology, psychology, and social history of drugs. It points out what psychoactive drugs do, how they do it, who uses them, and why. The author, a professor of psychology, was advised by a number of authorities regarding his presentation. The following chapters are included: 1) Introduction, 2) Fundamentals, 3) The nondrug drugs, 4) Psychotherapeutic drugs—their use and misuse, 5) The narcotic drugs, 6) The phantasticants, and 7) Conclusion.

The book is somewhat difficult to read and understand, and much technical material is included. However, a great many facts are presented, and if the reader is willing to study the text he can learn a great deal.

415. Sheehy, Gail. **Speed Is of the Essence**. New York, Pocket Books, 1971. 166p. $0.95pa. ISBN 0-671-77283-X.

This book, written by a journalist, explores three social concerns: drugs, revolution, and personal liberation. The stories presented appeared in *New York* magazine during an 18-month period beginning in 1969. The author calls the stories "sidewalk portraits drawn at a particular time on a particular sidewalk when the subjects were high-lighted by crisis." The largest section of the book does not highlight drug abuse; personal liberation gets the most attention. The only drug discussed at any length is "speed" (amphetamines), and it is pictured as the ultimate in dangerous drugs of abuse. While this viewpoint seems to exist in certain circles, and the drug is subject to considerable abuse, it does not appear to be more dangerous than most drugs of abuse. However, the theme of the book is "speed," used to describe some people's lives today as well as the drug, so perhaps the emphasis on amphetamines is suitable. Basically, the author is making a plea for tolerance and acceptance of the life style and views of groups similar to the hippies before the movement degenerated.

416. Smith, David E., and George R. Gay, eds. **"It's So Good, Don't Even Try It Once": Heroin in Perspective**. Englewood Cliffs, N.J., Prentice-Hall, Inc., 1972. bibliog. 208p. $4.95. LC 72-3966. ISBN 0-13-506592-5; 0-13-506584-4pa.

This editors of this collection of writings have been connected with the Haight Ashbury Free Clinic and have worked with several thousand heroin addicts in a variety of programs. Covering all aspects of heroin abuse, the authors attempt to define the problem and suggest a solution. They place the blame on the social-political system of our country, suggesting that we make changes in our national priorities. The drug addiction problem is presented clearly enough, but to this reviewer the solution leaves much to be desired. There really is no easy solution, and what is suggested in the book is vague and general, restating the same old overworked phrases and notions that have been offered as solutions for all social problems.

417. Speck, Ross V., and others. **The New Families: Youth, Communes, and the Politics of Drugs**. New York, Basic Books, 1972. 190p. index. $6.95. LC 78-174825. ISBN 0-465-05018-2.

The author of this book, a psychiatrist, visited youth communes along with a team of psychiatrists, psychologists, and anthropologists, in an effort to understand them and what their members were achieving. The book describes the daily activities of the communal life, the sexual patterns, the role of women, household arrangements, and especially the use of drugs, which seemed to be the main bond between the members of the groups. The author is quite tolerant of drug abuse by young people and believes that the new life styles and new values are preparing for the future of our world in a basic new humanistic way. He thinks that acceptance of their ideas may even be necessary for survival.

The youth groups were studied from 1966 to 1969. At the present time it does not appear that the youths and their new life styles, communes, and the like have had as much influence as the author felt they would. However, the scene as presented and the point of view expressed probably were "relevant" at the time of the study.

The reviewer cannot resist a comment on the role of the women as the book (probably accurately) reports it. The girls were unbelievably passive, nonassertive, and dependent. The women's liberation movement could find no comfort here!

418. Stimson, Gerry V. **Heroin and Behavior: Diversity among Addicts Attending London Clinics.** New York, Halsted Press, a division of John Wiley and Sons, 1973. bibliog. index. $11.50. LC 73-174. ISBN 0-470-82530-8.

There has been a feeling that the British system of prescribing heroin to addicts on a controlled basis in clinics could be validly applied in other countries. This book presents research on behavior patterns among addicts in London clinics. The common stereotype of the addict did not fit all the individuals studied. It was found that there were four types classified by behavior patterns. The first, called the Stables, were characterized by a high degree of employment with legitimate income, low degree of criminal activity, and a low degree of involvement with other addicts. They also had the most control over their drug use and were relatively conventional in their behavior and appearance. The second group, the Junkies, were opposites of the Stables in almost all respects. The third group, the Loners, were like the Junkies in that they were unemployed, but they did not support themselves by stealing. They seemed to be cut off from other addicts and also from the conventional world. The last group, the Two-Worlders, had a high degree of employment but also had a high degree of criminal activity. In addition, they had a high level of contact with other addicts. It is suggested that a different method of treatment for each of the four groups might be most effective.

419. U.S. National Institute on Drug Abuse. **Effects of Labeling the "Drug Abuser": An Inquiry.** By Jay R. Williams. Washington, GPO, 1976. 39p. bibliog. (DHEW Publication No. (ADM) 76-320; National Institute on Drug Abuse Research Monograph Series. No. 6). For sale by the National Technical Information Service, Springfield, Va. 22161. $4.00pa.; microfiche $2.25. S/N PB 249-092. LC 76-3101.

The original purpose of the study upon which this report is based was to attempt to determine whether arrest or otherwise labeling a person a "drug abuser" caused increased alienation. Since attitudes have been changing about marihuana use, it was decided this was not a serious problem, and that a large-scale study would not be feasible. However, the problem is of continuing interest, so this publication was produced.

The section headings are as follows: 1) Introduction, 2) Drug abuse as a crime, 3) The labeling perspective, 4) The labeling process and self-concept, 5) Resisting labeling, 6) The effect of apprehension, 7) Self-concept antecedent to apprehension, 8) Self-concept antecedent to drug abuse, 9) Drug abuse, 10) Drug abuse and drug laws, 11) Drug abuse, apprehension, self-concept and subsequent behavior, and 12) Concluding remarks. A 14-page bibliography is included.

The results of the study were not altogether conclusive. Many factors were found to neutralize the labeling process. The one-time or experimental drug user, however, was found to lose more self-esteem upon apprehension than a user committed to an ideology that views drug abuse positively.

420. U.S. National Institute on Drug Abuse. **Recent Surveys of Nonmedical Drug Use: a Compendium of Abstracts.** By William A. Glenn and Louise G. Richards. Washington, GPO, 1974. 101p. bibliog. index. (DHEW Publication No. (ADM) 75-139).

This work is to some extent a continuation of two earlier publications (D. Berg, 1970. *Illicit Use of Dangerous Drugs in the United States: a Compilation of Studies, Surveys and Polls.* Washington, Bureau of Narcotics and Dangerous Drugs; and a 1972 edition with the same title by Berg and L. Broecker). In addition to the quantitative information, this 1974 compendium also examines methodological questions essential for interpreting and using the findings of surveys, and it summarizes the major patterns and trends they reveal. The following sections are included: 1) Introduction, 2) Developing the compendium, 3) A preview of survey terminology, 4) Summary and interpretation of findings, 5) Comments on survey methods, and 6) Cited references. There are seven appendices: A) Abstracts—Nationwide Surveys, B) Abstracts— Surveys of High School Populations, C) Abstracts—Survey of University Populations, D) Abstracts—Surveys of Other Populations, E) Master List, F) Author Index, and G) Index of Reports Containing Statistical Information on Characteristics Other Than Extent of Drug Abuse. The abstracts, which are presented in tabular fashion, make up the largest part of the publication.

421. Waldorf, Dan. **Careers in Dope**. Englewood Cliffs, N.J., Prentice-Hall, Inc., 1973. 186p. bibliog. index. $5.95. LC 72-13655. ISBN 0-13-114660-2.

The author of this work points out that his book does not deal with the horrors of drug abuse. Rather it is about the addict and his life at the hands of society, describing the addict and his "career in dope." It covers how the addict begins to use heroin and becomes addicted; how he supports himself and raises money to support his need; how he suffers at the hands of society; how he gets arrested and goes to jail or for treatment. Occasionally the addict gives up heroin and rises above the status society has demoted him to.

The data and the information in the book came mainly from interviews and a periodic check of records kept by treatment programs to show progress being made by individual addicts. All of the programs and addicts concerned were located in New York City.

The following is a list of the chapter headings: 1) Addiction as a career, 2) Becoming a heroin addict, 3) Supporting a habit, 4) It's not all getting high, 5) Going to treatment, 6) New York's big push, 7) Methadone maintenance, 8) Life without heroin, 9) Rock bottom, and 10) Women versus men. The book takes a more sympathetic view of addiction than is often found. The author is a sociologist who blames society's laws and behavior for the addicts's problems.

The last chapter, which discusses women addicts as compared to men, is noteworthy, containing material not frequently found. Women, the author concludes, have been more deterred by the criminalization of addiction than men, and far fewer women addicts exist.

422. Weil, Andrew. **The Natural Mind: A New Way of Looking at Drugs and the Higher Consciousness.** Boston, Houghton Mifflin Co., 1972. 229p. bibliog. index. $5.95. LC 76-189331. ISBN 0-395-13936-8.

This book was written by a physician who became interested in drugs while still a medical student in the 1960s. The viewpoint of this book is that one can use drugs of abuse to advantage as a path to heightened consciousness, but that this can better be achieved in other ways. Drug use should be only a temporary means to this end. The author thinks drugs are with us to stay and that we should not fight them but accept them and turn them into nonharmful if not beneficial forces. Dr. Weil is interested in the ritual use of drugs by Amazon tribes of South America and includes a chapter on this topic also.

The author cautions in his introduction that his views are unorthodox and revolutionary.

423. Wilder Smith, A. E. **The Drug Users: The Psychopharmacology of Turning On.** Wheaton, Ill., Harold Shaw Publishers, 1969. 294p. bibliog. index. $5.95. LC 73-96528.

This book is divided into two parts. The first, "The Drug Factor," discusses drugs in widespread use at the present time and their clinical effects. The second part, "The Environmental Factor," explores societal and religious patterns to find out why people feel the need for drug experience. The following chapters are presented: 1) Lysergic acid diethylamide-25: its pharmacology, 2) Clinical experiments with LSD, 3) Possible toxicity of and uses for LSD, 4) Properties of marijuana and hashish (cannabis drugs), 5) The tranquilizers, 6) The amphetamines, 7) The morphine drugs, 8) The human mind and mind-at-large, 9) Psychic phenomena, 10) Psychical structure of the human individual, 11) The importance of motivation, 12) Dr. Timothy Leary and psychedelic drugs, and 13) The implication of hallucinogenic drugs. The author is a pharmacologist and chemist. However, he feels that the answer to the drug abuse problem lies in Christian teachings, and he urges youth to accept the Christian challenge. Beside it, he says, the artificial challenge of drugs will pale.

424. Winick, Charles, ed. **Sociological Aspects of Drug Dependence.** Cleveland, Chemical Rubber Co., 1974. 327p. bibliog. index. $39.95. ISBN 0-87819-057-0.

This book, an overview of the trends, developments, concepts, research findings, and problems in the sociological aspects of drug dependence, offers chapters contributed by noted specialists. Material is presented in five sections: 1) Theory, 2) Education and mass communications, 3) Some dimensions of users and prevalence, 4) Treatment and resocialization of the drug dependent, and 5) Social costs. Among the subjects specifically dealt with are: career lives of drug dependent individuals, incidence and prevalence, factors relating to drug dependence in youths, the family of the drug user, occupational skills and life-styles of addicts, the therapeutic community, methadone maintenance, drug education, drug dependence among nurses, and the drug abuse-crime syndrome. Two chapters deal with alcoholism.

425. Woodley, Richard. **Dealer: Portrait of a Cocaine Merchant.** New York, Holt, Rinehart and Winston, 1971. 210p. $5.95. LC 79-155538. ISBN 0-03-086584-0.

This account, written by a journalist, is the story of the daily life of a cocaine dealer in Harlem. The author accompanied the dealer on his rounds and became well acquainted with the life, dreams, and philosophy of the hustler. The account is rather sympathetic to the dealer in spite of the many sordid details of his existence.

11. Production, Control, Public Policy, and Legal Factors

This large section contains numerous titles on legal matters, many of them critical of recent and past handling of drug control. One often-expressed view is that laws have been too restrictive. There has been much propaganda about the merits of legalizing, or at least decriminalizing, marihuana use, and comparisons are made between marihuana prohibition and alcohol prohibition. It is sometimes pointed out, however, that the repeal of prohibition did not end the alcohol problem, since alcohol is said to be the biggest drug abuse problem of all. There is much disagreement on the advisability of lessening restrictions on any drug use, even among experts and scientists. Attitudes, however, may be changing because of the relatively widespread use of marihuana.

The titles included in this section provide a good approach to the problems surrounding the production, control, public policy, and legal aspects of drug abuse. However, practical solutions to the problems are not so evident. In general, more permissive laws and policies than presently exist are advocated. Perhaps the most enlightened view is that social pressure will be more effective in controlling drug abuse than formal laws.

426. Bailey, F. Lee, and Henry B. Rothblatt. **Handling Narcotic and Drug Cases**. Rochester, N.Y., Lawyers Co-operative Publishing Co.; San Francisco, Bancroft-Whitney Co., 1972. 549p. index. $35.00. LC 72-84855.

The senior author of this work is a celebrated defense attorney known for defending such clients as Patty Hearst. Ths book is designed to prepare the defense attorney to defend his client in almost any kind of federal or state narcotics prosecution. There is nothing sensational or flamboyant about the presentation; it is a serious and well-documented book on law. There are chapters on the law of possession, sale, and importation of narcotics, with discussion of the Uniform Narcotic Drug Act and the Drug Abuse Prevention and Control Law. The book also deals with the exclusionary rule and its application to admissibility of evidence and confessions in drug prosecutions. There are discussions of drugs and simplified explanations of new chemical testing procedures. The useful appendices include a Directory of Narcotic Addiction Treatment Agencies in the U.S. and Aftercare Contract Agencies. Supplementary material has been issued to accompany the basic volume.

427. Bean, Philip. **The Social Control of Drugs**. New York, Halsted Press, a division of John Wiley and Sons, 1974. 198p. bilbiog. index. (Law in Society Series). $11.95. LC 74-1342. ISBN 0-470-06090-5.

This book, concerned with the sociology of law, attempts to fill some gaps in the sociological literature of drug use in Great Britain and, to some extent, in the United States. It offers a picture of the historical development and present operation of the control system. The book is in two parts, "The Control System," and "The Control System in Operation." The following chapters are included: 1) Introduction 2) Development of the control system, 3) The international control system up to 1970, 4) The British system up to 1945, 5) Major changes since 1945, 6) The drug takers 1920-1970, 7) The role of the medical professions, 8) Secondary aspects of change, and 9) An assessment of control. There are also some appended materials, such as a "Chronological Summary of Major Events in the Control of Drugs in England and Wales" and the "Number of Drugs Controlled under Dangerous Drugs Acts from 1921-1970." There is also an essay appended on the "Prevalence of Drug Taking and Its Relation to Crime" which reports little conclusive evidence one way or the other.

The author wants to see laws on drug taking as part of wider issues about law, sociology, and politics. He also suggests that the sociology of law is well placed to produce important insights into these areas and to concern itself with older questions of legitimate and illegitimate authority.

428. Blum, Richard H., and Associates. **The Dream Sellers: Perspectives on Drug Dealers.** San Francisco, Jossey-Bass, Inc., 1972. 384p. bibliog. index. $12.50. LC 79-184960. ISBN 0-87589-119-5.

The author and his associates have produced several books on various aspects of drug abuse. Focusing on the drug dealer and the phenomenon of drug distribution, the book explores the subject in considerable depth, as the contents will show: 1) A variegated population, 2) Evolution of dealing, 3) Dealing life and community, 4) Capsule case histories, 5) Psychological case studies, 6) Commentary on dealers, 7) Arrested and nonarrested dealers, 8) Active and inactive dealers, 9) Big dealers and Mafia dealers, 10) Pushers, 11) Sins of the father, 12) Violence, 13) Drugs in the budget, 14) A commune, 15) English dealers, 16) Phases of a ghetto career, 17) The social structure of a heroin copping community, 18) Dealers on a campus, 19) Dealers on another campus, 20) American collegian abroad, 21) Holy Rock Bible College, 22) College faculty, 23) Dealers in high school, 24) Dealers in junior high school, 25) Physicians, 26) Pharmacists, 27) Pharmaceutical salesmen, 28) Narcotics officers.

In spite of the comprehensive treatment, the reviewer could draw few conclusions from the book. It did appear, however, that individuals who have access to drugs but who also have strong commitments to their work or professions (such as pharmacists, physicians, pharmaceutical salesmen, and professors) were seldom involved in illicit drug dealing.

Other volumes to be prepared by the authors will present further research results on this subject.

429. Blum, Richard H., and Associates. **Drug Dealers–Taking Action.** San Francisco, Jossey-Bass Publishers, 1973. 312p. bibliog. index. $10.00 LC 76-187065. ISBN 0-87589-166-7.

This work is a companion volume to several others produced by the same group, whose aim is to provide information and perspective that will help improve present international drug activities and will be useful in planning new legislation and programs to reduce drug abuse problems. In this particular volume, concerned with drug traffic, the authors point out that policies need to be attuned to regional realities. Several chapters deal with international problems and look at the worldwide situation. There are four sections: 1) Traffic, 2) Policing, 3) After arrest, and 4) Policy.

Chapters cover the following specific topics: problems associated with drug-dealing; substances in illicit drugs; marijuana use, distribution, and control; international opiate traffic; considerations on law enforcement; the narcotics law in action: a college town; the narcotics law in action: a major city; juvenile detention centers; prisons; drug-dealing and the law; corrections and treatment; social response to drug problems; future research and policy action; responsibilities of the pharmaceutical industry; action in the schools; and taking action. The book ends with a plea for nations to share their successes in the hope of finding better solutions to this international problem.

430. Brown, Clinton C., and Charles Savage, eds. **The Drug Abuse Controversy.** Baltimore, National Educational Consultants, Inc., 1971. 270p. bibliog. $8.50. LC 77-185832. ISBN 0-87971-002-0.

This book is a collection of formal presentations made at a symposium held October 16, 1970. The speakers were psychiatrists, psychologists, sociologists, ministers, lawyers, and administrators who were familiar with some facet of the topic. They discussed the ways organized society could restrict, prevent, punish, prohibit, modify, alter, dissuade, and eliminate the growing practice of drug abuse. According to the preface, the "controversy" mentioned in the title refers to the differences of opinion between one group who uses drugs which are said to temper and restrict life's experiences and the other group which is vehement in its contention that individuals are suppressed by both law and tradition and seek enlightenment, liberation, and extended vision through drugs. The reviewer presumes that this is another way of identifying the "establishment" and the new, young, group of drug abusers. There is no mention of a group who does not use drugs or who use practically none. It should also be pointed out that most scientists hold the view that drugs do not give one "extended vision," hallucinations being a more accurate term. The book is perhaps noteworthy, however, for exploring a viewpoint that is sometimes presented. Topics covered are as follows: 1) Drugs and the law: a legal controversy, 2) Drugs and the individual: a controversy of ethics, 3) Drugs and the new order: a controversy of change, 4) Drugs and doctors: a treatment controversy, and 5) Drugs and conclusions: an unfinished answer.

431. Brown, James W., Roger Mazze, and Daniel Glaser. **Narcotics Knowledge and Nonsense: Programmed Disaster versus a Scientific Model.** Cambridge, Mass., Ballinger Publishing Co., 1974. 109p. bibliog. index. $11.00. LC 74-1237. ISBN 0-88410-016-2.

This book was written by social scientists who hold positions in American universities and whose concern is heroin abuse in the United States. Their viewpoint is that the heroin problem hinges on the prolonged attempt to control it by prohibitions and penalties, the failure to do adequate research and evaluation, and the lack of adequate financial support for such research. They offer five recommendations that they believe will give assistance to mature addicts: 1) Reclassify heroin use as a medical problem and declassify it as a criminal offense, 2) Provide methadone or heroin maintenance for all addicts who request it, 3) Expand evaluation and basic research on treatment programs, 4) Expand basic research on the causes and consequences of addiction, and 5) Consciously expand conventional life style opportunities for former addicts.

As can be seen from the above, the book is highly critical of the way the United States handles the drug abuse problem. Some of the criticism is possibly justified, but the authors offer little evidence to support their statement that "programmed disaster" has been planned. In addition, an overly simple view of the drug abuse problem is evidenced by such statements that "the first step toward control of drug abuse [should] be the decriminalization of the addict, thereby giving him the choice of either being drug-free or continuing the habit." Drug users do not have much "choice" after addiction sets in.

432. Bruun, Kettil, Lynn Pan, and Ingemar Rexed. **The Gentlemen's Club: International Control of Drugs and Alcohol.** Chicago and London, University of Chicago Press, 1975. 338p. bibliog. index. $12.50. LC 74-21343. ISBN 0-226-07777-2.

The material for this book was prepared under the auspices of the International Research Group on Drug Legislation and Programs. The viewpoint of the authors is that prejudiced pressure groups and egotistical national representatives have combined courteously to preclude effective international control of the growth, manufacture, export, and distribution of opium, heroin, cannabis, psychotropic drugs, and alcohol. Recommendations are offered to turn the gentlemen's club into an effective international instrument of social control. The presentation is in several parts as follows: 1) Perspectives from the past, 2) The system, 3) Case studies, and 4) A choice of futures. Much useful information is included about the national and international organizations that have been involved with narcotics and drug control.

433. Chein, Isidor, Donald L. Gerard, Robert S. Lee, and Eva Rosenfeld. **The Road to H: Narcotics, Delinquency, and Social Policy.** New York, Basic Books, Inc., 1964. 482p. index. $12.50. LC 63-17342.

This is a report on studies that attempt to show how and why addiction happens and what, if anything, should be done about it. The bulk of the book is based on studies carried out at the Research Center for Human Relations of New York University with assistance from grants made by the National Institute of Mental Health. An interdisciplinary team of researchers concentrated mainly on 16- to 20-year-old male drug users in New York City. Large amounts of data are presented on the neighborhood distribution of juvenile drug use; the familial, social, economic, and cultural influences on the users; and the personality characteristics of addicts. Law enforcement efforts and resources for rehabilitation and treatment are considered.

The book is in two parts; the first deals with the "Epidemiology of Drug Use," the second with "What To Do." Also included are several appendices, such as a copy of the questionnaire used, summary tables, and various notes on how the studies were conducted.

The book is aimed at those who are seriously concerned with the drug abuse problem, such as lawmakers, behavioral scientists, police officers, social case workers, psychiatrists, personnel of correctional institutions, and social agencies.

The volume records much valuable and interesting information. The ideas about treatment and prevention, however, offer nothing new, unusual, or perhaps even convincing—just that society should provide a multipronged program of special services. A detailed outline of such a program, though, is beyond the scope of the book.

434. Cuskey, Walter R., Arnold William Klein, and William Krasner. **Drug-Trip Abroad: American Drug-Refugees in Amsterdam and London.** Philadelphia, University of Pennsylvania Press, 1972. 205p. bibliog. $6.95 LC 73-182497. ISBN 0-8122-7653-1.

The treatment of drug addicts in the United States is contrasted with treatment in Great Britain and Holland. The American system is depicted as harsh, the British permissive (although the clinic system provides very strict controls), and that of Amsterdam lenient. Although the addicts themselves prefer the foreign systems, the authors suggest that the Dutch are rather naive about the physiological effects of drug use, thinking it does no harm as they use largely "soft drugs"; and the British almost never effect cures or get to the roots of the problems of the addicts, since they merely maintain them.

A great many American drug abusers have fled to Europe from the United States, and this book contains many case histories and testimonies of these individuals who seem to have found a refuge from the American police. Obviously, addicts are far more inclined to seek refuge than to seek cures.

435. Danaceau, Paul. **Pot Luck in Texas: Changing a Marijuana Law.** Washington, Drug Abuse Council, Inc., 1974. 70p. $1.25pa.

Written by a journalist, this is an account of the political and legislative history of changing the marijuana possession law in Texas. Prior to the 1973 change, Texas had the most severe law in the country. The new law, incidentally, did not make sweeping changes, but limited its changes to those already made by other states. The author takes the view that it was unfortunate that the political climate was not ready for decriminalization.

436. Drug Abuse Institute for Trial Court Judges. **Proceedings. Vol. 1, General Sessions. Vol. 2, Small Group Discussions.** San Diego, Calif., Judicial Council of California, 1972. 2v.

These volumes present the papers and discussions (somewhat abridged and edited) of a meeting of June 22-24, 1972. The purpose of the meeting was to make available to California judges the most current medical, social, and legal information on narcotics, and to improve the administration of justice in cases involving drug abusers. At the outset, physicians furnished much background information, then legal problems were presented. The reports are interesting in that they present a practical point of view on how offenders can be dealt with.

437. **Drug Abuse Law Review.** New York, Clark Boardman Co., Ltd., 1971-1973. 2v. $32.50/v. ISBN 0-87632-045-0 (v.1); 0-87632-096-5 (v.2).

This series attempted to collect the best periodical writing on the legal aspects of narcotic drug abuse, presenting in each volume about 30 articles from about 25 leading legal and related periodicals. Some of the topics covered were the debate over marijuana, the legislative approach to drug control, the British approach, issues in drug prosecutions, treatment modalities, getting the addict to treatment, and legal issues in treatment. Evidently the series ceased publication with volume 2 in 1973.

438. Duster, Troy. **The Legislation of Morality: Law, Drugs, and Moral Judgment.** New York, The Free Press, a division of the Macmillan Co., 1970. 274p. bibliog. index. $6.95. LC 72-80469.

This book examines the connection between laws and morals by tracing the history and evolution of narcotic laws. The author cites many documents to support his view that narcotics morality was a direct consequence of legal change. The traditional idea is opposite to this—namely, that morality is followed by its codification in law. The author, who is a sociologist, believes his theory also holds for other current issues and problems.

It is hoped that the volume contributes to both social science theory and to policy decision on reform of narcotics legislation and the treatment of addicts. The study should interest sociologists, political scientists, psychologists, lawyers, legislators, and those interested in the narcotics problem.

439. Edwards, Carl N. **Drug Dependence: Social Regulation and Treatment Alternatives.** With a Foreword by The Honorable Franklin N. Flaschner. Published in association with John A. Calhoun and the Justice Resource Institute. New York, Jason Aronson, 1974. 206p. bibliog. index. $10.00. LC 73-17739. ISBN 0-87668-117-8.

First published in 1973 under the title *Justice Administration and Drug Dependence: Issues and Alternatives*, this work examines the issues involving drug abuse and the alternatives to our present course of action. The author suggests that, although we have looked on drug use as both a crime and a disease, the available medical evidence and best legal interpretation support neither viewpoint. The author hopes that society will develop alternative models for providing the convicted offender with an opportunity both to pay his debt to society and to develop his own human potential.

Other treatments, such as pre-trial and post-trial diversions operating in residential or nonresidential settings, are suggested as alternatives to treatments now used such as medical maintenance and self-help abstinence models.

440. Goshen, Charles E. **Drinks, Drugs, and Do-Gooders**. New York, The Free Press, 1973. 268p. illus. bibliog. $7.95. LC 72-93309. ISBN 0-02-912620-7.

This book provides historical and comparative views of the current drug problem and the alcohol problem. The author feels that, since prohibition of alcohol was a failure, prohibition of drug use will be (or already is) a failure also. He presents some practical solutions that he thinks offer reasonable prospects for success in the areas of public education and sponsoring and financing preventive programs. The reviewer does not find the author's presentation of his views very persuasive, although the historical material presented is interesting. For instance, there are numerous illustrations and quotations from old prohibition publications and other documents of the past.

441. **Governmental Response to Drugs: Fiscal and Organizational**. Washington, Drug Abuse Council, Inc., 1974. 48p. bibliog. LC 74-83626.

This publication is made up of two papers. The first, by Sibyl Cline, "The Federal Drug Abuse Budget for Fiscal Year 1975," presents and explains the budget of the federal Executive Branch. The second paper, by Peter Goldberg and Carl Akins, "Issues in Organizing for Drug Abuse Prevention," recounts the continuing bureaucratic shifts, mainly at the federal level, in governmental drug abuse prevention efforts. It also analyzes the policy implication of these changes. The analysis presented in each of these two papers is intended to throw light on important changes in federal drug policy directions in order to assist those responsible for implementing such policies. There are many charts, tables, and graphs.

442. Great Britain. Advisory Committee on Drug Dependence. **The Amphetamines and Lysergic Acid Diethylamide (LSD)**. Report to the Home Office, Department of Health and Social Security. London, Her Majesty's Stationery Office, 1970. 51p. 6s Op. pa. ISBN 0-11-340338-0.

This report was made as a definitive account of the particular problems associated with the misuse of amphetamines and LSD and also as an indication of the wider, general problems of drug misuse that confront society at the present time. In addition to a general discussion, there are separate sections on amphetamines and LSD. At the time the report was submitted the government was about to introduce new legislation to control drug abuse, and a summary of the Committee's recommendations are included. For amphetamines these are: control of trafficking on certain premises; control of doctors' prescribing and supplying; scrutiny of prescribing; and treatment, rehabilitation and prevention measures. In regard to LSD the suggestion is made that the substance should not be withheld from doctors if legitimate use can be claimed, and research should be allowed by licensed scientists. The question of controlling precursors of LSD should be explored. General recommendations deal with penalties and encouragement of research.

443. Group for the Advancement of Psychiatry. Committee on Mental Health Services. **Drug Misuse: A Psychiatric View of a Modern Dilemma.** New York, Charles Scribner's Sons, 1971. 93p. bibliog. index. $4.95. LC 70-162785. ISBN 0-684-12556-0cl; 0-684-12555-1pa.

This concise book, directed toward a wide audience of educators, law enforcement officers, legislators, health care personnel, and parents, offers an excellent presentation of the drug problem. Clearly stating the pros and cons of various conflicting opinions, it explores the following areas: 1) Drug misuse today, 2) Factors contributing to the problem, 3) What is known and not known, 4) Medical-legal considerations, 5) If marijuana were legalized, and 6) What should be done.

The conclusions about what should be done are reasonable and well stated. They include such things as the support of more research into all aspects of drug abuse, modification of laws that hamper scientific investigation, improved education of the medical profession, law enforcement activities directed toward preventing illegal manufacture and distribution of dangerous drugs, help for addicts, and public education to make drug use unattractive. This book is highly recommended.

444. Helcon, Inc. **Federal and State Laws Pertaining to Methadone.** Rockville, Md., National Institute on Drug Abuse, 1974. 199p. (DHEW Publication No. (ADM) 74-62).

This manual is intended for use by those who are involved with methadone treatment programs for drug addicts. Since methadone is itself a controlled substance, adherence to federal and state laws is necessary. The Food and Drug regulations and the National Institute on Drug Abuse methadone program guidelines have been included in the manual. In addition, there is a state-by-state analysis which consists of a statement of each state's licensing requirements for physicians, pharmacists, and nurses.

445. Hellman, Arthur D. **Laws against Marijuana: The Price We Pay.** Urbana, University of Illinois Press, 1975. 210p. bibliog. index. $10.00. LC 74-34150. ISBN 0-252-00438-8.

This book is only about marijuana *laws*. There is no argument about whether the use of the substance is desirable or even harmless. However, the author does argue that in the light of what is known and likely to be learned about the drug, society is injured far more seriously by law enforcement efforts than by the drug iself. The heart of the book is a study of practices used by the police in enforcing laws against marijuana. The author feels that the way to control the drug is through regulation and licensing.

446. Inciardi, James A., and Carl D. Chambers, eds. **Drugs and the Criminal Justice System.** Beverly Hills, Calif., Sage Publications, Inc., 1974. 249p. bibliog. index. $15.00. (Sage Criminal Justice System Annuals. V. 2). LC 72-98036. ISBN 0-8039-0200-X.

This book attempts to increase the reader's knowledge of the relationship between drug use and criminal behavior. Material covers the effect of legal controls upon drug abuse, the probable success of treatment methods and their cost, and the changing characteristics of the drug-using population, and the substances it uses. The authors, who are well known in the fields of psychiatry, law, sociology, and economics, present somewhat controversial views. They discuss such issues as public policy, funding, experimentation, methodology, and myths. The last chapter, written by the editors, presents forecasts for the future, suggesting the desirability of reducing crime by increasing the number of addicts in treatment; the need to improve social conditions, particularly in urban settings; the belief that some social/recreational use of drugs will become "normal" behavior; and the need for appropriate planning in the areas of treatment and control.

446a. Judson, Horace Freeland. **Heroin Addiction in Britain: What Americans Can Learn from the British Experience**. New York and London, Harcourt Brace Jovanovich, 1974. 200p. bibliog. index. $6.95. LC 74-11236. ISBN 0-15-140098-9.

The author of this work, who is an American newswriter, observed the British system of treating heroin addicts and compares the British approach with that used in the United States. He also points out that the British have medical uses for heroin and that we do not, as we seem to fear the drug.

Our heroin abusers are usually treated as criminals, but the British have established a system of giving registered addicts maintenance doses of heroin. These doses seem to keep the addicts reasonably content (at least they do not have withdrawal symptoms). It is admitted, however, that some users supplement their maintenance doses with illegal drugs.

The author feels that the British system works because the drug situation seems almost stable, and the addict can live without fear.

447. Kalant, Harold, and Oriana Josseau Kalant. **Drugs, Society and Personal Choice**. Don Mills, Ontario, Paper Jacks, in association with the Addiction Research Foundation, Toronto, 1971. 160p. bibliog. index. $1.95. ISBN 0-7737-7001-1.

The authors, who are scientists in the fields of pharmacology and physiology, are members of the staff of the Addiction Research Foundation of Ontario. The book outlines the facts about the actions of alcohol and other drugs and the effects of prolonged or heavy use. The authors attempt to be objective and do not try to win others to any specific point of view. The work, which is intended for the use of the general public, gives factual information, points out matters which require a value judgment, and shows ways in which the two interact. The hope is that the reader will make his or her own evaluation of social policy. Chapter headings are as follows: 1) Identifying the problems, 2) Drugs and their effects, 3) Reasons given for non-medical drug use, 4) Physical consequences of drug use, 5) Psychological consequences of chronic drug use, 6) Social consequences of chronic drug use, 7) Evaluating the effects of drug use, 8) Role of government in drug use, and 9) Drawing a balance.

448. Kaplan, John. **Marijuana—the New Prohibition**. New York and Cleveland, World Publishing Co., 1970. 387p. bibliog. index. $8.50. LC 70-115804.

The author finds the present laws against marijuana use analgous to those against the use of alcohol, the Prohibition of the 1920s and '30s. He makes a case for liberalization of the present marijuana laws, based mainly on the view that the benefits of the laws are not worth the cost.

Chapter headings are as follows: 1) Marijuana as a symbol, 2) The cost of the marijuana laws, 3) The "ordinary" effects of marijuana, 4) Marijuana and aggression, 5) The dangers of marijuana use, 6) Marijuana and dangerous drugs, 7) Marijuana and heroin addiction, 8) Marijuana and alcohol, 9) Marijuana control, and 10) The future of marijuana criminalization.

449. Kerr, K. Austin, ed. **The Politics of Moral Behavior: Prohibition and Drug Abuse**. Reading, Mass., Addison-Wesley Publishing Co., 1973. 275p. bibliog. $4.50pa. LC 72-580.

In this collection of primary and secondary readings, the editor attempts to demonstrate through his selections something about the prohibition movement in this country and its significance for the current situation on drug abuse. The editor points out that there was strong sentiment throughout most of the nineteenth century to prohibit the sale and manufacture of alcoholic beverages, but it was most active from the 1890s through the 1920s. This book focuses on the latter period. The editor's view is that there was conflict between the dominant Anglo-Americans and the newer immigrants from Europe, who had a different religious and cultural background and a more lenient view toward the use of alcohol. Prohibition was an attempt to control the behavior of the "foreign" peoples. The situation is seen as analogous to the drug abuse problem of today. American society has seen the rise of the so-called "counterculture," the members of which espouse a different system of values and practice a different kind of behavior. It is assumed that this question will continue to plague Americans in the future.

The book contains the following sections: 1) The problem of control in a democratic society, 2) Prohibition as a problem of control, 3) The rhetoric of cultural conflict, 4) The clash of cultures: the 1920s, 5) The politics of counterculture, and 6) Conclusion.

450. King, Rufus. **The Drug Hang-Up: America's Fifty-Year Folly**. New York, W. W. Norton, 1972. 389p. bibliog. index. $8.95. LC 75-39810. ISBN 0-393-0-1093-7.

The author, a lawyer who has been involved in drug matters since 1956, feels that outlawing drug use has been destructive and ineffective. He uses the old analogy comparing alcohol prohibition with the drug abuse legislation of today. Thus, he feels that legalizing drug use, so that it won't be a crime anymore, will solve the problem (as the alcohol problem was solved?). In spite of the dubious reasoning, the book's tracing of the history of anti-drug legislation is fairly interesting. Also included is a chronological outline of events relating to the subject.

451. Kobler, John. **Ardent Spirits: The Rise and Fall of Prohibition**. New York, G. P. Putnam's Sons, 1973. 386p. illus. bibliog. index. $8.95. LC 73-78586. ISBN 0-399-11209-X.

This history of the temperance movement and prohibition in the United States covers the period from the seventeenth century up until 1933. The Anto-Saloon League, the Women's Christian Temperance Union, the Prohibition Party, and other such organizations are discussed. The book is filled with anecdotes, quotes, and personal narratives relating to the prohibition movement. The book is interesting, particularly to one who has lived through the prohibition years, 1919-1933. However, if the author is attempting to convey any message or point of view, this is not obvious.

452. Kunnes, Richard. **The American Heroin Empire: Power, Profits, and Politics**. New York, Dodd, Mead and Co., 1972. 215p. index. $5.95. LC 72-3930. ISBN 0-396-06697-6.

The author's view is that heroin addiction is not a medical problem but a political and economic one. Presumably it is "created by, and controlled for, wealthy criminals with political connections, and political officials with corporate and criminal connections, and corporate officials controlling the priorities of our society." The book sets out to show how this is the case, but it is not entirely convincing.

453. Lennard, Henry L., Leon J. Epstein, Arnold Bernstein, and Donald C. Ransom. **Mystification and Drug Misuse: Hazards in Using Psychoactive Drugs**. San Francisco, Jossey-Bass, Inc., 1971. 133p. bibliog. index. $6.75. LC 79-148657. ISBN 0-87589-091-1.

This book takes up the problem of the abuse of psychoactive drugs that are legally prescribed by physicians. Its viewpoint is that, while occasional warnings are issued that the increased use of such drugs constitutes a public health hazard, in general these warnings have not been heeded. The prevailing attitude is that taking a drug will solve all ordinary everyday problems. The groups that are blamed for perpetuating this attitude are the pharmaceutical industry, the medical profession, and the youth culture.

454. Levine, Harvey R. **Legal Dimensions of Drug Abuse in the United States**. Springfield, Ill., Charles C. Thomas, 1974. 196p. index. (Publications of the Criminal Law Education and Research Center. v.7). LC 73-5545. ISBN 0-398-01876-1.

This book, a study of the dangerous drug laws of the United States, points out the legislative problems that have arisen, such as differences in existing penalties for the same or similar offences. The efficacy of legislation is also put in perspective. It is pointed out that drugs are classified and defined differently. Chapter headings are as follows: 1) Introductory note, 2) Definitions and classifications contemplated by drug abuse laws, 3) Federal law aimed at controlling drug abuse, 4) State drug abuse laws, 5) Present trends reflecting increased utilization of the Uniform Controlled Substances Act, 6) The enforcement of dangerous drug laws: a consideration of exclusionary rules of evidence and the defense of entrapment, 7) Civil commitment of drug addicts.

The book points out that synthesized efforts by legislators, judges, law enforcement agents, pharmacological experts, behavioral scientists, and educators are essential to the control of drug abuse.

455. Levine, Samuel F. **Narcotics and Drug Abuse: Being a Volume of the Criminal Justice Text Series.** Cincinnati, W. H. Anderson Co., 1973. 438p. illus. (col.). bibliog. index. $12.00. LC 73-80937.

Written by a law officer, this book's aim is to help police officers and others who are involved with drug abuse problems (such as legislators, physicians, educators, scientists, and governmental enforcement agencies). The book will assist the reader in understanding the practical mechanics of drug investigation and bring about some understanding of the broader social context in which the problem must be encountered and dealt with. Chapter headings are as follows: 1) Introduction, 2) The drugs of abuse, 3) Development of illicit traffic in narcotic drugs, 4) The evolution of narcotics and dangerous drug laws, 5) Comprehensive drug abuse prevention and control act, 6) International and national police organizations, 7) State and local enforcement organizations, 8) Case initiation and objectives, 9) Effective case development, 10) Field tests and abuser identification, 11) The crime of addiction, 12) Comprehensive treatment and rehabilitation, 13) Abuse prevention and youth, 14) Officers' case experience. Appended are a glossary of terms and a section on community programs for the prevention of drug abuse.

456. McCoy, Alfred W. **The Politics of Heroin in Southeast Asia.** With Cathleen B. Read and Leonard P. Adams II. New York, Harper and Row, 1972. 464p. illus. bibliog. index. $10.95. LC 70-182807. ISBN 0-06-012901-8.

The authors based this narrative on first-hand research on illicit heroin traffic in Asia and Europe. Much of the research, however, seems to have been conducted in the form of interviews. The story of opiate drug traffic is traced from the end of World War II until 1972. The thesis of the book is that drug traffic has been vital to many of the political regimes in the Southeast Asian area and that the United States, which supported them, did little that was effective in stopping the illegal flow of drugs into the United States.

The authors felt that the United States should cease its military and economic aid to governments of Southeast Asia. They admitted that Communist governments might come to power in such case, but they reasoned that such governments might change the tolerant attitudes toward heroin traffic, which would stop the great flow of opiates to this country. Looking at this notion from the vantage point of 1976, when the United States is no longer involved in Southeast Asia, it is not evident that opiate traffic has lessened in this country with the change in regimes in Asia.

457. Morgan, H. Wayne, ed. **Yesterday's Addicts: American Society and Drug Abuse, 1865-1920.** Norman, University of Oklahoma Press, 1974. 220p. bibliog. $7.95. LC 73-7421. ISBN 0-8061-1135-6.

Offering an historical perspective on drug abuse, this work shows that public concern about the problem has passed through many cyclical stages and that public attitudes have shaped regulatory legislation. The book brings together a collection of documents from an earlier period which are oriented toward social attitudes and personal experiences rather than pharmacy, medicine, or law. The papers are grouped under the following general headings: 1) The extent of addiction, 2) Causes, 3) The addicts, and 4) The demand for regulation. The essays are well selected, interesting, and worth reading.

The editor concludes that little is new in the continuing debate on controlling drug abuse and that the explanations given to explain the increased usage are often variations of earlier explanations. Fear of drug abuse rests on long-established belief that it threatens national ideals and individual happiness. The editor predicts that prohibition will not now succeed unless the public becomes willing to tolerate a kind of law enforcement that threatens individual liberties to some extent. Such enforcement will also be expensive. Proponents of maintenance programs will fare little better unless drugs become unattractive to potential new users. Drug users will also become less cavalier as statistics accumulate to show that so-called "harmless" substances have side-effects not readily noticed. The editor feels that social pressures will be more effective than formal laws.

458. Musto, David F. **The American Disease: Origins of Narcotic Control.** New Haven, Yale University Press, 1973. 354p. bibliog. index. $10.95. LC 72-75204. ISBN 0-300-01537-2.

This well-documented historical work explores the various early attempts to solve the drug abuse problem on the international, federal, and local levels. It discusses the attempts at reform and control and the relationships between legislative processes and various interested groups such as social reformers, politicians, the American Medical Association, pharmacists, manufacturers, addicts, and others. There is emphasis on the way laws have actually worked out in practice. The author is also concerned about what to do with addicts—punish them, attempt to cure them, maintain them as they are, or what? The history of "cures" for drug addiction is presented, and the author concludes that for the most part they have failed. Clinics are discussed, and the relation of drug control to alcohol prohibition receives attention. Most of the book deals with the 1920s and 1930s, but the subject is brought up to the present time with special emphasis on marijuana. The author, who is a historian and physician, has made a thorough study of the subject and has located much material.

459. Perlman, Harry S., and Peter A. Jaszi. **Legal Issues in Addict Diversion: A Technical Analysis.** Washington, Drug Abuse Council, Inc., and American Bar Association Commission on Correctional Facilities and Services, 1975. 129p.

Designed primarily for lawyers seeking to deal with legal aspects of diversion programs for addicts, this work includes extensive citations. Diversion programs for drug abusers provide for the referral of individuals from the criminal justice system to treatment services. Legal problems may arise as a consequence. The analysis presented here attempts to set out various legal perspectives of diversion programs, particularly since diversion techniques fall between diverging lines of authority. The following sections are included: 1) Legal issues in addict identification: drug use interviews and urinalysis, 2) Legal issues in selection and admission of persons into diversion programs, 3) The right to counsel, 4) The role of the prosecutor and court in diversion programs, 5) Addiction treatment records and confidentiality, and 6) Termination of diversion.

The sponsors of the publication hope that the concept of "addict diversion" as a human, effective, and just alternative to criminal conviction can be refined and accepted as a permanent component of the criminal justice process.

460. Rachin, Richard L., and Eugene H. Czajkoski, eds. **Drug Abuse Control: Administration and Politics.** Lexington, Mass. D. C. Heath and Co., 1975. 181p. bibliog. index. $14.50. LC 74-15540. ISBN 0-669-95679-1.

This book presents seven original essays written by social scientists. The presentations include some of the themes of critical criminology and concentrate on the organizations and bureaucracies that surround (and, the editors feel, sometimes support in veiled ways) the drug problem. However, organizational efforts at drug control are not altogether condemned, nor are drug offenders entirely excused. There is an attempt to present a perspective on the problem.

The chapter titles are as follows: 1) Drug control: agenda for repression; 2) Narcotics and marijuana laws: two case studies in bureaucratic growth and survival; 3) The medico-penal model of drug abuse control: the English experience; 4) Choice in the enforcement of drug laws: organization and discretion in police work; 5) Organizing drug abuse treatment and training programs for the college and the community; 6) Advocate, activist, agitator: the drug abuse program administrator as a revolutionary-reformer; and 7) Heroin and society: an economist's perspective on public policy.

It is pointed out that there is a direct relationship between official attention paid to the drug problem and its expansion and severity. However, the conclusion reached is not necessarily that a laissez-faire approach to the problem is best. The crux of the matter is that law is effective in direct relationship to its recognition and acceptance by those subject to its provisions. Why drug abuse controls are not accepted is not made clear, if indeed they are not accepted. The implication is that drug abuse is not really harmful, a difficult view for most to accept, or we would not have drug abuse laws.

461. Regush, Nicholas M. **The Drug Addiction Business: A Denunciation of the Dehumanizing Policies and Practices of the So-Called Experts.** New York, Dial Press, 1971. 141p. illus. bibliog. $4.95. LC 70-163592.

The author is said to be presenting us a "new reality" in this book, with the view that drug abuse is a political phenomenon. Basic to his thesis is that the welfare state itself prevents the solution to drug addiction, by administering programs that assure the survival of the problem and by failing to eliminate the problem and maintaining a hold over an otherwise threatened population.

These are the actions called for to alleviate the drug problem: 1) The federal and state governments should declare that drug addiction is no longer a criminal act, 2) All government-sponsored research on the psychological and/or sociological characteristics of heroin users should be stopped and the funds rechanneled to hospitals, 3) Funds for psychiatric purposes to private or public agencies should be terminated except for persons who believe they can benefit from such therapy, 4) Hospitals should be given federal and state funds for the creation of detoxification units and methadone maintenance programs, 5) Methadone maintenance treatment should be declared a temporary national program, 6) A National Medical Information Center should be established, 7) The government should disband present drug agencies and charge the American Medical Association to establish a Council for the study of drugs and narcotic antagonists, and 8) A federal commission should be established to help unemployed "drug workers" find other work.

462. Schroeder, Richard C. **The Politics of Drugs: Marijuana to Mainlining.** Introduction by Dr. Thomas E. Bryant, President of the Drug Abuse Council. Washington, Congressional Quarterly Inc., 1975. 216p. bibliog. LC 75-21500. ISBN 0-87187-081-9.

This book examines myths, facts, and attitudes about drug abuse. Marijuana is discussed in detail, with emphasis on the pros and cons of its legal status. In addition to chapters on law enforcement and public policing issues, there are discussions of addiction, trade, control of the illicit traffic, and treatment of addiction.

The author's view is that the demand for drugs, not the illicit supply, lies at the heart of America's drug problem. Emphasis should be on providing alternatives to drugs rather than on laws prohibiting or regulating their use. The views are well presented, and considerable documentation has been provided.

463. Seymour, Whitney North, Jr. **The Young Die Quietly: The Narcotics Problem in America.** New York, William Morrow and Co., 1972. 192p. index. $5.95. LC 78-166344.

The author's point of view is that although there has been a great deal of public attention, many treatment programs, much research, and millions spent to solve the drug problem, these efforts have been ineffective. The problem has only grown. He says that common sense can solve it. It is somewhat unclear how common sense is to be applied in any innovative ways, but he outlines a program stressing these areas: 1) Prevention, 2) Treatment, 3) Law enforcement, 4) Education, and 5) Emphasis on the role of the family.

464. Siragusa, Charles. **The Trail of the Poppy: Behind the Mask of the Mafia.** As told to Robert Wiedrich. Englewood Cliffs, N.J., Prentice-Hall, Inc., 1966. 235p. LC 66-22098.

This is a personal account of the work of an officer of the Federal Bureau of Narcotics and his crusade against the drug-smuggling members of the Mafia. The author, himself of Sicilian ancestry, was easily able to infiltrate the Mafia-controlled gangs and to identify, time and time again, the drug pusher, the peddler, and the small-time dope overlord. The author had learned to hate the cruel Mafia mobsters early in life as a school boy. He tells a fascinating story of how he, although of slum background, rose to the second-highest position in the U.S. Federal Bureau of Narcotics and "proved that a Sicilian doesn't have to be a gangster." Much inside information is given about the workings of illegal drug traffic and how the federal agents attempt to control it. A short glossary of drug terms is inlcuded.

465. Stepanian, Michael. **Pot Shots**. With drawings by R. Crumb. Delacorte Press/Seymour Lawrence Book, 1972. 223p. LC 71-38898.

The author of this publication is a lawyer who has specialized in defending drug abusers. His point of view is that our young people are being victimized and that marijuana use should be legalized so that users would not be breaking the law. He believes that anti-drug use laws interfere with basic rights. In addition to being an expression of protest, the book advises lawyers who defend the young drug abusers and also gives tips to the young to avoid being arrested. The book is difficult reading for one poorly schooled in the language of the drug culture.

466. Susman, Jackwell, ed. **Drug Use and Social Policy: An AMS Anthology**. New York, AMS Press, 1972. 595p. bibliog. $30.00. LC 72-3121. ISBN 0-404-10301-4; 0-404-10351-0pa.

This publication brings together recent articles on various aspects of drug abuse. About 40 articles have been included, collected from a number of sources and written by individuals often well known in the field. The articles are presented under these subject headings: I) Some parameters of drug use, II) Possible consequences of drug use; III) Institutional, social and psychological factors associated with the use of drugs; IV) Studies of the legal control of drug users; V) Treatment programs and their efficacy; VI) Characteristics of drug users and physicians, with implications for treatment; VII) Efforts at prevention of drug use; and VIII) Notes toward a future social policy. The first of these sections attempts to show how pervasively drugs are used in our society, and the second explores possible consequences of drug use, with an emphasis on social, not medical, consequences. Section III examines clues as to why drugs are so widely used in our society. Section IV begins an examination of societal reaction to drug users and raises questions about discretion and corruption in law enforcement and attitudes of the community. Sections V and VI focus on strengths and weaknesses in treatment efforts. Section VIII offers some ideas of what the future social policy of drug use could be.

The editor's opinions and predictions are expressed in an introduction. He believes that society's present condemnation of drug use will change in the future and approach some state which he considers ideal. The use of drugs will be a personal matter, he feels, and formal controls over them will disappear. The book presents a reasonably good collection of articles which give much interesting data. The editor's interpretation of the material may be open to question, however.

467. Teff, Harvey. **Drugs, Society, and the Law**. Lexington, Mass., Lexington Books, 1975. 219p. bibliog. index. $19.50. ISBN 0-347-01079-2.

This book, based on the author's doctoral thesis written at the University of London in 1973 contains the following chapters: 1) Legal and social perceptions, 2) The development of control, 3) Causes of dependence, 4) Sanctions and treatment, 5) The social response to drug use, 6) Towards a rational perspective, 7) Cannabis, and 8) The paradox of drug control. In addition, tables of cases, statutes, statutory instruments, and treaties have been provided, along with some statistical tables on drug users.

It is difficult to determine just what the author's point of view is. He dwells on the ambiguity of society's attitudes about drug use, and he also seems to suggest that there really is not much of a drug problem. No "solution," if such is called for, is presented. The legitimate function of the law in the matter of drug abuse control is questioned.

468. Uelmen, Gerald F., and Victor G. Haddox. **Cases, Text and Materials on Drug Abuse and the Law**. St. Paul, Minn., West Publishing Co., 1974. 564p. index. LC 74-3664.

This book was written for students of law and students of the criminal justice system. The authors feel that law students must acquaint themselves with the effects of various drugs and with the laws regulating their use, since they will often be called upon to defend abusers. Also, the student will need to be able to evaluate the virtues and limitations of the legal system dealing with drug abuse.

The subject matter is dealt with in the following chapters: 1) Introduction, 2) Drugs of abuse, 3) Legal classification of drugs, 4) Criminal offenses, 5) Constitutional limits on the criminal sanction, 6) Enforcing the criminal sanction, 7) Sentencing the drug offender, 8) Alternatives for treatment. There are two appendices: selected provisions of the Uniform Narcotic Drug Act and selected provision of the Federal Comprehensive Drug Abuse Prevention and Control Act of 1970 (Title 21, United States Code Annotated). In addition, there is a table of cases, with references to page numbers.

469. U.S. Bureau of Narcotics and Dangerous Drugs. Drug Control Division. **International Narcotics Control: A Sourcebook of Conventions, Protocols, and Multilateral Agreements, 1909-1971**. Arthur D. Little, Inc., BNDD Contract #71-28. Washington, GPO, 1972. 82p. (SCID-TR-5, Vol. 4).

This sourcebook contains the text of a number of international instruments pertaining to narcotics control; it is not complete, since some documents have been omitted. The compendium is particularly useful because the texts of parallel documents have been placed side by side on the large pages, allowing ready comparisons. Insights can be gained from the presentations. The last four pages are charts showing the status of multilateral treaties.

470. U.S. Drug Enforcement Administration. **Drug Enforcement**. Vol. 2, No. 2, Spring 1975, special issue on Drugs of Abuse. Washington, GPO, 1975. 41p. illus. (col.) bibliog. index.

This is a simple guide to a complex subject. It is short but useful, including the following sections: 1) The Controlled Substances Act, 2) Narcotics, 3) Depressants, 4) Stimulants, 5) Hallucinogens, 6) Cannabis, and 7) Product identification. The illustrations, all in color, are particularly outstanding. Commonly abused drugs are pictured in crude and in tablet and capsule form. These photographs should be of considerable assistance in identifying drugs of abuse.

471. U.S. National Institute on Drug Abuse. **Federal and State Laws Pertaining to Methadone**. Washington, GPO, 1976. 199p. (DHEW Publication No. (ADM) 75-180).

This is a convenient reference for the administrator who wants to be sure his program of methadone treatment is in compliance with legal provisions. Federal requirements are indicated first, followed by a state-by-state analysis.

472. U.S. President's Commission on Law Enforcement and Administration of Justice. Task force on Narcotics and Drug Abuse. **Task Force Report: Narcotics and Drug Abuse.** Annotations and Consultants' Papers. Washington, GPO, 1967. 158p. bibliog. $1.00pa.

In 1967 the President's Commission on Law Enforcement and Administration of Justice issued a general report called *The Challenge of Crime in a Free Society*. Chapter 8 of that report presented findings and recommendations relating to narcotics and drug abuse. That chapter is reproduced at the beginning of this publication, with the addition of annotations indicating source materials considered. The volume also contains six publications submitted to the Commission by well-known outside consultants. Some material from them was used in the chapter, and they are also of value as source material. The chapter from the Commission's general report contains recommendations concerning enforcement of drug laws and research and education.

473. U.S. Senate. Committee on the Juciciary. **Drug Abuse: The Pharmacist.** Hearing before the Subcommittee to Investigate Juvenile Delinquency of the Committee on the Judiciary, United States Senate, 93rd Congress, Second Session, pursuant to S. Res. 255, Section 12, Investigation of Juvenile Delinquency in the United States. The Comprehensive Drug Abuse Prevention and Control Act of 1970 (P. L. 91-513) and its Relationship to the Pharmacist. March 28, 1974. Washington, GPO, 1974. 452p. $3.30pa. S/N 5270-02428.

These materials were assembled to assess the effectiveness of the drug control laws of the United States. The pharmacist's role in the battle against drug traffic and abuse is the focus of the presentations. A number of prominent representatives of pharmaceutical organizations present testimony, and the document also reproduces articles, pamphlets, statements by experts, legal documents, and statistical information.

The pharmacist's major concerns are such matters as drug thefts, illegal production and distribution of drugs, and the unethical practices of some professionals. Much useful information has been collected in this publication.

474. U.S. Strategy Council on Drug Abuse. **Federal Strategy for Drug Abuse and Drug Traffic Prevention, 1973.** Washington, GPO, 1973. 150p. $1.50pa. S/N 5203-00001.

The Strategy Council on Drug Abuse was established to develop a federal strategy for all the drug abuse prevention and drug traffic prevention functions of the federal government in accordance with the Drug Abuse Office and Treatment Act of 1972. Realizing the difficulties of the problem because of changing societal attitudes and beliefs with respect to drugs, the Council's goals did not go beyond present resources or current capacity to modify factors encountered. The document describes the federal government's efforts to achieve three major objectives: 1) to reduce drug abuse in America, 2) to reduce the adverse social consequences of drug abuse, and 3) to concentrate federal government efforts on those forms of drug abuse which cause the greatest harm to society.

The report is in four sections: 1) Introduction, 2) Drug abuse problems: causes and responses, 3) Federal programs: present and projected, and 4) Summary. The strategy outlined is to be reviewed continuously.

475. Weston, Paul, and Robert W. Cole. **Case Studies of Drug Abuse and Criminal Behavior**. Pacific Palisades, Calif., Goodyear Publishing Co., Inc., 1973. 172p. illus. bibliog. $6.50pa. LC 72-89415. ISBN 0-87620-159-1.

These 22 case studies from real-life situations were developed from trial transcripts, court records, and the reports of probation and correctional personnel. They are grouped into six chapters on the basis of a specific type of criminal activity or accounts of persons who engage in similar activities to support their drug habits. The chapter headings are as follows: 1) Ghetto and barrio—crime and drug abuse, 2) Wayward girls—runaways, 3) Play groups of the drug scene—crime gangs, 4) Armed robbery, 5) Dealing in drugs, 6) Drug sellers. At the end of each study are questions that offer guidelines for inquiry, probing, and attempting to achieve a better understanding of the lifestyle and behavior of the addicts.

The authors hope that the case studies as presented will clarify cause-and-effect relationships in the drug scene and will offer clues for helping drug abusers. They conclude that drug abusers do not commit crimes because drug dependence militates against steady employment. Rather, they participate in criminal activities because no other means of supporting their habits are available for persons of little training, skill, or work experience. Drugs cost money, and it is this expense rather than dependence which turns drug abusers into criminals. A plea is made to get help to addicts, but little advice is offered about how to help except to suggest that therapeutic communities have had some success.

476. Zinberg, Norman E., and John A. Robertson. **Drugs and the Public**. New York, Simon and Schuster, 1972. 288p. bibliog. index. $8.95. LC 71-189748. ISBN 0-671-21165-X; 0-671-21196-Xpa.

This book pleads for what is called a "more rational drug policy"; specifically, it advocates the careful and restrained availability of abused drugs in the hope that this will alleviate the drug abuse problems of the world for the common good. Chapter headings are as follows: 1) What is the drug issue? an overview, 2) Public attitudes toward illegal drug use, 3) Drug use and drug users, 4) The problem of research, 5) The British experience, 6) The drug laws, 7) The costs of the drug laws, 8) Alternatives for drug control. Many will not agree with the authors' reasoning. The reviewer does not find it convincing, although it is a permissive point of view recently advocated by some.

12. Pharmacology, Chemistry, Research, and Medical Aspects

These are perhaps the outstanding titles presented in this bibliography. Many of the works are highly technical and most are written for the high-level reader. Although it is sometimes said that little research is being done in this field and that more is badly needed, it is more likely the case that the sensational materials have overshadowed the numerous scientific publications. Once the sensational has been excluded, the research appears to be of high quality and significance.

Some of the areas that have received attention as research topics include: mechanisms of drug action, the nature of drug dependence, the addiction process, how the state of mind influences drug effects, drugs and behavior, physiologic effects of drugs, social effects of drug abuse, the epidemiology of drug abuse, methods of narcotic research, LSD and other hallucinogenic drug research, treatment of addicts, detection of drugs in the body, analysis of drugs, medical problems, the search for narcotic antagonists, drugs and sexual behavior, drugs and athletic performance, drugs and highway safety, and the actual experience of drug intoxication.

477. Abel, Ernest L. **Drugs and Behavior: A Primer in Neuropsychopharmacology**. New York, Wiley-Interscience Publication, John Wiley and Sons, 1974. 229p. illus. bibliog. index. $13.95. LC 74-8969. ISBN 0-471-00155-4.

This book helps the reader understand the mechanisms of drug action and appreciate the way drugs can be used to elucidate the mechanisms' underlying behavior. More than a cursory overview of the principles of neuropharmacology is supplied, but the book is written primarily for students rather than professionals. The author believes that those interested in how drugs affect behavior must also understand the principles involved in drug action, since otherwise there can be no real understanding of the matter. The following chapters are presented: 1) The structural and functional basis of behavior, 2) Biological factors affecting the activity of drugs, 3) Mechanisms of drug action, 4) Sources of variability in drug activity, 5) Pharmacology of the CNS.

478. Ayd, Frank J., and Barry Blackwell, eds. **Discoveries in Biological Psychiatry**. Philadelphia, J. B. Lippincott Co., 1970. 254p. illus. bibliog. index. $6.50. LC 78-124542.

This work is not, strictly speaking, a drug abuse book. It is a collection of papers by world-famous scientists who are discoverers of drugs of major importance in the area of biological psychiatry. The accounts of the original drug discoveries are related by the scientists themselves. Probably the account of greatest value to those interested in drug abuse is the one by Albert Hofmann on "The Discovery of LSD and Subsequent Investigations on Naturally Occurring Hallucinogens." There is also an interesting chapter on "The Impact of Biological Psychiatry" by the senior editor. To quote from this section: " . . . it is imperative that we realize the immense power we now possess to intervene in the nonintellectual functions of the brain and to alter moods and emotional states. . . . An increasingly extensive and precise influence over how a person thinks, feels, and behaves surely will be possible."

479. Ban, T. A., and others, eds. **Psychopharmacology, Sexual Disorders and Drug Abuse.** Proceedings of the Symposium held at the VIIIth Congress of the Collegium Internationale Neuro-Psychopharmacologicum, Copenhagen, August 14-17, 1972. Amsterdam, North-Holland Publishing Co., 1973. 727p. bibliog. $40.40. LC 73-86075. ISBN 0-444-10560-3.

A few of these papers are written in French or German. The title of the book is somewhat deceptive, since only one of the twelve sections presented is concerned with sexual disorders and one with drug abuse (on the psychopharmacology of cannabis). The remaining sections are concerned with other diversified psychopharmacological topics. The papers are of somewhat uneven quality, although they are scientifically oriented.

480. Barger, George. **Ergot and Ergotism.** A monograph based on the Dohme Lectures delivered in Johns Hopkins University, Baltimore. London, Gurney and Jackson, 1931. 279p. illus. bibliog. index.

This valuable classic work was an outgrowth of lectures instituted "to promote the development of a more intimate relationship between chemistry, pharmacy, and medicine." There has been an upsurge of interest in ergot of recent years, since LSD is a derivative of it, and research is in progress to find derivatives that may have medicinal value.

The following chapters are included: 1) Ergot: historical, 2) Ergotism, 3) Botanical, 4) Chemical, 5) Pharmacological and clinical, and 6) Pharmaceutical and forensic.

The bibliography is noteworthy for its inclusion of references to much of the earlier literature.

481. Barr, Harriet Linton, Robert J. Langs, Robert R. Holt, Leo Goldberger, and George S. Klein. **LSD: Personality and Experience.** New York, Wiley-Interscience, 1972. 247p. bibliog. index. $10.00. LC 72-37641. ISBN 0-471-05403-8.

This work describes a research study into the nature of altered states of consciousness, the personality factors related to the specific manifestations of such states as experienced by a given person, and the manner of functioning in these states. This research was carried out with the use of LSD-25 before adverse publicity about the drug brought a halt to all legal experimenting with it. Much interesting and authentic material is presented. The authors found in a follow-up of their research that no ill effects of their moderate doses were found—no genetic damage and no teratogenic or carcinogenic effects. Neither, however, did they observe any lasting benefit, in spite of claims made by several subjects immediately after taking the drug that they had gained remarkable and personally useful insights.

Chapter headings are as follows: 1) Introduction: a research strategy for studying personality and differences in drug response, 2) The design of the study and the subjects, 3) General drug effects-subjective reactions and observable behavior, 4) The effects of the LSD states on experimental test performance, 5) LSD states and personality, 6) Conclusions. Also much of the test data has been included in appendices.

The book is of particular value to clinicians, social workers, and researchers in psychopharmacology, but it should also be of interest to anyone who needs information on drugs and behavior.

482. **Behavioral and Social Effects of Marijuana**. Papers by Ernest L. Abel and others. New York, MSS Information Corp., 1973. 175p. bibliog. index. $15.00. LC 72-13500. ISBN 0-8422-7093-0.

These research papers cover various aspects of the chemistry of marijuana. All were previously published in leading scholarly periodicals (between 1970 and 1972). Although the articles are somewhat technical for the average reader, they provide the basis for a chemical understanding of the drug. Papers are grouped under the following broad subject areas: 1) Effects of marijuana on memory and other aspects of mental performance, 2) "Marijuana psychosis" and various perceptual and behavioral responses to marijuana, 3) Personality and attitude among marijuana users, and 4) Sociological and legal aspects of the marijuana problem.

483. Black, Perry, ed. **Drugs and the Brain: Papers on the Action, Use, and Abuse of Psychotropic Agents.** Baltimore, Johns Hopkins Press, 1969. 403p. bibliog. index. $10.00. LC 68-31642. ISBN 0-8018-1002-7.

This publication is based in part on a conference sponsored by Friends of Psychiatric Research, Inc., Baltimore, held in 1967. The papers indicate the status of psychopharmacology at the time of writing. The subject is important because centrally acting drugs pose a growing problem to medical science and to society because of their potential for abuse. Some of the papers present critical reviews of the subject, and some report on detailed research. The book is divided into six parts: 1) Basic considerations, 2) Psychochemotherapy, 3) "Memory enhancers," 4) LSD, 5) Alcoholism, and 6) Drug abuse. The work is suitable primarily for general medical and paramedical readers, but much of it can be understood by the general reader.

484. Bové, Frank James. **The Story of Ergot: For Physicians, Pharmacists, Nurses, Biochemists, Biologists and Others Interested in the Life Sciences.** Basel, S. Karger, 1970. 297p. illus. bibliog. $15.85.

This book relates the story of ergot, an important drug that has been used for centuries; coverage of the fungus material is from ancient times to the present. At the present time, scientists are developing newer synthetic and biosynthetic derivatives from ergot, and these have been used for such things as childbirth complications, migraine headache, psychiatric conditions, and old age disturbances. Another ergot derivative is LSD, and a short section is devoted to it.

The three sections describe the pharmacognosy, chemistry, and physiology of the substance. Besides being interesting to read, the book provides investigators with a valuable source of data. Each chapter is a complete documentation of a phase of the subject. The book is suitable for intelligent laymen as well as scientists.

485. Braude, Monique C., and Stephen Szara, eds. **Pharmacology of Marihuana.** New York, Raven Press, 1976. 2v. bibliog. index. $50.00. ISBN 0-89004-067-2.

These two volumes contain the proceedings of a symposium sponsored by the National Institute on Drug Abuse held in December 1974, in Savannah. It is a major scientific and technical work, bringing together many papers on aspects of the pharmacology of cannabis and its derivatives. Some of the areas covered include chemical and metabolic aspects; cellular, immunological, and hormonal effects; autonomic effects; neuropharmacological effects; behavioral pharmacology and interactions; long-term effects; genetics and reproduction; and therapeutic potentials as well as background material. The publication furnishes a state-of-the-art review and can have a marked effect on the direction of future scientific research on the subject.

486. Brown, F. Christine. **Hallucinogenic Drugs**. Springfield, Ill., Charles C. Thomas, 1972. 154p. illus. bibliog. index. $10.50. LC 74-164878.

Presenting material on the history, biogenesis, pharmacology, toxicity, and psychoactivity of hallucinogenic drugs, this work is organized around the chemical distinctiveness of the drugs (the author is a biochemist). The following topics and/or drugs are considered: 1) General considerations, 2) Phenylakylamines: mescaline and amphetamines, 3) Lysergic acid derivatives, 4) The indoles, 5) Marihuana, 6) Piperidyl benzilate esters and related compounds, and 7) Some minor hallucinogens.

The text is rather technical but can be understood reasonably well by those without advanced scientific training.

487. Byrd, Oliver E. **Medical Readings on Drug Abuse**. Reading, Mass., Addison-Wesley Publishing Co., 1970. 274p. index. $3.95pa. LC 77-100856.

These readings cover primarily the effects of a variety of drugs, including alcohol and tobacco, on human behavior. The following chapters are included: 1) Effects of drugs, 2) Tobacco, 3) Alcohol, 4) Drugs used in medicine, 5) Vapor sniffing, 6) Marijuana, 7) Barbiturates, 8) Tranquilizers, 9) Amphetamines, 10) Methamphetamine, 11) LSD, 12) Some other hallucinogens, 13) Heroin and the opiates, 14) Psychiatric relationships, 15) Treatment, and 16) Professional viewpoints. The readings are rather short, averaging about a page in length. The materials, taken from a variety of sources (mostly medical journals), have been well selected and should prove useful to those seeking evidence that will help them decide what attitude to take toward drug abuse.

488. Byrd, Oliver E., and Thomas R. Byrd. **Medical Readings on Heroin.** San Francisco, Boyd and Fraser Publishing Co., 1972. 252p. index. $3.95pa. LC 72-182679. ISBN 0-87835-040-3.

This book contains more than 150 condensed and simplified reviews of professional papers. They have been selected from a variety of sources, but most come from the best known medical journals. The papers are presented under these headings: 1) Prevalence and significance, 2) Some biological considerations, 3) Addiction as an occupational hazard, 4) The heroin addict, 5) Detection of the heroin addict, 6) Effects associated with heroin addiction, 7) Withdrawal symptoms, 8) Sudden death from the injection of heroin, 9) Multiple drug usage by heroin addicts, 10) Treatments without methadone, 11) Methadone, and 12) Multiple responsibilities. Each section is introduced by a one-page monograph. Besides being interesting and well selected, the papers are authentic and informative. This important material will interest the general reader as well as members of the medical profession.

489. Caldwell, Anne E. **Origins of Psychopharmacology: From CPZ to LSD.** Springfield, Ill., Charles C. Thomas, 1970. 225p. bibliog. index. $12.00. LC 72-103574.

This book about the origins of psychotropic drugs tells how the drugs were discovered (by chance, by serendipity, or by design) and who introduced them into psychiatry. In covering the century-long historical development of these drugs, the author points out that psychiatrists tried to make use of them, but the drug was always wrong until 1952, when chloropromazine (CPZ) was discovered. It was discovered by design, synthesized according to specification and for a specific purpose-to alleviate anxiety and stress in surgical patients. The stories of this drug and a number of others are told in chronological order.

The accounts are interesting, and the documentation is outstanding. A lengthy section of "notes" has been included. The author used the vast collection at the National Library of Medicine to substantiate essential facts and to cite the original publications.

490. Cappell, H. D., and A. E. Le Blanc, eds. **Biological and Behavioural Approaches to Drug Dependence**. General Editor: S. L. Lambert. Toronto, Alcoholism and Drug Addiction Research Foundation of Ontario, 1975. 179p. bibliog. index. $6.50pa. ISBN 0-88868-008-2.

These papers were presented at an International Symposium on Alcohol and Drug Research by the participants noted for their work in the drug abuse field. The papers are somewhat technical; they cover interdisciplinary areas of the behavioral and biological sciences and show connections between laboratory research and clinical work.

The last chapter is Harold Kalant's overview of the material covered in the volume, pointing out several themes that recur in the presentations: the need for a definition of drug problems in terms that permit experimental testing; the relation between physical dependence and the broader picture implied by the term "drug dependence"; and the question of which kinds of therapeutic research can be based on our present concepts of dependence. The work addresses a wide range of conceptual issues, and both scientists and practitioners will find it instructive.

491. Cholden, Louis, ed. **Proceedings of the Round Table on Lysergic Acid Diethylamide and Mescaline in Experimental Psychiatry**. Held at the Annual Meeting of the American Psychiatric Association, Atlantic City, N.J., May 12, 1955. New York, Grune and Stratton, 1956. 85p. bibliog. index. $3.00. LC 56-8731.

For the most part, these papers were written by scientific experts in medicine, pharmacology, and psychiatry. At the time the work was published, it was hoped that drugs had been found (LSD and mescaline) that could artificially produce temporary psychotic states such as schizophrenia. The drugs would furnish a tool to make it possible to study mental disease and its treatment in a way not possible previously. Some good basic information, both descriptive and scientific, is presented in the book; needless to say, however, these drugs have not yet proven to be the hoped for tools.

492. Clouet, Doris H., ed. **Narcotic Drugs: Biochemical Pharmacology**. New York, Plenum Press, 1971. 506p. bibliog. index. $28.00. LC 76-128503. ISBN 0-306-30495-3.

Not much material has been available in book form on the responses of the body and its tissues to narcotic drugs at the level of biochemical pharmacology. The molecular history of the drug in the body and the biochemical consequences of its presence in the tissues has not been written about extensively except in periodical literature. This book treats that subject. There has been a need for such information in order to understand addiction processes, and it is possible to do so more fully at this time because of recent advances made in the field of molecular biology. The material, which is presented by noted authorities, is divided into the following sections: 1) The chemistry of narcotic analgesic drugs, 2) The metabolic disposition of narcotic analgesic drugs, 3) The effects of narcotic analgesic drugs on general metabolic systems, 4) The effects of narcotic analgesic drugs on specific systems, 5) Sites of action of narcotic analgesic drugs, 6) Tolerance and dependence, 7) Electrophysiological studies in man, and 8) Pharmacologically based therapeutic programs in man. Some chapters are of interest to scientists working on the basic aspects of drug dependence, and some provide background for clinicians interested in therapy for addicts. The material is quite technical and is suitable mainly for biochemists, pharmacologists, behavioral and social scientists, neurobiologists, medical researchers, and public health officials.

493. Cochin, Joseph, ed. **Drug Abuse and Contraception.** Basel, S. Karger, 1973. 330p. bibliog. index. (International Congress on Pharmacology. 5th, 1972. Pharmacology and the Future of Man. Proceedings. v.1). $22.35. ISBN 3-8055-1470-0.

This is the first of the five volumes that present the complete proceedings of the meeting on Pharmacology and the Future of Man, International Congress on Pharmacology, held in San Francisco, July 23-28, 1972. The papers, which were presented by experts, are quite scientific and technical and somewhat difficult for the average reader. This volume presents first fourteen papers on "Drugs and Society." (The second part of the volume, which is on "Contraceptive Drugs," is not concerned with abuse of them.) The fourteen papers on drug abuse are as follows: 1) Introduction to the Symposium on Drugs and Society, behavioral and clinical aspects, 2) General introduction to the Symposium on Drugs and Society, 3) An experimental framework for evaluation of dependence liability of various types of drug in monkeys, 4) Sources of reinforcement for drug using behavior–a theoretical formulation, 5) Acute and chronic behavioral effects of *Cannabis sativa*, 6) Pharmacological and behavioral variables in the development of alcohol tolerance, 7) Developing a national response to drug abuse problems, 8) Pharmacological mechanisms of drug dependence, 9) Brain neurohormones in morphine tolerance and dependence, 10) Amphetamine-induced changes in the regulation of neurotransmitter biosynthetic and receptor functions in the brain, 11) Biochemical models of drug psychosis-focus on amphetamines, 12) Central nervous sites of action of morphine on dependent and non-dependent rabbits, 13) A search for the opiate receptor, and 14) Report of the discussion of the Symposium on Drugs and Society.

494. Cohen, Sidney. **The Beyond Within: The LSD Story**. Foreword by Gardner Murphy. New York, Atheneum, 1966 (c.1964). 268p. bibliog. index. $6.95. LC 64-25848.

The author of this book is a physician and researcher who has investigated many aspects of LSD and other hallucinogens and has published many articles. The book relates the experiences of some who have used LSD, describing the phantasies, visions, and feelings of the users. The LSD state was found to be extremely variable, highly subjective, and hard to measure. The author's hope is that drugs like LSD will reveal something of the expanse of the mind and suggest what its vast potential really is. He feels that the mind ordinarily functions at only a fraction of its full effectiveness and that the promise of the future is that we can learn how to alter this fraction to our advantage. Caution is urged, however, as this type of drug can be extremely dangerous.

495. Cole, Jonathan O., and J. R. Wittenborn, eds. **Drug Abuse: Social and Psychopharmacological Aspects.** Springfield, Ill., Charles C. Thomas, 1969. 170p. bibliog. index. $9.50. LC 69-14784.

This material is drawn from reports presented at the Fifth Annual Meeting of the American College of Neuropsychopharmacology held in San Juan, Puerto Rico. The papers presented have no primary focus but are representative of current research and thought on the subject in question. Following is a list of the papers: 1) Long-lasting effects of LSD on normals, 2) Patterns of response to self-administration of LSD, 3) Amphetamine use and abuse in psychiatric patients, 4) Incidence of non-narcotic drug addictions at a large city hospital, 5) Normal drug use: an exploratory study of patterns and correlates, 6) Factors affecting withdrawal response to certain minor tranquilizers, 7) Adverse reaction to marijuana, 8) Marijuana smoking and the onset of heroin use, 9) Intermittent patterns of narcotic usage, 10) Role of enzyme induction in drug tolerance, 11) Effect of morphine on protein and ribonucleic acid metabolism in brain. Although the papers are scientifically oriented, they can be understood reasonably well by the general reader.

496. Costa, E., and S. Garattini, eds. **International Symposium on Amphetamines and Related Compounds.** Proceedings of the Mario Negri Institute for Pharmacological Research, Milan, Italy. New York, Raven Press, 1970. 962p. illus. bibliog. index. $35.00. LC 77-84114. ISBN 0-911216-08-1.

The 58 chapters in this work cover many aspects of the amphetamines which are of present interest. The presentations are highly technical with emphasis on pharmacological, physiological, biochemical, and metabolic aspects of the subject. However, there are implications for those interested in the sociological and behavioral aspects of abuse of this drug. The contributors are well-known experts in their respective fields. The material is grouped into eight main subject areas: 1) Structure-activity relationships of amphetamines and halogenated amphetamines, 2) Distribution and metabolism of amphetamines, 3) Interaction of amphetamines with biogenic amines, 4) Physiological significance of the interaction of amphetamines with biogenic amines, 5) Effects of amphetamines on the cardiovascular system, 6) Effects of amphetamines on food intake and lipid metabolism, 7) Effects of amphetamines on the central nervous system: experimental, and 8) Effects of amphetamines on the central nervous system: clinical.

It is brought out that some amphetamines elicit specific and lasting biochemical changes in the central nervous system. On the other hand, some were found to be devoid of central stimulatory effects and to be therapeutically valuable. The editors hope that the book may give a better understanding of possible solutions to the problems involved in amphetamine use. Much information is presented, and the work is of high quality.

497. Denber, Herman C. B., ed. **Psychopharmacological Treatment: Theory and Practice.** Proceedings of a Symposium on Psychopharmacologic Treatment in Psychiatry, University of Florida, College of Medicine, Departments of Psychiatry and Pharmacology, Gainesville, Florida. New York, Marcel Dekker, Inc., 1975. 294p. (Modern Pharmacology-Toxicology Series. Vol. 2). bibliog. index. $19.75. LC 74-78968. ISBN 0-8247-6229-0.

It is of note that psychoactive drugs have now been used in the field of psychiatry for more than 20 years. At the present time some doctors are seriously questioning the advisability of their frequent use. This book, written for professionals, directs attention toward the technical aspects of psychopharmacology. Each chapter considers a different type of drug (e.g., antidepressants, antianxiety agents, neuroleptics, and hallucinogenic drugs), with pharmacological and clinical sections and discussions of the indications, limitations, and specific contraindications of each drug. The viewpoint of the book is that poor prescribing practices can and will be corrected and that the kind of drug under consideration makes a major contribution to the treatment of the mentally ill.

498. **Drug Abuse: Medical and Criminal Aspects.** Papers by Francis Braceland, David Freedman, Karl Rickels, *et al.* New York, MSS Information Corporation, 1972. 221p. bibliog. index. $15.00.

These papers, which have been reprinted from leading scientific and medical journals, have been divided into two sections as follows: 1) Psychotropic drug addiction or withdrawal in man, and 2) Drug abuse and crime. Twenty-eight articles are included.

499. Eddy, Nathan B. **The National Research Council Involvement in the Opiate Problem, 1928-1971**. Washington, National Academy of Sciences, 1973. 313p. bibliog. index. $10.50. LC 73-3392.

This is a report on the work of the Committee on Problems of Drug Dependence (previously known by other similar names) of the National Research Council. This Committee was for 42 years concerned with the support of laboratory and clinical research on problems related to drug addiction and dependence. More recently it has offered its wisdom and experience to government agencies responsible for traffic in drugs and concerned with the problems of addicts. The author, a well-known scientist, spent the major portion of his career involved in activities relating to narcotics and the affairs of the Committee. The book is a running account of the work of the Committee, the work done under its auspices, its deliberations, and conclusions. The Committee made important contributions in structure-action relationships of drugs and in fostering a better understanding of drug dependence and addiction. In addition, it has been a major force in promoting cooperation among government and private agencies, including industry, in the interests of public health and of avoiding a health hazard. The bibliographies, which list articles that report on work supported by the Committee, are very extensive and are indexed separately. A few letters and documents of interest are reproduced in an appendix, along with facts concerning Committee meetings, memberships, research funds, and grant programs.

500. Ehrenpreis, Seymour, and Amos Neidle, eds. **Methods in Narcotics Research**. New York, Marcel Dekker, Inc., 1975. 408p. bibliog. index. (Modern Pharmacology-Toxicology Series. Vol. 5). $29.75. LC 75-23586. ISBN 0-8247-6308-4.

These articles, prepared by researchers primarily in the field of pharmacology, outline representative methods of determining the effects of narcotic drugs on both laboratory animals and human beings. The work covers biochemical, pharmacological, and behavioral methods, and both the tissue and molecular levels are considered. Some of the topics included are as follows: intracerebral administration of opiates, problems in the experimental evaluation of narcotic analgesics, the tail-flick test, morphine-withdrawal aggression, and the determination of opiates in urine.

The book, which should be of considerable value to pharmacologists, neurochemists, biologists, physiologists, biochemists, and others concerned with addictions, will make it easier to track down an experimental procedure.

501. Einstein, Stanley, and Gerald G. De Angelis, eds. **The Non-Medical Use of Drugs: Contemporary Clinical Issues**. Sponsored by the Institute for the Study of Drug Addiction and Pfizer Pharmaceuticals. New York, Institute for the Study of Drug Addiction, 1972. 83p. (Monograph Series, No. 1).

This booklet was prepared for the physician who is increasingly being called upon to deal with drug abusers in a number of capacities. The papers presented were written by physicians and researchers well known in the field. The titles of the papers are as follows: 1) Acute treatment of heroin addiction with special reference to mixed addictions: I. Acute treatment; II. Withdrawal; 2) Human pharmacology of drugs of abuse; 3) Neuropsychopharmacology of drugs of abuse; 4) Acute drug reactions in perspective; 5) Peer pressure and drug abuse; 6) The role of the physician in community drug abuse programs; and 7) Alternatives to drug abuse: an analysis.

The material presented is quite perceptive, providing many insights into the behavior of drug users and many practical suggestions and tips on dealing with addicts. Although written for physicians, it will be valuable to anyone interested in the drug problem. The material on how to handle medical emergencies, particularly overdosage, is noteworthy.

502. Epstein, Samuel S., ed. **Drugs of Abuse: Their Genetic and Other Chronic Non-Psychiatric Hazards.** Based on a Symposium co-sponsored by the Center for Studies of Narcotic and Drug Abuse, National Institute of Mental Health, and by the Environmental Mutagen Society, San Francisco, Oct. 29-30, 1969. Cambridge, Mass., MIT Press, 1971. 228p. bibliog. index. $15.00. LC 78-148969. ISBN 0-262-05009-9.

This material is based on the second conference which was concerned with the non-psychiatric hazards of drugs of abuse. Like the first, this conference contributed to an awareness of what is needed for an adequate assessment of the possible mutagenic, teratogenic, and carcinogenic aspects of drug abuse. The work reviews existing toxicological information on drugs of abuse, defines the areas of ignorance about their hazards, and indicates productive strategies for future research.

Some of the material presented is highly technical, but much of it will also be of considerable interest to the general reader. There is discussion of the chemistry and sources of drugs such as marijuana, LSD, the amphetamines, barbiturates, heroin, and less well-known drugs such as sernyl, STP, mescaline, datura, DMT, psilocybin, ibogaine, and harmala. Medical, physiological, and pharmacological aspects of multiple drug use are treated, and there are articles on the chronic biological hazards of drug abuse–the carcinogenic, teratogenic, and genetic. The last section of the work deals with methods for mutagenicity testing of drugs. Concern is expressed and evidence given that many drugs of abuse are indeed hazardous to man in the areas under consideration.

503. Fox, Ruth, ed. **Alcoholism: Behavioral Research, Therapeutic Approaches.** New York, Springer Publishing Company, Inc., 1967. 340p. bibliog. index. $9.50. LC 66-22518.

This book, an outgrowth of several scientific conferences sponsored by the National Council on Alcoholism, is edited by the medical director of the Council. The aim of the book is to assist in the prevention of alcoholism, although treatment of those already addicted is given attention. The hope is that research into the alcoholic condition can help identify the vulnerable individuals and reach them before they become addicted.

The first section of the book is on behavioral research (11 pages) and the second on therapeutic approaches (19 pages). These outstanding papers, written by those well-known for their work in the field, provide much psychological insight as well as practical information and suggestions. The book has been widely used.

The editor concludes all the successful treatment modalities discussed have one common denominator: namely, that the therapist must get across to the patient that he is a worthwhile person who can be helped. It is a great relief to the alcoholic to find the therapist objective, firm, nonjudgmental, as well as compassionate, understanding, and hopeful.

504. Garattini, S., and V. Ghetti, eds. **Psychotropic Drugs.** (Proceedings of the International Symposium on Psychotropic Drugs, Milan, May 9-11, 1957.) Amsterdam, Elsevier Publishing Co., 1957. 606p. illus. bibliog. index. $15.00. LC 57-13476.

This volume contains a large number of scientific papers presented at an international meeting; the authors are noted scientists from all over the world. Most of the papers are in English, but a few are written in other Western languages such as French, German, or Italian. Contributions are arranged under five main headings: 1) Biochemistry of normal and altered cerebral functions, 2) Behavioral effects of psychotropic drugs on animals, 3) Electrophysiological basis of normal and altered cerebral function, 4) Pharmacological aspects of central acting substances, and 5) Clinical experiences. In addition, there is an introductory historical chapter on the mandrake, one of the most famous plants of the ancient pharmacopoeia, seldom used now although its active ingredients have been defined. It is of note that several papers on LSD are included.

505. Gilbert, R. M., and J. D. Keehn, eds. **Schedule Effects: Drugs, Drinking, and Aggression.** Toronto, University of Toronto Press for the Addiction Research Foundation, 1972. 259p. illus. bibliog. $12.50. LC 70-189607. ISBN 0-8020-3286-9.

The papers upon which this volume is based were presented at a 1970 symposium sponsored by the Addiction Research Foundation. The topic of the symposium was schedule-induced and schedule-dependent phenomena. The papers in this volume are only part of those presented at the symposium. Papers included here cover phenomena associated with schedule of reinforcement: 1) Schedule-dependent effects: effects of drugs, and maintenance of responding with response-produced electric shocks; 2) Conditioned anxiety and operant behaviour; 3) Drugs as reinforcers: schedule considerations; 4) Schedule-dependence, schedule-induction, and the Law of Effect; 5) Schedule-induced polydipsia: an analysis of water and alcohol ingestion; 6) Drug effects upon behaviour induced by second-order schedules of reinforcement: the relevance of ethological analyses; 7) The nature and determinants of adjunctive behaviour; 8) Schedule-independent factors contributing to schedule-induced phenomena; 9) Side-effects of aversive control.

As can be seen, the material is intended primarily for the advanced student and professional in the fields of psychology and pharmacology.

506. Gordon, Maxwell, ed. **Psychopharmacological Agents. Vol. 4, Use, Misuse, and Abuse.** New York, Academic Press, 1976. 215p. bibliog. index. (Medicinal Chemistry; a Series of Monographs, Vol. 4, Pt. 4). LC 64-17794. ISBN 0-12-290559-8 (v.4).

The first three parts of this treatise deal primarily with medical use of psychoactive drugs. This volume summarizes the chemistry, pharmacology, and clinical manifestations of psychoactive drugs that are abused. To some extent historical, legal, regulatory, and sociological aspects of such drug use are presented as well as treatment modalities. Each of the six sections is written by a different expert in the field, and the material is of high quality. The presentations contain many literature references and are, for the most part, for the scientist and researcher.

507. Greene, Mark H., and Robert L. Dupont, eds. **The Epidemiology of Drug Abuse.** Washington, American Public Health Association, 1974. 56p. bibliog. (Supplement of the American Journal of Public Health, Vol.64, pt.2, December, 1974.) $2.50.

Epidemiologic techniques and methodologies can be applied to such phenomena as drug abuse. They can serve the useful purpose of separating fact from fantasy, and in addition the product of such research can have a significant impact on drug abuse policy development. This publication assembles a group of papers in which the epidemiologic approach to problem solving has been focused on drug abuse. The titles of the papers are 1) An epidemiologic assessment of heroin use, 2) The high drug use community: a natural laboratory for epidemiological experiments in addiction control, 3) Recent spread of heroin use in the United States, 4) The New York City Narcotics Register: a case study, 5) Drug use during and after high school: results of a national longitudinal study, 6) How permanent was Vietnam drug addiction?, 7) Methadone maintenance treatment five years later–where are they now?, 8) Criminality in heroin addicts before, during and after methadone treatment.

The results of the research indicated that Vietnam drug addiction was not as permanent as had been supposed. In addition, one group found that methadone maintenance programs have for the most part made patients socially productive, although the last paper presents disparate results in its finding that there was no reduction of criminal activity among addicts while in treatment. The study on drug use among high school students indicates that illegal drug use among this group was less than the media have suggested although the "counter-culture" syndrome is in evidence.

508. Harris, Robert T., William M. McIsaac, and Charles R. Schuster, eds. **Drug Dependence.** Austin, University of Texas Press for the Faculty for Advanced Studies of the Texas Research Institute of Mental Sciences, 1970. 342p. bibliog. index. (Advances in Mental Science II). $10.00 LC 76-121127. ISBN 0-292-70043-1.

This publication contains the proceedings of the second in a series of international symposia sponsored by the Texas Research Institute of Mental Sciences. The 24 papers included were presented by leading experts in medicine, law, research science, social work, and the U.S. Bureau of Narcotics and Dangerous Drugs. The papers are divided into five general subject areas: 1) Biological aspects of drug dependence, 2) Pharmacological aspects of drug dependence, 3) Behavioral aspects of drug dependence, 4) Therapeutic programs for drug dependence, and 5) Social aspects of drug dependence.

Most of the material presented is highly technical, discussing recent research findings on marihuana, LSD, STP, other hallucinogens, and areas such as treatment of addicts by narcotic antagonists and the research for analgesics that will reduce dependence capacity.

The book suggests that the root of today's drug problem may lie in man's curiosity and his eternal search for conquest of new horizions. The ingenuity that brought about in a single generation the development and discovery of more psychoactive compounds than were known in all previous ones is evidence of this desire to explore unknowns.

509. **Immunoassays for Drugs Subject to Abuse**. Edited by S. J. Mulé and others. Cleveland, CRC Press, 1974. 126p. bibliog. index. $23.00. LC 73-88630. ISBN 0-87819-121-6.

The increase in the use and abuse of drugs of recent years has created a need for rapid, reliable, sensitive, specific, and inexpensive methods to detect and identify drugs in the fluids of the body. Such data help to identify the drug dependent person and to make early treatment possible. Immunoassay techniques, along with other methods of detection, have been used for this purpose since the early 1970s.

This volume contains the proceedings of a meeting on immunoassays for drugs subject to abuse, sponsored by the Center for Studies of Narcotic and Drug Abuse, National Institute of Mental Health, held in March 1973. The papers, presented by a select group of individuals, were limited to general methodologies and omitted most technical detail. The book is divided into two parts: 1) Immunoassays: current state of the art, and 2) Evaluation of immunoassays for the detection of drugs subject to abuse.

The purpose of the monograph is to help workers in the field stay up to date on new developments. Pharmacologists, toxicologists, forensic scientists, clinical chemists, and clinicians who have concern or responsibility for the analysis of psychoactive drugs will find the book of particular value.

510. International Narcotic Research Club Conference, May 21-24, 1975. **The Opiate Narcotics: Neurochemical Mechanisms in Analgesia and Dependence.** Executive Committee Secretary, INRC, Avram Goldstein. New York, Pergamon Press, 1975. 270p. bibliog. index. $20.00. LC 75-15864. ISBN 0-08-019869-4.

It was decided to publish these papers of a scientific meeting because it was recognized that rapid strides had been made in the understanding of the subject. The papers, written on the advanced research level, are suitable only for those working in the field on that level. The following sections are included: 1) Brain substances with affinity for the opiate receptor, 2) Opiate receptors and their interactions with opiate agonists and antagonists, 3) Cyclic nucleotides and mechanism of opiate action, 4) Effects of opiates on neurotransmitters and neuromodulators, 5) Effects of opiates on single neurons, 6) Hypotheses on neurochemical mechanisms of opiate action in analgesia, and 7) Conference summation. The summary chapter points out areas where there is agreement in research results, where there is disagreement, methodological differences to be solved, and some points of interest for future research orientation.

511. Iverson, Susan D., and Leslie L. Iverson. **Behavioral Pharmacology**. New York and Oxford, Oxford University Press, 1975. 310p. bibliog. index. $10.95; $5.95pa. LC 74-22879.

This book describes the achievements of the field of psychopharmacology in providing behavioral methods for analyzing drug action and gives a résumé of the subject matter of neuropharmacology, emphasizing the use of objective methods for analyzing normal and abnormal behavior. There are five sections: 1) The analysis of behavior, 2) Basic neuropharmacology, 3) Determinants of drug action, 4) Drugs and behavior, and 5) Animal models and the neuropharmacological basis of nervous and mental discorders in man. Section 4, which is about one-third of the book, is perhaps of most interest to those concerned with drug abuse. Amphetamines, barbiturates, mood-modifying drugs, opiates, minor tranquilizers, antipsychotic drugs, and hallucinogenic drugs and cannabis are all discussed in some detail.

The work is technical and suitable mainly for psychologists and pharmacologists. It is important because it inquires into a relatively new area—how the state of mind can influence the effect of drugs.

512. Karczmar, A. G., and W. P. Koella, eds. **Neurophysiological and Behavioral Aspects of Psychotropic Drugs**. Springfield, Ill., Charles C. Thomas, 1969. 199p. illus. bibliog. index. $12.50. LC 69-14789.

These papers were presented at a workshop meeting of the American College of Neuropsychopharmacology in 1966 and were updated and revised for publication through 1968. The book offers a bird's-eye view of the ramifications of the field, pointing out rapid progress made, the concomitant possibilities for conceptualizations, and the interdisciplinary character of the field. The following papers have been included: 1) Neurophysiological action of LSD; 2) Effects of pemoline and magnesium hydroxide on acquisition and retention; 3) Clinical and neurophysiologic aspects of barbiturate addiction; 4) EEG patterns of cyclazocine, a narcotic antagonist; 5) Quantitative EEG and behavior changes after LSD and Ditran; 6) Cyclic response to repeated LSD administration; 7) Evoked response studies of schizophrenic thinking; 8) One trial learning in the mouse: its characteristics and modifications by experimental-seasonal variables; 9) Learning and effect of drugs on learning of related mice genera and strains; and 10) Drug effects on behavior and evoked potentials in fixated rats. Also included is a directory of the American College of Neuropsychopharmacology.

513. Keup, Wolfram, ed. **Drug Abuse: Current Concepts and Research.** Springfield, Ill., Charles C. Thomas, 1972. 467p. bibliog. index. $1.50. LC 70-172459. ISBN 0-398-02331.

This book presents the proceedings of a meeting of the Eastern Psychiatric Research Association held November 7-8, 1970. It gives an overview of drug abuse at the time and presents some recent concepts, scientific findings, and treatment possibilities. There are summary papers and original contributions. The book is in the following sections, each of which contains several papers: 1) Introductory papers, 2) Physical and medical aspects, 3) Psychological and sociological aspects, 4) Psychopharmacological aspects, and 5) Clinical and treatment aspects.

The book ends with a look into the future regarding the management and care of drug abusers. The author believes we need a program of care for the recovering addict in an arrangement of outpatient services flanking the hospital, and that counseling and psychotherapy must be made available to the patient.

514. Leavitt, Fred. **Drugs and Behavior.** Philadelphia, W. B. Saunders Co., 1974. 404p. illus. bibliog. index. $7.95pa. LC 73-89182. ISBN 0-7216-5695-1.

This introduction to the field of psychopharmacology, the science which deals with the effects of drugs on behavior, is suitable for home study or for classroom use. Although no prior knowledge of drug actions or of psychological principles is assumed, the material is presented on a rather advanced level. The chapter headings are as follows: 1) Classification of drugs, 2) Principles of drug action, 3) Effects of drugs, 4) Dangers of drugs, 5) Profiles of drug users, 6) Therapy for drug abuse, 7) Psychopharmacotherapy, 8) Developmental aspects, 9) Methodological issues, 10) Sensory phenomena, 11) Learning and memory, 12) Creativity, 13) Sex and reproduction, 14) Aggression, 15) Sleep and dreams, and 16) Electrical stimulation of the brain. There are two appendices: 1) A brief introduction to organic chemistry, and 2) A glossary of psychoactive drugs.

The work can be used as a summplementary text for courses in such fields as physiological psychology, sociology, experimental design and methodology, and pharmacy, as well as for a one-semester course in psychopharmacology.

515. Madow, Leo, and Laurence H. Snow, eds. **The Psychodynamic Implications of the Physiological Studies on Psychomimetic Drugs.** Springfield, Ill., Charles C. Thomas, 1971. 81p. bibliog. $7.75. LC 70-165890.

These papers were presented at the third annual symposium on the psychodynamic implications of various studies in physiology. The participants attempt to shed some light on and raise some questions about fundamental problems in the entire issue of drug usage. One of the basic questions discussed is "why is there an enormous drive to drug oneself?" More specifically, why are hallucinogenic agents popular? What is the appeal of rendering oneself psychotic, and why is there a drive toward self-destruction? The papers, which are written by psychiatrists, are as follows: 1) Theories on the psychic effects of the psychomimetics, 2) Some special features of the LSD reaction, 3) Studies in marijuana, 4) Psychophysiology of hallucinogenic drug action, and 5) Some psychodynamic considerations of drug choice.

The papers are interesting and enlightening, as are the discussions, which have also been included. As might be expected, however, the questions posed are not answered completely. The subject matter is of particular interest to psychiatrists and other medical personnel, educators, behavioral scientists, and those in related professions.

516. Marshman, Joan A., ed. **Street Drug Analysis and Its Social and Clinical Implications.** Toronto, Alcoholism and Drug Addiction Research Foundation, 1974. 120p. bibliog. index. $5.50pa. LC 74-81878. ISBN 0-88868-000-7.

This publication contains papers presented at an International Symposium on Alcohol and Drug Problems. With the increasing widespread illegal use of psychoactive drugs during the past few years, it has become apparent that drugs purchased "on the street" do not always contain the pharmacologically active materials alleged to be present. Recognition of the problems brought about by this practice prompted the establishment of street drug analysis programs in both Europe and North America. This symposium brought together individuals involved in street drug analysis efforts so their experiences could be shared, achievements of such programs determined, and future endeavors considered.

In conclusion it appeared that benefits as follows might accrue from systematic street drug analyses: 1) better education of the user about potentially hazardous drugs on the market, 2) assistance to physicians in treating the adverse consequences of drug use, 3) epidemiological information about trends in drug use, and 4) assistance to law enforcement agencies about the comparative availability of the different substances. In addition, ways to set up centers for drug analysis were explored in some detail.

517. Mechoulam, Raphael, ed. **Marijuana: Chemistry, Pharmacology, Metabolism, and Clinical Effects.** New York, Academic Press, 1973. 409p. bibliog. index. $24.50. LC 72-77349. ISBN 0-12-487450-9.

The aim of this book is to present the state of the art in the chemistry, pharmacology, and clinical aspects of *Cannabis sativa L.* preparations which include marijuana, hashish, and the cannabinoids. A great deal of scientific progress in these areas has been made in the past few years because of the interest aroused by the increased use of these drugs and the associated problems.

Chapter headings are as follows: 1) Cannabinoid chemistry, 2) Structure-activity relationships in the cannabinoid series, 3) Analytical aspects of cannabis chemistry, 4) Labeling and metabolism of the tetrahydrocannabinols, 5) The pharmacology of cannabis in animals, 6) The actions of cannabis in man, 7) Clinical aspects of cannabis action. There is also an appendix of "Formulas of known natural cannabinoids and metabolites and some synthetic cannabinoids." The work is a scientific presentation that includes much technical data. It should be of special interest to researchers in pharmacology, psychology, medicine, and chemistry, and also of some interest to sociologists and criminologists.

The editor and the contributors have not attempted to draw a picture from which a clear-cut decision on social and legal problems can be made. The material has been presented objectively by a group of noted scientists.

518. Mendelson, Jack H., A. Michael Rossi, and Roger E. Meyer, eds. **The Use of Marihuana: a Psychological and Physiological Inquiry**. New York, Plenum Press, 1974. 202p. bibliog. index. $14.95. LC 74-17169. ISBN 0-306-30895-3.

This work reports on a controlled research project which yielded a mass of data on a number of separate aspects of the drug's effect on human subjects. Leading research workers examined the effects of marihuana on such things as motivation, aggression, group interaction, problem-solving, mood states, memory and time estimation, and psychological reactions. Some years ago Professor Mendelson and his collaborators did a study similar to this one on alcohol use. Comparison of acute and repeat dose effects of marihuana and alcohol showed some differences. The marihuana study showed that in tolerant individuals marihuana intoxication over a period of three weeks and with increased doses produced little disturbance, but the results with alcohol were quite different. However, cannabis was shown definitely to produce tolerance, a question that has been debated. The authors conclude that how marihuana use interacts with and affects the complex phenomenon of "dropping out" by some young people may never be determined. This study has been highly commended as a competent piece of scientific investigation.

519. Miller, Loren L., ed. **Marijuana: Effects on Human Behavior**. New York, Academic Press, 1974. 406p. bibliog. index. $24.50. LC 74-10216. ISBN 0-12-497050-8.

This is a summary of recent research on the effects of marijuana on individual behavior. Each of the 14 chapters reports the contributor's original research, with a review of previous research in the particular area. The papers are authoritative and interesting, and the book is probably the best of its kind. The contributors are well-known researchers, and the book is designed for clinical investigators, researchers in pharmacology, psychiatrists, and sociologists. But it will also interest lawyers, legislators, and the general public. The writing is objective.

There are chapters on the drug's influence on memory and attention, the relationship of use to aggressive behavior, progression to more dangerous drugs, the development of mental illness, effects on driving, and a number of other topics. In general, the research results indicate that the use of marijuana is detrimental in almost all instances.

520. Mulé, S. J. and Henry Brill, eds. **Chemical and Biological Aspects of Drug Dependence**. Cleveland, Ohio, CRC Press, 1972. 561p. illus. bibliog. index. $39.95. LC 72-191695. ISBN 0-8789-011-2.

This monograph was produced because drug dependence has reached epidemic proportions and its treatment and prevention have brought mainly disappointing results. As a reference work, it provides the scientist with basic knowledge and background information on the chemical and biological basis of drug dependence. The characteristics of each class of drug are described and, as much as possible, correlated with the capacity to induce drug dependence. The work offers theories on how tolerance and dependence develop, with attention to biochemical mechanisms as well.

Many experts contributed these technical papers, which are arranged in the following sections: 1) Significance and characteristics of drug dependence, 2) Criteria for evaluating drug dependence, 3) Chemical aspects of drug dependence, 4) Physiologic and pharmacologic aspects of drug dependence, and 5) Biochemical aspects of drug dependence. While most of the papers in the book are too technical for the average reader, there is much information of general interest.

521. Nahas, Gabriel G., ed. **Marihuana: Chemistry, Biochemistry, and Cellular Effects**. Co-editors: William D. M. Patron and Juhana E. Idapaan-Heikkila. New York, Springer-Verlag, 1976. 556p. illus. bibliog. index. $19.80. LC 75-37724. ISBN 0-387-07554-2.

This book presents the Proceedings of the Satellite Symposium on Marihuana of the Sixth International Congress of Pharmacology held July 26, 1975 in Helsinki, Finland. Papers discuss the biochemical and cellular effects of long-term marihuana use.

Although a good deal of publicity has been given to the supposedly harmless effects of marihuana use, some experts feel that scientific evidence points to long-term effects. Investigators have shown experimentally that some of the substances in marihuana inhibit cell proliferation, growth, and sperm formation and impair the immunity system.

The papers contained in this book describe interactions between the biologically active molecules in marihuana and the basic components and processes of living cells. It is hoped that these technical, scientific papers will help the biologist and physician assess the long-term effects of the drug's use on such things as reproduction, embryological development, learning, growth, and numerous physiological functions. It is stressed that there is still much to be learned about the effects of marihuana.

Micromethods for detecting the substance in body fluids, urine, plasma, and saliva have been included.

522. Nahas, Gabriel G. **Marihuana—Deceptive Weed**. Rev. ed. New York, Raven Press, 1975. 334p. bibliog. index. $12.50. LC 72-76743. ISBN 0-911216-39-1.

The author of this work has come to the conclusion, shared by many scientists, that the innocuousness of marihuana is being overstated and its dangers underestimated. This book presents a general account of the plant, the history of its use, and the scientific and medical evidence about it, offering evidence that prolonged daily use of cannabis preparations is associated with mental and physical deterioration. The author is a physician and pharmacologist.

Chapter headings are as follows: 1) From Bhang to Delta-9-THC: four thousand years of history, 2) Botany—the unstabilized species, 3) Chemistry: The elusive Delta-9-THC and its active metabolites, 4) Toxicology and pharmacology, 5) Clinical pharmacology, 6) Cannabis intoxication and mental illness, 7) Social aspects, and 8) General summary and conclusion. The book is important because it gives a realistic, medically responsible approach with a somewhat different outlook in a controversial field. The author's view is that marihuana intoxication is not just another youthful fad—it is symptomatic of disillusioned youth seeking new values. He warns that intoxication cannot lead to any lasting fulfillment, and he opposes making cannabis or any hallucinogenic drug available for use. He also wonders how long a political system can endure when drug taking becomes one of the prerequisites of happiness. To quote: "If the American dream has lost its attraction, it will not be retrieved through the use of stupefying drugs. Their use only delays the young in their quest to understand the world they now live in and their desire to foster a better world for tomorrow."

523. National Research Council. Committee on Problems of Drug Dependence. **Report, 1974.** Proceedings of the thirty-sixth annual scientific meeting. Washington, National Research Council, 1974. 1245p. bibliog. index. ISBN 0-309-0244-4.

This publication contains papers of a meeting of the Committee on Problems of Drug Dependence. The papers are reports of ongoing research and projects and are not definitive works on the subjects under consideration. Special sessions in the following subject areas were presented: clinical studies relating to drug dependence, treatment and rehabilitation, opiate receptor and pharmacology, other research in drug abuse, and sociology and epidemiology. Among the 94 papers included are presentations on such matters as methadone analysis, synthetic substitutes for morphine, narcotic antagonists, heroin addiction, Vietnam drug addiction, effects of maternal narcotic addiction, analgesic studies on cancer patients, alcoholism, early precursors of teenage drug abuse, and adverse reactions and recurrences from marihuana use. (See the next entry for a report of the 1975 annual scientific meeting of the same group.)

524. National Research Council. Committee on Problems of Drug Dependence. **Problems of Drug Dependence, 1975.** Proceedings of the thirty-seventh annual scientific meeting, Committee on Problems of Drug Dependence, Washington, D. C., May 19-21, 1975. Washington, National Research Council, 1975. 1212p. bibliog. index. LC 75-29630. ISBN 0-309-02417-X.

Most of these scientific papers are reports of on-going research. Some of the subject areas covered are: sociology and epidemiology, clinical studies, clinical pharmacology, opiate receptors, treatment and rehabilitations, drug dependence animal studies, and animal pharmacology.

525. Paton, W. D. M., and June Crown, eds. **Cannabis and Its Derivatives: Pharmacology and Experimental Psychology.** Proceedings of a Symposium arranged by the Institute for the Study of Drug Dependence, London, May 1972. London, Oxford University Press, 1972. 198p. illus. bibliog. index. $16.00. ISBN 0-19-26115-1.

This publication presents the papers and an edited version of the discussions of the second symposium organized by the Institute for the Study of Drug Dependence. Chemists, biochemists, pharmacologists, and experimental psychologists from a number of countries participated. Laboratory work is emphasized, and the papers are highly technical. Major aspects covered are recent advances in chemistry, general and neuropharmacology, toxicity, and experimental psychology in man and animals.

526. Praag, H. M. Van, ed. **Biochemical and Pharmacological Aspects of Dependence, and Reports on Marihuana Research.** Symposium organized by the Interdisciplinary Society of Biological Psychiatry held in Amsterdam, September 1971. Haarlem, Bohn, 1972. 213p. bibliog. $13.00. ISBN 90-6051-439-4.

The first group of papers presented here discuss various aspects of drug dependence. The second group discuss reports on research on marihuana and its derivatives. Only scientific matters are considered; social views are not presented. The short summary included with each paper makes it possible to scan the material quickly. The following papers are presented: 1) Dependence: symptom and cause, 2) Complexity of the dependence problem, 3) A pharmacological analysis of drug-dependence, 4) Factors which might modify morphine dependence in rats, 5) Biochemistry of alcoholism and models of addiction, 6) Experimental and clinical studies on amphetamine dependence, 7) Opiate dependence, 8) The chemical pharmacology of the active constituents of cannabis, 9) Some new cannabis-constituents, 10) Analysis of illicit drugs, 11) Marihuana and health, 12) The acute mental effects of marihuana, 13) Cannabis and alcohol: effects on simulated driving, 14) The use and cannabis: East and West, 15) Cannabis psychosis, and 16) The progression hypothesis: myth or reality?

527. Richter, Ralph W., ed. **Medical Aspects of Drug Abuse.** New York, Harper and Row, 1975. 399p. illus. bibliog. index. $17.50. LC 74-23052. ISBN 0-06-142264-9.

The contributors to this volume, medically trained individuals who are experienced in the medical problems of drug abuse, outline recent progress in the clinical and basic science aspects of the abuse of hallucinogens, opiates, stimulants, and other mind-altering drugs. Subjects treated are: management of infections, withdrawal states, overdose, and toxic reactions. Use and abuse of drugs in Vietnam and other military sites are analyzed. The information learned from the Vietnam experience was found to be especially startling. The book is divided into four parts: 1) Clinicopharmacological aspects of mind altering and addictive drugs, 2) Treatment modalities, 3) Medicosurgical management, 4) Therapeutic and educational approaches.

The editor hopes that this book will become a standard training text for health professionals. He emphasizes that all aspects of the drug abuse problem are important—social and rehabilitative as well as medical—but that this book deals mainly with medical problems. However, the last section of the work presents material of broader interest: 1) Odyssey House: a prototype therapeutic community, 2) Treatment of the addict in correctional institutions, and 3) Medical school education in the addictive disorders.

528. Sandler, Merton, and G. L. Gessa. **Sexual Behavior: Pharmacology and Biochemistry.** New York, Raven Press, 1975. 354p. bibliog. index. $22.50. LC 74-14478. ISBN 0-89004-005-2.

These brief scientific papers, contributed by various authors, report the effects of drugs and other substances on sexual behavior. A number of papers report research carried out with laboratory animals as subjects, but most involve humans. It is becoming apparent that sexual behavior is not only dependent on classic hormonal influences but also can be influenced by some rather recently discovered drugs, which can stimulate or influence such behavior. The aim of this book is to report such findings. Some of the major subject areas covered are: neuroendocrinology and pharmacology of sexual behavior, drug abuse and sexual behavior, influence on sexual behavior of drugs acting on monoaminergic or cholinergic mechanisms, sex offenders (pharmacological, psychological, and legal problems), influence on sexual behavior of steroid and peptide hormones, sexual behavior in psychiatric disorders, and drugs affecting behavior in humans (hormones, drugs, and monoamines). The book is of interest because it covers a subject area about which relatively little has been written.

529. Sapira, Joseph D., and Charles E. Cherubin. **Drug Abuse: A Guide for the Clinician**. Amsterdam, Excerpta Medica; New York, American Elsevier Publishing Co., 1975. 443p. illus. bibliog. index. $55.95. ISBN 90-219-2067-0; 0-444-16711-0 (American Elsevier).

Medical problems associated with drug abuse have become so prevalent that a book of this kind serves a real need. Written by physicians, it helps the physician handle these problems and helps educate him to the pharmacologic and personal situations that may confront him as he works with drug addicts. Social problems as well as medical ones are considered, although the emphasis is on the latter.

The first part of the book deals with medical complications of drug abuse; the second discusses the types of drugs abused and includes discussion of the effects of withdrawal; and the third, a miscellaneous section, includes a discussion of treatment modalities, pharmacologic tests for drugs, and the causes of death in narcotic addicts.

The chapter headings of the first 11 chapters, which discuss the effects of drugs of abuse on various organs and systems of the body, are as follows: 1) Cardiovascular, 2) Pulmonary, 3) Gastrointestinal, 4) Hematologic, 5) Endocrine, 6) Renal, 7) Connective, 8) Skin, 9) Systemic infections, 10) Neurological, and 11) Reproduction. Headings for the next chapters, which discuss the drugs, are: 12) Receptor theory, 13) Narcotic analgesics, 14) Narcotic analgesic withdrawal, 15) Hypnotic-sedatives, 16) Hypnotic-sedative withdrawal, 17) Sympathomimetics, 18) Hallucinogens, and 19) Miscellaneous intoxicants. The "Potpourri" section includes these chapters: 20) Long-term treatment modalities, 21) Nalorphine and Naloxone testing, and 22) Causes of death in narcotic addicts.

The work is quite comprehensive and the bibliographies included are extensive. The literature on the subjects covered has been reviewed exhaustively, particularly in the medical sections. The treatment of the social problems of drug abuse is not so well handled. However, the parts dealing with medical complications are quite outstanding, and the chapter on the causes of death is most welcome. If the index were more detailed, the work could be used more easily for reference.

530. Singh, Jasbir M., Lyle Miller, and Harbans Lal, eds. **Drug Addiction. Vol. 1, Experimental Pharmacology; Vol. 2, Clinical and Socio-Legal Aspects.** Mount Kisco, N.Y., Futura Publishing Co., Inc., 1972. 2v. illus. bibliog. index. $14.95; $13.75. LC 72-189180.

These two volumes contain papers presented at the International Symposium on Drug Tolerance, Addiction, Abuse, and Methadone Treatment at the College of Pharmacy, Xavier University of Louisiana. Some papers by other researchers are also included. The subject matter of the first volume deals with behavioral studies of drug addiction, pharmacological aspects of drug addiction, environmental interactions with drug addiction, and the mechanism of drug addiction. Volume two contains papers on social and legal aspects of drug addiction, human pharmacodynamics, methadone treatment, and recent innovations in the treatment of addiction. The papers present a multidisciplinary approach to the problem, although most are at least somewhat scientific. The authors are for the most part professors who are only moderately well known.

The summary chapter suggests that continued research of a multidisciplinary nature is essential if one is to acquire the knowledge needed for intelligent treatment, education, and legislation to deal with this problem. Although this is true, it is not a novel proposal.

Other volumes are appearing in this seris. Volumes three and four present papers from the Second International Symposium on Drug Addiction. Volume three is on neurobiology and influences on behavior, and volume four on new aspects of analytical and clinical toxicology.

531. Snyder, Solomon H. **Drugs, Madness, and the Brain**. London, Hart-David MacGibbon, 1975. 287p. illus. bibliog. index. £6.00. ISBN 0-246-10822-3. (Originally published as *Madness and the Brain.* McGraw-Hill, 1974).

This book is about the disease schizophrenia rather than about drug abuse. However, there is a connection, since several drugs of abuse produce schizophrenia-like symptoms, and some have also been used as treatment for the condition. The material is presented for the layman. Recent research into the biology and treatment of schizophrenia are discussed. In Part I the author outlines the concepts of insanity, the treatments for schizophrenia, and the effects of psychedelic drugs like mescaline and LSD, which are similar to but different in several crucial respects from schizophrenia. Part II presents a nontechnical description of the behavior of the schizophrenic patient. It is pointed out that the psychosis induced by repeated high doses of amphetamine is similar to the mental state of paranoid schizophrenia. The use of tranquillizers is explored and questioned. Well written and balanced in opinion, the book is recommended for laymen and health professionals.

532. Sternberg, Hannah, ed. **Scientific Basis of Drug Dependence: A Symposium.** London, J. and A. Churchill Ltd., 1969. 429p. illus. bibliog. index. £5.00. ISBN 0-7000-1394-6.

These papers, written by scientists from several disciplines, deal with numerous aspects of the drug dependence problem, including definitions, general principles, approaches to laboratory experiments, and clinical and social factors. Opiates were formerly the traditional drugs of dependence. Now they have been joined by barbiturates, amphetamines, cocaine, cannabis, and alcohol (which has traditionally been a socially accepted drug). The pharmacological actions of these drugs differ, and it is not known at this time how much these properties are responsible for creating dependence and addiction. Perhaps some explanations must be sought elsewhere, but there is good evidence to suggest a scientific basis. Much of this evidence is presented and discussed in this book.

533. U.S. Bureau of Narcotics and Dangerous Drugs. Drug Control Division. **A Survey of Analytical Methods for Determination of Controlled Drugs in Body Fluids.** By F. J. Bullock and others of the Arthur D. Little Co. staff. Final Report, BNDD Contract No. 72-22. Washington, GPO, 1972. 237p. index. (SCID-TR-8).

Reliable methods of determining the presence of controlled drugs in the human body are frequently needed in drug abuse treatment programs, overdose treatment, and in doing post-mortem examinations. The purpose of this work was to survey and evaluate published methods for determining the presence in body fluids of certain drugs included in the Controlled Substances Act of 1970. Indexing and abstracting publications were used to locate pertinent articles, and the literature was searched from 1960 to August 1972. The methods outlined in the book are presented in the following sections: 1) Quantitative methods of choice, 2) Alternative quantitative methods, 3) Methods of uncertain reliability, 4) Qualitative detection methods, 5) Metabolic and biological data, and 6) Supplementary information and comments. About each method the following information is included in outline form: principle, specimen, procedure, conditions for chromatography, precision, sensitivity, reliability, specificity, interferences, and notes.

Because there is great variability in the method of publishing such data, standardization and experimental evaluation of methods in this area of forensic science are needed. Also, it is pointed out that no quantitative analytical methods are available for many substances covered in the Controlled Substances Act.

534. U.S. National Institute on Drug Abuse. **Cannabinoid Assays in Humans.** Edited by Robert E. Willette. Washington, GPO, 1976. 120p. bibliog. (DHEW Publication No. (ADM) 76-339; Research Monograph Series 7). For sale by the National Technical Information Service, $6.00pa., $2.25 microfiche. Stock Order #PB 251 905. LC 76-15843.

These papers describe methods of determining qualitatively and quantitatively the constituents of marihuana in the human body. These methods are important in research investigations and also in practical areas such as determining the presence of cannabinoids in drivers suspected of being under the influence of the drug. The methods described are grouped under three major headings: 1) Immunoassay techniques, 2) Chromatography, and 3) Mass spectrometry.

535. U.S. National Institute on Drug Abuse. **Drugs and Addict Lifestyles: Lifestyle Histories of Heroin Users.** Edited by Patricia Ferguson, Thomas Lennox, and Don J. Lettieri. Washington, GPO, 1974. 263p. bibliog. index. (DHEW Publication No. (ADM) 75-189; Research Issues Series No. 7). $3.30pa.

This publication is made up of reviews or summaries of articles reporting on research findings of the past 15 years. The material has been divided into five sections: 1) Life styles, 2) Natural history of addiction, 3) Characteristics of heroin addicts, 4) Drug use patterns, and 5) Theories of addiction. The summaries, which are two or three pages long, include comments on methodology, findings, and conclusions about each article.

536. U.S. National Institute on Drug Abuse. **Drugs and Death: The Nonmedical Use of Drugs Related to All Modes of Death.** Edited by Patricia Ferguson, Thomas Lennox, and Dan J. Lettieri. Washington, GPO, 1974. 151p. bibliog. index. (DHEW Publication No. (ADM) 75-188; Research Issues Series 6). $2.25pa.

This publication presents summaries of articles that report major findings of the last 15 years. The reviews have been arranged under headings as follows: 1) Classification and reporting systems, 2) Suicide and homicide, 3) Opiate related death: incidence and cause, 4) Opiate related death: infectious disease, 5) Opiate related death: pathological findings, and 6) Other drug-related death. With each citation the following information is given: a summary, methodology, findings, and conclusions. Most of the reviews are at least two pages long.

537. U.S. National Institute on Drug Abuse. **Drug and Pregnancy: The Effects of Nonmedical Use of Drugs on Pregnancy, Childbirth, and Neonates.** Edited by Patricia Ferguson, Thomas Lennox, and Dan J. Lettieri. Washington, GPO, 1974. 147p. bibliog. index. (DHEW Publication No. (ADM) 75-187; Research Issues Series No. 5.) $2.15pa.

This publication presents summaries of articles reporting major research findings of the last 15 years. The reports have been arranged under the following headings: 1) Overviews, 2) LSD, 3) Heroin, 4) Methadone, 5) Methadone and heroin; comparative studies, and 6) Selected annotated studies. The following information is usually included with each citation: a summary, methodology, findings, and conclusions. In general, the reports indicate that a high rate of problems is found with infants of drug-addicted mothers.

538. U.S. National Institute on Drug Abuse. **Drugs and Sex: The Nonmedical Use of Drugs and Sexual Behavior.** Edited by Patricia Ferguson, Thomas Lennox, and Don J. Lettieri. Washington, GPO, 1974. 80p. bibliog. index. (DHEW Publication No. (ADM) 75-184; Research Issues Series No. 4). $1.45pa.

This publication is one of a series that summarizes articles reporting major research findings of the past 15 years. The reviews are arranged under the following headings: 1) Multi-drug, 2) Marijuana, 3) Amphetamines, 4) LSD, and 5) Heroin and methadone. The reviews, which are usually two pages or more in length, include a summary, methodology, findings, and conclusions. Major clearinghouses, data bases, library collections, and previous bibliographies were searched to find references for inclusion.

539. U.S. National Institute on Drug Abuse. **Narcotic Antagonists: Naltrexone Progress Report.** Editors, Demetrios Julius and Pierre Renault. Washington, GPO, 1976. 181p. bibliog. (DHEW Publication No. (ADM) 76-387; Research Issues Series No. 9). LC 76-40692. For sale by the National Technical Information Service, Order No. PB 255 833. $7.50pa.; microfiche $2.25.

This volume contains the papers presented at the National Academy of Science's Satellite Naltrexone Conference, held June 6 and 7, 1976, in Richmond, Virginia. The participants were individuals well known for their work in the drug abuse field. The papers provide reviews of research problem areas and techniques and indicate the state-of-the-art in developing better treatment methods for opiate dependence with the use of a narcotic antagonist.

The presentations have been grouped into the following subject sections: 1) The federal role in naltrexone development, 2) The NAS double-blind study, 3) The NIDA clinical studies, 4) The NIDA behavioral studies, and 5) Current status of naltrexone safety data.

The studies resulted in some interesting conclusions: the drug is generally safe, although there are some side effects; it is for the highly motivated only; the goal of treatment should be focused on change of lifestyle; and the patient maintained on naltrexone must eventually face a crisis when he attempts to maintain control in the absence of naltrexone and heroin is again available.

540. U.S. National Institute on Drug Abuse. **Narcotic Antagonists: the Search for Long-Acting Preparations.** Robert Willette, editor. Washington, GPO, 1976. 45p. illus. bibliog. (DHEW Publication (ADM) 76-206; National Institute on Drug Abuse Research Monograph Series No. 4). $1.10pa. LC 75-29949. S/N 017-024-00488-0.

This document reviews the current state-of-the-art of developing pharmaceutical preparations that will give sustained or long-acting effect (through the use of such materials as implanted discs or microcapsules injected intramuscularly), thus making it possible to deliver a narcotic antagonist that will allow weeks or even months between doses. Using narcotic antagonists in opiate addiction is based on the concept that a pharmaceutical agent taken during an addict's rehabilitation can block the reinforcing properties of a dose of an opiate. The antagonist blocks the "high" and makes it pleasureless, thus removing the addict's incentive for continued use of the narcotic. The drug naltrexone is the most promising at the present time, and it is the one used in this study.

541. U.S. National Institute on Drug Abuse. **Operational Definitions in Socio-Behavioral Drug Use Research, 1975.** Editors: Jack Elinson, David Nurco. Washington, GPO, 1975. 58p. bibliog. (DHEW Publication No. (ADM) 76-292; National Institute on Drug Abuse Research Monograph Series No. 2). LC 75-29022.

This monograph is an outgrowth of the efforts of the Special Action Office for Drug Abuse Prevention and the National Institute on Drug Abuse to achieve greater comparability across socio-behavioral research studies. It has in the past been difficult to compare the results of one research effort with another, at least partly because research terms have not been agreed upon. The concerns, admonitions, and recommendation expressed in this document are limited to survey research on human populations. (Questions are asked of respondents, and the resulting data are self-reports of behavior, experience, attitudes, and values.)

The following chapters, written by various experts, are included: 1) Introduction, 2) History of drug use, 3) Functional taxonomy of drugs, 4) Definition of addiction liability associated with different patterns of drug use, 5) Measures of currency or recency (in drug use surveys), 6) The measurement of "ever use" and "frequency-quantity" (in drug use surveys), 7) Defining the term "polydrug use," 8) Conditions of drug use, 9) Some words of caution on subjective concepts: "Interest in trying, maintaining or changing use," "Reasons for use," "Reasons for non-use," 10) Effects of drug use. Appended materials, which make up more than half the volume, include operational definitions used in recent socio-behavioral research on drugs and examples of questionnaires.

542. U.S. National Institute on Drug Abuse. **Rx: 3 x/week LAAM; Alternative to Methadone**. Jack D. Blaine and Pierre F. Renault. Washington, GPO, 1976. 127p. bibliog. For sale by the National Technical Information Service. $6.00pa.; $3.00 microfiche. (NIDA Research Monograph 8; DHEW Publication No. (ADM) 76-347). LC 76-20257. S/N PB 253-763.

This publication reviews the development and assesses the value of the new drug LAAM (levo-alph-acetyl methadol) as a replacement for methadone in the treatment of heroin addiction. The drug is now ready for widespread use after years of development and clinical trials. The hope is that there will be fewer problems connected with its use than there have been with methadone. Reports are given on the chemistry, pharmacology, and toxicology of LAAM and on preclinical and clinical experience with it.

543. Vesell, Elliot S., and Monique C. Braude, eds. **Interactions of Drugs of Abuse**. New York, New York Academy of Sciences, 1976. 489p. bibliog. (New York Academy of Sciences. Annals. v.281). LC 76-54861. ISBN 0-89072-027-4.

The papers presented in this volume are the proceedings of a conference held March 9-11, 1976, sponsored by the New York Academy of Sciences and the National Institute of Drug Abuse. It was the first conference on Interactions of Drugs of Abuse. The subject matter treated is of growing importance because of the increase in polydrug use and the ever-present use of alcohol. The authors of the papers, who are expert scientists, analyze the many complexities of the neuronal, extra-neuronal, and genetic factors involved, explore the behavioral aspects, and examine the clinical effects. The material is of high quality.

The papers are divided into two sections: "Molecular, Cellular, and Clinical Aspects of Drug Interactions" and "Interactions Involving Drugs of Abuse." The following drugs are covered: marihuana, narcotics and narcotic antagonists, depressants, stimulants, and hallucinogens.

544. Wider, François. **Psychoactive Drugs, including Combinations.** Basel, S. Karger, 1974. 264p. bibliog. index. (Data Processing in Medicine, Vol. 3). $44.00. ISBN 3-9055-1740-8.

This work contains summarized data on more than 650 psychoactive substances. The drugs have been divided into five primary classes as follows: 1) Neuroleptics, 2) Tranquillizers, 3) Antidepressants, 4) Psychostimulants, and 5) Psychodysleptics (hallucinogenics, psychotomimetics). Within the five classes, arrangement is by the chemical point of view. The following information is given with each entry: the name, with an indication of its source (such as British Approved Name or a U. S. Adopted Name); additional customary trivial names and other unofficial names; the chemical structural formulae; the chemical abbreviated formulae; trade names and the manufacturers and country in which the name is used. In addition, an alphabetical index of about 7,000 names and an abbreviated formula index have been provided. The introduction to the work is given in English, French, and German.

Although this material can be found elsewhere (notably in Martin Negwer, *Organisch-Chemische Arzneimittel und ihre Synonyma.* Bd. 1-2. Berlin, Akademie-Verlag, 1971), Wider's work gives more consideration to combination drugs.

545. Williams, Melvin H. **Drugs and Athletic Performance**. Springfield, Ill., Charles C. Thomas, 1974. 199p. bibliog. index. $10.75. LC 73-19709. ISBN 0-398-03064-2.

This book attempts to synthesize the specific research concerning the effects of various drugs on athletic performance. It also considers the ethics of using drugs to improve athletic performance. Chapter headings are: 1) Introduction to the drug problem in athletics, 2) Drugs affecting the nervous system–stimulants, 3) Drugs affecting the nervous system–depressants, 4) Drugs affecting the muscular system, 5) Drugs affecting the cardiovascular system, and 6) Research and the doping problem.

No solution to the problem is presented. The drugs that consistently improve athletic performance are not known, and the way in which they act is also unknown. So far the research has been inconclusive, although some of the studies outlined in the book may provide insight or assist in making valid interpretations of data. There is an excellent bibliography of about 550 references. The work is of particular value to athletes, physical educators, coaches, sports physicians, sports administrators, and others who are interested in the subject.

546. Wisconsin State University (Stevens Point, Wisconsin). **Drug Use and Highway Safety: A Review of the Literature**. Prepared for the U.S. Department of Transportation, National Highway Traffic Safety Administration by James L. Nichols. Washington, GPO, 1971. 110p. bibliog. $1.25pa. S/N 5003-0050.

The purpose of this report is to provide a comprehensive review of the literature concerning the relationship between drug use and traffic safety. The report includes any study that received publicity in traffic safety periodicals, circulated research reports, or through the news media. Topics covered include the effects of drugs, types of drug users, research problems in assessing risk, laboratory findings on effects of drugs, survey findings, toxicological investigations, and legal aspects of drug-driving laws.

On the basis of the information presented in this review, the recommendation is made that emphasis be place on adequate research concerning drug-driving phenomenon and not on more rigorous legislation and enforcement procedures.

The following research recommendations are made: 1) it will be necessary to develop methods for the detection of hallucinogens in users; 2) it will be necessary to develop improved screening methods for the detection of all drugs; 3) more sophisticated research designs must be incorporated into investigations of the drug-driving phenomenon; and 4) research concerning the impact of drugs on traffic safety should be conducted in conjunction with ongoing Alcohol Safety Action Programs.

547. Zinberg, Norman E. **"High" States: A Beginning Study**. Washington, Drug Abuse Council, 1974. 51p. bibliog. $1.25pa. LC 74-20155.

This phenomenological study describes the actual experience of intoxication with opiate and psychedelic drugs. The experience is placed within a social and psychological context. The author, a physician well known in drug abuse work, includes the following chapters: 1) Introduction; 2) Morality; 3) Drug, set, and setting; 4) Theoretical framework; 5) The drug states; and 6) Discussion. The author makes a case for studying the processes of perception by observing altered states of consciousness.

13. Employee Problems in Business and Industry

This section lists titles covering the problems of drug abuse and employment, which have received attention recently. Detection, treatment, and rehabilitation of the drug-using employee are given emphasis. Also work has been used as a rehabilitative factor in the lives of addicts and ex-addicts. It has become evident, however, that legal entanglements are quite possible when socially conscious employers hire drug users.

548. Carone, Pasquale A., and Leonard W. Krinsky. **Drug Abuse in Industry**. Springfield, Ill., Charles C. Thomas, 1973. 172p. index. $11.50. LC 73-228. ISBN 0-398-02801-X.

The material in this book is based on papers and discussion presented at a conference, "Drug Abuse in Industry," held at South Oaks, Long Island, New York, in April 1972. The topic is quite timely. Representatives of both management and labor, the academic community, psychiatrists, psychologists, physicians, medical directors of companies, and directors of state agencies were participants. Four basic aspects of drug abuse were covered: 1) The physiological effects, 2) Clinical and treatment aspects, 3) Labor-management views of the problem, and 4) Legal aspects. Discussions covered therapeutic community models as contrasted with methadone maintenance units; criteria for employment and re-employment; detection and treatment of the drug-using employee; findings of the medical examiner and neuro-pathologist; how the labor movement sees this major problem; and views and progress of the probation department.

549. Chambers, Carl D., and Richard D. Heckman. **Employee Drug Abuse: A Manager's Guide for Action**. Boston, Cahners Books, 1972. 222p. bibliog. index. $12.50. LC 73-183372. ISBN 0-8436-0718-1.

Since drug abuse in business and industry is widespread, managers in all organizations and on all levels are confronted with problems of detection, prevention, drug education, and involvement with rehabilitation. This guide helps managers define and implement a program of action, with actual examples of what companies do. There are sections on the following subjects: 1) Policy in the making, 2) Treatment and rehabilitation of drug abusers, 3) About employee education, and yours, 4) Co mmunicating with supervisors, 5) An avocation ends, 6) As one manager sees it, 7) The extent of drug abuse in business and industry, and 8) Organizing a community drug program. Appended are a list of "Selected Printed Reference and Audio Visual Materials," a "Drug Glossary," and a list of "Sources for Information about Drug Abuse."

The senior author, a Ph.D. medical sociologist, has had considerable experience in the field of employee drug abuse. The co-author is a freelance writer specializing in business and industry subjects. They have produced a useful book.

550. Goldberg, I. Ira. **Employment and Addiction: Perspectives on Existing Business and Treatment Practices.** Final report of a research and development project under Department of Labor grant #92-25-71-05. Cambridge, Mass., Harvard University, 1972. Available from the National Technical Information Service, Springfield, Va. 181p. bibliog. $3.00.

The purpose of this study was to assess and analyze business practices when there was drug use by employees. In addition, employer relationships with manpower and drug addiction control agencies were studied, in the hope of developing models for coordinating employer-manpower development-drug rehabilitation activities to enhance employment stability of drug users and ex-addicts. Practices of both employers and drug treatment programs were surveyed by means of questionnaires.

The conclusions reached were, for the most part, disappointing. Few drug programs in the area under consideration (Massachusetts) made use of "world of work" concerns, and few employers hired drug users or ex-addicts. However, if such programs are undertaken, this study provides suggestions on how to proceed.

The survey questionnaire, a list of drug programs, the employers contacted, and a bibliography have been appended.

551. Halpern, Susan. **Drug Abuse and Your Company.** American Management Association, Inc., 1972. 145p. index. (An AMA Research Book). $11.50. LC 79-184053. ISBN 0-8144-5294-9.

The recent increase in drug abuse has made it a problem among every company's employees. The intent of the book is to make known the extent of the problem, the experiences of other companies, and what is being done to alleviate the situation. The material is based on surveys from 231 companies, interviews with about 75 executives in industry, and available literature.

There are four chapters: 1) Highlights for management, 2) Detection methods, 3) Dealing with the problem, and 4) Recommendations. The three appendices include a drug chart, a list of terminology, and legal questions and answers. A number of exhibits are also presented, such as sample laboratory procedure for urine screening for drugs, drug policies and policy statements of various companies, and excerpts from drug treatment programs. It is hoped that the information presented will help other companies implement their own policies and programs.

552. Scher, Jordan M., ed. **Drug Abuse in Industry: Growing Corporate Dilemma.** Springfield, Ill., Charles C. Thomas, 1973. 312p. index. $11.95. LC 73-227. ISBN 0-398-2809-5.

This work explores the extent and seriousness of the drug abuse problem in industry, examining such matters as serious thefts, accidents, poor work performance, chronic absenteeism, and lowered company morale and loyalty. The reader is told what signs and symptoms to look for when drug abuse is suspected, and ways of helping the drug user are suggested. The book is divided into seven main parts, with several chapters in each, written by various authors. The parts are: 1) General considerations, 2) Drugs in industry, 3) The impact of the drug abuser, 4) Law and drug abuse, 5) Rehabilitation and industry, 6) Alcoholics in industry, and 7) Special problems. Appended are definitions and a primer on drugs.

553. Shaw, Sue Olinger, ed. **Drugs as a Management Problem**. A management seminar sponsored by the College of Business Administration of the University of Akron and the Akron Area Chapter of the American Society for Personnel Administration, in cooperation with the School of Law and the College of Nursing of the University of Akron. Akron, Ohio, College of Business Administration, University of Akron, 1971. 70p.

This publication contains four addresses, two by physicians, one by a lawyer, and one by a personnel administrator. The presentations are popular and somewhat elementary, but they contain much practical information on an important aspect of the drug problem.

554. Stewart, W. Wayne, ed. **Drug Abuse in Industry**. Symposium, May 18-19, 1970, Philadelphia. Miami, Halos and Associates, Inc., 1970. 268p. illus. bibliog. $11.50. LC 70-134794.

This book identifies and explores the basic problems of drug abuse in industry. The papers were written by authorities in the field of medicine and by representatives of various industries and government agencies. There are sections on drugs and their effects, identification of drugs, writing a policy on drug abuse, and program planning within the company. In addition there are appended materials as follows: legal controls, where to get help, sources of drug abuse information, glossary of slang terms and definitions, and questions and answers.

Abstracts of the papers are given in both English and Spanish.

555. Trice, Harrison M., and Paul M. Roman. **Spirits and Demons at Work: Alcohol and Other Drugs on the Job**. Ithaca, New York, New York State School of Industrial and Labor Relations, Cornell University, 1972. bibliog. index. $5.00. LC 72-619517. ISBN 0-87546-034-8.

Since the literature on drug abuse is growing at such a rapid rate, the authors hope this guide to the material will be of value for both work-organization personnel and behavioral scientists. They also offer a program of action for work organizations for the management of alcohol and drug abuse. Alcohol is the primary focus of this book, as it is seen to be America's major drug problem. The material, based on research studies from scholarly journals and monographs, is arranged under the following chapter headings: 1) Drinking, deviant drinking, and work; 2) Drugs, youth, and the work world; 3) Opiates, non-opiates, and their users; 4) Job-based risks for deviant drinking and drug use; 5) Job behaviors of deviant drinkers and drug abusers: specific impacts in the work place; 6) Reactions of supervisors to deviant drinkers and drug users; 7) The strategy of constructive confrontation; 8) Union-management cooperation and conflict, 9) Therapeutic alternatives for deviant drinkers and drug users.

556. U.S. National Institute on Drug Abuse. **Drugs and Employment: Nonmedical Use of Drugs in Occupational and Industrial Settings.** Edited by Patricia Ferguson, Thomas Lennox, and Dan J. Lettieri. Washington, GPO, 1974. 107p. bibliog. index. (DHEW Publication No. (ADM) 75-183; Research Issues Series No. 1). $1.80pa.

This publication presents reviews of the major research findings of the past 15 years. With each literature reference is given a summary of the article, methodology employed, findings, and conclusions. The material is divided by subject area as follows: 1) Overviews and issues, 2) Drug use in specific professions (medical, sports, aviation), 3) Surveys of drug use in companies, 4) Surveys of drug use among addicts, 5) Drug use in the labor force, and 6) Programs. The subject is well covered.

557. Ward, Hugh. **Employment and Addiction: Overview of Issues.** New York, The Drug Abuse Council, 1973. 55p. bibliog. $1.25pa. LC 73-83861.

Focusing primarily on the situation in New York, the author traces the comparatively short history and development of programs designed to use work as a rehabilitative factor in the lives of drug addicts and ex-addicts. The author also describes the evolution of employer attitudes and practices from 1970 until the time the book was written. The problems that stem from the shifting and often contradictory policies of local, state, and national governments are reviewed. There are examples of what are called "brighter signs," and a list of recommendations regarding future policy formation and program development. The author is skeptical of much of the research being done by academicians in the field of addiction and employment, but the reason for his skepticism is not made clear.

The book is readable, and it presents a fairly good analysis of a problem. However, there are no easy answers, since employers most often do not feel obligated to assist in the rehabilitation of drug addicts.

558. Willig, Sidney H. **Legal Considerations: Drug Abuse in Industry and Business.** Miami, Symposium Enterprises, 1971. 101p. $7.75pa. LC 77-151994.

This publication defines the statutes, regulations, and court decision that apply to the problems of employment of a drug mis-user in industry. It has become apparent that legal entanglements are quite possible, perhaps likely, when socially conscious employers have employed these people. Some of the legal problems considered are: 1) issues of substantive law of agent and principal, master and servant; 2) labor, contract law, and product liability; 3) Constitutional issues (1st, 4th, 5th, and 14th amendments); 4) Workmen's Compensation; 5) responsibility for criminal violations of drug and narcotic laws; 6) negligence, malpractice, and gross negligence; assault and battery, defamation, invasion of privacy; torts law and remedies; 7) pertinent decisional law.

14. Religion and Drugs

Certain psychoactive plants have been used since early times in the religious ceremonies of primitive peoples. These drugs and the peoples who still use them today are subjects of recent interest. Examples are the peyote cactus used by some of the Indians of Mexico and the Native American Church of the United States, and the sacred mushrooms (such as the Psilocybe and the *Amanita muscaria*). Some experts (see Clark, *Chemical Ecstasy*, entry 562) believe that there is a definite connection between psychedelic drugs and authentic religious experience. Clark feels that these drugs bring about religious insight and lasting conversion. Others reject the idea. Still others believe that hallucinogenic drugs have a place in society, although there is usually agreement that they must be used with caution.

559. Allegro, John M. **The Sacred Mushroom and the Cross: A Study of the Nature and Origins of Christianity within the Fertility Cults of the Ancient Near East.** New York, Bantam Books, Inc., published by arrangement with Doubleday and Co., Inc., 1971. 355p. index. $2.00.

Although this book is intended primarily for the general reader, the author acknowledges that the technical data included may be outside the scope of this group. The copious notes at the end of the book explain many passages referred to in the text.

The book's thesis is that Judaism and Christianity are, after a fashion, cultic expressions of the endless pursuit by man to discover instant power and knowledge. These present-day religions, he says, are logical developments from the older, cruder fertility cults. Primitive people thought that the drug-herbs provided the way to God and a fleeting view of heaven; the science of cultivating and using these drug-herbs had accumulated over centuries of observation and dangerous experiment. The sacred mushroom referred to in the title is known today as the *Amanita muscaria* or fly-agaric, and it has been used from early times. The ancients saw in its phallic form the replica of the fertility god, and it was, in fact, thought to be God himself manifest on earth. The mystics believed that the mushroom was the divinely given means of entering heaven, that God had come down in the flesh to show the way to himself. This mushroom, of course, contains a powerful hallucinatory substance.

The book is a scholarly presentation written by a lecturer in the Old Testament and inter-testamental studies at the University of Manchester. He was the first British representative on an international team currently preparing the Dead Sea Scrolls for publication. Some experts feel that the work is of doubtful authenticity, however, as the sacred mushroom referred to is not known to have grown in the Near East.

560. Benítz, Fernando. **In the Magic Land of Peyote.** Introduction by Peter T. Furst; translated by John Upton. Austin and London, University of Texas Press, 1975. 198p. illus. bibliog. index. $9.75. LC 74-23171. ISBN 0-292-73806-4.

This work was first published as part of the second volume of the author's *Los Indios de Mêxico*, a four-volume work published from 1970 to 1974. The author is a well-known Mexican journalist-historian, editor, and social critic who is interested in the surviving Indian cultures of his country. He has had the experience of going with the Huichol Indians on a sacred peyote hunt (as a few anthropologists also have had in the recent past), and this work describes the long pilgrimage to the magic land to gather peyote buttons for use in religious ceremonies. There are detailed descriptions of the life and social customs of the Indians, as well as their religious ceremonies. In addition, the book offers a comparison between the use of hallucinogenic drugs in our modern society and their use in a primitive society that is ruled by a mythical way of thinking. The book is illustrated with photographs of the Huicholes. The following chapters are included: 1) Why do we study Indians?, 2) Scenes of the desert, 3) Other religions, other inquisitions, 4) The pilgrims, 5) In the beginning was the deer, 6) Difficulties in San Andres, 7) A concise itinerary of the pilgrimage, 8) The return of the peyote pilgrims, 9) The festival of the parched corn, 10) The blood sacrifice.

561. Castaneda, Carlos. **The Teaching of Don Juan: A Yaqui Way of Knowledge.** New York, Ballantine Books, Inc., published by arrangement with the University of California Press, 1968. 276p. $1.25. LC 68-17303.

This book purports to recount the experiences of a graduate student in anthropology at UCLA while gathering information on peyote and medicinal herbs used by Indians of Sonora, Mexico. The author claims to have spent five years with a Yaqui Indian medicine man, don Juan, learning of the uses of peyote, jimson weed, and other hallucinogenic plants in "opening the doors of perception." The first part of the work is called "The Teachings "; the second, "A Structural Analysis."

The book has been widely acclaimed by reviewers in such publications as the *New York Times* and *Publishers Weekly* as an extraordinary document destined for fame and likely to become a classic. Unfortunately, the work was later exposed as a hoax, written to embarrass unwary anthropologists who might be taken in by the account. The book is readable and reasonably interesting, but experts in the area of the use of hallucinogenic drugs have not been fooled by it. The hoax is revealed in Richard de Mille's *Castaneda's Journey* (see entry 563).

562. Clark, Walter Houston. **Chemical Ecstasy: Psychedelic Drugs and Religion.** New York, Sheed and Ward, 1969. 179p. bibliog. index. $5.00. LC 74-82600. ISBN 0-8362-0412-3.

The author of this work is a scholar who has held university positions in both psychology and the psychology of religion. His point of view is that there is a definite connection between psychedelic drugs and authentic religious experience—that is, that the drugs do bring about genuine, self-transcending religious insight, ecstasy, and lasting conversion. He examines the religious experience of the Native American Church and its use of peyote, the experiments of Timothy Leary at Harvard, and claims of others who have used drugs to bring about religious experience. Although admitting the dangers of such drug use, Dr. Clark calls for more experimentation with the substances and hopes that churches will take some notice of the drug movement.

563. de Mille, Richard. **Castaneda's Journey: The Power and the Allegory.** Santa Barbara, Calif., Capra Press, 1976. 205p. illus. bibliog. index. $4.95pa. LC 65-26030. ISBN 0-88496-067-6; 0-88496-068-4pa.

This publication exposes the work of Carlos Castaneda as a hoax (see entry 561 for an example of his work) and outlines his unorthodox career at UCLA. However, the author points out that there are noteworthy aspects to Castaneda's writings (he wrote four best sellers) and that he has made a contribution to the mystical literature on religion and drugs. He is said to have done his homework very well, even though his books are fiction rather than fact as purported.

564. Furst, Peter T., ed. **Flesh of the Gods: The Ritual Use of Hallucinogens.** New York, Praeger Publishers, 1972. 304p. illus. bibliog. index. $10.00. LC 78-143970.

These ten noteworthy essays were written by well-known scholars of the world who have specialized in the subject under consideration. The contributors write from an anthropological, botanica, or psychological point of view. The view is taken that hallucinogenic substances have potentials for both good and evil and that the potential realized depends on who uses the drug, in what contexts, for what purposes, and under what kinds of control, as well as the chemical properties of the drug itself.

Chapter titles are as follows: 1) An overview of hallucinogens in the Western Hemisphere, 2) Tobacco and shamanistic ecstasy among the Warao Indians of Venezuela, 3) The cultural context of an aboriginal hallucinogen: *Banisteriopsis Caapi*, 4) The San Pedro cactus in Peruvian folk healing, 5) To find our life: peyote among the Huichol Indians of Mexico, 6) The divine mushroom of immortality, 7) What was the soma of the Aryans?, 8) Ritual use of *Cannabis Sativa L.*: a historical-ethnographic survey, 9) *Tabernanthe Iboga*: narcotic ecstasies and the work of the ancestors, and 10) Hallucinogens and the shamanic origins of religion.

The editor points out that the use of psychotropic drugs to achieve religious ecstacy goes back almost to the beginning of human culture. It is of note that the content of psychedelic experience in Western culture today has been found to be similar to early religious pilgrimages. But a significant difference is that the early cultures used the drug "trip" as a means to an end, a quest for confirmation of traditional values and unity with tribal ancestors. In present-day Western society the trip is an end in itself and a rejection of society's values. In spite of this, the editor feels that the role of hallucinogens in societies other than our own has relevance to our time and place.

565. Harner, Michael J., ed. **Hallucinogens and Shamanism.** New York, Oxford University Press, 1973. 200p. illus. bibliog. index. $8.50. LC 72-92292.

These ten field studies by anthropologists explore the use of hallucinogens in shamanism, the ancient practice of invoking a trance state in order to perceive and manipulate the supernatural. The varieties of drug-induced shamanism are presented in the following sections: 1) In the primitive world: the upper Amazon, 2) In cultures undergoing Westernization, 3) In the traditional Western world, and 4) Hallucinogens and shamanism: the question of a trans-cultural experience. Section one deals with primitive people; section two with such groups as the North American Indian and urban slum-dwellers; section three with the role of hallucinogens in medieval European witchcraft; and section 4 with two very different cultures, the South American Indians and 35 white urban volunteers who used a hallucinogenic drug in a laboratory setting. The latter two groups had similar visions, showing that local tradition did not have as much influence as the state induced by the drug.

The editor hopes that the contributions of this book will rectify the inadequate attention given to native hallucinogens by anthropologists.

566. Marriott, Alice, and Carol K. Rachlin. **Peyote.** New York, Thomas Y. Crowell Co., 1971. 111p. bibliog. index. $5.95. LC 75-146284. ISBN 0-690-61697-X.

This work is an account of the peyote religion of the Indians of the Southwest. Although the religion has been somewhat underground from time to time because of its involvement with drug use, it has been institutionalized in the form of the Native American Church and has spread among many Indian tribes of the United States. The book, a descriptive and historical account, includes little scientific material, although it does suggest that long-term use of peyote seems to be harmful. The authors are anthropologists who have participated in peyote ceremonies, and their descriptions of the effects of the drug and the rituals used in the rites are authentic.

567. Mortimer, W. Golden. **Peru History of Coca: "The Divine Plant" of the Incas.** With an introductory account of the Incas, and of the Andean Indians of today. New York, J. H. Vail and Co., 1901. 576p. illus. bibliog. index.

This classic work undertakes to trace the associations and uses of coca (the plant from which cocaine comes) from the earliest accounts to the time the book was written. The story begins with the Empire of the Incas and shows a connection between these people and the history of use of the plant. The industries, science, arts, poetry, drama, laws, social system, and religious rites of the Incas are all interwoven with the uses and applications of coca. Mortimer's work includes the accounts of contemporary travellers and scientists, as well as the scientific material about the plant that was known at the time. The following chapters are presented: 1) An introduction to the history of coca, 2) The story of the Incans, 3) The rites and acts of the Incans, 4) The conquest of the Incans, 5) The physical aspect of Peru, 6) The history of coca, 7) The present Indians of Peru, 8) The botany of coca, 9) In the coca region of Peru, 10) The products of the coca leaf, 11) The production of alkaloids in plants, 12) Influence of coca upon muscular energy, 13) Action of coca upon the nervous system, 14) The physiological action of coca, 15) Adaptation of coca to voice production, 16) The dietetic influence of coca. There are some additional appended materials, such as results of a collective investigation among several hundred physicians on the physiological action and the therapeutic application of Coca. This monumental book, which includes 178 illustrations, is quite interesting to read.

568. Myerhoff, Barbara G. **Peyote Hunt: The Sacred Journey of the Historical Indians.** Ithaca and London, Cornell University Press, 1974. 285p. illus. bibliog. index. LC 73-16923. ISBN 0-8014-0817-2.

This book is one of a series on symbol, myth, and ritual, the aim of which is to bring to public attention works by anthropologists on these subjects. This work describes an annual pilgrimage made by members of the Huichol Indian tribe of Mexico to their sacred land of Wirikuta to hunt peyote. The myth, rituals, religious symbols, and culture of the people are all painstakingly treated by the author who accompanied the Indians on their trip.

This interesting account does not focus entirely on the effects of the hallucinogenic agents in the peyote. It treats peyote as only one constituent in the Huicholes' ritual complex. This complex is made up of the deer, maize, and peyote as symbols in a sacred unity.

569. Nahal, Chaman, ed. **Drugs and the Other Self: An Anthology of Spiritual Transformations.** New York, Perennial Library, Harper and Row, 1971. 241p. $1.25pa. LC 74-146802.

This book presents material drawn exclusively from the experiences of mature, well-known writers. Some of it is reprinted from other sources. Section I is the editor's introduction to the drug phenomenon. Section II presents selections on drug experiences from the writings of Fitz Hugh Ludlow, Havelock Ellis, Aldous Huxley, R. C. Zaehner, and Christopher Isherwood. Section III, called "Limitations," presents writings by Heinrich Klüver, Charles Baudelaire, and William Blair. Section IV, "The Way Out," is made up of passages by the editor and Ralph Waldo Emerson.

In the introduction the editor comments on each essay and concludes that we can combat the drift toward the pseudo-mysticism that the drug culture has set in motion only by a renewal of the true religious ends of life.

570. Reichel-Dolmatoff, G. **The Shaman and the Jaguar: A Study of Narcotic Drugs among the Indians of Colombia.** Philadelphia, Temple University Press, 1975. 280p. illus. bibliog. index. $15.00. LC 74-83672. ISBN 0-87722-038-7.

The author of this well-documented work, an internationally known ethnologist, is chairman of the Department of Anthropology at the University of the Andes in Colombia. The main theme of the book is the use of certain narcotic drugs among Colombian Indians and the shaman-into-jaguar transformation which is related to it. Jaguar-people play key roles in the religious rites of these tribes. The study offers subjective and objective accounts of the hallucinogenic drug experiences used in the religious ceremonies of the Indians, presenting the botanical, chemical, and physiological properties of the drugs, although they are not always specifically described chemically or botanically. The author thinks it is important to study the lore of these Indians, since modern civilization is bringing about changes in the traditional way of life, and much of the information and experience of the older generation may be lost to posterity.

The first chapter is an historical survey of the use of narcotic snuff among the Indians. Chapter 2 refers to narcotic drinks made from a jungle vine. Chapter 3 discusses the relationship between narcotic substances and shamanistic practices, including jaguar imagery and symbolism. Early Spanish sources were used in compiling these chapters. Chapter 4 is an introduction to the local environment and rain forest Indian inhabitants of the Colombian Northwest Amazon. Chapters 5 to 10 consist mostly of accounts recorded in the field and commented upon by the Indians themselves.

The author concludes that studying the hallucinogenic plants and the use of native shamans provides a key to understanding many basic cultural processes.

571. Roseman, Bernard. **The Peyote Story**. 1972 ed. Hollywood, California, Wilshire Book Company, c1972. 90p. illus. $2.00pa.

The first part of this small book describes the author's experience when he joined a group of Navajo Indians who were members of the Native American Church of North America in a peyote ceremony. The second part is about the battle this church has waged for religious freedom. The third section sketches the beliefs of the Peyote Indians. Also included is reprinted material from the 38th Annual Report of the Bureau of American Ethnology to the Secretary of the Smithsonian Institution, which reports on the use of drugs by Indian groups. The last section, an article reprinted from the *Los Angeles Times* of August 17, 1967, reports, along with other information about the Indians' religion, that 45 percent of the Navajos accept the peyote-oriented church.

572. Schleiffer, Hedwig. **Sacred Narcotic Plants of the New World Indians: An Anthology of Texts from the 16th Century to Date**. Riverside, N.J., Hafner Press, 1974. 160p. illus. index. $5.95pa. ISBN 0-02-851780-6.

Many of the selections included here are from material that is scarce or unobtainable in libraries today. The anthology preserves a culturally and historically balanced sampling of diverse points of view, since hallucinogens have been both praised and condemned in the past. The earliest selections date back to the Europeans who first encountered these plants; other items cover the cultural disruptions brought upon the American Indians by the European civilization; finally, selections reflect today's resurgence of interest in hallucinogens.

The book is probably of most interest to the general reader, but students, teachers, and research workers in anthropology, botany, ethnobotany, pharmacology, psychology, and medicine may also benefit from reading it. The two indexes, one of Latin names of genera and species of plants and one of vernacular names of plants and plant products, give the work some reference value.

573. Wasson, R. Gordon. **The Hallucinogenic Fungi of Mexico: An Inquiry into the Origins of the Religious Idea among Primitive Peoples.** Cambridge, Harvard University, 1960. pp. 137-162. bibliog. (Botanical Museum Leaflets, Harvard University, vol. 19, no. 7, 1961).

This paper was presented as the Annual Lecture of the Mycological Society of America at Stillwater, Oklahoma, August 30, 1960. The author and his wife are known for their studies of hallucinogenic mushrooms, particularly the religious role the mushrooms have played among primitive peoples.

Explaining his interest in the subject and outlining the historical background, Wasson then describes the drug-induced religious experience. An appended list of the hallucinogenic mushrooms of Mexico cites literature references to the publication place of the earliest report of use.

574. Wasson, R. Gordon, George Cowan, Florence Cowan, and Willard Rhodes. **María Sabina and her Mazatec Mushroom Velada.** New York and London, Harcourt Brace Jovanovich, a Helen and Kurt Wolff Book, 1974. 282p. illus. (part col.) index. (Ethno-Mycological Studies No. 3). $82.50. LC 74-964. ISBN 0-15-157202-X. (Four cassettes which record Maria Sabina's mushroom velada and a musical score to accompany the text and records are furnished with the book.)

This attractive book, a collector's item, presents the text of a shamanic ceremony performed on the night of July 12-13, 1958 by María Sabina in the Mazatec village of Huautla de Jimenez, in the Sierra Madre Oriental, in the northern part of the State of Oaxaco, Mexico. Such sessions are called "velada" (a night vigil) by the Mazatec who speak Spanish. The complete text of the session is given in the Mazatec language with a translation into English and Spanish. Also included are linguistic commentaries, the musical notation of the chanting and singing, the sound track of the session, ethnographic notes prompted by the text, and a photographic record of the events of that night. Except for the observers recording the event and a few others, those at the ceremony were under the influence of the divine inebriant, a species of the mushroom genus, Psilocybe.

The performance is held on behalf of a youth who is seriously ill. (He died about six weeks later.) The climax of the ceremony comes when the mushroom (Jesus) says through María Sabina that the boy must die.

The intellectual content of the transcript of the performance is not noteworthy, but it furnishes a major document for anthropological study of the Mazatec. For the ethno-musicologist and the ethno-mycologist, it is of interest because it opens doors not known to exist. This is the first complete shamanic document from the Mazatec country and perhaps from all of the Americas.

575. Wasson, R. Gordon. **Soma: Divine Mushroom of Immortality**. New York, Harcourt Brace Jovanovich, Inc., ca. 1971 (c1968). 381p. illus. (part col.) bibliog. index. (Ethno-Mycological Studies No. 1). $15.00. LC 68-11197.

This scholarly work was written by a retired banker who is a noted specialist on the cultural role of mushrooms in history. He has travelled to many parts of the world studying the use of hallucinogenic mushrooms and particularly their role in religious ritual. The exact identity of a plant called *Soma* in the ancient Aryan religion has never been known. It has sometimes been known as a plant, the juice of that plant, and sometimes a god. This book advances the theory and documents the thesis that *Soma* was the fly-agaric (*Amanita muscaria*), a hallucinogenic mushroom.

About two years and a half before this edition of Wasson's work was published, a lavishly printed, deluxe, limited edition of the work was issued at the price of $200.00.

576. Zaehner, R. C. **Zen, Drugs and Mysticism**. New York, Pantheon Books, 1972. 223p. index. $6.95. LC 72-11871. ISBN 0-394-48540-8.

The British edition of this book was published under the title *Drugs, Mysticism and Makebelieve*. The author is a noted authority on Eastern religions who has written other works on mysticism and Hinduism, but his book is aimed at a wider audience. The book is a critique of contemporary mystical beliefs. The author contrasts the claims of drug enthusiasts with the spiritual discipline and principles of real mystical experience. He thinks there are a variety of both drug-induced and mystical states, and that the two seldom overlap. In addition, he finds little significance in contemporary solutions to problems. He is critical of nearly all of them–the religious, the scientific, and those that make use of drugs. However, Professor Zaehner is not entirely despairing about the possibility that man can have knowledge about the spiritual world.

15. Hallucinogens

This section contains more material about LSD than about other hallucinogens, although others such as peyote and psilocybin warrant attention. The early works on LSD and some of the other hallucinogens suggest that great good may come from their use: the unconscious might be explored, in the hope of healing troubled minds, providing psychological insights and spiritual uplifting, treating alcoholism, elevating moods, and revealing the ultimate aim of human life. The LSD "trip" was highly acclaimed by such high priests of the psychedelic as Timothy Leary (see entries 589, 590). Though it is true that research has been slowed because of bad publicity, the studies that have been done nevertheless do not bear out the great claims. The thoughts expressed by subjects under the drug's influence were found to be commonplace, although the subjects may have felt them to be profound. The great risk to the user and fear of genetic damage have made this class of drugs less appealing to drug abusers than some others. Much work remains to be done on the possible therapeutic value of these drugs or their derivatives.

577. Aaronson, Bernard, and Humphry Osmond, eds. **Psychedelics: The Uses and Implications of Hallucinogenic Drugs.** Garden City, N.Y., Anchor Books, Doubleday and Co., 1970. 512p. bibliog. index. $2.45. LC 70-103788.

Some of these articles about psychedelics, or hallucinogenic drugs, have been published previously. Using a psychological rather than physiological or medical approach, the papers outline the implications of using these drugs and point up some of the problems. The attitudes expressed are in general sympathetic to the use of these "mind-expanding" substances, although a more controlled development of their use is hoped for. Articles are arranged under the following section headings: 1) Introduction, 2) The nature of the experience, 3) Anthropoligcal considerations, 4) Effects of psychedelics on religion and religious experience, 5) Psychedelic effects on mental functioning, 6) Non-drug analogues to the psychedelic state, 7) Therapeutic applications, 8) Sociology of psychedelics in the current scene, and 9) Conclusion.

The viewpoints expressed in the book seem a bit out of date at this writing. There is now a growing feeling that the use of at least some of the hallucinogenic drugs is very risky, since permanent damage to the user is likely and genetic damage possible.

578. Brimblecombe, Roger W., and Roger M. Pinder. **Hallucinogenic Agents.** Bristol, Wright-Scientechnica, 1975. 272p. bibliog. index. £12.50. ISBN 0-85608-011-X.

This is a collection of material on several aspects of hallucinogenic drugs: the chemical, biochemical, and pharmacological knowledge. One author is a neuropharmacologist and the other a medicinal chemist.

The following chapter titles are included: 1) Introduction, 2) Evaluation of hallucinogenic activity, 3) Phenylalkylamines and their derivatives, 4) Indolealkylamines and related compounds, 5) Cannabis, 6) Drugs affecting cholinergic systems, 7) Miscellaneous hallucinogens, and 8) Mechanisms of action of hallucinogenic agents. The material presented is for the most part technical and scientific, although the introductory chapter covers such areas as nomenclature and classification, the hallucinogenic experience, and source of hallucinogenic drugs. The material all appears to be of high quality.

The authors think it unlikely that all types of hallucinogenic drugs share a common mode of action. They believe the drugs can be grouped into three categories: the sympathomimetic amines, the cannabinoids, and the antiacetylcholine drugs. Within these classes it is likely, however, that the mechanisms are similar if not identical. In summary, though, they say that the effects of hallucinogenic drugs remain as mysterious as the mechanisms by which the body and mind react to mediate them.

Of particular value for research workers interested in drug actions in the central nervous system, the book will also appeal to psychiatrists, psychologists, sociologists, and those interested in the role of drugs in modifying behavior.

579. Caldwell, W. V. **LSD Psychotherapy: An Exploration of Psychedelic and Psycholytic Therapy**. New York, Grove Press, 1968. 329p. bibliog. index. $3.95pa. LC 68-22006.

The first part of this book surveys the history of LSD and its use in therapeutic and other contexts, based on the author's interviews and research carried out in the United States and other countries. The second part of the book describes and classifies what are said to be universal images and fantasies brought on by the use of hallucinogens. The author's viewpoint is that psychedelic drugs are too potent to be safe for do-it-yourself experiments but that through their use the unconscious can be explored with the hope of healing troubled minds.

580. Crocket, Richard, R. A. Sandison, and Alexander Walk, eds. **Hallucinogenic Drugs and Their Psychotherapeutic Use**. Proceedings of the Quarterly Meeting of the Royal Medico-Psychological Association in London, February, 1961. London, H. K. Lewis and Co., Ltd., 1963. 191p. bibliog. index.

These papers were presented at a meeting that covered topics from several disciplines. At the time of the meeting the area of hallucinogenic drugs was relatively new and had not been explored extensively. There were six sessions: 1) The historical and psycho-pharmacological background,

2) Hallucinogenic agents and their general application, 3) Techniques and methodology, 4) The use of hallucinogens in specific conditions, 5) Clinical observations and phenomenological interpretation, and 6) The moral, religious and social significance of experience under hallucinogenic drugs.

Research into the properties and potentialities of LSD and related compounds was intense from about 1943 until the 1960s, when such research slowed down because of the potential for abuse of the drug. The organizers of this conference hoped to assist in interpreting the remarkable psychic changes that accompany administration of the hallucinogens. Some of the papers are significant. An attempt was made to examine the philosophical, ethical, and religious implications of these drugs for mankind.

581. DeBold, Richard C., and Russell C. Leaf, eds. **LSD, Man and Society**. Middletown, Conn., Wesleyan University Press, 1967. 219p. illus. bibliog. $5.00. LC 67-24111.

This book contains the papers presented at a public symposium held at Wesleyan University in March 1967, as well as the discussions that followed the presentations. The papers, although delivered by nine experts, can easily be understood by intelligent laymen. The work has been arranged in three sections: the first, on LSD and the individual, considers the motivations of those who use the drug, the consequences of its use, and its therapeutic potential; the second discusses the religious, legal, and medical impact of the drug on society; the third concerns LSD itself, its pharmacologic properties and its effects.

The book points out that the folklore of LSD, as publicized by the news media, is characterized by half-truths that are seductive and dangerously misleading to many, particularly the young. The purpose of this book is to counter this folklore and present some scientific, objective data on the subject.

582. Efron, Daniel H., ed. **Psychotomimetic Drugs**. Proceedings of a Workshop organized by the Pharmacology Section, Psychopharmacology Research Branch, National Institute of Mental Health, held at the University of California, Irvine, on January 25-26, 1969. New York, Raven Press, 1970. 365p. illus. bibliog. index. (Workshop Series of Pharmacology Section, National Institute of Mental Health No. 4). $15.95. LC 73-89388. ISBN 0-911216-07-3.

Psychotomimetic drugs are those which cause a state that mimics naturally occurring psychosis. They are perhaps more frequently called hallucinogenic drugs. The problems caused by these substances receive much attention today because of social, political, moral, legal, and perhaps even economic implications. This book, however, is concerned only with the scientific aspects of the subject, because the editor feels that only scientific data and research can solve the problems. Neurologists, pharmacologists, psychologists, physiologists, and psychiatrists took part in the workshop, in the hope of bringing out new views and pointing to research possibilities in this difficult area. Papers were presented in four sessions: 1) Chemistry; 2) Pharmacology; 3) Physiology, neuropathology, and neurochemistry; and 4) Clinical considerations. The last part of the book contains a general discussion, a summary, and closing remarks.

For the most part, the presentations are highly technical, but the discussions that follow each part are of general interest.

583. Fuller, John G. **The Day of St. Anthony's Fire**. New York, Macmillan Company, 1968. 310p. index. $5.95. LC 68-23632.

This is the true story of a small French village where, on a night in 1951 hundreds of inhabitants were struck with a strange illness that caused them to suffer hallucinations, go totally mad, or die. Little by little, the story behind the tragedy is unfolded. Such outbreaks have occurred throughout history, as far back as the Middle Ages. They were called 'St. Anthony's Fire' because it was believed that only by prayers to this saint could the disease be held in check. Since rather early times, however, it has been known that the cause of St. Anthony's Fire is ergot, a mold found on grain. The mold is ingested if bread is made from the contaminated grain. LSD, which is derived from ergot, was coming to the attention of scientists about the same time as the tragedy in the French village. It has been presumed that the form of ergot which poisoned the villagers was akin to LSD, since the effects were so similar.

584. Gamage, James R., and Edmund L. Zerkin, eds. **Hallucinogenic Drug Research: Impact on Science and Society**. Proceedings of the First Annual Symposium of the Student Association for the Study of Hallucinogens. Beloit, Wisc., STASH Press, 1970. 139p. bibliog. index. $2.95pa. LC 72-133456.

The papers presented in this volume are authored by experienced researchers in the field of hallucinogenic drugs. Some are ardent proponents of the drugs; others are skeptics. Like the STASH organization which sponsored the symposium, all of the researchers claim to be unbiased in their views and anxious to "find out" about these drugs. There is a hope that hallucinogens may play a part in providing insights into relations of mind and brain. Titles of the papers are as follows: 1) Problems and prospects of research with the hallucinogens, 2) The psychological state produced by the hallucinogens, 3) Potential dangers of the hallucinogens, 4) The hallucinogens and embryonic malformations, 5) LSD treatment in alcoholism, 6) The experimental use of psychedelic (LSD) psychotherapy, 7) Treatment of psychosis with LSD, 8) The influence of "psychedelic" experience on contemporary art and music, and 9) Social aspects of research with psychoactive drugs. The sixth paper has been reprinted from the *Journal of the American Medical Association.*

585. Hicks, Richard E., and Paul Jay Fink. **Psychedelic Drugs**. Proceedings of a Hahnemann Medical College and Hospital Symposium sponsored by the Department of Psychiatry. Consulting editor, Van Buren O. Hammett. New York, Grune and Stratton, 1969. 249p. bibliog. index. $16.75. LC 73-79951.

This work presents a comprehensive multidisciplinary view of psychedelic (or hallucinogenic) drugs. The discussions presented at the symposium suggest that the initial furor over these drugs has subsided, and that attempts are being made to study them scientifically. The viewpoint presented is neither wildly enthusiastic nor totally despairing. Material is arranged in the following sections: 1) Research with psychedelic drugs, 2) Known or suspected hazards from non-medical use of psychedelic drugs, 3) Legal issues related to the use of psychedelic drugs, 4) Socio-cultural considerations of the non-medical use of psychedelic drugs, and 5) The clinical use of psychedelic drugs. Each section contains several papers, all written by noted authorities. Overall, the work provides a view of the current knowledge and opinion on the subject. The book should be of particular interest to physicians, mental health professionals, and others who are concerned with the problem. The level of the presentation is not too technical for the average intelligent reader.

586. Hoffer, A., and H. Osmond. **The Hallucinogens.** With a contribution by T. Weckowicz. New York, Academic Press, 1967. 626p. bibliog. index. $34.00. LC 66-30086.

This work, perhaps the most definitive in the field, describes the chemistry, biochemistry, pharmacology, and toxicology of all known classes of drugs known as the hallucinogens. Emphasis is on LSD and its effects on schizophrenic patients, its use in psychotherapy, the psychedelic experience, and the sociological implications of its use. The last chapter takes up animal studies of hallucinogenic drugs; this is an increasingly important area because it affords better control of all experimental variables and the possibility of using a wider range of doses than can be used with human subjects.

The book was written for chemists, biochemists, psychologists, sociologists, research physicians, and social workers involved with drug abuse.

587. Hollister, Leo E. **Chemical Psychoses: LSD and Related Drugs.** Springfield, Ill., Charles C. Thomas, 1968. 190p. bibliog. index. $8.00. LC 67-18340.

Hallucinogenic drugs are classified and discussed in the following chapters: 1) Historical perspectives; 2) Types of psychotomimetic drugs; 3) Clinical syndromes of the chemical psychoses; 4) Psychological effects of psychotomimetic drugs; 5) Electroencephalographic and neurophysiological studies; 6) Physiological, biochemical and metabolic studies; 7) Chemical theories of psychosis and the model psychoses; 8) Chemical psychoses as therapy; and 9) Drugs and our culture.

The author presents evidence for and against the therapeutic use of these drugs for such conditions as psychoneuroses, schizophrenia, depression, and alcoholism. The author points out that these drugs have had a long history of use, and the recent upsurge of extensive use in Western society today is of great importance. Despite the claims made for them, the evidence either for or against their use is inconclusive. The acceptance of such drugs in our society is a marked departure from previous attitudes about them. Paradoxically, this trend has developed at a time when scientific advance has been greatest. Some feel that this accepting attitude represents anti-intellectualism in a new and dramatic guise.

588. La Barre, Weston. **The Peyote Cult.** New Haven, Conn., Yale University Press, 1938. 188p. illus. bibliog. (Yale University Publications in Anthropology. No. 19).

This well-documented publication is probably the most important classic work on the subject of the hallucinogen peyote and its use by Indians of Mexico and the southwestern United States. The work is partially based on field work done in 1935 and 1936 with funds granted by Yale University and the American Museum of Natural History. The following Chapters are presented:

I) Botanical and physiological aspects of peyote, II) The ethnology of peyotism, III) Comparative study of Plains peyotism, IV) Psychological aspects of peyotism, and V) Historical interpretations. In addition, these appendices are included: 1) Peyote in Mexico, 2) Peyote and the mescal bean, 3) Peyote and Teo-nanacatl, 4) "Plant worship" in Mexico and the United States, 5) Chemistry of peyote, 6) Physiology of peyote, 7) John Wilson, the revealer of peyote, 8) Christian elements in the Peyote Cult, and 9) The Native American Church and other peyote churches. A 14-page bibliography is also furnished. The publication is of special value now because of the growing interest in (and abuse of) hallucinogenic drugs.

589. Leary, Timothy. **The Politics of Ecstasy**. New York, G. P. Putnam's Sons, 1965. 371p. $6.95 LC 68-29674.

This work, written by the "high priest of the psychedelic," is a collection of essays defending and describing the charms of the psychedelic way of life. Leary was dismissed from the faculty of Harvard University in 1963 when it was learned that he had been experimenting on himself and others with psychedelic drugs. In spite of the bad publicity, he still believes that anyone who wants to have a psychedelic session should be allowed to. This book is an attempt to explain his views.

590. Leary, Timothy, Ralph Metzner, and Richard Alpert. **The Psychedelic Experience: A Manual Based on the Tibetan Book of the Dead**. New Hyde Park, N.Y., University Books, 1964. 159p. $6.00. LC 64-19705.

The authors of this work (all Ph.D.'s) were engaged in experimental programs using LSD and other hallucinogenic drugs at Harvard University when adverse national publicity and legal difficulties led to the suspension of the experiments and the dismissal of the authors from the school. Since then they have, at least to some extent, continued their work underground and without academic auspices.

The authors' point of view is that a drug is only one component of a psychedelic session. Equally important is mental and spiritual preparation, before and after taking the drug. They further feel that there is no need to invent new materials for this purpose, since the great literature of meditation lends itself to this use. The manual presents preparation materials based on the *Tibetan Book of the Dead*, which is a "book describing the experiences to be expected at the moment of death, during an intermediate phase lasting forty-nine (seven times seven) days, and during rebirth into another bodily frame."

The manual is divided into four parts: 1) the introduction, 2) a step-by-step description of a psychedelic experience based directly on the *Tibetan Book of the Dead*, 3) practical suggestions on how to prepare for and conduct a psychedelic session, and 4) instructive passages adapted from the *Tibetan Book of the Dead*, which may be read to the voyager during the session, to facilitate the movement of consciousness. Included in the introductory section are commentaries on the *Book of the Dead* by W. Y. Evans-Wentz (a translator-editor of four treatises on Tibetan mysticism), Carl Jung (the Swiss psychoanalyst), and Lama Govinda (an initiate of one of the principal Buddhist orders of Tibet).

591. Ling, Thomas M., and John Buckman. **Lysergic Acid (LSD 25) and Ritalin in the Treatment of Neurosis.** London, Lambarde Press, 1963. 172p. illus. bibliog.

This book purports to indicate the potentialities, safeguards, and contraindications for the clinical use of LSD with the drug Ritalin (a mood-elevator). Most of the book consists of case histories that attempt to show how these agents have been beneficial in treating migraine, writer's block, frigidity, sexual perversion, pathological gambling, immaturity, character disorder, anxiety, and psoriasis. The authors contend that this form of treatment has great potentialities for the right patient in the right surroundings. At the time this book was written it did appear that LSD might have great therapeutic value. Subsequent research still leaves doubts. The other drug, Ritalin, is still used, but it is a very mild mood-elevator that, according to some, has much value.

592. Masters, R. E. L., and Jean Houston. **The Varieties of Psychedelic Experience.** New York, Dell Publishing Co., 1966. 326p. $1.95pa.

This book is principally concerned with the psychedelic drug-state as it is experienced by the normal individual, not by psychiatric patients. The authors are optimistic that good can come from further investigation of these drugs and their ability to push human consciousness beyond its present limitations. However, they are realistic also, and do not seem to believe that such drug use will reveal the ultimate aim of human life. The drugs studied were mainly LSD-25 and peyote (before such studies became illegal), and the materials presented are based on first-hand observation and interviews with subjects who have taken the drugs.

The book gives a balanced account of the complexities of the psychedelic experience and something of the technique used in working with the users and the drugs.

A section of notes includes references to many classic works.

593. Pollard, John C., Leonard Uhr, and Elizabeth Stern. **Drugs and Phantasy: The Effects of LSD, Psilocybin, and Sernyl on College Students.** Boston, Little, Brown and Co., 1965. 205p. bibliog. $7.50. LC 65-27627.

The authors of this work feel that a lot of nonsense has been written, of a nonscientific sort, about the wondrous effects of hallucinogenic drugs. In this book they attempt to show the actual effects of these drugs on normal people. A controlled experiment was conducted in which three students took LSD-25, psilocybin, and Sernyl on different occasions and then described their changing feelings and perceptions as they actually occurred. The subjects made recordings in which they talked about everything that happened to them while under the influence of the drugs. The bulk of the book is made up of the narrative of these students.

The reports of the drug experiences are interesting and perhaps enlightening, although nothing startling happened to them, and their thoughts were, for the most part, commonplace. The authors are critical of those who want to douse society in these drugs, but they also criticize those who tend to look away from the drug problem and do research in safer areas.

594. Roseman, Bernard. **LSD, the Age of Mind.** 1973 ed. Hollywood, California, Wilshire Book Company, 1963. 172p. bibliog. index. $2.00pa.

This curious book deals with how to expand the existing senses to their fullest potential. The point of view expressed is that psychedelic drugs have shown that the senses can be improved, and this book attempts to make the reader aware of these "aids" and how to apply them.

Although the author by his own account is not well educated scientifically, he claims to have made a large amount of LSD which he allowed a very "select group of doctors and psychiatrists" to experiment with. This and many of the other accounts presented sound like the imagination at work or something akin to childish bragging.

In addition to the LSD material, there are chapters on such topics as the "Battle for Religious Freedom as Waged by the Native American Church," culture, mysticism, carbon dioxide, America's sacred mushrooms, airplane glue, and hypnosis. Much of the material makes no sense, although the writing is not illiterate. For example the statement: "Carbon Dioxide is for the most part the experience of death." Unfortunately, the book is an example of what has sometimes passed for serious writing on hallucinogenic drugs.

595. Sankar, D. V. Siva. **LSD–A Total Study.** Westbury, N.Y., PJD Publications Ltd., 1975. 960p. illus. bibliog. index. $29.50. LC 72-95447. ISBN 0-9600290-3-6.

This comprehensive volume is a compilation of the works of Dr. Sankar and a number of other authorities, including Dr. Albert Hofmann, who first synthesized LSD-25. The book considers not only the scientific aspects of LSD but also the cultural and sociological effects of using this kind of drug. Historical and philosophical material is also presented.

The book is divided into the following sections: Molecular investigations; LSD, past imperfect, future indefinite; Psychological investigations; Neurological and physical investigations; Genetic investigations; Biochemical investigations; Pharmacological investigations; Psychiatric investigations; Patterns and profiles of non-medical use, sociodynamic investigations; Religion, law and public education; Drugs of past and future. Appendices cover classification of drugs, effects of abused drugs, identification of drug abusers, legal penalties, slang terminology, and available literature on drug education.

In general, the author's point of view can be summed up as follows: the concern that has been shown about the non-medical use of LSD is completely justified. He does feel, however, that there are certain situations where small doses may be beneficial when given under trained supervision. He also believes basic research on the drug should not be hindered because, although it is a very potent chemical, it has considerable potential for unraveling neurochemical mechanisms not now fully understood.

596. Schultes, Richard Evans, and Albert Hofmann. **The Botany and Chemistry of Hallucinogens.** With a Foreword by Heinrich Klüver. Springfield, Ill., Charles C. Thomas, 1973. 267p. illus. bibliog. index. $14.75. LC 72-187675. ISBN 0-398-02401-4.

The two authors of this book, a botanist and a chemist, are particularly well qualified to write such a work. Dr. Schultes spent 12 years in the field acquiring information on the plants, and Dr. Hofmann is the discoverer of LSD. The book is in five chapters: 1) Hallucinogenic or psychotomimetic agents: what are they?, 2) The botanical distribution of hallucinogens, 3) The chemical distribution of hallucinogens, 4) Plants of hallucinogenic use, and 5) Plants of possible or suspected hallucinogenic use. The first three chapters are quite short. Chapter 4, "Plants of hallucinogenic use," the longest section of book, systematically names, describes, and pictures the plants. Chapter 5, which is rather short, follows the style of Chapter 4. There is a bibliography of more than 450 literature references included.

Some of the plants described are well known, and some are quite obscrure. The primary thrust of the book is toward the botany and chemistry of the hallucinogenic plants, but other aspects of the subject, such as the ethnobotanical, historical, pharmacological, and psychological, are also considered. Theories on the biogenetic pathways of many of the active principles of the plants are discussed, and information on the synthesis of some of the better known compounds is reviewed in the hope of encouraging further research. This is an outstanding and unique book.

597. Siegel, R. K., and L. J. West, eds. **Hallucinations: Behavior, Experience, and Theory**. New York, John Wiley and Sons, 1975. 322p. illus. (part col.) bibliog. index. $25.00. LC 75-12670. ISBN 0-471-79096-6.

This work explores hallucinations in several contexts: anthropological, psychopharmacological, clinical, and social. The phenomenon is examined as part of a continuum of experience ranging from sensations through dreams, fantasies, thoughts, and "real" perceptions. The book views hallucinations as abstractions involving neurochemical, neurophysiological, behavioral, imaginal, experimental, and cognitive systems. Also presented are reports of current research that explains possible mechanisms of action involved in hallucinogenic experiences.

The chapters, which are surprisingly readable despite being scientific and technical, were written by well-known experts. Titles and authors are as follows: 1) Anthropological perspectives on hallucinations and hallucinogens, by Western La Barre; 2) The continuum of CNS excitatory states and hallucinosis, by Wallace D. Winters; 3) Dreams and other hallucinations: an approach to the underlying mechanism, by Ernest Hartmann; 4) Drug-induced hallucinations in animals and man, by Ronald K. Siegel and Murray E. Jarvik; 5) Hallucinations: an information-processing approach, by Mardi J. Horowitz; 6) Cartography of inner space, by Roland Fischer; 7) The social context of hallucinations, by Theodore R. Sarbin and Joseph B. Juhasz; 8) The continuity of perceptual and cognitive experiences, by C. Wade Savage; and 9) A clinical and theoretical overview of hallucinatory phenomena, by Louis Jolyon West.

The book includes a number of excellent colored plates and some black and white artistic works depicting hallucinatory experiences, done by David Sheridan and Yando (Hildebrando de Rios). This is an outstanding work.

598. Smart, Reginald G., and others. **Lysergic Acid Diethylamide (LSD) in the Treatment of Alcoholism: An Investigation of Its Effects on Drinking Behavior, Personality Structure, and Social Functioning.** Toronto, University of Toronto Press for the Addiction Research Foundation, 1967. 121p. (Brookside Monograph of the Addiction Research Foundation No. 6). bibliog. index. $6.00.

This study, sponsored by the Addiction Research Foundation, reviews the effects of LSD and its possible role as a therapeutic agent in the treatment of alcoholism. Before the study was undertaken there was a widely held opinion that LSD was a useful agent in therapy for alcoholics. The study did not bear this out. The following chapters are presented: 1) Discovery and early use of LSD, 2) Use of LSD in psychiatric treatment, 3) LSD in the treatment of alcoholism, 4) Methods of the A.R.F. investigation, 5) Results of the A.R.F. investigation, 6) Discussion and conclusions, and 7) Direction of future research with LSD.

As a whole, the results of the study fail to indicate that LSD is an effective adjunct in the treatment of alcoholism. Also, it had no effect on the personality variables or social stability of the individual.

599. Solomon, David, ed. **LSD: The Consciousness Expanding Drug.** Introduction by Timothy Leary. New York, G. P. Putnam's Sons, 1964. 273p. bibliog. index. $5.95. LC 64-18016.

These essays are about drugs that are said to be consciousness-expanding, such as LSD. Although these drugs have in the past been used to treat alcoholism and some emotional disorders, much controversy has surrounded their use and they are now controlled substances. The book investigates the complex problems surrounding the use, distribution, and controls of the drugs. The editors and contributors to the volume for the most part believe that the drugs should be used because they are important in revealing the reality of man and his environment—that is, they believe that the hallucinations the drugs produce are reality, and that the world as one normally sees it is not real.

Other contributors to the volume doubt the advisability of psychedelic drug use. To illustrate, note this quote from the essay of Cole and Katz, "It is, of course, difficult to determine whether or not some of the bizarre behavior of such individuals [drug users] are a product of the drug itself or a product of the underlying personality aberrations which lead the individuals to seek out these agents. In any case, there is no evidence that uncontrolled self-administration is either safe or desirable. There has also been concern over the possibility that investigators who have embarked on serious scientific work in this area may have been subject to the deleterious and seductive effects of these agents."

The essays presented are as follows: 1) Psychopharmacology: the manipulation of the mind, by Humphry Osmond; 2) Culture and the individual, by Aldous Huxley; 3) The hallucinogens: a reporter's objective view, by Dan Wakefield; 4) A visit to inner space, by Alan Harrington; 5) How to change behavior, by Timothy Leary; 6) A psychedelic experience: fact or fantasy?, by Alan Watts; 7) A review of the clinical effects of psychotomimetic agents, by Humphry Osmond; 8) Do drugs have religious import?, by Huston Smith; 9) Points of distinction between sedative and consciousness-expanding drugs, by William S. Burroughs; 10) LSD, transcendence, and the new beginning, by James Terrill, Charles Savage, Donald D. Jackson; 11) Mescaline, LSD, psilocybin and personality change, by Sanford M. Unger; 12) Lysergic acid diethylamide: an editorial, by Roy R. Grinker; 13) The psychotomimetic drugs: an overview, by Jonathan O. Cole, Martin M. Katz; 14) Pain and LSD-25: a theory of attenuation of anticipation; 15) LSD and psychotherapy: a bibliography of the English-language literature, by Sanford M. Unger.

600. Solursh, Lionel P., and M. John Solursh. **Illusinogenic Drugs: Their Effect on Criminal Responsibility**. Toronto, Canadian Mental Health Association, n.d. 37p. bibliog. $2.00pa.

This short monograph presents material on the following aspects of the subject: the concept of criminal responsibility, relevant effects of illusinogenic drugs, and illusinogenic drug states as a defence to criminal responsibility.

The authors examine some possible implications of the recent increase in street use of hallucinogenic drugs, particularly in the area of criminal responsibility. Characteristics of the drugs are outlined, and the necessity for considering each case individually is stressed. The hope is expressed that adequate legislation and continued adaptation of it by the courts will be continued.

601. Stafford, P. G., and B. H. Golightly. **LSD, the Problem-Solving Psychedelic**. New York, Award Books, 1967. 288p. index. $0.75pa.

This book, written for laymen, is an account of some of the positive uses of psychedelics. The authors feel that many individuals have incorrectly been led to believe that use of these drugs is harmful while in reality a great many social problems can be solved through their proper use.

The style of writing is straightforward with little of the vague other-worldliness and mysticism that appears in many of the publications encouraging and defending the use of psychedelics.

602. Tarshis, Maurice S. **The LSD Controversy: An Overview**. With a Foreword by Herman A. Dickel. Springfield, Ill., Charles C. Thomas, 1972. 80p. bibliog. index. $6.50. LC 72-75931.

Much of the material in this short monograph is based on a paper that the author published previously. Each of the chapters answers a specific question on the topic: 1) Introduction; 2) Terminology; 3) General chemical characteristics; 4) Is LSD addictive?; 5) How is LSD used, stored, and transported? What does it cost on the black market?; 6) What are some of the major effects and complications from the use of LSD?; 7) Does LSD affect human and animal cells, tissues, and pregnancy?; 8) Who are the users of LSD not under medical supervision and what are the patterns of abuse?; 9) Are there any medical uses of LSD?; 10) What are some of the opinions regarding the medical safety and abuse of LSD?; 11) Summary.

Some of the author's views are interesting. He feels that much further research is necessary before any conclusions can be drawn on the therapeutic potentialities and limitations of LSD. Many investigators feel that LSD is too unpredictable to use even under the most exacting supervised medical setting. Others are not in agreement on this matter and feel that it can be used in properly selected patients by experienced investigators. Self-administration of the drug and use when its source and purity are unknown magnifies the complications and makes them even more serious.

603. U.S. Bureau of Narcotics and Dangerous Drugs. **LSD-25: A Factual Account; Layman's Guide to the Pharmacology, Physiology, Psychology and Sociology of LSD.** By Louise G. Richards, Milton H. Joffe, and George R. Spratto. Washington, GPO, 1969. 44p. bibliog. $0.30.

The aim of this booklet is to give the public factual and enlightened information on LSD. The material is presented in reasonably simple terms, although it was written by experts and/or scientists. The following subject areas are discussed: actions of LSD in body and brain, major drug effects, current research on LSD, reactions and risks, and LSD abuse and the social problem. Also included are a question-and-answer section; some definitions of terms; a short section showing chemical structure relationships of LSD; and a list of references to books, articles, films, and laws.

604. U.S. National Clearinghouse for Mental Health Information. **Adverse Reactions to Hallucinogenic Drugs with Background Papers.** Conference held at the National Institute of Mental Health, Chevy Chase, Md., September 29, 1967. Roger E. Meyer, ed. Washington, GPO, 1969. 111p. bibliog. (U.S. Public Health Service Publication No. 1810.) $1.25pa.

This publication consists of the proceedings of a conference plus significant background papers. The purpose of the meeting was to discuss the psychological and biological sequelae of LSD and similar drug use. Few definitive answers emerged from the discussions by noted experts in the field, but major questions were defined and research strategies proposed. What was known at the time of the conference is brought out in the publication.

605. Ward, R. H. **A Drug-Taker's Notes.** London, Victor Gollancz Ltd., 1957. 222p. $4.50.

The author took LSD experimentally on six different occasions and under medical supervision. The present work is not a scientific account, but consists of the author's notes on his thoughts and feelings, as recorded while under LSD's direct influence. Afterward he made some additional comments, which are interspersed through the original notes. The first and last chapters were written shortly after the experiments took place and provide explanation and analysis. Six "experiments" (which make up the bulk of the book) are presented, outlining the drug-induced thoughts, actions, reminiscences, and feelings. Each experiment lasted for about eight hours, the period of time the author was under the drug's influence. Understandably the writing done during this time is curious and disconnected. It is very interesting, and perhaps provides insights. The author believes psychological alterations were brought about.

In the last few pages the author states his conclusions very well. He feels that those who use drugs to escape have failed to see that there are no short cuts to a new and inward world of consciousness. The way to such a world is the long and narrow way of discipline in the renewal of the mind. Narcotics provide an escape only in the negative and uncourageous sense. The only real way to liberation, he feels, is through God in what seems to the reviewer to be conventional religion.

606. Watts, W. David, Jr. **The Psychedelic Experience: A Sociological Study.** Beverly Hills, Calif., Sage Publications, 1971. 258p. bibliog. index. $8.95. LC 78-127007. ISBN 0-8039-0081-3.

This work, based on the author's master's thesis accepted by the Sociology Department of the State University of New York at Buffalo, explores the relationship between the nature of the psychedelic experience and that of religious mysticism. It also studies attitudes toward mental illness and those concerning use of hallucinogens. The ideologies of diverse groups are described. Chapter headings are as follows: 1) Social control and drugs, 2) Mysticism and the psychedelic experience, 3) Psychedelic experience and mental illness, 4) A sociological interpretation of the psychedelic experience, 5) Social control, social definition, and the psychedelic experience, 6) Some sociological considerations of psychedelic drug use, 7) Conclusions. There are few real conclusions about what should be done regarding the use of hallucinogenic drugs. The hope is expressed, however, that a review of the present situation will result in the judicious use of such drugs for the treatment of such conditions as alcoholism and psychoneuroses and that additional uses may be discovered so these agents will be assets to society instead of liabilities. It is only fair to point out, though, that "judicious use" of these drugs may not prove to be helpful in treating psychological or any disorders; they may be worthless.

607. Weil, Gunther W., Ralph Metzner, and Timothy Leary, eds. **The Psychedelic Reader**. Selected form the *Psychedelic Review.* Secaucus, N.J., Citadel Press, 1973. 260p. illus. bibliog. index. $3.95pa. ISBN 0-8065-0255-X.

The material presented here was taken from the *Psychedelic Review*, a quarterly periodical inaugurated in 1963 as a forum for the exchange of information and ideas in the area of psychedelic drug use. The essays included here are from the first four issues of the journal. They discuss the philosophical, religious, and social aspects of psychedelic drug use, the pharmacology and dosage, psychotherapeutic applications, and the history of the drug use in ancient culture. Some personal experiences with drug use are related also. Several of the authors are well known in literary and scientific circles, such as R. Gordon Wasson and Julian Huxley. Others are well-known proponents of the drug culture such as Alan W. Watts, Timothy Leary, and Ralph Metzner. Most of the material had been reprinted from other sources when it appeared in the *Psychedelic Review.*

608. Wells, Brian. **Psychedelic Drugs: Psychological, Medical and Social Issues.** With a Foreword by Humphry Osmond. Baltimore, Penguin Education, 1973. 250p. bibliog. index. $1.95pa.

This book may serve as a starting point for exploring a social issue—the part that mind-altering drugs have in society. It also pulls together much basic material on the drugs themselves. The following chapters have been included: 1) Prospect, 2) Minor psychedelics, 3) Major psychedelics, 4) Therapeutic applications, 5) Pathogenic aspects 6) Psychedelic philosophy, 7) Sex and sexuality, 8) Crime and aggression, 9) Creativity, 10) Religion, 11) Retrospect.

The possibilities of both the good and the bad effects of psychedelics are considered. The author is convinced that the specific effect of this kind of drug depends largely on the motivations and expectations of the user and the settings in which the drugs are taken. The author, as a scientist himself, would like to see fewer restrictions on research with psychedelic drugs. However, he believes that some are potentially so dangerous that no sane society would ever contemplate their use outside of a laboratory.

16. Marihuana

The numerous recent books on marihuana included here attest to the fact that the drug has attracted a great deal of attention. Both spellings of the word are used—"marihuana" and "marijuana"; the former is the official spelling. There is considerable controversy over whether or not the drug is really harmful and what the legal restrictions, if any, should be. Some of the books on the subject contain a good deal of propaganda, and a few, such as the titles by Drake (entries 612 and 613), are underground-type books. The best scientific evidence available suggests that marihuana is at least somewhat harmful, although the direct health implications are still not certain. The better scientific treatises on this subject are listed in the section entitled "Production, Control, Public Policy, and Legal Factors" (pp. 161-179).

609. Bloomquist, E. R. **Marijuana**. Beverly Hills, Calif., Glencoe Press, 1968. 215p. illus. bibliog. $1.25pa. LC 68-54641.

This well-done book was a bestseller, and a revised and expanded edition has also been published (see next entry). It includes the following chapters: 1) From cannabis to marijuana, 2) The history of the weed, 3) The world of marijuana, 4) The marijuana trip, 5) The major controversies, 6) The literature of cannabis use, 7) The law and Mary Jane. In addition, there is a "Glossary of the Jargon of the Drug World" and an unusually good section of "Arguments Pro and Con: Questions and Answers on the Use of Cannabis." There are numerous amusing cartoons.

610. Bloomquist, Edward R. **Marijuana: The Second Trip**. Rev. ed. Beverly Hills, Calif., Glencoe Press, 1971. 434p. illus. bibliog. index. $6.95. LC 75-171360.

This book is a revised and expanded edition of the preceding entry, which was widely read. The author, who is a physician, has served as an expert on dangerous drugs for a number of years and is in great demand as a lecturer. His interesting book reports on the dangers of marijuana use and its effect on youth and society. All aspects of the subject are surveyed, in easy-to-understand language. The chapter headings are as follows: 1) From cannabis to marijuana, 2) The history of the weed, 3) The world of marijuana, 4) The pleasant effects, 5) Physical effects, 6) Bummers, 7) Bad trips, 8) The major controversies, 9) The literature of cannabis use, 10) The law and Mary Jane, 11) The non-drug aspects of pot, and 12) First person singular: is there a rational approach? In addition, there is a "Glossary of the Jargon of the Drug World," and an unusually good appended section "Arguments Pro and Con: Questions and Answers on the Use of Cannabis." As a special feature cartoons are scattered throughout the book, many of them different from those found in the first edition.

In Chapter 12 Dr. Bloomquist presents his own feeling about how to resolve the problem of dealing with marijuana use. His point of view is rather conservative. He believes that marijuana is too often the master rather than the servant of those who use it. However, he thinks many of the present laws are too harsh. He feels that pharmacologic evidence is against the use of the drug; more and more adverse effects are being discovered. He does have some hope that society can make decisions that will to some extent alleviate the problem. He warns, however, that we should consider two previous tragic lessons as we attempt to solve the problem of drug abuse; the first was the legalization of alcohol, and the second involved addiction to opium and its "treatment" with morphine and later with heroin as substitutes. Perhaps some safe chemical substitute will be found for addictive drugs. America evidently needs a cheap, safe, effective tranquilizer, but the author's feeling is that it is possible that once again, with professional assistance, we may be climbing "fool's hill." Chapter 12 is especially worthwhile because its approach is more conservative, though more compassionate, than the usual approach.

611. Bonnie, Richard J., and Charles H. Whitebread, II. **The Marihuana Conviction: A History of Marihuana Prohibition in the United States.** Charlottesville, University Press of Virginia, 1974. 368p. illus. bibliog. index. $12.50. LC 73-89907. ISBN 9-8139-0417-X.

This history of marihuana use and prohibition in the United States begins with the first anti-marihuana laws in 1915 in Utah and California and traces prohibition in other parts of the country up to the present time. Dividing the history into five different phases, the authors predict that we are about to enter the sixth phase, during which public attitudes will be reshaped and there will be a "reform" (liberalization) of the laws. The authors' view is that marihuana is a reality and that the nation should adopt a social policy of official neutrality toward the recreational use of marihuana. Heavy or irresponsible use should be discouraged by controls, though these should not resemble the controls now placed on alcoholic beverages. Their view is that the drug should be distributed through a government-controlled or -regulated monopoly, with taxes used as a control device. No advertising or commercial inducement should be permitted. Lastly, the authors say they do not urge immediate adoption of a regulatory scheme; they prefer evolutionary reform.

612. Drake, Bill. **The Cultivator's Handbook of Marijuana.** 1st ed. rev. Eugene, Ore., Agrarian Reform Co., 1970. 92p. illus. bibliog. $2.00pa.

This curious publication contains presumably accurate and helpful information on how to grow the best marijuana plants and how to harvest and dry marijuana. Interspersed throughout are inspirational gems, both poetic and philosophical, and oriental-looking illustrations are scattered here and there, with no explanation of their significance.

The following sections are presented: 1) Introduction: myths–fact and fiction; 2) Overview of the plant; 3) Soil, water, nutrition and environment; 4) Seeds, seedlings, germination and transplantation; 5) Lighting effects and growth patterns; 6) Harvesting and drying; 7) Making a good plant better; 8) Producing an unrecognizable hybrid. A bibliography contains references to early literature on the subject and appended materials tell how to recognize and detect adulteration, and also cover the use of opiates in early patent medicines.

613. Drake, William Daniel, Jr. **The Connoisseur's Handbook of Marijuana.** San Francisco, Straight Arrow Books, 1971. 252p. illus. bibliog. $3.95pa. LC 75-158516. ISBN 0-87932-021-4.

This book offers information on all aspects of marijuana, under the following chapter headings: 1) We took Bhang and the Mystery I Am he grew plain: some literature of the cannabis from several countries; 2) A brief ramble through the history of hemp in various cultures; 3) The Indian Hemp Drugs Commission Report, Appendices I and II: The Report, 1893-94; 4) Marijuana in America: a "scientific" confrontation; 5) Botany and cultivation: a complete and extraordinarily useful course; 6) Cannabis cookery; 7) Further reading.

Much of the material makes little sense; the illustrations are depressing; and many of the scientific statements conflict with the information the reviewer obtained from pharmacologists and pharmacognosists.

614. Goode, Erich, ed. **Marijuana.** New York, Atherton, 1969. 197p. bibliog. index. $6.95. LC 68-56981.

This unique anthology presents a variety of opinions on the subject, pro and con. There are selections by lay writers, sociologists, psychologists, one pharmacologist, and several journalists. Some of the papers have been published previously. Most of the articles are concerned with social behavior; papers on the agriculture, chemistry, and medical aspects of marijuana have been excluded. There is some historical material. Each article deals with a controversial aspect of the subject, presenting one side or the other of the question. The papers are intended to be of interest to both scholars and lay people, though only Western countries are considered. Section headings are: 1) The question of motivation, 2) Physiological effects of marijuana, 3) The connection between marijuana and heroin, 4) The dealer: buying and selling marijuana, 5) Marijuana in the schools, 6) The question of legalization, and 7) The epistemology and esthetics of pot.

615. Goode, Erich. **The Marijuana Smokers.** New York, Basic Books, Inc., 1970. 340p. bibliog. index. $10.00. LC 78-126949. ISBN 0-465-04381-X.

This book, written by a sociologist, is based on a survey of 200 marijuana users and on direct observation. It depicts the life and viewpoints of the marijuana smoker and analyzes the views of those concerned with marijuana policy. A few sections of the book have appeared in print previously. Chapter headings are as follows: 1) Overview; 2) A profile of the marijuana smoker; 3) Marijuana and the politics of reality; 4) The smoker's view of marijuana; 5) Physicians on marijuana use; 6) Turning on: becoming a marijuana user; 7) The effects of marijuana; 8) Multiple drug use among marijuana smokers; 9) Marijuana, crime, and violence; 10) Using, selling, and dealing marijuana; 11) Marijuana and the law; and 12) Epilogue: models of marijuana use. A glossary of terms is included.

The author hopes that his book will clarify misconceptions and calm widespread fears over the morals and lifestyles of drug users. Some readers may be reassured by what they find in the book about the current drug scene, but the reviewer found it quite depressing.

616. Grinspoon, Lester. **Marihuana Reconsidered.** Cambridge, Harvard University Press, 1971. 443p. bibliog. index. $9.95.

The author of this well-documented account says he is not attempting to establish that marihuana is a harmless drug, since it is not possible to claim that for any drug at this time. However, he does imply that there has been much mythology, distortion of facts, and hyperemotionalism surrounding the drug. The book, which includes much historical material, is addressed to the non-specialist reader, though one chapter, "Chemistry and Pharmacology," requires some scientific background. The following chapters are presented: 1) The history of marihuana in the United States; 2) From plant to intoxicant; 3) Chemistry and pharmacology; 4) The acute intoxication: literary and other reports; 5) The acute intoxication: its properties; 6) Motivation of the user; 7) Turning on; 8) The place of cannabis in medicine; 9) Addiction, dependence, and the "stepping stone" hypothesis; 10) Psychoses, adverse reactions, and personality deterioration; 11) Crime and sexual excess; 12) The campaign against marihuana; and 13) The question of legalization.

Dr. Grinspoon advocates legalizing the social use of marihuana, though his reasoning may seem peculiar: he believes (and cites evidence from other cultures) that when a psychoactive substance is outlawed, a more harmful one is increasingly used.

617. Grupp, Stanley E., ed. **Marihuana.** Columbus, Ohio, Charles E. Merrill Publishing Co., 1971. 302p. $5.50pa. LC 72-157698. ISBN 0-675-09834-3.

In collecting these 25 papers on marihuana use, the editor has attempted to avoid the insipid and sentimental and to present well-argued and clearly-presented materials that cover a range of viewpoints. Papers are arranged under four general headings: 1) Its nature and use, 2) Value perspectives, 3) Research reports, and 4) The question of control. This is a good collection of reprinted papers.

618. Grupp, Stanley E. **The Marihuana Muddle.** Lexington, Mass., D. C. Heath and Co., 1973. 181p. bibliog. $12.50. LC 72-13550. ISBN 0-669-84863-8.

The author presents these materials, based on various research endeavors, in the hope of clarifying some of the issues that confront society in regard to marihuana use and control. Several chapters of the book are written by contributors, most of whom are individuals active in the social sciences. Some of the chapters are reprinted from other sources, while some appear for the first time in this volume.

The presentation is divided into three parts: Initiation to marihuana smoking, epidemiology of marihuana use, and marihuana and heroin. The chapter headings are as follows: 1) Marihuana as a social object, 2) Predicting who will turn on, 3) Marihuana use in the small college: a Midwest example, 4) Black and white experienced marihuana smokers, 5) Observation on experienced and exclusive marihuana smokers, 6) Multiple drug use in a sample of experienced marihuana smokers, 7) Experience with marihuana in a sample of drug users, 8) Experienced marihuana smokers and receptiveness to heroin, 9) Prior criminal record and adult marihuana arrest dispositions, 10) The "Marihuana Muddle" as reflected in California arrest statistics and dispositions, 11) Criminal record characteristics of 1960 and 1969 California adult marihuana arrestees, 12) Police and illicit drug markets: some economic considerations, 13) Deterrence and the marihuana smoker.

One cannot come to many conclusions about the marihuana problem on the basis of this descriptive and exploratory material, which raises questions and perhaps suggests avenues for future investigations. The chief value of the publication is that it presents a great deal of data, much of it in tabular form, that may be of interest.

619. Indian Hemp Drugs Commission. **Marijuana Report, 1893-1894.** Introduction and glossary by John Kaplan. Silver Spring, Md., Thos. Jefferson Publishing Co., 1969. 503p. $28.50. LC 74-84211.

This classic work had been almost completely unavailable in the United States until recently. The Indian Hemp Drugs Commission was charged in 1893 by the government of India to investigate whether marijuana should be criminalized. The Commission's Report is reproduced here in full, except that only a small part of the appended materials have been included. The original report was published in seven volumes with two subsequently issued supplementary volumes. The complete work is also now available, having been reprinted in 1971 by the Johnson Reprint Corporation.

The chapter headings are as follows: 1) Introductory; 2) Important points connected with the natural history of the hemp plant (Cannabis sativa); 3) The existence, prevalence, and character of the spontaneous growth; 4) Extent of cultivation, and its tendency to increase or decrease; 5) Methods of cultivation and matters connected therewith; 6) Preparation of the raw drugs from the cultivated wild plant; 7) Trade and movement of the hemp drugs; 8) Extent of use and the manner and forms in which the hemp drugs are consumed; 9) Social and religious customs: 10) Effects–General observations; 11) Effects–physical; 12) Effects–mental; 13) Effects–moral: general summary of conclusions; 14) The policy of hemp drug administration; 15) Existing systems described; 16) Provincial systems examined; 17) Systems of native states; and 18) Summary. Appended are an extract from the "Mysore Memorandum," which tells how ganja (a marijuana product) was prepared, a report on animal experiments with marijuana and dhatura (in the U.S. called jimson weed), and a memorandum on the religious aspects of hemp drugs in India. There is also a glossary of Indian and Anglo-Indian terms (prepared by the editor of this recent edition).

In summary, the Commission concluded that total prohibition of the cultivation of the hemp plant for narcotics and of the manufacture, sale, or use of drugs derived from it was not necessary. The policy advocated was one of control and restriction. The dissenting note that was included expressed the feeling that the evidence did show the use of the drug to be deleterious, although opinions differed as to the extent of the dangers. The differences were explained this way: "On the one hand, the patriots and philanthropists in their excessive zeal for the welfare of the people are generally apt to magnify the existing evils which corrode society, however small they may appear to the naked eye; while, on the other hand, another class, with a view to serve the interests of the State, generally make the evils appear very much smaller, like things seen through the wrong end of the binocular glass, forgetting that the interest of the Government could be best served by serving the interest of the people."

In the introduction to the edition being reviewed, the editor makes a plea for lessening controls today on marijuana use because this Report found that the drug is not very harmful.

620. Lewis, Mark F., ed. **Current Research in Marijuana.** New York and London, Academic Press, 1972. 219p. bibliog. $10.00. LC 72-88343.

These papers were presented at a symposium held at the Aeronautical Center, Oklahoma City, June 13-15, 1972, a meeting sponsored by the Office of Aviation Medicine of the Federal Aviation Administration. The topics covered, however, do not concern the aviation community alone, being of interest also to those who wish to evaluate the effects on human behavior of short-or long-term marijuana use. The papers include the following: 1) Tolerance, state-dependency and long-term behavioral effects of delta-9-THC; 2) Delta-9 tetrahydrocannabinol: behavioral toxicity in laboratory animals; 3) Effects of delta-9-trans-tetrahydrocannabinol on simple and complex learned behavior in animals; 4) On the mechanism of tolerance to delta-9-THC; 5) 21-day administration of marijuana in male volunteers; 6) A comparison of the effects of marijuana and alcohol on visual functions; 7) Effects of altitude and psychological stress on the response of the rat to cannibolic compounds; 8) The effects of the chronic use of marijuana on sleep and perceptual motor performance in humans; 9) Marijuana and the naval aviator; 10) The effect of marijuana on driving performance; 11) Marijuana today: an overview.

The last paper sums up the results of the scientific studies. One noteworthy conclusion of the studies is that, among other effects, marijuana use interferes with central mechanisms, which implies that it impairs complex performances such as driving and flying.

621. **Marihuana: Biochemical, Physiological and Pathological Aspects.** Papers by Peter B. Dews and others. New York, MSS Information Corp., 1973. 289p. bibliog. index. $18.50. LC 72-13833. ISBN 0-8422-7094-9.

These papers cover various aspects of the chemistry of marijuana. With the exception of one article, they are all research papers, all published previously (1970-1972) in scholarly periodicals. The exception is a summary of the Second Annual Report to Congress from the Secretary of Health, Education and Welfare,

"Marihuana and Health" (1972). Many of the articles are somewhat technical for the average reader, but the first section, which takes up more general problems of marihuana and health, is not. In any case, the reports will help give the reader a chemical understanding of the drug's effects. Other sections of the book cover the following topics: 1) Pathological aspects of marihuana use, 2) Localization of cannabinol derivatives in brain and their effects on central nervous system metabolism, 3) Metabolism of cannabinol derivatives and various physiological effects, 4) Chemical identification and synthesis of cannabinol derivatives, and 5) Cannabis, the marihuana plant.

622. **Marijuana: Chemistry, Pharmacology, and Patterns of Social Use.** Edited by Arnold J. Singer. New York, New York Academy of Sciences, 1971. 269p. bibliog. (New York Academy of Sciences. Annals. Vol. 191).

These papers present the results of a conference held by the Academy on May 20-21, 1971. They are high-level, scholarly, research contributions to the literature. The material is presented in two sections, the first on chemistry and pharmacology and the second on psychopharmacology and sociology. The discussion that followed each presentation is also included.

623. Merlin, Mark David. **Man and Marijuana: Some Aspects of their Ancient Relationship.** Rutherford, N.J., Fairleigh Dickinson University Press, 1972. 120p. illus. bibliog. index. $8.00. LC 73-150239. ISBN 0-8386-7909-9.

In the last few years there has been a great interest in the hemp or marijuana plant, and many books have been published on the topic. This one is better than most and a bit different. Tracing the history of man's use of hemp, it describes botanical aspects in the first part of the book and then formulates a theory on man's earliest uses of the plant. Here, the economic, therapeutic, recreational, and spiritual uses are outlined, including use as a fiber source (particularly for rope), as food and oil, as medicine, and as a hallucinogen. The third and final section of the book traces the spread of use from central Asia to ancient China, India, Europe, and southwest Asia. Since many are unaware of the diverse and ancient uses of hemp, the author hopes to throw light on the subject. The book is interesting, well-documented, and well-written in a straightforward manner, making no attempt to influence one's thinking on the evils or possible benefits of use of the drug.

624. Mikuriya, Tod H., ed. **Marijuana: Medical Papers, 1839-1972.** Oakland, Calif., Medi-Comp Press, 1973. 465p. illus. bibliog. index. $15.00. LC 72-87736.

This diverse collection of papers (taken from professional journals) concerning the medicinal applications and scientific properties of marijuana products. Some of the papers, particularly the older ones, suffer from lack of documentation and difficult, archaic, or colloquial language. The editor feels that Western medicine has forgotten most of what it once knew about the therapeutic effects of cannabis, and that this book will recall some of the earlier findings.

The papers are presented under the following categories: 1) From East to West, 2) Personal experiences and speculations, 3) Therapeutic excursions, 4) Recent acute clinical studies, 5) Chemical and pharmacological studies, and 6) Social origins of the marijuana laws.

The papers are interesting, but many of them are personal accounts based on interviews rather than reports of scientific research.

625. New York (City). Mayor's Committee on Marihuana. **The Marihuana Problem in the City of New York**. By Mayor LaGuardia's Committee on Marihuana, with a foreword by Raymond P. Shafer and an introduction by Dana L. Farnsworth. Published under the auspices of the Library of the New York Academy of Medicine. Metuchen, N.J., Scarecrow, 1973. 220p. (History of Medicine Series, No. 38). bibliog. $7.50. LC 73-5924. ISBN 0-8108-0629-0.

This reprint of the 1944 edition, compiled and edited originally by G. B. Wallace and E. V. Cunningham, contains a new foreword.

During the late 1930s and early 1940s the mayor of New York City appointed a committee to study the marihuana problem because its use among Negroes and jazz musicians had been receiving considerable adverse publicity in the press. This book, a report of the Committee's investigation, includes observations from sociologists, psychologists, pharmacologists, and physicians. In general, the investigators found that the dangers of marihuana were exaggerated and unfounded, but public acceptance of the report was negative. It was felt that reissuing the publication in the 1970s, at a time whem marihuana use was more widespread, would result in a more receptive audience and would make available valuable historical material.

The foreword points out that the Committee's findings are similar to those reported in 1972 by the National Commission on Marihuana and Drug Abuse in its report *Marihuana: A Signal of Misunderstanding* (entry 636).

The 1970s audience for these findings does not seem to have been entirely receptive, however. As the book points out, there is still much concern about the long-range effects of the drug, especially on heavy users, and the evidence isn't all in yet.

626. Oursler, Will. **Marijuana: The Facts, the Truth**. New York, Paul S. Eriksson, Inc., 1968. 240p. index. $5.95. LC 68-18953.

Attempting to determine whether or not marijuana is dangerous, the author presents here what experts have reported and what users have said. Material, collected by interviews with authorities and users, includes case histories. The book's conclusions can be summed up as follows: It appears that some individuals can use the drug moderately and suffer few ill effects. Others cannot. A large percentage of those drawn to the use of marijuana are in some measure resentful, maladjusted, and disturbed, having had difficulty with the adult world in general and with their parents and families in particular. Drug use to many is a form of social protest, and some users are seeking avenues of escape, for a variety of reasons. Many are led to the use of stronger drugs. Users interviewed gave curiously contradictory statements regarding their drug use. They frequently spoke one way and acted another. Hallucinations were reported by very few users; most claimed they did not hallucinate even if their behavior indicated the opposite.

In his summary, the author says that he admires the younger generation for their concern with social problems, but that they will not find answers in marijuana or any similar drug. Solutions can be found only in the reality of action in the real world.

627. Rosevear, John. **Pot.** New York, Lancer Books, 1967. 158p. $2.00.

The author encourages the use of marijuana, evidently because he feels that is use is pleasurable, it relieves pressure on the individual, and it does no harm. First presenting a short history of the drug, he gives details on how to grow and care for the plant, then tells how to use the product. The author goes to some length to point out that marijuana users are ordinary peaceful individuals. He categorizes them as regular, occasional, and rare smokers. The book includes some appended materials such as a glossary, a short section on chemistry, and methods of legal identification of the drug.

628. Smith, David E., ed. **The New Social Drug: Cultural, Medical, and Legal Perspectives on Marijuana.** Englewood Cliffs, N. J., Prentice-Hall, Inc., 1970. 186p. bibliog. $5.95. LC 77-104863.

The editor of this collection of papers (which are reprinted from other sources) feels that the prohibition of alcohol and the illegality of marijuana use are similar situations. Viewing alcohol as the social drug of this generation and pot the social drug of the next generation, he thinks this situation has contributed to widening the generation gap in America.

The papers are divided into five subject sections as follows: 1) Pharmacology and classification, 2) The issue of marijuana abuse, 3) Marijuana as a social issue, 4) The issue of marijuana regulation, and 5) Marijuana as a political issue.

The book attempts to place this difficult problem in proper perspective, although it offers no good solution to it. It is felt that the present generation's "irrational" viewpoint will not be modified, but the prediction is made that the next generation will place marijuana in its "proper perspective." it is not made clear just what that "proper perspective" is.

629. Snyder, Solomon H. **Uses of Marijuana.** New York, London, Oxford University Press, 1971. 127p. illus. bibliog. index. $5.95. LC 70-161891.

Written by a professor of psychiatry and pharmacology, this book tells what is known about marijuana, particularly from the point of view of possible medical uses. The following sections are presented: 1) Marijuana as medicine, 2) A brief world history, 3) Behavioral effects, 4) Dangers, 5) Research progress, and 6) Legal turmoil. The use of the drug as a medicine in nineteenth century Europe and America is described. (It was prescribed as a pain killer and for the relief of headache, epilepsy, and insomnia). The author believes that further research on the substance may yield important scientific information. The tone of the book is sympathetic to the limited use of this drug, and present restrictive laws are criticized.

630. Solomon, David, ed. **The Marijuana Papers.** London, Panther Books, 1969. 475p. bibliog. index. $1.70.

This volume is divided into three sections: historical, sociological, and cultural papers are in the first, literary and imaginative papers in the second, and scientific papers in the third. Each section contains six to eight papers written by well-known scientists and/or literary figures.

The editor's point of view is that marijuana use should be legalized. His reasoning is that the drug has therapeutic applications and is at least as harmless as nicotine and alcohol. While the claim that the drug is harmless is still in question (the evidence is perhaps stronger the other way), this collection is noteworthy because many of the writings are well-documented classics, even including a selection from Rabelais's *Pantagruel.*

631. Tart, Charles T. **On Being Stoned: A Psychological Study of Marijuana Intoxication.** Palo Alto, Calif., Science and Behavior Books, 1971. 333p. bibliog. index. $7.95. LC 79-153848. ISBN 0-8314-0027-7.

This volume attempts to describe the feelings of marijuana users when they use the drug and the drug's effect on their senses, perception, and thinking. The work is based on a study of 150 experienced marijuana smokers, a study financed by the Public Health Service.

Much numerical and statistical information is included, but everything is written understandably so that general readers as well as researchers will find it interesting. The book does not settle any of the great underlying problems of drug abuse, but it does allow one to gain some understanding of marijuana use and altered states of consciousness in general. The research reported differs from earlier studies in that it deals with the effects of the drug in a social rather than laboratory setting.

632. Tinklenberg, Jared R., ed. **Marijuana and Health Hazards: Methodological Issues in Current Research.** New York, Academic Press, 1975. 178p. bibliog. index. $8.50. LC 75-13085. ISBN 0-12-691350-1.

This publication contains the proceedings of a conference sponsored by the Drug Abuse Council, held in Washington, D.C., on January 6, 1975. The contributors, 19 noted scientists presently studying the effects of marijuana, present their critical, state-of-the-art assessments of what is currently known about the consequences of marijuana use by humans. Five areas of concern and controversy are focused on: 1) marijuana and genetics, 2) marijuana and immunity, 3) marijuana and testosterone, 4) marijuana and the central nervous system, and 5) marijuana and psychiatric problems.

No really definitive conclusions are reached. The scientists point out areas where additional research is needed and express the view that no drug can be said to be really safe. The papers are rather technical in approach but can be understood reasonably well by the intelligent reader.

633. U.S. Bureau of Narcotics and Dangerous Drugs. **Marihuana, 1972.** Washington, GPO, 1972. 47p. illus. bibliog.

This pamphlet presents the Bureau of Narcotics and Dangerous Drugs' view of the marihuana problem. The Bureau feels that the available evidence and the research results are sufficient to warrant a public warning against lessening the controls on the drug. The following chapters are presented: 1) Background history and present use; 2) Marihuana's effects; 3) Risks, benefits and consequences; 4) Marihuana, the individual and society.

The booklet is well written and presents a reasonable view.

634. U.S. National Commission on Marihuana and Drug Abuse. **Drug Use in America: Problem in Perspective**. Second Report. Washington, GPO, 1973. 481p. bibliog. $2.60pa. S/N 5266-00003.

Public Law 91-513 gave the Commission a mandate to study the marihuana problem, and this report is the result. The Commission studied the roots of the country's drug problem, analyzed the assumptions upon which the present policy is based, and recommended policy directions for both the public and private sectors. The Commission believed that policy should focus on the behavioral concomitants of drug use rather than on the drugs themselves.

The report describes the phenomena of drug use, drug-induced behavior, and drug dependence and establishes a process for assessing their social impact. Recommendations for the present were submitted and speculations were made about policies that may prove useful in the future.

Included is an index of recommendations for both the first report and this (the second and final) report. The second report recommendations are presented in two parts, one for public institutions and one for private institutions. Predictably it was recommended that Congress should create a single federal agency to establish, administer, and coordinate all drug policy at the federal level; this agency would be the principal, if not sole, point of contact for state drug programs. Further, each state and most communities should establish unified drug agencies. Legal controls would be strengthened internationally as well as on the federal, state, and local levels. The federal government should have the major responsibility for treatment funding. Prevention and research would be given attention. The recommendations for private institutions include adding courses in schools of medicine and allied medical fields. Practitioners should expressly warn patients of drug use dangers, and drug manufacturers should undertake a major campaign to educate health professionals and the public. Retail pharmacies should vigorously enforce regulations, and the alcohol beverage industry should fund research. All industries should undertake studies of employee drug use. Colleges and universities should undertake expanded counseling programs. The mass media must re-examine the impact of informational messages on young people.

The Commission also prepared four volumes of appended materials to accompany this report (see following review).

635. U.S. National Commission on Marihuana and Drug Abuse. **Drug Use in America: Problem in Perspective**. Second Report. Appendices. Washington, GPO, 1973. 4v. bibliog. v.1, $11.85pa.; v.2, $6.15pa.; v. 3, $7.50pa.; v. 4, $7.45pa. S/N 5266-0004 to 5266-0007.

These large volumes present the technical papers of the Second Report of the Commission, containing most of the materials prepared for the Commission. The Commission hopes that researchers and lay audiences will find them informative, since they may suggest areas for further research and may provide policy makers with guideposts for decision-making.

The volume titles are as follows: I, Patterns and consequences of drug use; II, Social responses to drug use; III, The legal system and drug control; and IV, Treatment and rehabilitation.

636. U.S. National Commission on Marihuana and Drug Abuse. **Marihuana: A Signal of Misunderstanding**. First Report of the Commission. Washington, GPO, 1972. 184p. $1.00pa. S/N 5266-0001.

This report, prepared to conform with a mandate contained in Section 601 of Public Law 91-513, the Comprehensive Drug Abuse Prevention and Control Law of 1970, attempts to present the facts as they were known in 1972 and to place the problem in proper perspective. The following sections are presented in the Report: 1) Marihuana and the problem of marihuana, 2) Marihuana use and its effects, 3) Social impact of marihuana use, 4) Social response to marihuana use, 5) Marihuana and social policy. Readers who are interested in greater detail will want to investigate the two-volume appendix, which provides technical papers (see following review).

The Report concludes that while the use of marihuana should be discouraged, it does not rank very high in the range of social concerns. The Commission would de-emphasize marihuana as a problem.

637. U.S. National Commission on Marihuana and Drug Abuse. **Marihuana: A Signal of Misunderstanding. Appendix**. The technical papers of the First Report of the Commission. Washington, GPO, 1972. 2v. $10.75pa. S/N 5266-0002.

This appendix fully documents the methodological and substantive issues presented in the Commission Report (see review above). In addition to the technical data, it also contains the historical and philosophical foundation of the Report. There are six parts as follows: 1) Biological aspects, 2) Social aspects, 3) Legal aspects, 4) Response of the criminal justice system to marihuana use, 5) National survey, 6) Social policy aspects.

638. U.S. National Institute on Drug Abuse. **Marihuana and Health: Fifth Annual Report to the U.S. Congress from the Secretary of Heatlh, Education, and Welfare, 1975**. Washington, GPO, 1976. 145p. bibliog. index. (DHEW Publication No. (ADM) 76-314). $1.90pa. S/N 017-024-00501-1.

This edition of *Marihuana and Health*, the fifth in a series of annual reports, points out that although more data are available than previously, the direct health implications of marihuana are still not certain. In addition to a summary and overview, the following technical chapters are included: 1) Epidemiology of marihuana use, 2) Chemistry and metabolism, 3) Toxicological and pharmacological effects, 4) Preclinical effects: unlearned behavior, 5) Preclinical effects: learned behavior, 6) Preclinical chronic effects: unlearned and learned behavior, 7) Human effects, 8) Effects of marihuana on the genetic and immune systems, and 9) Therapeutic aspects.

The report says marihuana use poses significant hazards for drivers, pilots, and factory workers because psycho-motor performance is impaired. However, new research indicates the drug may be medically useful for treating such diseases as glaucoma, cancer, and asthma. The increased use of alcohol and marihuana simultaneously poses a threat that may be more hazardous than that of either drug used alone. Another finding is that marihuana use is continuing to increase in the U.S. but remains concentrated in the 18 to 25 age group. Twice as many males as females use it. The report does not answer all questions surrounding marihuana, but it does point to new medical research leads. It is frequently quoted.

639. World Health Organization Scientific Group. **The Use of Cannabis.** Geneva, World Health Organization, 1971. 47p. bibliog. (World Health Organization Technical Report Series No. 478.) $1.00pa.

This booklet is an authoritative examination of the scientific effects of cannabis on man. In addition, an attempt is made to indicate where further research is needed and to suggest possible approaches to such research. The following sections are presented: 1) Introduction, 2) Cannabis: broad perspectives, 3) Epidemiological aspects, 4) Effects on man of using cannabis, 5) Research needs, and 6) Research strategies.

17. Stimulants

Only a few titles are listed in this section. In view of the widely publicized (and condemned) use of amphetamines, however, it seemed advisable to place the material in a separate section. This class of drug has been used medically by prescription, notably as an appetite suppressant for obesity; but because of adverse publicity, physicians have almost completely stopped prescribing it. The large intravenous dose used by drug abusers, however, is enormous compared to the oral dose used medically. The drug has been condemned by drug abusers themselves as dangerous ("speed kills"). This adverse publicity probably stems from the fact that amphetamines, which are powerful stimulants, cause the user to be aggressive and impulsive, as opposed to narcotics and marihuana, which tend to make the user lethargic.

640. **Amphetamines: Medical and Psychological Studies**. Papers by Francis Antony Whitlock, K. D. Charalampous, Edward J. Lynn et al. In cooperation with the Smithsonian Science Information Exchange. New York, MSS Information Corporation, 1974. 265p. bibliog. index. $17.00. LC 74-8024. ISBN 0-8422-7129-5.

Amphetamine abuse has been reported since 1938, but only since the emergence of the drug subculture in the 1960s has it been classed as a problem drug. The papers collected in this volume, which have been reprinted from other sources, discuss the assumed and documented abuse of the drug. There seem to be two types of abusers, the first of which receives most of the publicity. These abusers use amphetamines with other drugs, experiment with drug combinations, and often take the drug intravenously. The second group comprised of patients who initially were given the drug for some clinical reason (such as obesity) and cannot stop its use. Studies have been undertaken to determine if there might be a predisposition to amphetamine abuse. One investigator describes the abuser as one who is "isolated, preoccupied with food, sleep, death, and longings for maternal care to the exclusion of mature relationships."

The papers have been grouped into the following sections: 1) General studies, 2) Medical use, 3) Drug abuse among psychiatric patients, 4) Personality factors, 5) Antisocial effects of amphetamine abuse, 6) Psychological effects, 7) Physiological effects. The last section of the volume presents summaries of current research projects, which were obtained from a search of the Smithsonian Science Information Exchange data base, a national collection of information on ongoing and recently completed research.

641. Grinspoon, Lester, and Peter Hedblom. **The Speed Culture: Amphetamine Use and Abuse in America.** Cambridge, Harvard University Press, 1975. 340p. bibliog. index. $15.00. LC 74-27257. ISBN 0-674-83192-6.

This book was written primarily to inform the general reader of the dangers of amphetamine abuse. Laws passed in 1971-1972 have controlled the drug rather strictly, since it had become evident that there had been considerable misuse of it. Much of this misuse was legal, as physicians before that time prescribed the substance rather freely. The book points out that social forces exist which have favored the use of these synthetic drugs: manufacturers are blamed, patients accept and desire the drugs, and they are medically convenient. What the book does not emphasize is that they also have legitimate medical use (although some feel that their disadvantages outweigh their usefulness). In any case, they have been used as appetite depressants, as stimulants, to control sleeping sickness, for psychopathic conditions and for alcoholism; they are still used to treat hyperkinetic children. While it is obvious that this type drug can be harmful, the reviewer feels that the book overdramatizes the harm that has resulted from their use. The case histories of the abusers indicate that they also used other drugs, which doubtless added to their problems.

The book has been carefully prepared with elaborate documentation, but somehow the subject doesn't seem to be worth the attention given it—particularly right now, when physicians, yielding to pressure, have for the most part stopped prescribing the drug, and manufacturers have limited production of it.

642. Kalant, Oriana Josseau. **The Amphetamines: Toxicity and Addiction.** 2nd ed. Toronto, University of Toronto Press, 1973. (Published and distributed in the U.S. by Charles C. Thomas). 188p. bibliog. index. (Brookside Monograph of the Addiction Research Foundation No. 5). $8.50. LC 70-185868. ISBN 0-8020-1835-1.

This work discusses the hazards associated with the misuse of the amphetamine drugs, the most serious of which have been presumed to be addiction and a schizophrenia-like reaction. When the first edition of the book was written in 1966, a survey of the literature on amphetamines was undertaken to find answers to these four question: 1) What are the physiological and psychological effects of the drugs in the normal individual?, 2) When can the drugs be used with advantage by a normal individual?, 3) What are the dangers from their use, either to the individual or to society?, and 4) What are the addicting properties of the drug? The book explores and attempts to answer these questions.

There are seven chapters: Introduction; Acute and subacute amphetamine intoxication; Toxic effects due to chronic consumption of amphetamines; Amphetamine psychosis; Amphetamine dependence, habituation, and addiction; Abuse of amphetamine-like drugs; and Social significance of amphetamine abuse. In order to update the first edition, three appendices have been added: an overview of recent developments, the psychopharmacology of amphetamine dependence, the nature and extent of speed use in North America.

While the book contains a good review of the literature on the subject, there are as yet no definitive answers to most of the questions surrounding amphetamine use.

643. Leake, Chauncey D. **The Amphetamines: Their Actions and Uses.** Springfield, Ill., Charles C. Thomas, 1958. 167p. bibliog. index. $4.50. LC 58-10277.

The author, a pharmacologist, wrote this book before amphetamines became notorious and widely abused. His intention was to present an introduction or survey of the drugs, pointing out what seemed at the time to be significant about them. He discusses several amphetamine substances, comparing them to compounds that have similar actions. Though his aim was mainly to help physicians in prescribing, he suggests that lawyers, sociologists, law-givers, administrators, and others might use the book to gain an understanding of how amphetamines act and how they may be used for individual and social benefit. These strong stimulants had at least reasonable success when used as appetite depressants and nasal decongestants or to treat narcolepsy and behavior problems in children. Today they are seldom used medically, probably because they have been so abused by addicts who take enormous doses.

644. Sjöqvist, Folke, and Malcolm Tottie, eds. **Abuse of Central Stimulants.** Symposium arranged by the Swedish Committee on International Health Relations, Stockholm, November 25-27, 1968. New York, Raven Press, 1969. 536p. bibliog. $9.75.

This book first presents some introductory material on the growth of widespread use of amphetamines and related drugs. These drugs were first used in the 1940s as weight-reducing agents, since they suppress the appetite. When they later became the fashion among young drug abusers, who obtained them illegally and injected massive doses, they were designated as dangerous narcotic drugs. This symposium, presenting the various views of outstanding experienced workers from many countries, throws light on the medical, biochemical, and pharmacological aspects of the use of these central stimulants. The papers are presented under the following subject areas: 1) abuse of central stimulants: general clinical aspects, 2) medical and social aspects of central stimulants, and 3) pharmacological and biochemical aspects of abuse of central stimulants. In addition, a panel discussion has been included on "The possibilities of chemical diagnosis of abuse of central stimulants." The material is all scholarly and advanced, although most of it can be understood by the general reader.

645. U.S. National Institute of Mental Health. **Current Concepts on Amphetamine Abuse.** Proceedings of a workshop, Duke University Medical Center, June 5-9, 1970. Edited by Everett H. Ellinwood and Sidney Cohen. Washington, GPO, 1972. 238p. illus. bibliog. index. (DHEW Publication No. (HSM) 72-9085). $3.50pa. S/N 1724-0231.

This workshop brought together a notable group of researchers and experts in the area of mood-altering drugs. The first part of the work covers "Correlated Studies on Amphetamine-Induced Behavior," and the second, "Clinical Aspects of Amphetamine Use and Abuse."

The summary of the papers points out that at least three kinds of amphetamine misuse can be identified today. The first is intermittent or consistent use of small amounts orally. These users are often athletes, truck drivers, and students who use the drug to cope with anticipated, prolonged periods of physical or mental stress. Those who have used the drug for weight control and are unable to discontinue it may fall in this class. The second misuse is a chronic, moderate dose, again taken orally. These users began with average amounts but have increased them over a period of time. The third misuse, a chronic, high dose, taken intravenously, can result in overdose or in liver and brain cell damage. Also, a paranoid psychosis resembling schizophrenia develops. With this is seen social disintegration, disorganization of thought, impulsive and violent behavior, and criminal activity.

In addition, the report includes material on the possible mode of action of the drug, although this is not fully understood at the present time.

18. Alcohol

This section is quite extensive, reflecting the availability of a great amount of material. Problems connected with alcohol use are not recent, so more older materials are listed here than in other sections of the bibliography. A recent upsurge of interest in alcoholism has occurred, however, with the realization that alcohol is the major drug of abuse–it is more widely used than any other drug, and much more widely accepted. In addition, society's attitude toward the use of alcohol is more ambiguous than its attitude toward any other drug, an ambiguity that young people no doubt sense. Nearly all of this bibliography's books on alcoholism and problem drinking have been placed in this special section, although some could reasonably go in other places, such as Section 12, where scientific and research studies have been placed, and in Section 5, with personal narratives. Despite the similarities between alcoholism and other forms of drug addiction, however, alcoholism is most often treated as a separate condition.

There seems to be better success with the treatment of alcoholism than with the treatment of other kinds of drug addiction. Whether this is because of something inherent in the drugs or whether it is because of more experience with the treatment of alcoholism is not clear. Actually, the acceptance of alcoholism as a medical problem has proceeded slowly. Only recently has it emerged as an appropriate subject for laboratory study and clinical investigation. Little work in these areas was done prior to the mid-1960s.

Emphasis in the field of alcoholism is on treatment of problem drinking rather than on prevention of alcohol use (in contrast to other drugs). Alcoholics Anonymous emerges as an outstanding treatment modality. A rising problem in this area is the growing use of alcohol in conjunction with other drug use, often with dangerous and disastrous results.

646. Addeo, Edmond G., and Jovita Reichling Addeo. **Why Our Children Drink.** Englewood Cliffs, N.J., Prentice-Hall, Inc., 1975. 191p. bibliog. $7.95. LC 75-20326. ISBN 0-13-959460-4.

Intended primarily for parents, this work presents the authors' conclusions about the alcohol problem among young people. Authoritative independent reports were the basis for the conclusions. The authors caution that hysteria and scare tactics will only alienate youth, but these scare tactics are used to some extent in the book. The material is presented in three parts: 1) Are teen-agers drinking?, 2) Why do our teen-agers drink?, and 3) What to do about it.

The book pulls together information about the problem, but there are few concrete suggestions about "what to do about it." Dr. Morris E. Chafetz says in the introduction: "Parents often send their children a confusing batch of signals about taking alcohol—signals which reflect the parents' own ambivalence and confusion about drinking." It is probably fair to say that the book is guilty of the same tactic.

647. **The Alcoholism Digest Annual.** v. 1– . Rockville, Md., Information Planning Associates, Inc. 1972-73– . Annual. $35.00.

These volumes are compilations of the 12 issues of the monthly publication *The Alcoholism Digest*. Each yearly volume consists of 400-500 pages of about 1,200 abstracts or summaries of reports, books, journal articles, and other publications. Every aspect of the subject is covered. The material is divided into broad subject areas, and author and subject indexes have been provided. Also included are a few full-length articles on alcoholism and a listing of federal treatment and rehabilitation programs and grants.

648. **Aspects of Alcoholism.** Volume 2. With a preface by Ruth Fox. Philadelphia, J. B. Lippincott Co., 1966. 80p. bibliog. index.

This book, a compilation of articles by Roche Laboratories, summarizes quite well the current knowledge about the many facts of alcoholism. The following chapters are presented: 1) Signs and symptoms, 2) Who will be an alcoholic?, 3) Profile of an alcoholic, 4) The "intelligent" alcoholic—why does he drink?, 5) Drinking, an international problem, 6) Alcoholism—18th century and today, 7) The problem drinker in industry, 8) The medical complications of alcohol, 9) Prevention—knotty problem, 10) Researchers speculate, 11) Drug treatment in general practice, and 12) The role of the family doctor.

It is brought out that the results of treatment for alcoholics have grown steadily better during the past 30 years or so.

649. Becker, Charles E., Robert L. Roe, and Robert A. Scott. **Alcohol as a Drug: A Curriculum on Pharmacology, Neurology and Toxicology.** Baltimore, Williams and Wilkins Co., 1974. 99p. illus. bibliog. index. $9.95pa. LC 74-6002. ISBN 0-8463-0134-2.

Said to be the first comprehensive treatise on the pharmacology, neurology, and toxicology of alcohol, this work was prepared by physicians who have both expertise in the subject and humanistic concern. Examining behavioral aspects of alcohol abuse, treatment, and intervention techniques, it provides an overview of the toxicology of alcohol abuse and its association with polydrug abuse disorders. The purpose of the work is threefold: first, to provide information to physicians who care for alcoholic patients; second, to dispel reluctance that many physicians feel with alcoholic patients by pointing out challenging problems and practical solutions; and third, to help the alcoholic patients themselves.

The following chapters are presented: 1) Introduction, 2) Pharmacology of alcohol, 3) Effects of alcohol on the central nervous system, 4) Effects of alcohol on specific organ systems, 5) Therapy of alcoholism, and 6) Other aspects of alcoholism. Also included are two self-test exercises.

Much good, practical material is conveniently presented in this publication, material that is not easy to locate elsewhere.

650. Block, Marvin A. **Alcohol and Alcoholism: Drinking and Dependence.** Belmont, Calif., Wadsworth Publishing Co., Inc. 1970. 63p. bibliog. index. (Basic Concepts in Health Science Series). $1.25pa. LC 74-107378.

This book provides basic information on the progressive nature of alcoholism and its related problems. The contents are as follows: 1) Why people drink, 2) What is alcohol?, 3) Effects of alcoholic beverages on the body, 4) What is excessive drinking?, 5) Alcoholism, 6) The treatment of alcoholism, and 7) Primary prevention of alcohol problems. The author's aim in writing the book was to make the character of alcohol and its potential for causing harm thoroughly understood. He feels that cultural patterns have become more relaxed and heavy drinking more acceptable, thus increasing the risk of alcohol abuse.

651. Block, Marvin A. **Alcoholism: Its Facets and Phases.** New York, John Day Co., 1965. 320p. index. $7.95. LC 65-13751. ISBN 0-381-98015-4.

This book, by a physician who has treated many alcoholics, is written in simple, non-technical language that can be understood by all concerned with the care and treatment of alcoholics. The author hopes that those in the medical and legal professions as well as sociologists, social workers, teachers, and other concerned individuals will become more understanding of alcoholic individuals.

The following chapters are included: 1) The illness called alcoholism, 2) Why people drink, 3) The problem as a public health matter, 4) How alcohol affects humans, 5) Alcoholism and the law, 6) Understanding the alcoholic, 7) Treating the alcoholic, 8) Medical treatment of alcoholism 9) Effect of alcohol on the body, 10) Treating the abstaining alcoholic, 11) Skid row: a socio-economic and public health problem, 12) Alcoholics Anonymous, 13) Women alcoholics, 14) The government and alcoholism, 15) The medical profession and alcoholism, 16) Alcoholism and industry, 17) The teacher and alcoholism, 18) The hospital and alcoholism, 19) Necessary components for an effective program on alcoholism, 20) The nurse, 21) The clergy, 22) Young people and drinking, 23) The spouse of the alcoholic, 24) Mass media and communications, 25) Lawyers and alcoholism, 26) The social workers and alcoholism, and 27) Alcoholism in other countries.

As can be seen, many facets of the subject are covered, but there is little depth to the coverage. Background information is provided and general suggestions are made, but there is no documentation, and few research results are reported. The author writes mainly from experience.

652. Blum, Eva Maria, and Richard H. Blum. **Alcoholism: Modern Psychological Approaches to Treatment.** Foreword by Morris E. Chafetz. San Francisco, Jossey-Bass, Inc., 1972. 373p. bibliog. index. $12.50. LC 67-13278. ISBN 0-87589-005-9.

Prepared by a husband and wife team who have had much experience in clinical psychology and the drug abuse field, this work discusses current methods for the psychological and social treatment of alcoholism. Individual, group, and community levels are considered, with special attention to such subjects as conditioning and learning, group therapies, motivation, and expectations and evaluation in treatment. The book has been divided into six parts: 1) What is treatment?, 2) The treatment process: stages and hurdles, 3) Kinds of treatment, 4) Treatment problems for special consideration, 5) Treatment evaluation, and 6) Recommendations.

The book is not a how-to-do-it treatment manual but a "treatment aid" for those who work with alcoholics, such as professionals in the healing arts, ministers, welfare counselors, civic leaders, concerned citizens, and those who have alcoholics in their families.

653. Bourne, Peter G., and Ruth Fox, eds. **Alcoholism: Progress in Research and Treatment**. New York, Academic Press, 1973. 439p. bibliog. index. $21.00. LC 72-82638.

The rising concern over drug abuse in the United States has brought about recognition of the fact that the major drug problem is alcohol. It is a drug that can be obtained easily and legally and that is socially acceptable. This volume, prepared by a number of experts, explores almost every aspect of the problem—biochemical effects, cross-cultural studies of drinking patterns, the behavior of alcoholics, the effect on family life, legal aspects, genetic aspects, and treatment. It evaluates treatment by private practitioners and non-physicians, and the success of Alcoholics Anonymous, stressing the need for more research and more effective treatment. Physicians, medical students, social workers, biochemists, and laymen will all be interested in this book, which is excellent. It leaves one not with the feeling that great progress is about to be made, but with the realization that there is much to be done.

654. Bridge, Carl J. **Alcoholism and Driving**. Springfield, Ill., Charles C. Thomas, 1972. 84p. index. $7.00. LC 78-187647. ISBN 0-398-02243-7.

The author's point of view is that the drunk-driving arrest can serve as a resource for a study of alcoholism and its relationship to driving. His study shows that most people arrested for drunk driving are alcoholics. He feels that further research along these lines could perhaps help to solve the current drunk driving problem.

The book reviews the general problems of alcoholism very well, discussing how deterioration, from subtle loss of judgment to extreme deterioration, correlates with driving characteristics. The author feels that alcoholics must be kept off the road until there is a definite remission of the illness. Statistics from other studies are cited, and new insights into alcoholism are described. Chapter headings are as follows: 1) Introduction, 2) Preliminary observations, 3) Conduct of the study, 4) Rating the disease, 5) Review of two hundred arrests, 6) Preliminary conclusions from this series, 7) Added illustrative case, 8) Alcoholism and mental illness, 9) Alcoholic drivers not arrested, 10) Alcoholics are drivers, 11) Drug abuse and driving, 12) Interpersonal relationships among alcoholics, 13) Stark realities, 14) The nature of alcoholism, and 15) How to deal with the problem.

655. Burton, Mary. **An Alcoholic in the Family**. Philadelphia, J. B. Lippincott Company, 1974. 175p. $6.95. LC 74-4366. ISBN 0-397-01016-8.

This personal narrative, told by the wife of an alcoholic, reads rather like a novel. The family problems, disappointment, and the assistance given by Alcoholics Anonymous make up the story.

656. Cahalan, Don, Ira H. Cisin, and Helen M. Crossley. **American Drinking Practices: A National Study of Drinking Behavior and Attitudes.** New Brunswick, N.J., Rutgers Center of Alcohol Studies, Publications Division, 1969. 260p. bibliog. index. (Rutgers Center of Alcohol Studies No. 6). $9.50. LC 70-626701. ISBN 0-911290-37-0.

The authors place the problems of alcohol use in realistic context, with a demographic analysis of alcohol users. They describe man in society using alcoholic beverages and having attitudes about that use. The study's methods are of as much interest as the results of the study. A large amount of statistical data is presented both in the text and in numerous charts and tables. The publication is a valuable and unusual contribution to the study of alcohol and man.

657. Cahalan, Don. **Problem Drinkers: A National Survey**. San Francisco, Jossey-Bass Inc., 1970. 202p. bibliog. index. $9.95 LC 73-133617. ISBN 0-87589-080-6.

This book, based on a national survey conducted in 1967 through interviews with 1,349 adults living in the United States, also reviews prior studies. Focusing on problem drinkers rather than alcoholics in institutionalized settings, the survey shows the prevalence of the various types of drinking problems; prevalence by various demographic characteristics; prevalence rates when social-psychological characteristics are taken into account; and conclusions and implications for public health, therapy, and behavioral research. The chapter headings are as follows; 1) Problem drinking vs. alcoholism, 2) Defining drinking problems, 3) Identifying problem drinkers, 4) Social and personality characteristics, 5) Predicting problem drinking, 6) Patterns of change, 7) Summing up the national survey, and 8) New directions. The appendix discusses the sampling and field procedures.

Only a few of the study's results can be mentioned here: Almost all types of problem drinking are found among people in their early twenties. Drinking problems taper off after age fifty. Women tend to become heavy drinkers later in life than men. Men of lower socioeconomic status contribute more than their share of the severe types of problem drinkers. Those residing in the larger cities had a higher rate of problem drinkers. Social reasons were said to motivate heavy drinking more often than increase of tension or problems of living. This is an interesting and significant book.

658. Cahn, Sidney. **The Treatment of Alcoholics: An Evaluative Study**. New York, Oxford University Press, 1970. 246p. bibliog. index. $7.50. LC 75-83032.

Prepared by a member of the Cooperative Commission on the Study of Alcoholism, this is a study of state and local programs and services for alcoholics, covering governmental, voluntary, and private agencies. The study discusses the strengths and weaknesses of the various approaches to treating alcoholics and suggests ways to improve treatment. A major theme of the book is that treatment for alcoholics must be viewed in the context of total community health and welfare activities. The material for the study is based on visits to various communities in the United States and Canada, and on interviews with persons working with alcoholics. The problems of alcoholics are described and analyzed, with particular reference to variations in social class. Although treatment of alcoholics has not been notably successful, the author's recommendations for improvements will be welcomed by those who are working with the problem and by those who are interested in it.

659. Catanzaro, Ronald J., ed. **Alcoholism: The Total Treatment Approach.** Springfield, Ill., Charles C. Thomas, 1968. 508p. bibliog. index. $22.50. LC 67-18335. ISBN 0-398-00295-9.

These 42 chapters, written by 54 authors who are well known in the field, present multidisciplinary material covering all phases of treatment of the alcoholic. The collection of well-documented articles is impressive. Pragmatic, empiric, and experimental approaches are taken. The book contains the following sections: 1) General aspects of alcoholism, 2) General aspects of treatment, 3) Special treatment methods (psychotherapeutic, pharmacologic, other unique contributions, and experimental), 4) Special treatment settings, 5) Treatment research studies, 6) Prevention and planning future rehabilitation programs, and 7) Treatment in neighboring cultures.

The editor had in mind two types of readers when he assembled the book: the person engaged in treatment programs, large or small, and the person desiring a comprehensive guide to treating alcoholics. Intended primarily for professionals in the area of rehabilitation of alcoholics, the book can be understood by laymen as well. The work was sponsored by the Research Committee of the North American Association of Alcoholism Programs.

660. Chafetz, Morris E., and Harold W. Demone, Jr. **Alcoholism and Society.** New York, Oxford University Press, 1962. 319p. bibliog. index. $9.95. LC 62-9823. ISBN 0-87668-026-0.

The principal objective of this book is to inform a wide audience of lay and professional readers about alcoholism and alcoholics. The authors, a noted psychiatrist and a social scientist, feel that the problem cannot be solved unless it is faced openly. The work is in four sections: Alcoholism and society, A review of previous work, Contemporary alcoholism programs, and The concept of alcohol prevention. In addition, there is a substantial section of representative case histories that have been expertly analyzed by the authors.

The authors present their own "methods of prevention," many of which are concerned with attitudes of society. Some of their comments are: alcohol should not be singled out for special significance and defined as a magical substance to meet all needs and all problems; drinking should not be fitted into a system to demonstrate masculinity; drinking should be used to enhance social relations, not to meet life's problems; alcohol should not be set up in the family as the motivation for rebellion; social attitudes should not force alcohol on an individual; and family physicians, doctors in industry, personnel in general hospitals, social workers, ministers, police, and others should receive training in the detection of alcoholism.

Although the book was written a number of years ago, little new basic knowledge has emerged since, and the work is still widely read.

661. Chafetz, Morris E., Howard T. Blane, and Marjorie J. Hill, eds. **Frontiers of Alcoholism.** New York, Science House, 1970. 424p. bibliog. index. $15.00. LC 79-91171. ISBN 0-87668-026-0.

The volume describes research and clinical progress dealing with psychoanalytically oriented psychotherapy for alcoholics during a 10-year period. The material is presented in two parts: "Understanding and facilitating psychotherapy with alcoholics," and "New directions in research and clinical action." The first part deals with a series of studies that arose from a central program of research, and the second describes several approaches, including clinical action and research and evaluation projects, that are consequences of the earlier work.

The editors conclude that real progress will be made only when alcohol problems are treated as humanely as any other condition and when the need for segregated facilities no longer exists. There is a need for innovative teaching programs for those who work with alcoholics. More study of successful programs is needed, and new people must be attracted to the field. Alcoholics should be identified and treated earlier than they usually are. The editors feel that much progress has been made in attitude and interest concerning alcoholic people and that much new knowledge has come to light. However, the field is still in the frontier stage. Among the notable bibliographies accompanying the text is "An Annotated Bibliography of Studies Evaluating Psychotherapeutic Techniques, 1952-1963."

662. Chafetz, Morris E. **Liquor, the Servant of Man.** Boston, Little, Brown and Co., 1965. 236p. bibliog. index. LC 65-15238.

The author, a physician, has worked in the field of alcoholism since 1954. He has undertaken extensive research and made major contributions to the field, but this book is not one of them. Rather than a scientific treatise, it is "just a pleasant look at liquor"–an unusual viewpoint, particularly for someone in Chafetz's position. He makes the point that man can–and should–drink with pleasure and without fear. Problem drinking is not considered.

663. Clinebell, Howard J., Jr. **Understanding and Counseling the Alcoholic through Religion and Psychology**. Rev. and enl. ed. Nashville, Abingdon Press, 1968. 336p. bibliog. index. $5.95. LC 68-11710.

This book was written for those who need to know what to teach concerning alcoholism and how to handle the alcoholic who seeks counsel. Religious resources are stressed. The work is presented in three parts: Understanding the problem of alcoholism, Some religious approaches to alcoholism, and The minister's approach to alcoholism. The first part presents scientific facts and describes the various factors in the etiology and development of this complex illness. The second part helps the reader profit from the experience of religious groups which have been concerned with helping alcoholics, presenting and evaluating various types of religious approaches, and giving a psychological analysis of them. The final part applies understanding of alcoholism that should be gained from reading the first two parts, emphasizing practical implications for the religious worker and presenting a strategy for working with alcoholics.

This work, which has been widely read by those working with alcoholics and their families, is highly recommended.

664. Cole, Jonathan O., ed. **Clinical Research in Alcohol.** Scientific papers of a Research Conference held December 26-27, 1966, Washington, D. C., under the Joint Auspices of the American Association for the Advancement of Science and the American Psychiatric Association's Committee on Research 1965-66. Washington, American Psychiatric Association, 1968. 178p. bibliog. (Psychiatric Research Report No. 24). $5.00. LC 68-21711.

These papers, written by well-known individuals in the field of clinical research on alcohol, provide an overview of various approaches to research. The following papers are included: 1) Trends in the prevention of alcoholism, 2) Comparison of abstainers and heavy drinkers in a national survey, 3) Prognostic factors in alcoholism, 4) Drug and placebo responses in chronic alcoholics, 5) Group therapy with alcoholics, 6) Maryland alcoholics: follow-up study 1, 7) Drinking patterns of chronic alcoholics: gambling and motivation for alcohol, 8) Fatty liver, cirrhosis, and metabolic effects related to problem drinking, 9) Sleep disturbances in the acute alcoholic psychoses, 10) Central effects of Metronidazole, 11) A review of the use of a Thiazole derivative (Hemineurin) in delirium tremens and allied conditions, and 12) The National Center for Prevention and Control of Alcoholism, NIMH.

665. Cull, John G., and Richard E. Hardy, eds. **Alcohol Abuse and Rehabilitation Approaches.** Springfield, Ill., Charles C. Thomas, 1974. 203p. bibliog. index. $12.75. LC 73-14851. ISBN 0-398-03017-0.

This is one of a series of books on social rehabilitation psychology. Like the others in the series, it contains chapters (some reprinted from other sources) by numerous authors. The chapter titles are as follows: 1) An overview of research in alcohol abuse, 2) Causes of alcohol abuse, 3) The psychological approach to the understanding of alcoholism, 4) Behavioral group therapy with alcohol abusers, 5) Individual counseling and therapy with the alcohol abuser, 6) A description of some selected treatment approaches in alcohol abuse, 7) Vocational satisfaction among alcoholics, and 8) Predicting rehabilitation outcome in alcohol abuse. The third chapter, which makes up about one third of the book, is probably the most valuable; it attempts a global synthesis of the problems of alcoholism.

666. Filstead, William J., Jean J. Rossi, and Mark Keller, eds. **Alcohol and Alcohol Problems: New Thinking and New Directions.** Cambridge, Mass., Ballinger Publishing Co., 1976. 304p. bibliog. index. LC 76-7401. ISBN 0-88410-115-0.

This book is an outgrowth of a symposium held at the Alcoholism Rehabilitation Center of the Lutheran General Hospital, Park Ridge, Illinois, in the spring of 1973. Reflecting the current state of knowledge in the alcohol field, it offers a critical analysis of what has not been done and makes challenging suggestions for what might be done to meet the problems facing the field. It is hoped that these suggestions will form the bases for new thinking and new directions in alcohol studies of the near future. The symposium participants are well known in the field, and the papers are of high quality.

Chapter headings are as follows: 1) Problems with alcohol: an historical perspective, 2) Problem drinking in the perspective of social change, 1940-1973, 3) Concepts, 4) Some possible origins of alcoholism, 5) Some issues in research on the biology of alcoholism, 6) "Treating" the treatment issues: some general observations about the treatment of alcoholism, 7) Evaluation of alcoholism treatment programs, and 8) The prevention of drinking problems.

Like most books on this subject, this one shows that the problems are more evident than the solutions. Emphasis is on the need for experiments in preventing alcohol problems.

667. Forney, Robert B., and Francis W. Hughes. **Combined Effects of Alcohol and Other Drugs.** Springfield, Ill., Charles C. Thomas, 1968. 124p. bibliog. index. $6.50. LC 68-18293.

Written by two pharmacologists and toxicologists, this is a reference source for those interested in the effects of alcohol or alcohol in conjunction with another drug. Exploring published research data, it also evaluates the impact of mixed medication on biological activity, including levels of mental and motor performance. The following chapters are presented: 1) Introduction, 2) Terminology, 3) General pharmacologic effects of ethanol, 4) Alcohol with other depressants, 5) Alcohol with stimulants, 6) Other alcohol-drug combinations, 7) Legislation concerning alcohol-drug combinations, and 8) Epilogue.

The subject under consideration in this book is of considerable importance because of the widespread use of alcohol.

668. Forrest, Gary G. **The Diagnosis and Treatment of Alcoholism.** Springfield, Ill., Charles C. Thomas, 1975. 257p. bibliog. index. $12.75. LC 74-13224. ISBN 0-398-03307-2; ISBN 0-398-03306-4pa.

This work offers a comprehensive treatment approach to alcoholism, in three sections: the first provides background information and initial clinical considerations, the second presents eight chapters, each on a particular strategy of treatment, and the third contains short clinical readings on the treatment of alcoholism. Titles of the eight chapters in the second section are: Individual psychotherapy, Group psychotherapy, Alcoholics Anonymous, Residential treatment, Behavior therapy, The recovery issue, and Toward a causative theory of alcohol addiction. These readings supply the reader with in-depth understanding of both clinical and theoretical issues germane to the treatment of alcoholics. A broad spectrum of issues is covered. While the book may be weak in certain areas (such as documentation), it gives evidence that treatment is going on, has successes, and is worthwhile. The author, writing as a clinical psychologist, stresses the psychological role in treating alcoholism, a role that is sometimes neglected. Some valuable insights are provided.

669. Forsander, Olof, and Kalervo Eriksson, eds. **International Symposium, Biological Aspects of Alcohol Consumption**, 27th-29th September, 1971, Helsinki. New Brunswick, N.J., Rutgers University Center of Alcohol Studies, 1972. 291p. illus. bibliog. (The Finnish Foundation for Alcohol Studies, vol.20). $6.50.

These papers provide a perspective on the current research problems concerning the biological aspects of alcohol consumption. The participants represent a number of disciplines, and the papers have been grouped in these broad subject areas: 1) Metabolic aspects of alcohol consumption, 2) Genetic aspects of alcohol consumption, and 3) Central nervous system and alcohol consumption. The papers are technical and scientific, and each includes a short abstract. The editor's remarks that summarize each session can be readily understood by the general reader.

670. Fort, Joel. **Alcohol: Our Biggest Drug Problem.** New York, McGraw-Hill Book Co., 1973. 180p. illus. bibliog. index. $6.95. LC 72-12746. ISBN 0-07-021598-7; 0-07-021599-5pa.

The author, a physician, has crusaded for the recognition of alcohol as a drug and as a major drug problem and for an end to alcohol advertising. He treats alcohol in the same context as marijuana, heroin, or cocaine, and he calls for better treatment for alcoholics. In addition, the flourishing alcohol industry is severely criticized. The book's viewpoint is somewhat new, and it is one that is currently getting attention.

671. Fox, Ruth, and Peter Lyon. **Alcoholism: Its Scope, Cause and Treatment.** New York, Random House, 1955. 208p. $6.95. LC 55-8170. ISBN 0-394-41454-3.

The senior author of this work is a physician widely known for her work in the field of alcoholism. Although this book is more than 20 years old, most of what is written has not changed.

The prevalence and extent of alcohol use are discussed, followed by alcoholism and problem drinking. The author analyzes why such behavior comes about and explores treatment and assistance for the alcoholic. A "Sources of Help" section lists Information Centers and Treatment Centers, by state.

The authors point out that "nowhere in the annals of medicine or public health has there been a sickness, a disorder, the course of which was so influenced or the treatment of which so compromised by social sanctions." As for the frequently asked question of whether alcoholism can be cured, the authors say that it does not seem that talk of a "cure" is meaningful. Alcohol is a toxic drug. "It is incorrect to say that he is a completely well person who is able to drink a toxic drug without doing himself damage. It would seem more correct to say he is a complete well person who, understanding why once he needed such a toxic drug to get along in life, now no longer has any slightest desire to depend on it."

672. Gammage, Allen Z., David L. Jorgensen, and Eleanor M. Jorgensen. **Alcoholism, Skid Row, and the Police.** Springfield, Ill., Charles C. Thomas, 1972. 82p. bibliog. index. $6.00. LC 71-180813. ISBN 0-398-02288-7.

This small book presents the problem of the public drunkenness offender on skid row and the manner in which he has been handled. Such offenders have variously been ostracized, confined, ridiculed, pitied, treated, and ignored. At the present time the police, courts, and public opinion seem to agree that the offender should usually be locked in jail, dried out, and released. Quite recently, however, programs have been initiated to rehabilitate the skid rower. This book reviews the skid row subculture and its inhabitants, concluding with a proposal for a police-sponsored, community program for treatment and rehabilitation.

673. Gerard, Donald L., and Gerhart Saenger. **Out-Patient Treatment of Alcoholism: A Study of Outcome and Its Determinants.** Toronto, University of Toronto Press for the Alcoholism and Drug Addiction Research Foundation of Ontario, 1966. 249p. bibliog. (Brookside Monograph No. 4). $10.00 ISBN 0-8020-3153-6.

This report is based on a study undertaken from 1957 to 1962 to determine the results of treatment services for alcoholics. The main objectives were to secure a picture of contemporary clinic treatment of alcoholism in the United States and to develop suitable standards for evaluating the treatment offered in alcoholism clinics. The following questions were asked and answered: 1) what kinds of patients come to state supported alcoholism clinics?, 2) what kind of treatment is offered?, 3) what changes take place in the patients?, and 4) to what extent is change related to the characteristics of patients and/or the treatment provided? Some of the findings will surprise therapists. For instance, drugs such as barbiturates, vitamins, and tranquillizers in out-patient treatment were not very effective, although Antabuse (Disulfiram) was found to be rather effective. Psychiatric therapy was not as effective as treatment by internists. Perhaps more significant was the finding that the therapy used should match the pathology of the patient. His personality structure, social and cultural milieu, and attitude toward himself and the world should be considered. Cutting across the disciplines of psychiatry, public health, sociology, and psychology, the study should be of value to professionals in these fields and to laymen who are interested.

674. Gibbins, R. J., with the assistance of B. W. Henheffer and A. Raison. **Chronic Alcoholism and Alcohol Addiction: A Survey of Current Literature.** Toronto, Alcoholism Research Foundation, 1953. 57p. bibliog. (Brookside Monograph No. 1). $6.50. LC 55-31954. ISBN 0-8020-7014-0.

This publication makes a distinction between "chronic alcoholism" and "alcohol addiction." The outstanding characteristic of the latter condition is the inability to break with the habit. Addicts are designated as primary, or true, addicts and secondary addicts. The editor does explain, however, that the articles use a variety of classifications of "abnormal drinkers." Exploring the literature of the subject and reporting the findings of researchers, the book, despite its age, is pertinent and still of interest, perhaps because relatively little progress has been made in dealing with the problem of alcoholism. The material is presented in three parts: etiology, psychological investigation of alcohol addiction, and treatment.

675. Gibbins, Robert J., and others, eds. **Research Advances in Alcohol and Drug Problems.** Vol. 2. New York, Wiley, 1975. 348p. bibliog. index. $24.00. LC 73-18088. ISBN 0-471-29738-0.

This second volume in an annual series covers quite a different selection of topics than the first. The whole book is devoted to various alcohol problems, under the following chapter headings: 1) A critical review of ethnographic studies of alcohol use, 2) An appraisal of drug education programs, 3) The drinking driver and the law: legal countermeasures in the prevention of alcohol-related road traffic accidents, 4) Acute effects of ethanol and opiates on the nervous system, 5) An evaluation of tension models of alcohol consumption, 6) Cost of alcoholic beverages as a determinant of alcohol consumption, and 7) Methods for the treatment of chronic alcoholism: a critical appraisal.

The papers are scholarly and have excellent bibliographies.

676. Grad, Frank P., Audrey L. Goldberg, and Barbara A. Shapiro. **Alcoholism and the Law.** Dobbs Ferry, N.Y., Oceana Publications, Inc., 1971. 311p. bibliog. $14.85. LC 72-116057. ISBN 0-379-00457-7.

This report is based on an 18-month study conducted by the Legislative Drafting Research Fund of Columbia University under contract with the National Institute of Mental Health. The purposes of the study were to examine the present state of the law relating to the problem of alcoholism, to evaluate the effectiveness of present legal mechanisms in the light of current knowledge of the causes and treatment of the disorder, and to attempt to provide a basis for sounder legal approaches to reach desirable social ends. The research of this work was used in developing the model Alcoholism and Intoxication Treatment Act, which has been included in the book.

The study is in three parts. The first concerns the legal and practical alternatives in dealing with persons found intoxicated in public, particularly persons in need of medical help. The second part discusses the legal devices currently available to deal with alcoholism and proposes methods for legal treatment of alcoholics. The third part treats miscellaneous legal problems of alcoholism, particularly problems relating to criminal law.

677. Gross, Milton M., ed. **Alcohol Intoxication and Withdrawal: Experimental Studies.** New York, Plenum Press, 1973. 422p. bibliog. index. (Advances in Experimental Medicine and Biology. v.35.) $24.00. LC 73-80327. ISBN 0-306-39035-1.

This work is based on a symposium entitled "Experimental Studies of Acute Alcohol Intoxication and Withdrawal," a part of the Proceedings of the 30th International Congress on Alcoholism and Addiction, held in Amsterdam, September 11-15, 1972. The symposium's purpose was to share the most recent findings on alcohol intoxication and to stimulate others to join in the effort. For the most part, the papers included present new data, and the authors are well-known experts.

The papers, which are highly technical, scholarly, and of excellent quality, have been grouped in five sections: Basic mechanisms of tolerance and physical dependence, Biochemical aspects, Experimental studies in animals, Experimental studies of sleep, and Human experimental studies.

678. Gross, Milton M., ed. **Alcohol Intoxication and Withdrawal: Experimental Studies II**. New York, Plenum Press, 1975. 667p. bibliog. index. (Advances in Experimental Medicine and Biology. v.59.) $37.50. LC 75-16174. ISBN 0-306-39049-0.

This publication contains the Proceedings of a symposium on Alcohol Intoxication and Withdrawal: Experimental Studies, held in Manchester, England, June 24-28, 1974, as part of the 20th International Institute on the Prevention and Treatment of Alcoholism, International Countil of Alcoholism and Addiction. It is planned that international symposia of this type will be held every two years. The first was held in 1972, and the proceedings were published as volume 35 of the Advances in Experimental Medicine and Biology series (see preceding entry). The purpose of the meetings is to present recent findings in order to show the state-of-the-art and to encourage further research. The papers included present new data. The authors are established researchers in the field of alcoholism, and the material presented is quite technical and of high quality.

The papers have been grouped in five sections: 1) Neurochemistry, 2) Biochemistry, 3) Experimental studies in animals, 4) Studies of sleep, and 5) Human studies.

679. Himwich, Harold E., ed. **Alcoholism: Basic Aspects and Treatment**. Washington, American Association for the Advancement of Science, 1957. 212p. bibliog. index. $5.75. LC 56-12631.

Presented here are the papers of a symposium held under the auspices of the American Association for the Advancement of Science in cooperation with the American Psychiatric Association and the American Physiological Society and presented at the Atlanta, Georgia, meeting, December 27-28, 1955. The discussions held after the presentation of the papers have not been included. The participants were some of the best-known experts at that time in the fields of physiology, biochemistry, pharmacology, and medicine and psychiatry.

680. Hornik, Edith Lynn. **You and Your Alcoholic Parent**. New York, Association Press, 1974. 119p. $2.95pa. ISBN 0-8096-1881-8pa.; 0-8096-1841-9 hard cover.

This book, written for teenagers who have an alcoholic parents, gives useful information about the disease and methods of coping with it. Young people are approached as responsible individuals, and they are even given criteria to help them diagnose the illness in the parents. The last chapters describe resources available to such young people, giving positive suggestions on how to cope. The reader learns of the frustrating situations that emerge, and he also is made to realize that no one solution will be useful for everyone and that there are subtle differences in situations.

This kind of book certainly serves a purpose, since the situation described is relatively common. However, the book's suggestions place a large responsibility on the teenager.

681. Israel, Yedy, and Jorge Mardones. **Biological Basis of Alcoholism.** New York, Wiley-Interscience, 1971. 453p. bibliog. index. $24.00. LC 73-159285. ISBN 0-471-42900-7.

These papers, by researchers in alcoholism, give recent findings and personal views of the researchers in the context of their particular disciplines. Titles of the papers are as follows: 1) The metabolism of ethanol, 2) Effects of alcohol on the nerve cell, 3) Effect of ethanol in neuroamine metabolism, 4) The experimental approach to alcoholic liver damage, 5) Mechanisms of liver and pancreas damage in man, 6) Influence of ethanol on the metabolism of the pathological liver, 7) Effects of alcohol on cardiac and muscular function, 8) The importance of congeners in the effects of alcoholic beverages, 9) Tolerance to, and dependence on, ethanol, 10) Experimentally induced intoxication in alcoholics: a comparison between programmed and spontaneous drinking, 11) Appetite for alcohol, 12) Genetic aspects of alcoholism, 13) Nutrition factors in alcoholism and its complications, 14) The psychological and pharmacological basis for the treatment of alcohol dependence, and 15) The epidemiology of alcoholism.

The book is probably of most value to researchers and clinicians involved with the problems of alcoholism, but because of the wide scope it will also interest physicians, behavioral scientists, and others interested in the condition.

682. Johnson, Vernon E. **I'll Quit Tomorrow.** New York, Harper and Row, 1973. 168p. $5.95. LC 72-11356. ISBN 0-06-064172-X.

The author, a recovered alcoholic, founded the Johnson Institute in Minneapolis in 1966 to assist in the treatment of alcoholics. The Institute has two basic goals: to design specific programs for alcoholics through applied research, and to educate the public in methods of intervention. It is believed that alcoholics should be treated in general hospitals. The first part of the book describes the process by which the social drinker develops a chemical dependence and becomes alcoholic. The methods of treatment developed by the Johnson Institute are then outlined, using a multidisciplinary approach: physical, mental, psychological, and spiritual. The presentation provides a great many insights into the nature of alcoholics, and the book should be quite useful.

A number of helpful appendices have been included: patient's handbook, group therapy handbook, patient's self-evaluation, counselor's initial interview, meaningful person evaluation form, first step preparation, outpatient's handbook, hospital personnel training handbook, and clergyman's handbook.

683. Kissin, Benjamin, and Henri Begleiter, eds. **The Biology of Alcoholism.** New York, Plenum Press, 1971-1976. 5v. illus. bibliog. index. $37.50/vol. LC 74-131883. V.1, Biochemistry, ISBN 0-306-37111-1; v.2, Physiology and Behavior, ISBN 0-306-37112-X; v.3, Clinical Pathology, ISBN 0-306-37113-8; v.4, Social Aspects of Alcoholism, ISBN 0-306-37114-6; v.5, The Treatment and Rehabilitation of the Chronic Alcoholic, ISBN 0-306-37115-4.

This five-volume work presents a comprehensive examination of the current knowledge of alcoholism, particularly the biological aspects. The authors of the various chapters are well-known experts in their fields. The work should prove very valuable to scientists concerned with alcoholism, such as biologists, biochemists, medical research workers, and behavioral scientists.

The material in the first volume emphasizes the biological interaction of alcohol with man and animals at given levels of activity, volume two considers treatment of the neurological and psychological effects of alcohol, discussing such topics as alcohol and sleep and alcoholism and learning. The third volume emphasizes the clinical and practical aspects of the subject rather than the theoretical and experimental. Almost all the material deals with the human condition rather than that of experimental animals. Physicians will be especially interested in this volume.

In contrast to the first three volumes, the fourth deals largely with the psychological and social aspects of alcoholism. Although the original intention was to present "hard" scientific data in the volumes of the set, a later decision was made to include more "soft" data in the interest of completeness. This volume considers the social forces leading to alcoholism and the consequences of the condition. The following topics are covered: alcohol use in tribal societies; anthropological perspectives on the social biology of alcohol; drinking behavior in the United States; alcoholism in women; youthful alcohol use; family structure and behavior in alcoholism; the alcoholic personality; alcoholism and mortality; alcohol and unintentional injury; alcohol and crimes of violence; alcohol abuse and work organizations; education and prevention of alcoholism; and effects of legal restraint on drinking.

It is planned that Volume 5, like Volume 4, will deal with social and psychological factors more than with biological factors.

This is an outstanding, comprehensive work.

684. Larkin, E. J. **The Treatment of Alcoholism: Theory, Practice, and Evaluation**. Toronto, Addiction Research Foundation of Ontario, 1974. 73p. $2.95pa.

Intended for use by individuals in alcoholism therapy or for those seeking a brief overview of the field, this work is so brief that it serves mainly as an introduction to the subject, with synopses only of the literature dating from 1945 to 1973. The bibliographies are valuable. The six chapters cover causes and cures, the disease concept, treatment programs, voluntary termination of psychotherapy, behavior modification, and evaluation models for measuring the success of treatment programs.

685. MacAndrew, Craig, and Robert B. Edgerton. **Drunken Comportment: A Social Explanation**. Chicago, Aldine Publishing Company, 1969. 197p. bibliog. index. $5.95. LC 68-8154.

This book reconsiders the conventional attitudes that exist in regard to man's relationship to alcohol. The prevailing view, according to the authors, is that the toxic effects of the drug on the central nervous system cause individuals to lose control of themselves and do things they would not otherwise do. For this reason, they are to some extent excused for their behavior. However, the authors' view is that nowhere is it the case that once one is drunk, anything and everything goes. Certain limits are set, although those limits may be sometimes beyond reasonable toleration. What is fundamentally at issue are the learned relations that exist among men living together in a society. The final statement of the book sums it up thus: "The moral is this. Since societies, like individuals, get the sort of drunken comportment that they allow, they deserve what they get."

The authors make a good case for their viewpoint and use many examples of behavior from contemporary society and from the American Indian groups. Probably the message of the book could have conveyed just as effectively in simpler language, however.

686. McClelland, David C., William N. Davis, Rudolf Kalin, and Eric Wanner. **The Drinking Man**. New York, The Free Press, 1972. 402p. illus. bibliog. index. $10.00. LC 79-143504.

The authors and contributors to this work are for the most part clinical psychologists in academic institutions. The book reports the results of a ten-year program of psychological investigation of the role of alcohol in human life, some of it supported by federal grants. The book is divided into four sections: 1) Social drinking, 2) Motives for drinking, 3) Drinking and the need for power, and 4) Explaining alcoholism. The 15 chapters, which are mostly technical presentations on diverse topics do not always support or relate to the final conclusions that the authors reach (although they are of interest).

The authors' conclusion, based on the accumulated evidence of why men drink, is stated in non-technical terms in a summary chapter. They believe that men who drink to excess do so to get desired feelings of strength and power. The man who drinks excessively needs personalized power and for a variety of reasons has chosen drinking as an outlet for it rather than some other alternative. The sense of responsibility is decreased, however. It follows that the simplest way to cure men of excessive drinking is to socialize their power drives. It is of note that this is what Alcoholics Anonymous does. The theory as presented is convincing.

687. McIlwain, William. **A Farewell to Alcohol**. New York, Random House, 1972. 143p. $5.45. LC 72-5121. ISBN 0-394-47610-7.

This book is a personal narrative about an alcoholic and his treatment at Butner, a rehabilitation center for alcoholics in North Carolina. The story is well written (the author is an outstanding writer and newspaper editor) as well as honest and touching. The methods of treatment used are of interest, and while the author does not claim successful results for most of the patients, some were apparently cured as he himself was.

688. Maddox, George L., ed. **The Domesticated Drug: Drinking among Collegians**. New Haven, College and University Press, 1970. 479p. bibliog. index. $9.00. LC 78-92543.

This book attempts to present a balanced view of drinking among American college students. The collegian is seen as a commentary on the generation that produced him and as a prophecy of the generation that will provide leadership in the near future. The editor sees alcohol as, at best, a partially domesticated drug; while much alarm has been expressed about drug abuse among the young, much more trouble continues to be associated with alcohol use. He feels that there is some slight comfort, however, in that the situation is not as bad as it might be, given the peculiarities of the American way of drinking. The book is a collection of papers divided into three sections. The first group constitutes a perspective; the second is a group of empirical studies; and the third contains several articles on implications. Each paper is by a different expert; a few have been published previously. The material should prove of particular interest to the college student and to college administrators and research investigators, especially in the social sciences.

689. Madsen, William. **The American Alcoholic: The Nature-Nurture Controversy in Alcoholic Research and Therapy**. Springfield, Ill., Charles C. Thomas, 1974. 248p. bibliog. index. $11.50. LC 73-8975. ISBN 0-398-02926-1.

This book explores the problem of alcoholism from several viewpoints—the biological, psychological, and cultural. The author urges a holistic approach and a synthesis of all possible interpretations.

The work consists of two parts: "Thesis and Antithesis: Body and Mind" and "An Attempt at Synthesis." The chapter headings are: 1) The nature-nurture conflict, 2) The blurry world of alcoholism, 3) The alcoholic's mind, 4) The alcoholic's body, 5) To drink or not to drink, 6) The cultural milieu: the anxious American, 7) The American alcoholic: I, 8) The American alcoholic: II, 9) A.A.: birds of a feather.

A good deal of attention is given to Alcoholics Anonymous, with an analysis of why it works. Much case material has been included in the work. The author sees in A.A. a hope for alcoholics.

690. Majchrowicz, Edward, ed. **Biochemical Pharmacology of Ethanol.** Proceedings of the American Chemical Society symposium on Biochemical Pharmacology of Ethanol, held in Chicago, August, 1973. New York, Plenum Press, 1975. 367p. bibliog. index. $29.50. LC 75-8369. ISBN 0-306-39056-5.

These scientific papers make known some basic facts about the biological chemistry and pharmacology of alcohol. Each presentation is followed by a summary and a long list of references. The following papers are included: 1) Mammalian liver alcohol dehydrogenases; 2) Microsomal ethanol oxidation: activity *in vitro* and *in vivo*; 3) Pathways of ethanol metabolism in perfused rat liver; 4) Rate-limiting steps in ethanol metabolism and approaches to changing these rates biochemically; 5) Metabolic correlates of ethanol, acetaldehyde, acetate and methanol in humans and animals; 6) Comparison of the effects of ethanol on liver and brain metabolism; 7) Alcohol and aldehyde metablism in brain; 8) Effects of ethanol on brain metabolism; 9) Effects of ethanol on protein synthesis; 10) The effects of aliphatic alcohols on the biophysical and biochemical correlates of membrane function; 11) Interaction of ethanol with cyclic AMP; 12) Alcohol, aldehydes and biogenic amines; 13) Interaction of biogenic amines with ethanol; 14) Some endocrine aspects of alcoholism; 15) Marihuana vs. alcohol: a pharmacologic comparison; 16) Induction of physical dependence on alcohol in rodents; 17) Induction of physical dependence upon alcohol in nonhuman primates; and 18) Genetic determinants of alcohol addiction.

Much of the material presented in the volume is highly technical and can be thoroughly understood only by experts.

691. **Nature and Nurture in Alcoholism**. Edited by Frank A. Seixas and others. New York, New York Academy of Sciences, 1972. 229p. bibliog. (New York Academy of Sciences. Annals. Vol. 197).

These papers were presented at a conference called Nature and Nurture in Alcoholism, held by the National Council on Alcoholism on April 27-28, 1971. The central topic of the meeting was how to explain the large number of alcoholics who have a parents or family member who is also an alcoholic. The papers assess the research in this area and attempt to stimulate further activity. The material, presented on the scholarly research level, has been divided into chapters, each representing a separate phase of either research design or topic. The chapter headings are as follows: 1) Animal studies, 2) Metabolism, 3) Chromosomes and immunoglobulins, 4) Family and human twin studies, 5) Genetic markers, 6) Congenital factors, 7) Ego ideals, 8) Nonparental forces, and 9) Study methods. The book explores a subject area in which a good deal more research is required.

692. O'Briant, Robert G., Henry L. Lennard, and others. **Recovery from Alcoholism: A Social Treatment Model**. Springfield, Ill., Charles C. Thomas, 1973. 93p. bibliog. index. $6.95. LC 73-194. ISBN 0-398-02830-3.

This book discusses alcoholism and its treatment, describing in particular an effective alcoholism program that is being used in San Joaquin County, California. The authors' view is that alcoholism is sustained or arrested by social arrangements and human associations. Further they maintain that when alcoholics do recover it is as a result of taking part in social networks that insulate them from the social forces that encourage alcohol use. The plan that is presented takes these beliefs into account. The program includes a residential detoxification center, a drug free program, the construction of new social networks, and reterritorializing the alcoholic.

693. Popham, Robert E., ed. **Alcohol and Alcoholism**. Papers presented at the International Symposium in memory of E. M. Jellinek, Santiago, Chile. Toronto, published for the Addiction Research Foundation by University of Toronto Press, 1970. 421p. illus. bibliog. index. $15.00. LC 71-487568. ISBN 0-8020-3241-9.

This volume presents the highly specialized papers of an international symposium held in 1966 also published in Spanish as Supplement 3 of the *Archivos de Biológia y Medicina Experimental*, they stress pharmacology, pathology, and psychiatry. The material has been updated, since the meeting was held several years before publication of this volume. The 50 papers have been grouped into these sections: 1) Biochemical and pharmacological aspects, 2) Etiological and clinical aspects, 3) Organic complications of alcoholism, and 4) Epidemiological and preventive aspects. Also included is a section of tributes to the late E. M. Jellinek for his work in the field of alcohol and alcoholism, with a list of his publications on the subject.

694. Roach, Mary K., William M. McIsaac, and Patrick J. Creaven, eds. **Biological Aspects of Alcohol.** Published for the Faculty for Advanced Studies of the Texas Research Institute of Mental Sciences. Austin, University of Texas Press, 1971. 471p. bibliog. index. (Advances in Mental Science III.) $12.50. LC 78-165915. ISBN 0-292-70144-6.

This book contains the proceedings of an international symposium that annually brings together scientists from different disciplines to discuss topics in the field of mental health. More work has been done on alcohol than on any other drug, but controversy over the etiology of its dependence still remains. Many feel that the answer to the problem is biological, at the cellular or subcellular levels, and this is the basis for the studies presented. Eighteen technical papers are presented on such topics as alcohol's interaction with other drugs, studies of its effect on behavior, and new hypotheses regarding the role of alkaloids formed in the body after alcohol is metabolized. The material is suitable mainly for scientists involved in research in the field, and the papers are on very specialized aspects of the subject.

695. Roebuck, Julian B., and Raymond G. Kessler. **The Etiology of Alcoholism: Constitutional, Psychological and Sociological Approaches**. Springfield, Ill., Charles C. Thomas, 1972. 260p. bibliog. index. $11.95. LC 71-87672. ISBN 0-398-02392-1.

This book presents various points of view on the causes of alcoholism, examining theories that appeared in the literature from 1940 to 1971. Three major categorical approaches are explored, the constitutional, the psychological, and the sociological. The authors suggest that an interdisciplinary approach to the problem is the best one, and they present a plan for further studies along these lines.

696. Rothschild, Marcus A., Murray Oratz, and Sidney S. Schreiber, eds. **Alcohol and Abnormal Protein Biosynthesis: Biochemical and Clinical**. New York, Pergamon Press, 1975. 519p. illus. bibliog. index. $25.00. LC 74-5308. ISBN 0-08-017708-5.

This book describes complications of alcoholism, particularly nutrition disorders that affect the liver, heart, skeletal muscles, and the brain. The interrelationships among alcohol, malnutrition, and protein synthesis are explored, with a description of the entire clinical syndrome produced by alcohol and an indication of the research concepts of nutritional management. The book, which is scientific and technical, is suitable mainly for students of biochemistry and for medical practitioners concerned with the treatment of alcoholics.

697. Rubington, Earl. **Alcohol Problems and Social Control.** Columbus, Ohio, Charles E. Merrill Publishing Co., 1973. 200p. bibliog. $4.95. LC 72-86515. ISBN 0-675-09046-6.

Most of this book deals with the public drunkenness offender. The work is in five parts. "Definition of the problem" surveys alcohol problems, discusses the nature of social problems, and covers alcohol and social responsibility. The second part, "The Deviant Career," takes up the hidden alcoholic, types of offenders, and the alcoholic and the jail. Part three, "The Street," discusses the bottle gang, the changing Skid Row scene and the "revolving door" game. Part four, "Personal Change," takes up relapse and the chronic drunkenness offender, reports a case study of an alcoholic's relapse, and discusses organizational strains and key roles. Part five, "Organizational Change," discusses the halfway house, legal commitment, and hospital behavior.

The material presented is illuminating and realistic. There is little stress on new solutions to the drinking problem, since the author feels the knowledge for solution already exists.

698. Schmidt, Wolfgang, Reginald G. Smart, and Marcia K. Moss. **Social Class and the Treatment of Alcoholism: An Investigation of Social Class as a Determinant of Diagnosis, Prognosis and Therapy.** Published for the Addiction Research Foundation. Toronto, University of Toronto Press, 1968. 111p. bibliog. index. (Brookside Monograph of the Addiction Research Foundation No. 7). $6.00. ISBN 0-8020-3207-9.

This is the report of a study that observed public clinic patients in order to determine the influences of class position on the therapy used in each case. Drinking patterns and the clinical picture of alcoholism differed among the social classes and, as might be expected, the treatments assigned differed. The book is important because there has been a rapid increase in the number of public institutions that treat alcoholism, and the possibility that class status affects the diagnosis and care of the patient should be explored in order to discover new and better methods of treatment.

699. Seixas, Frank A., Remi Cadoret, and Suzie Eggleston, eds. **The Person with Alcoholism.** New York, New York Academy of Sciences, 1974. 177p. illus. bibliog. (New York Academy of Sciences. Annals. v.233). $24.00.

These papers were delivered by well-known individuals at a conference co-sponsored by the National Council on Alcoholism and the George Washington University School of Medicine on April 3-4, 1973. Stressing the psychiatric aspects of alcoholism, the papers have been divided by subject: "What Is the Alcoholic Mix," is subdivided into two parts, covering "Alcoholism in the Presence of Individual Differences and Psychiatric States" and "Organic and Physiologic States Modifying the Alcoholic's Psychiatric Presentation." "What Can Be Done Psychiatrically," is subdivided into three parts: "Varied Psychotherapeutic Approaches," "Alcoholics Anonymous and Beyond," "Biofeedback and Meditative Techniques."

The papers are somewhat technical but most can be readily understood by an educated reader. The material is of high quality. The methods used by Alcoholics Anonymous and the use of meditation to control anxiety after sobriety have been found to be effective approaches to therapy.

700. Siegel, Harvey H. **Alcohol Detoxification Programs: Treatment Instead of Jail**. Springfield, Ill., Charles C. Thomas, 1973. 94p. illus. index. $8.75. LC 73-206. ISBN 0-398-02820-6.

This book is a procedural manual to help community workers develop alcohol detoxification programs. The author feels that such programs will benefit the police, social agencies, taxpayers, and alcoholics. Chapter headings are as follows: 1) The existing system of alcohol treatment/punishment, 2) History of detoxification treatment, 3) How to develop an alcohol detoxification program in your community, 4) Where to get funds for detoxification programs, 5) Where to locate a detoxification program within the community, 6) Transitional management facilities, 7) An in-depth look at the problem–alcoholism, 8) Summary, conclusion, and future for detoxification programs. The five appendices include a summary of National Institute on Alcohol Abuses and Alcoholism as conceived by its sponsor, Senator Harold E. Hughes; Law Enforcement Assistance Administration regional offices (a list); Indiana Comprehensive Criminal Justice Plan; Illinois Criminal Justice Plan; provisions of Illinois Department of Mental Health.

701. Staub, George E., and Leona M. Kent, eds. **The Para-Professional in the Treatment of Alcoholism: A New Profession**. Springfield, Ill., Charles C. Thomas, 1973. 170p. bibliog. index. $8.50. LC 73-5518. ISBN 0-398-02860-5.

These papers were written by individuals active in alcoholism treatment programs. The term "para-professional" is not specifically defined in the work; the whole book is said to be a definition of what the para-professional is and does. The publication presents thoughts and philosophies on the best way to treat alcoholics, with emphasis on the attitudes that make a successful para-professional in this field. It is suggested that too often "professionals" will not concern themselves about the miserable alcoholic as a person, although Alcoholics Anonymous has shown that the personal but firm approach is necessary.

The following chapters are presented: 1) Attitude: key to successful treatment, 2) A differential view of manpower resources, 3) Systems development and role changes needed for acceptance of the para-professional in al alcoholism treatment program, 4) In-service training of the para-professional in the field of alcoholism, 5) Policies important to personnel, 6) The para-professional in a medical setting, 7) The para-professional in the poverty community, 8) Non-alcoholic versus recovered personnel, 9) Alcoholics Anonymous members as alcoholism counselors, 10) Understanding and relating to Alcoholics Anonymous, 11) For those who wear two hats, Alcoholics Anonymous guidelines, 12) Alcoholics Anonymous training groups–a suggested group format to be used by the para-professional, 13) Thoughts to ourselves.

702. Steed, Ernest H. J. **The Answer to Alcoholism**. Washington, Narcotics Education, Inc., 1971. 96p. illus. LC 96-158113.

This small book was written by a Seventh-day Adventist minister who has been active in community service work for the treatment of alcoholism. The booklet's educational and rehabilitation plan is called the Four-Dimensional Key to the Cause of Alcoholism. The four dimensions are: physical, mental, social, and spiritual. Presenting a plan for better living in seven steps, the book is religious in tone.

703. Steiner, Claude. **Games Alcoholics Play: The Analysis of Life Scripts.** New York, Grove Press, Inc., 1971. 173p. bibliog. index. $5.95. LC 74-139254. ISBN 394-47583-6.

The author, a clinical psychologist who has had much experience with alcoholics and drug addicts, applies Eric Berne's Transactional Analysis to the behavior displayed by alcohol users and the individuals they are associated with. It explains the basic aspects of TA and will be of value to counselors and those who treat or deal with alcoholism in some way. The book presents a somewhat new theory about alcoholism (and emotional disorders in general) and a method of treatment that follows this theory. The theory, a "decision theory" rather than a disease theory of alcoholism, is based on the idea that some people make conscious decisions in childhood that influence and make predictable the rest of their lives. Persons whose lives are based on such a decision are said to have a "script," and the script may involve various kinds of life plans, mostly destructive, such as alcoholism, suicide, mental illness, or drug addiction. The book describes the various aspects and stages of life scripts and their treatment. Examples of case histories are included, and there are sections on the alcoholic game and the part associates unconsciously play. Treatment methods for alcoholics are included. The book is unusual and the methods innovative, but the psychology presented rings true. The three types of heavy drinkers Steiner describes can be recognized and distinguished by almost everyone.

704. Straus, Robert. **Escape from Custody: A Study of Alcoholism and Institutional Dependency as Reflected in the Life Record of a Homeless Man.** New York, Harper and Row Pubs., Inc., 1974. 388p. $15.00. LC 73-14066. ISBN 0-06-014149-2.

This book is a well-written account of the life of Frank Moore, an intelligent and sensitive person who loses the battle with alcoholism and institutional dependency. The work covers his unhappy life from birth to age 68, when he dies. The author based his work on correspondence he received from Moore and from additional material supplied by the subject's mother and others. The story is particularly touching because Moore is an appealing, sympathetic character, much brighter and more literate than his skid row associates. He is comfortable neither in competitive society nor on skid row.

The aim of the book seems to be to show how society with its system of treatment and rehabilitation and institutionalization of alcoholics has failed individuals like Frank Moore despite his potential.

705. Thomsen, Robert. **Bill W.** New York, Harper and Row, 1975. 373p. $10.95. LC 74-1861. ISBN 0-06-014267-7.

This personal, readable work is the biography of Bill Wilson, an alcoholic who was involved in the early development of Alcoholics Anonymous and who is known as a co-founder of the organization. He was a failure in a military academy but showed a talent for leadership in World War I. He rose in the world of Wall Street, but crashed with the stock market in 1929. Then began a long struggle toward recovery, with the help of his wife, friends, and classical literature in the fields of psychology, philosophy, and religion.

The history of AA as told has many interesting aspects. It is of note that the concept of anonymity developed, partially at least, because it removed the threat of individuals competing for power. By the time of Bill's death in 1971, AA had become the most successful treatment avenue available for alcoholic individuals. It was Wilson's wish that Thomsen write this book, although he himself was the author of books on Alcoholics Anonymous.

706. U.S. National Institute on Alcohol Abuse and Alcoholism. **Recent Advances in Studies of Alcoholism: An Interdisciplinary Symposium**. June 25-27, 1970. Editors: Nancy K. Mello and Jack H. Mendelson. Washington, GPO, 1971. 920p. bibliog. index. (DHEW Publication No. (HSM) 71-9045). $3.75pa. S/N 1724-0143.

This publication, a state-of-the-art report on alcoholism research presents reviews and reports by well-known researchers on the biological, psychological, and sociological factors of alcoholism. The papers are arranged in the following sections: 1) Biochemical research, 2) Physiological research, 3) Behavioral research: animal models for studies of addiction, 4) Behavioral research: effects of alcohol intoxication, 5) New treatment techniques: behavioral approaches, 6) New treatment techniques: pharmacological approaches, 7) Social science research, and 8) Training for health services.

The publication is important because it illustrates progress that has been made that can affect treatment and prevention of the alcoholic condition. It is of note that only recently has alcoholism emerged as an appropriate subject for laboratory and clinical investigation. Little work of this kind was done prior to the mid-1960s.

707. U.S. National Institute on Alcohol Abuse and Alcoholism. **Second Special Report to the U.S. Congress on Alcohol and Health**. June 1974. New Knowledge. Morris E. Chafetz, Chairman of the Task Force. Washington, GPO, 1975. 170p. bibliog. (DHEW Publication No. (ADM) 75-212.) $2.25pa. S/N 017-024-00399.

The *First Special Report to the U.S. Congress on Alcohol and Health* (DHEW Publication No. (HSM) 72-9099) in 1971 described certain areas of knowledge about alcohol, its historical and contemporary uses and misuses, drinking and problem drinking, theories of the causes of alcoholism and its treatment. It also reviewed effects of alcohol on the nervous system and the legal status of intoxication and alcoholism. The second report concentrates on highlighting certain advances in knowledge gained since the earlier report. For the most part material in the first report is not repeated, so the second report does not supersede it or make it obsolete. The two should be used together. The following chapters are included: 1) Alcohol use and misuse by adults and youth, 2) Alcohol and older persons, 3) Economic costs of alcohol-related problems, 4) Alcoholism: heredity and congenital effects, 5) Some health consequences of alcohol use, 6) Alcohol and highway safety, 7) Trends in treatment of alcoholism, 8) Problem drinkers on the job, 9) Alcoholism and health insurance, and 10) The enhancement of health. A list of findings has also been included. The main common finding was that alcohol-related problems have been neglected, although they are of far greater magnitude than other drug problems. The report suggests some new directions that may be taken to deal with alcoholism and problem drinking.

708. U.S. National Institute on Alcohol Abuse and Alcoholism. **Seminar on Alcoholism Emergency Care Services. Proceedings.** Edited by George G. Pavloff. Washington, GPO, 1975. 98p. (DHEW Publication No. (ADM) 76-265).

This publication contains the abridged results of a seminar held at the National Institute of Mental Health on March 24, 1972. The publication suggests a variety of models or settings through which emergency care services can be delivered to alcoholic individuals with varying needs within communities of various resources. The conclusion is reached that general hospitals are best equipped to meet this need and should be encouraged to undertake this responsibility. Program failures are analyzed.

The following papers were selected for inclusion: 1) Detoxification in a comprehensive community alcoholism treatment program, 2) Recommendations for detoxification services, 3) The training of professionals for meeting the needs of alcoholics and problem drinkers, 4) The role of a detoxification service in an alcoholism treatment program, 5) Recommendations for alcohol detoxification services. In addition, the abridged proceedings of the Seminar on Alcoholism Emergency Care Services are included, as is a summary of the Seminar conclusions.

709. U.S. National Institute on Alcohol Abuse and Alcoholism. **Seminar on Public Health Services and the Public Inebriate. Proceedings.** Washington, GPO, 1975. 74p. bibliog. (DHEW Publication No. (ADM) 75-218).

This seminar examined the role of public health services in the skid row subculture, in an effort to help develop guidelines or policies for community services to public alcoholic people. Three papers are included: 1) Public health services and the culture of skid row bums, 2) The role of the law in improving the quality of the public inebriate's life, and 3) Interaction between skid row people and law enforcement and health professionals. In addition, the proceedings of a discussion session are included. The publication is of value because little material is available on this aspect of alcoholism.

710. Valles, Jorge. **From Social Drinking to Alcoholism.** Dallas, Tane Press, 1969. 226p. bibliog. LC 79-87915.

This book analyzes alcoholism and discusses causes, symptoms, complications, and treatment of the condition. The author, a physician who has had a good deal of experience with alcoholics, bases the book mainly on his observations and experience. The reader may gain some insights, although the approach offers little that is new. The author's hope is that the book may assist in identifying the youthful alcoholic so that steps may be taken to divert him from the path he is taking.

711. Allgren, Henrik, and Herbert Barry, III. **Actions of Alcohol**. Vol. 1, Biochemical, Physiological and Psychological Aspects; vol.2, Chronic and Clinical Aspects. New York, American Elsevier Publishing Co., Inc. 1970. 2v. bibliog. index. $75.00/set. ISBN 0-444-40877-0; 0-444-40902-5.

This comprehensive summary and evaluation of the scientific knowledge about the actions of alcohol reviews the acute and chronic effects at all levels of functioning of living organisms. Contributions from a number of diverse specialties have been included and synthesized.

The following chapters are presented: 1) Introductory comments, 2) Some basic data on the chemistry and pharmacology of ethyl alcohol, 3) Ethanol in the metabolism, 4) Effects of ethanol on various physiological functions, 5) Cellular basis of ethanol action on the nervous system, 6) Integrative functions of the CNS, 7) Complex behavioral effects, 8) Voluntary selection of alcohol, 9) Prolonged exposure to alcohol, 10) Drug actions in relation to alcohol effects, 11) Understanding and treatment of alcoholics, and 12) Conclusions.

Most of the material is highly technical, but the discussion of alcohol programs and treatment of alcoholics is of general interest. Topics of special potential interest in research programs are pointed out, such as prevention of alcoholism, early detection, early treatment, and the beneficial effects of alcohol.

712. Whitney, Elizabeth D. **The Lonely Sickness**. With a Preface by Robert Fleming. Boston, Beacon Press, 1965. 178p. $4.00. ISBN 0-8070-2794-4.

The author has been active in community work, specializing in assistance to the alcoholic. Instead of speculating on the underlying causes of alcoholism, the book stresses how to help. Several personal narratives are presented, with details about the victims' lives, the development of the alcoholic problem, how help was sought, the rocky road to recovery, backsliding, and then successful treatment. The need for professional assistance is stressed, and the planning of community services is encouraged. There is a chapter on how to get help, and a list of agencies providing assistance is appended. The book reads well and provides insights and encouragement. The last section of the book, made up of frequently asked questions about alcoholism, supplies good answers.

713. Whitney, Elizabeth D., ed. **World Dialogue on Alcohol and Drug Dependence**. Boston, Beacon Press, 1970. 400p. bibliog. index. $12.50. LC 76-101329. ISBN 0-8070-2776-6.

These essays, written by world experts in the field of alcohol and drug dependence, reflect the latest thinking and investigation on these problems. The first part discusses the approaches used in France, Scandinavia, Australia, Italy, Czechoslovakia, and the United States. The second part presents methods of attacking addictions. Alcoholics Anonymous, office treatment, the minister's role in recovery, the use of pharmacological adjuncts, and special facilities for youths are some of the approaches discussed. Part three, "New Dimensions," explores new approaches and new research underway in various parts of the world. The emphasis is on innovation and interdisciplinary cooperation.

714. Wilkins, Rodney H. **The Hidden Alcoholic in General Practice: A Method of Detection Using a Questionnaire.** London, Paul Elek (Scientific Books) Ltd., 1974. 241p. bibliog. index. $10.75.

This book is based on research carried out for a M.D. thesis submitted to the University of Manchester in 1972. For a period of one year a questionnaire was administered to a group of patients with the aim of detecting the abnormal drinker and examining some aspects of the behavior of drinkers. Questions were asked regarding the quantity/frequency of drinking alcohol, the patient's opinion of his own drinking, the problems arising from alcohol abuse, and the symptoms of alcohol addiction. The results were validated by the clinical assessment of patients by psychiatrists. The book contains a great deal of statistical information and documentation.

It was concluded that general practitioners, by asking patients questions about alcohol abuse, could detect a considerable proportion of the "hidden alcoholics." The hope is that general practitioners will be able, through sympathy and understanding, to persuade the alcoholic that he needs guidance.

715. Wilkinson, Rupert. **The Prevention of Drinking Problems: Alcohol Control and Cultural Influences.** New York, Oxford University Press, 1970. 301p. bibliog. $10.00. LC 78-83057.

This book reports research carried out (in 1962-66) while the author was a research assistant to the Cooperative Commission on the Study of Alcoholism, a body financed by the National Institute of Mental Health. The author surveys American patterns of drinking, arguing that the way Americans drink and their attitude toward it may be factors in problem drinking and may influence the country's high rate of alcoholism. He outlines ways by which public and private agencies might influence the climate of drinking for the better.

The work is in four parts: 1) Drinking patterns and the prevention of drinking problems, 2) The alcohol industry and its regulation: the present system, 3) Proposals, 4) Freedom and responsibility: some ethical questions. In addition there are several appendices: Early drinking experiences: direct comparisons of "normal" and "problem" drinkers; Wet background, dry background; American ethnic groups; Italy and France; A perspective from anthropology; and Statistical comparisons: official data.

The proposals for preventing drinking problems stress few restrictions, better education, tax reforms, and measures to ensure that state and federal alcohol control officials are free of domination by a few interest groups. Like most of the works on alcohol and drug problems, the problem is reasonably well analyzed, but the solution is not impressive.

716. Williams, Richard L., and Gene H. Moffat, eds. **Occupational Alcoholism Programs.** Springfield, Ill., Charles C. Thomas, 1975. 282p. bibliog. $18.50. ISBN 0-398-03282-3.

There has been a growing interest in programs that have successfully treated workers with drinking problems. These seven papers report on various approaches to the problem. The first chapter, an historical perspective of alcoholism in industry, is followed by a summary of the literature, which stresses the need for evaluating rehabilitation programs. The remainder of the book describes programs that have been used in dealing with alcoholic employees in the United States and Canada. Included are programs adopted by the Bell Telephone Company of Canada, Canadian National Railways, Gulf Oil Canada Limited, the Illinois Bell Telephone Company, the Boston Edison Company, the New York City Police Department, and the Kennecott Copper Corporation. The various program had similar outcomes. From 57 to 77 percent of the employees were considered "recovered" or "rehabilitated." In general, the programs described stressed the "troubled employee" or "occupational mental health" approach rather than the alcoholism or drug abuse approach.

The book is of particular value for those in personnel work or management. Although it has limitations and is somewhat repetitive, it can serve as a guide in industrial situations in establishing alcohol treatment programs.

19. Tobacco

All of the limited number of material on tobacco which are included in the bibliography have been placed in this section. There are perhaps few parallels between tobacco use problems and those of the major drugs of abuse, since tobacco has little effect on behavior and its use is not a serious social problem. However, it has been widely condemned because of its carcinogenic and other deleterious physiological effects, and many smokers have stopped smoking or at least attempted to break the habit. The campaign against its use the past few years has been a notable success, considering how firmly the habit was established in our society. Most of the publications included in the bibliography are concerned with smoking and health, although such aspects as behavior and political implications are also considered.

717. Diehl, Harold S. **Tobacco and Your Helath: The Smoking Controversy.** New York, McGraw-Hill Book Co., 1969. 271p. index. $5.50. LC 69-13216.

The author, retired Dean of Medical Sciences and Professor of Public Health at the University of Minnesota, feels that many individuals do not accept the overwhelming evidence that smoking is harmful. The purpose of his book is to explore the questions concerning tobacco and to give answers that will allow the reader to take informed and meaningful action. He presents scientific and medically accepted information and judgment on the subject.

The following chapters are included: 1) Responsible opinions about tobacco and health; 2) The use of tobacco; 3) Suspicions and early medical evidence; 4) Prospective studies–general death rates; 5) Substances in tobacco smoke and their immediate effects; 6) Tobacco and cancer; 7) Tobacco and cardiovascular disease; 8) Tobacco and chronic bronchitis, emphysema, and certain other diseases; 9) Tobacco–illness and disability; 10) Dissenting opinions; 11) Who smokes and why?; 12) Giving up smoking; 13) Government responsibility; 14) Efforts to reduce smoking; 15) Counterattacks; and 16) A personal decision. Several appendices are also included. There is a glossary and a chart showing tar and nicotine contents of certain brands of cigarettes, and the author gives suggestions that may help a smoker break the habit.

718. Dunn, William L., Jr., ed. **Smoking Behavior: Motives and Incentives.** Washington, V. H. Winston and Sons, 1973. Distributed by the Halsted Press Division of John Wiley and Sons. 309p. bibliog. index. $9.95. LC 72-13271. ISBN 0-470-22746-X.

This publication is made up of papers presented at a conference sponsored by the Council for Tobacco Research–U.S.A., Inc., in January 1972.

The conferees, who were a representative group of life, behavioral, and social scientists, were asked to reply to the question, "What are the motivational mechanisms sustaining cigarette smoking behavior?" Most experts agree that a pharmacological effect, probably mediated by nicotine, is sought by the smoker under conditions that have an emotional impact. The authors of the papers attempt to outline the underlying mechanisms and processes to explain why 35 percent of American adults smoke. The papers cover such topics as neuropsychopharmacology of nicotine and tobacco smoking; additional characteristic EEG differences between smokers and nonsmokers; personality and the maintenance of the smoking habit; the relationship of smoking and habits of nervous tension; effects of nicotine on avoidance, conditioned suppression and aggression response measures in animals and man; the effects of smoking on mood change; smoking attitudes and practices in seven preliterate societies; motivational conflicts engendered by the on-going discussion of cigarette smoking; smoking behavior 1953 and 1970: the midtown Manhattan study; the social sciences and the smoking problem.

719. Friedman, Kenneth Michael. **Public Policy and the Smoking-Health Controversy: A Comparative Study**. Lexington, Mass., D. C. Heath and Co., 1975. 216p. bibliog. index. $14.00. LC 75-604. ISBN 0-669-98160-5.

The author, a professor of political science, analyzes the impact on governmental policy of key political forces—that is, the actions of health interest groups, the economic interests engaged in the growing of tobacco, and the strategies of the tobacco industry. Next he looks into trends in smoking, their possible health significance, and the possible impact on them of governmental policies, health interest group actions, and tobacco industry tactics. In addition, the smoking-health controversy is comparatively analyzed in three countries, the United States, Canada, and Great Britain.

It was apparent that more vigorous governmental efforts were undertaken where agencies and levels of government were relatively autonomous and competitive. It was also found that the problem raised by the anti-smoking interests is far from being solved everywhere.

720. Fritschler, A. Lee. **Smoking and Politics: Policymaking and the Federal Bureaucracy**. 2nd ed. Englewood Cliffs, N.J., Prentice-Hall, Inc., 1975. 180p. bibliog. index. LC 74-12381. ISBN 0-13-815019-2.

Consumer interests have received more and more attention in recent years. Controversy developed in 1964 over the proposed requirement that a health warning label should appear in advertisements and on packages of cigarettes. The interactions among such agencies as Congress, the President, the courts, interest groups, and the general public are given attention in this book. The first edition of the title appeared in 1969, and this new edition bring the material up to date.

The following chapters are presented: 1) Cigarettes and the policy process, 2) Smoking and administrative politics, 3) The advisory committee and the new policy directions, 4) Development of administrative policymaking powers,

5) Procedures used in administrative policymaking, 6) The rulemaking hearings, 7) Congressional power and agency policymaking, 8) Congress and the bureaucracy: a balance of power? In addition there are appended materials as follows: a chronology of important events in the cigarette labeling controversy, and the Federal Trade Commission's trade regulation rules on cigarette labeling and advertising.

721. Mausner, Bernard, and Ellen S. Platt, with the assistance of Judith S. Mausner. **Smoking: A Behavioral Analysis.** New York, Pergamon Press, 1971. 238p. bibliog. index. $14.00. LC 72-119599. ISBN 0-08-016397-1.

This book was written by two experimental social psychologists. The study they describe is of interest because it helps one understand why the community at large applies or ignores scientific advances. The first part of the book is a study of the natural history of smoking. Material drawn from questionnaires and interviews shows that children start to smoke because they see it as adult or adventurous. This eventually leads to full addiction. The second part of the work considers role-playing in an attempt to induce change of smoking habits. One subject acts as patient and the other as doctor in a contrived situation where one attempts to persuade the other to stop smoking. The "doctors" reduced their cigarette consumption more than the "patients," although only 10 percent and 5 percent respectively, actually stopped.

A number of conclusions can be drawn from the study regarding attitudes and behavior, with implications for research into designing control programs in other areas in which people must sacrifice immediate gratification for long-range benefits. The book will be of interest to those involved with public health problems and preventive medicine who are attempting to convince the public that the prevention of many illnesses now lies in the hands of the patient. It is interesting to note that the physician is a powerful persuasive force in changing the behavior of a smoker.

722. U.S. National Clearinghouse for Smoking and Health. **Bibliography on Smoking and Health. 1972.** Washington, GPO, 1973. 314p. index. (DHEW Publication No. (HSM) 73-8719; Public Health Service Bibliography Series No. 45.)

This bibliography includes items added to the Technical Information Center of the National Clearinghouse for Smoking and Health from January to December 1972. Earlier volumes were published, beginning in 1968. There are author, organizational, and subject indexes. Most of the citations are to scholarly journal articles, and each includes a rather detailed abstract.

723. U.S. National Clearinghouse for Smoking and Health. **Directory of On-Going Research in Smoking and Health, 1974.** Compiled by Herner and Company. 5th ed. Washington, GPO, 1974. 331p. index. (DHEW Publication No. (CDC) 74-8739) $3.35. S/N 017-023-00088-8.

This is an international directory of research pertaining to smoking and its relationship to health. Research résumés from 38 countries are included, covering activities in the agricultural, biochemical, medical, behavioral, psychological, and related fields. Over 700 research projects are described, arranged alphabetically by the name of the country, and by state and/or city within the country. There are indexes for principal investigator, organization, sponsor, and subject. Each description includes the following: name and address of the organization, the principal investigators, project title, objective, methods or approach, results to date, future plans, project dates, source of financial support, and references.

724. U.S. National Clearinghouse for Smoking and Health. **Smoking, Tobacco, and Health**. Rev. ed. Prepared by James L. Hedrick of the Resource Management Corporation, Bethesda, Md. Washington, GPO, 1969. 134p. $1.25pa. (U.S. Public Health Service Publication. No. 1931).

This material was taken almost entirely from data published by various agencies of the U.S. government. Topics such as health effects of cigarette smoking, the importance of cigarettes and tobacco farming to our economy, and the revenues contributed by cigarette sales to the federal, state, and local governments are covered. Much tabular and graphic material is presented.

725. U.S. Public Health Service. **The Health Consequences of Smoking.** January 1973. Washington, GPO, 1973. 261p. index. (DHEW Publication No. (HSM) 73-8704.) $1.85. S/N 1723-00064.

This report is the seventh in a Public Health Service series that reviews and assesses the scientific evidence linking cigarette smoking to disease and premature death. This report reiterates, strengthens, and extends the findings of earlier reports that smoking is a health hazard. Contents are as follows: 1) Cardiovascular diseases, 2) Nonneoplastic bronchopulmonary diseases, 3) Cancer, 4) Pregnancy, 5) Peptic ulcer disease, 6) Pipe and cigar smoking, and 7) Exercise performance.

AUTHOR AND TITLE INDEX

SUBJECT INDEX